£14.95

Transport Economics
2nd Edition

ONE WEEK LOAN

Transport Economics
2nd Edition

Kenneth J. Button

Professor of Applied Economics and Transport
Loughborough University
and
VSB Visiting Professor of Transport and the Environment
Tinbergen Insititute, Free University of Amsterdam

Edward Elgar

Published by
Edward Elgar Publishing Limited
Gower House
Croft Road
Aldershot
Hants GU11 3HR
England

Edward Elgar Publishing Company
Old Post Road
Brookfield
Vermont 05036
USA

First published 1982
Second edition 1993

Reprinted 1994

British Library Cataloguing in Publication Data
Button, K. J.
  Transport Economics. – 2 Rev. ed.
  I. Title
  388

Library of Congress Cataloguing in Publication Data
Button, Kenneth John.
    Transport economics/Kenneth Button. — 2nd ed.
      p.   cm.
    1. Transportation.   I. Title.
  HE151.B9   1993
  388—dc20   93–22689
                                                                   CIP

Printed in Great Britain at the University Press, Cambridge

ISBN 1 85278 521 7
       1 85278 523 3 (paperback)

Contents

Preface

The first edition of this book appeared over a decade ago and a lot has happened in the world during the intervening period. The aim of the original book was to '...show how modern economics can be applied to the transport sector' and that has not changed. Nor, surprisingly, when rereading some of the theoretical material in the original book, has much of the basic microeconomic theory. What has changed is the perception of the nature of some of the problems confronting those concerned with transport; in particular the problem of the environment has come more to the fore. Further, there have been changes in the ways in which we approach some transport topics; and here the matter of the appropriate degree and nature of regulation has received much more attention. There have also been technical developments in transport modelling and forecasting reflecting an improvement in the way economic theory is being applied in practice. These developments help enrich our understanding of both important causal linkages influencing current transport patterns and assist policy makers develop better strategies to cope with emerging trends. Finally, changing political and macro-economic considerations mean that matters relating to transport in the post-communist states and in developing countries has attracted increasing interest within the transport fraternity.

This new edition of *Transport Economics* provides an up-dating of the original book together with a considerable amount of new material. As before the level of exposition is intended to pose few problems for those who have completed an introductory course in economics. In particular, the amount of mathematics is kept to a minimum and, where it is introduced, can easily be skirted round by those who wish without losing the thread of an argument. Additional reading, together with a short bibliography at the end of each chapter should enable those who wish to go into topics in a little more depth. The overall structure of the book, however, remains the same; it is framed around the key concepts of economics rather offering a set of chapters on individual modes. In doing this it highlights the generality of applying economic principles to all forms of transport rather than seeing each mode of transport as requiring specialised treatment.

I am afraid that I am a very selfish person and the production of this book has meant that I have sadly neglected my family as usual! Once again I must thank my wife, Elizabeth, and two offspring, Alexandra and James, for putting up with me.

Kenneth Button

1   Transport and Economics

1.1   Transport economics

Over a decade ago I opened the first edition of *Transport Economics* with a quote from an address to the Chartered Institute of Transport by K.J.W. Alexander (1975) which made the rather sober point that despite the importance of transport in the economy, '....the number of academic economists who specialise exclusively in transport could probably be counted on two hands. If one adds to these economists the applied economists employed in the transport business and the specialist consultants working exclusively in that field I would be surprised if the total number exceeded sixty or seventy.' This was the situation as seen in the mid-1970s and highlighted the fact that many transport economic issues were under-researched and poorly understood. The situation has changed somewhat since that time, as witnessed by the introduction of a number of serious academic journals which regularly publish papers on transport economics, but, compared to many areas of economic study, transport remains relatively neglected. None the less, Winston (1985) when examining recent developments in transport economics is able to comment on 'a current intensity [*of interest in the field*] not witnessed for more than fifty years'.

This relative lack of interest is surprising because transport problems have in the past stimulated major developments in economic theory (for example, the development of the notion of consumer surplus by French economists/engineers such as Dupuit, in the 1840s, the refinement of cost allocation models by US economists such as Clark and Taussig in the early part of this century and refinements of the marginal cost pricing principle to improve the charging of rail service) and, more recently, have encouraged work on applied econometrics (for example, the development of discrete choice models in consumer theory and refinements to flexible form cost functions). In part, the relatively small number of clearly identifiable specialist transport economists may be attributed to the diverse nature of some sections of the industry, such as road haulage and taxicabs, which are characterised by numerous small firms without resources to employ full-time specialists. It may also be explained by the tendency, which to some extent still remains, for physical planners and transport engineers to dominate substantive investment decision-making within the sector. The emphasis in this case being on the physical manifestation of travel, namely trips and journey numbers, rather than the demand for movement and the ability of the system to meet these aspirations where, economics is used it is often the engineering framework and carried through by engineers. This situation has only gradually been changing with innovations in management and planning.

The recent upsurge in interest in transport economics began slowly about thirty years ago. Up until that time, as Rakowski (1976) points out, 'the field had essentially been in a state of semi-dormancy since the 1920s', and while considerable institutional studies had been conducted very little analytical work had been attempted. If one looks for a watershed in transport economics at that time it would probably be the publication of Meyer *et al.*'s (1959) *Economics of Competition in the Transportation Industries* which provided a state-of-the-art review of resource allocation problems in the sector coupled with rigorous statistical analysis. While never easy to explain the timing of change, the reasons for the renewed research interest in the 1960s, especially in the USA, Rakowski attributes to (i) 'the problems of physical distribution and the development of a new field which has come to be called business logistics', (ii) 'expanded interest in all phases of urban transportation' and (iii) 'a great deal of research in the areas of transportation in the developing countries.' Gwilliam (1980) echoes these themes but places particular emphasis on the growing problems of urban transport in the 1960s and the recognition that land-use and transport needed to be considered together, and usually simultaneously, if the problems were to be successfully tackled. As a result of this, he argues, 'the boundaries between transport economics and urban and regional planning were obscured'. More recently, changing political attitudes and, especially, the general withdrawal of state intervention has resulted in the need for increased understandings of how transport functions in much more liberalised market conditions.

It is important to emphasise at the outset that transport economics is not distinct from all other branches of economics but rather, as our knowledge has increased, it has become difficult, if not impossible, for economists to follow developments in all branches of their discipline and, hence, increased specialisation has occurred. Transport economics has a long history but, as Alexander, Rakowski, and others suggest, it has only recently become a major field of academic study within universities and only recently has a substantial body of specialists emerged.

The scope of each of the sub-disciplines within economics (for example, agricultural economics, development economics, public sector economics, etc.) is determined not by particular schools or philosophies but rather by the type of subject matter examined and the problems tackled. Transport economists are interested in the economic problems of moving goods and people – they are not normally so concerned with either the industries producing the vehicles and infrastructure (aircraft manufacturing, road construction, ship building, etc.) nor with the very wide implications of transport policy (for example, on the balance of payments). Of course, this does not mean that transport issues are viewed in complete isolation from their wider context but it does mean that the main emphasis and thrust of analysis is directed towards the more immediate transport implications.

The main 'tools' of the transport economist are taken directly from the kit-bag of standard microeconomic theory. Having said this, however, one should add that the actual implements used by transport economists have changed significantly over the years. The pre-war emphasis centred on the transport industries (that is, the railways, road haulage, shipping, etc.) and, in particular, on ways in which the transport market could be improved so that conditions of free competition would ensure that maximum benefit would be derived from public and private transport operations. The situation was summarised by one geographer who felt that transport economics at that time was concerned almost entirely with 'matters of organisation, competition and charging, rather than with the effects of transport facilities on economic activities' (O'Connor, 1965). To some extent – particularly in relation to international transport and, to a lesser extent, inter-urban transport – this interest has remained. It has, however, more recently been supplemented by concern with the wider welfare and spatial implications of transport. Greater emphasis is now placed on the environmental and distributional effects of the transport system and, in some cases, market efficiency is seen as an undesirably narrow criterion upon which to base major decisions. As Alexander argued, in the speech cited above, one of the most important roles for economists is to make clear the overall resource costs of transport rather than just the accounting costs. It is no accident, perhaps, that much of the early work in cost benefit analysis was in the transport field.

Transport economics has, like virtually all other branches of economics, become more quantitative in recent years. The dominant pre-war idea that economics is concerned mainly with establishing broad principles (for example, that quantity demanded rises, *ceteris paribus,* as price falls) has given way, with the advent of econometric techniques and the computer age together with improved data sources, to attempts at detailed measurement (that is, a rise of *x* tons in the quantity demanded will, *ceteris paribus,* follow from a £*y* fall in unit price). Transport economists are now heavily involved in trying to assess the precise quantitative effect of different policy options and with forecasting likely changes in transport demand. The increasing sophistication of transport operations, combined with both the long lead times which are required for full policy implementation and the financial costs involved, place mounting strains upon economists to produce useful, quantified predictions of future trends.

From the relatively small base of the 1960s, transport economists are now becoming established in both public and private enterprises, in addition to assisting in national transport policy formulation. Their increased interest in the overall welfare consequences of different transport strategies, together with a willingness to attempt some form of quantitative assessment, has led to transport economists becoming closely involved in major transport planning exercises. They have an established role in advising on appropriate actions at the national policy formulation level (for instance, in the US economists have chaired both the Interstate Commerce Commission and the Civil Aeronautics Board) but this has also spread down to a more specific function at the local planning level. At the strategic level, transport economists, for example, made a significant contribution to the Greater London Development Plan of the late 1960s and have subsequently been involved in many detailed appraisals of traffic management schemes (both in developed and less developed countries).

The particular advances made in transport investment appraisal – most notably the development of cost-benefit analysis (CBA) techniques as practical tools of analysis – led to the adoption of economic criteria for the assessment of many large-scale investment projects in the 1960s and 1970s (for example, the Third London Airport scheme and Victoria Underground Line in the UK). Recent refinements have resulted in rather more standardisation, and uniform CBA procedures are employed as a standard method of small-scale transport project appraisal (for example, the COBA package used in UK trunk road investment appraisal and the procedures favoured by the World Bank for appraising transport schemes in low income countries). The recent surge of regulatory reform and market liberalisation which is discussed in Chapter 11 stems, at least partly, from the empirical work of applied economists and the resultant new regimes are largely economics based.

The dichotomy between the wealth of the industrial nations and the poverty of third world countries has resulted in large-scale programmes being initiated to stimulate the economic development of the third world. Much of this aid has been in the form of monies and resources to improve transport provision. Over 20 per cent of World Bank lending, for example, goes on transport projects as does about 15 per cent of total Bank assistance – grants, expertise, etc. Although it is not altogether agreed that aid actually stimulates growth (for example, see Baur, 1971) nor that, if it does, transport investments are the most suitable projects to finance, it is nevertheless important that within the narrow confines of transport efficiency these monies are spent wisely. Transport economists have become increasingly involved in the third world in transport project appraisal work.

The remainder of this introduction is concerned with setting the scene for the body of the book. Initially, some of the main economic features of the transport sector are discussed. The intention is, however, not to point to the uniqueness of transport but rather to highlight the particular characteristics of the sector which pose special problems for economists. Recent trends in transport are then reviewed and commented upon. To keep the subject matter manageable, much of the focus will be on the UK situation, although experiences elsewhere will not be neglected. This is followed by a brief review of what appear to be some of the longer-term factors which are going to attract the attention of transport economists. Finally, a detailed contextual section explains the format of the book and outlines briefly the rationale for the structure adopted.

1.2   The economic characteristics of transport

Possibly the most important characteristic of transport is that it is not really demanded in its own right. People wish, in general, to travel so that some benefit can be obtained at the final destination. The trip itself is to be as short as possible. Of course, there are 'joy riders' and 'tourists' but they tend to be in the minority. Similarly, users of freight transport perceive transport as a cost in their overall production function and seek to minimise it wherever possible. The derived nature of the demand for transport is often forgotten in everyday debate but it underlies all economics of transport.

While the demand for transport has particular, if not unique, features certain aspects of supply are entirely peculiar to transport. More specifically part of the plant is 'mobile' – almost by definition – and is entirely different in its characteristics to the fixed plant (for example, rail-track, airports, etc.). The fixed component is usually extremely long-lived and expensive to replace. While most factories in the manufacturing sector may be thought to have a physical life-expectancy of a hundred years at most we still use ports and roads constructed in Roman times. Further, few pieces of transport infrastructure have alternative uses: some former waterways have been turned into leisure areas but these tend to be exceptions.

In contrast, most mobile plant is relatively short-lived and replacement usually occurs with physical obsolescence rather than technical obsolescence as with the fixed components. It is also cheap, with the prospect of alternative employment if demand declines in one market; for example, a bus can be transferred to another route or another form of service – in technical terms transport operators have few 'sunk costs'. Also, unlike fixed plant, the mobile components of transport are generally subject only to minimal scale economies. (Ships and aircraft may be seen as exceptions to this in some cases.) The fixed component, on the other hand, is normally subject to quite substantial economies of scale. Once a rail track is laid the marginal cost of using it falls until some maximum capacity is reached. This means that generally there is a minimum practical size below which the provision of transport infrastructure is uneconomical. There are minimum traffic flows, for example, below which it is not economically practical to build motorways.

As Thomson (1974) has pointed out, it is these features of the fixed and mobile components of transport which have influenced the present institutional arrangements in the sector. The high cost of provision, longevity and scale economies associated with the fixed components create tendencies towards monopoly control, while the ease of entry, flexibility and lack of scale effects tend to stimulate competition in the mobile sector. In common with many other countries official reaction in Britain to this situation has, in the past, tended to be the nationalisation and public ownership of transport infrastructure and the regulation of competition in the mobile sector. Nations differ in the degree to which fixed transport assets are publicly owned (there are private railways in some countries while several European states have privately operated motorways) and in the types of regulation imposed on mobile factors but the overall impression is consistent.

While the rationale of directly controlling the provision and sale of the fixed components of transport can be linked to the containment of any monopoly exploitation which may accompany private ownership (although British experience in the nineteenth century suggests that control might equally well be enforced through price regulation), the need to regulate the mobile component stems from another aspect of transport operations. Transport generates considerable external effects (most obvious of which are congestion and pollution); as Thomson (1974) says, it is an engineering industry carried on outside the factory. It is, therefore, felt important at least to contain the harmful effects of transport and at best to ameliorate them. Coupled with this is the imperfect knowledge enjoyed by operators and, in particular, their inability to foresee relatively short-term change in demand. Regulation is, therefore, often justified to ensure that excessive competition at times of depressed demand does not reduce the capacity of the transport system to an extent that it cannot meet higher demand during the upturn. Finally, there are political-economy arguments that transport is a social service which should meet 'need' rather than demand and, hence, traditional market forces need to be supplemented to ensure that this wider, social criterion of transport operations is pursued rather than the simple profit motive.

1.3 The transport sector
Some indications of recent global trends are seen in Table 1.1. The table gives a broad picture of the growth of world transport during recent years. It is quite clear that, despite the limitations of using this type of crude aggregated data, the growth has been substantial. The mercantile marine has nearly doubled between 1977 and 1988 while air passenger kilometres has risen more than threefold. The main difficulty with this type of data is the impossibility of devising a common unit of measurement for transport. It is possible to count physical units (for example, the number of cars or planes) but lack of homogeneity prevents meaningful comparisons over time for individual modes (for example, an average aircraft of ten years ago is different from the average aircraft of today), let alone contrast of trends to be made between modes. Output measures (for example, tonne-kilometres or pas-

senger kilometres), although appearing to circumvent problems of comparability over broad categories of transport, in fact tend to be equally inadequate. Such measures, in particular, ignore the quality and costs of alternatives. Despite these comments it is still possible to look at official statistics and obtain a general feel for the transport situation evolving in the more parochial context of Britain.

Table 1.1
World transport trends, 1971-1988

	1971	*1977*	*1982*	*1985*	*1988*
Motor vehicles (thousands)					
Cars	206110	285660	342574	373668	407959
Lorries	53660	76410	100360	115165	129593
Merchant shipping (thousands registered tons)					
Stream	78518	140100	120184	89857	67989
Motor	159684	253548	304558	326412	335417
Civil aviation					
Freight (million kms)	11590	21340	28750	37125	50613
Passengers (million kms)	406000	691000	964520	1178347	1492872
Passengers (thousands)	333000	517000	649870	785573	958135

Source: United Nations, *Statistical Yearbook* (various issues)

Transport forms a major component of the national output and accounts for between over 15 per cent of national expenditure in Great Britain. A substantial part of this is accounted for by consumer expenditure, the remainder is undertaken by firms. While the UK's relative expenditure on transport is roughly in line with that found in the US, it is slightly atypical within Europe where it is at the top end of the spectrum, for example, in Belgium 12.9 per cent of income was spent on transport in 1989, in Italy it was 12.9 per cent and in the Netherlands 11.3. Table 1.2 gives a more detailed breakdown of the relative importance of transport in overall expenditure during the 1980s and it is apparent that, given national income has been rising, the amount actually spent on transport has risen considerably.

Although the costs of transport increased slightly faster than the retail price index between 1981 and 1988, as can be seen in Table 1.3 there is also ample evidence that the main cause of the upward trend in expenditure on transport is due to a marked rise in the amount of travel undertaken and in the physical quantity of goods moved and the distances over which they are moved. As a rough guide (and making some allowance for short-term fluctuations which are not immediately apparent from Table 1.3), passenger transport has grown by about 35 per cent over the 1980s while freight transport has risen by around 20 per cent.

Table 1.3 also reveals another important set of trends, namely the changing relative and absolute roles played by the different, individual modes of transport. It is quite clear that travel by road has risen substantially. Car and motor cycle travel dominate personal transport both in terms of traffic carried and monies expended. We also see that the dominance of private (that is, motor car and motor cycle) transport over public modes is increasing both relatively and absolutely over time. As we see in Chapter 2, the rise in private transport use is closely related to higher car ownership levels – although the question of cause and effect is a complex one. What should also be remembered, however, is that while the use of private transport is rising, the role of public transport, especially for commuter trips into large cities is still very important. Table 1.4, for example, provides details of the modes used for morning peak period travel into London. As can be seen, private transport is the minority mode here. This, in fact, is often the picture found in many European cities where public passenger transport still fulfils a major transport function but is not the case in North America where private cars dominate commuter travel.

Table 1.2
Household expenditure in the United Kingdom

	1977	1980	1983	1986	1989
Housing	14.4	15.0	16.8	16.8	17.1
Fuel & lighting	6.1	5.6	6.5	5.9	4.7
Food	24.7	22.7	20.7	19.6	18.6
Alcohol	4.9	4.8	4.8	4.6	4.2
Tobacco	3.6	3.0	3.0	2.6	2.1
Clothing & footwear	8.0	8.1	7.0	7.5	6.8
Durable household goods	6.9	7.0	7.2	7.8	..
Other goods	7.4	7.9	7.6	7.8	..
Transport and vehicles	13.5	14.6	14.7	14.3	..
Services	9.7	10.8	11.3	12.7	..
Household goods	..	..	..	7.7	8.5
Household services	..	..	..	4.8	4.3
Personal goods & services	..	..	..	3.6	3.8
Motoring expenditure	..	..	..	11.9	13.6
Fares & other travel costs	..	..	..	2.4	2.4
Leisure goods	..	..	..	4.8	4.9
Leisure services	..	..	..	7.4	8.5
Miscellaneous	0.8	0.5	0.4	0.4	0.4

Source: Family Expenditure Survey

Table 1.3 also shows that inland freight transport is increasingly being dominated by road haulage which is, over time, taking a larger share of the total market. Also we notice that pipelines are gradually emerging as an important form of transport. Physical limits to the type of commodities which can be carried in this way, however, are likely to prevent pipelines from ever becoming more than a minority mode of transport. Rail transport tends to be declining irrespective of whether measured in absolute physical tonne-kilometres or in the real monetary value of the revenues obtained.

While these aggregate data reveal interesting trends they nevertheless hide quite important details. In particular, on the freight side the tonne-kilometres statistics do not show that much of the increase in road haulage is attributable to longer hauls in larger vehicles. The average length of haul by road rose by over 5 per cent between 1967 and 1977 while the average vehicle capacity increased

Table 1.3

Trends in transport in the United Kingdom 1970–1991

	1970	1976	1982	1988	1991
Passenger traffic (thousand million passenger-kms)					
Bus and coach	56	53	48	46	45
Car and motor cycle	330	363	418	543	596
Pedal cycle	5	4	6	5	5
Road sub-total	391	446	472	593	646
Rail	36	35	31	41	38
Air	2.0	2.4	2.9	4.6	4.8
Total	429.0	483.4	505.9	638.6	688.8
Freight transport (thousand million tonne-kms)					
Road	85.0	99.1	94.5	130.2	130.0
Rail	26.8	20.0	15.9	18.2	15.3
Waterborne	-	-	58.7	59.3	55.9
Pipeline	3.0	9.9	9.5	11.1	11.1
Total	114.9*	129.1	178.6	218.8	212.3

* Does not include coastal shipping or inland waterways
Source: *Transport Statistics Great Britain* (various issues)

Table 1.4

Commuters (thousands) into London during the traffic peak period[1]

Mode	1982	1985	1988	1991
Public transport				
British Rail	390	401	468	426
London Transport				
Rail	283	364	411	347
Bus	99	94	80	74
Coach/minibus	22	26	21	20
All public transport	794	885	980	867
Private transport				
Private car	197	171	160	155
Motor cycle	23	5	10	12
Pedal cycle	16	11	7	9
All private transport	236	197	177	175
All transport	1030	1082	1157	1042

[1] Refers to passenger traffic entering central London during the peak 0700 to 1000 hours in October/November.
Source: *Transport Statistics Great Britain* (various issues)

from 9.5 tons in 1973 to 10.3 tons in 1976. The explanation of this probably is in the greater geographical concentration of industry which has occurred, with a small number of production units now supplying the whole country rather than numerous small factories meeting the needs of local markets. Personal trips have also increased in length from an average of 6.1 miles in 1965 to 6.6 miles in 1975 and to 7.5 miles in 1985/6. Much of this is accounted for by longer journeys to work.

Table 1.5 draws upon Family Expenditure Survey data to show another aspect of transport, namely the share of household expenditure which goes on transport for different income groups. What is found is that the proportion of expenditure which is devoted to transport tends to rise overall with household income reflecting the 'superior good' nature of the activity. The same data source also reveals the use made by different income groups of the various modes. The railway mode is used primarily by those in the higher income groups, as is the private car. In contrast bus transport is used disproportionately more by the poorer sectors of the community. The Survey ignores business account travel which is likely to be undertaken mainly by the higher income groups.

Table 1.5
Household expenditure in the United Kingdom by income group (% of reported expenditure in 1989)

Household weekly income	Food	Housing	Fuel, light & power	Alcohol	Tobacco	Clothing & footware	House-hold goods	Transport & vehicles	Other goods
Under £60	27.2	14.1	10.0	3.7	4.3	5.2	12.5	6.8	13.1
£60 to £99	25.4	21.6	9.6	2.8	3.5	5.4	11.2	8.4	12.0
£100 to £149	23.0	22.2	7.2	3.7	3.3	6.6	10.5	9.3	14.2
£150 to £199	20.1	20.1	5.9	3.4	2.8	5.6	9.8	14.6	17.7
£200 to £249	20.5	19.5	5.6	4.7	2.8	6.2	10.9	14.8	15.0
£250 to £299	19.2	17.1	4.6	4.3	2.4	6.6	13.6	16.7	15.4
£300 to £349	19.3	17.1	4.8	4.8	2.4	6.8	11.5	17.0	16.3
£350 to £399	18.7	16.0	3.9	4.6	2.0	6.5	11.5	17.5	19.3
£400 to £524	17.7	15.6	3.9	4.6	1.9	7.1	11.8	18.4	19.0
£525 and over	15.8	16.4	3.1	4.5	1.2	7.9	12.1	18.3	20.7
All	18.8	17.4	4.8	4.3	2.2	6.9	11.7	16.2	17.8

Source: Family Expenditure Survey

The public sector plays an important role in transport. It both provides and maintains a considerable amount of infrastructure as well as being responsible for those modes operating within the nationalised transport sector. Total employment in the different transport industries and related activities is shown in Table 1.6. It is clear that transport is responsible for a substantial number of jobs in the national economy and that the public contribution, for example the railways, is significant. Additionally, in financial terms public expenditure on transport forms a major component of total UK public expenditure both at the local and national levels. Table 1.7 gives some indication of the general trends over recent years. It is worth noting that about 50 per cent of the public expenditure on roads, public transport and ports is by local rather than central government. These figures are, however, likely to hide some transport expenditures and should, thus, be seen as

Table 1.6
Employment (thousands) in transport in Great Britain

	1981	1984	1987	1989
Railways	174.3	153.6	138.8	128.6
Scheduled road passenger [1]	196.3	190.7	158.7	167.1
Other road passenger	13.8	11.5	11.5	17.2
Road haulage	194.8	217.3	211.6	240.2
Other road transport	2.7	1.9	0.9	0.8
Sea transport	65.1	37.6	33.3	33.2
Air transport	54.8	46.2	53.5	60.6
Supporting services	109.3	94.0	90.0	89.4
Miscellaneous & storage	158.3	149.3	165.0	185.0
All transport	969.3	902.1	863.4	922.2
Transport–related industries [2]	1141.9	988.3	925.4	...
All transport industries	2111.2	1890.4	1788.8	...

[1] Includes urban railways
[2] Includes such sectors as motor vehicles and parts, repair of vehicles and transport equipment.
Source: *Transport Statistics: Great Britain* (various issues)

Table 1.7
UK public expenditure (expressed as outturn figures in real terms at 1989-90 prices)

	1978–9	1981–2	1984–5	1986–7	1990–1*
Defence	17.5	19.4	22.5	21.5	20.5
Overseas services	2.5	2.2	2.2	2.3	2.5
Agriculture, fisheries, food & forestry	2.4	2.6	3.2	2.7	2.7
Trade & industry, energy & emploment	9.7	9.7	10.7	7.7	7.2
Transport	7.0	7.4	7.5	6.6	7.4
Housing	10.7	6.6	6.0	4.8	5.3
Other environmental services	6.4	6.2	5.9	6.6	7.1
Law, order & protective services	5.9	7.	8.2	9.0	10.6
Education & science	22.2	22.4	22.3	24.1	25.4
Arts & libraries	0.9	1.0	1.1	1.2	1.3
Health & other personal social services	21.6	24.5	25.7	27.9	30.5
Social security	39.6	45.5	52.2	55.6	54.2
Micellaneous expenditures	6.3	5.1	5.4	6.4	6.7
Total expenditure on services	152.7	159.7	172.7	176.4	181.4

* Estimated
Source: HM Treasury (1990)

lower limits. Transport, for instance, accounts, or is directly responsible, for additional expenditures under items such as law and order, environmental services and health. Also monies are lent to the nationalised transport industries. As we see from the data, public expenditure on transport fluctuates in the UK, as in other countries, in part due to the needs of macroeconomic policy-making.

External transport to and from the UK has also increased (Table 1.8) although reliance on physical measures often obscures the value or importance of goods traffic. Table 1.8 provides an indication of this measurement problem. The UK is typical of a developed economy which tends to import low-value, bulk raw materials and exports high-value, non-bulk manufactures. This explains the wide difference in the inward and outward flows of shipped tonnage. The growth in air traffic is due, to a large extent, to the growth of international tourism with a more gradual expansion of business travel.

Table 1.8
International transport to and from the United Kingdom

Mode	1982	1985	1988	1991
Foreign sea (million tonnes)				
Inwards	120.7	139.9	166.4	178.1
Outwards	130.3	147.8	141.7	142.7
Foreign air (thousand passengers)				
Inwards	6911	9413	10968	11341
Outwards	12031	13732	21026	20173

Source: *Transport Statistics Great Britain* (various issues)

1.4 Emerging trends

The world is not static and there are a number of emerging trends which are beginning to influence the issues which transport economists are addressing. The important trends can be isolated according to the nature of the economic environment of the countries involved.

First, in the established industrial world the long-term trend would seem to be for continued economic expansion. The recent past has already witnessed significant increases in traffic and vehicle ownership in these countries (Table 1.9) and there are reasons to expect this trend to continue. The Single Internal Market within the European Community and the North America Free Trade Area will, for instance, foster economic expansion. The natural growth in trade that is likely to accompany these developments will in itself create demands for more transport services but this inevitably will take place in the context of limted infrastructure capacity.

A lot has been written on probable impacts for transport of the creation of the Single European Market and certainly the new situation has implications for transport not only within the Twelve and with regard to a number of transit countries, such as Austria and Switzerland, but also to countries of the European Free Trade Area involved in the larger European Economic Space (see Chapter 10). The creation of the Single Internal Market alone will, it is forecast, lead to a 4.5–7 per cent rise in the Community's GNP – an increase of 30–50 per cent in transfrontier lorry traffic alone being predicted. A study for the European

Parliament forecast the overall growth in land transport will be 34 per cent between 1988 and 2000. The European Conference of Ministers of Transport suggests an even higher rate amounting to 3.5 per cent per annum into the next century. The problem is how to cater for such traffic growth in an efficient manner.

Table 1.9
Car ownership in industrialised countries

Country	Cars 1987(1975)	Goods vehicles 1987(1975)
Austria	2685(1721)	221(146)
Belgium*	3457(2614)	302(235)
Canada	11681(8870)	3222(2112)
Denmark*	1595(1295)	228(279)
Federal Republic of Germany*	27908(17898)	1305(1121)
France*	21970(15555)	3917(2325)
Greece*	1439(439)	667(198)
Irish Republic*	707(516)	108(54)
Italy*	22719(15060)	1926(1170)
Luxembourg*	162(115)	13(12)
Netherlands*	5118(3399)	465(332)
Norway	1623(954)	139(284)
Portugal*	1754(937)	522(204)
Spain*	10319(4807)	1821(1014)
Sweden	3367(2760)	246(157)
Switzerland	2733(1794)	218(139)
United Kingdom*	19799(14061)	1556(1820)
USA	137736(106706)	41250(25781)

* European Community Members 1993

Second, the liberalisation of Eastern Europe, coupled with the new political geography that is emerging, represents both problems and opportunities, for the countries in the region. Liberalisation means in particular that the overall 'transport market' in Europe will expand considerably in line with major new urban and industrial centres being brought within the market system. It means, therefore, that many more major transport links must now be considered as part of Europe's transport future. In many ways this may prove advantageous for the long-term development of European transport since it creates something more akin to a natural market for transport services than currently exists.

Short-term problems are likely to arise, though, because of the attitude regarding transport that has grown up in Eastern and Central Europe over the past forty years and the impact this has had on the physical transport infrastructure now in place. In particular, the transport systems of Eastern Europe are dominated by rail (which itself suffers from low productivity and over-manning), tend to be of poorer quality than in Western Europe and have been developed since the late 1940s to meet the trading patterns of the members of the Council for Mutual Economic Assistance. The indications are, however, that even on the basis of even a relatively conservative scenario, by the early part of the next century this pattern of trading activity will be transformed and with this will come the need for a different form of transport provision.

Third, it is not only in the industrialised nations and in the post-communist states that new conditions are emerging. If there is to be economic development in the low income countries of Africa, Asia and South and Central America then transport will inevitably change. There is some evidence that the economies of some of these states are beginning to expand, although not the lowest income countries. At present, see Table 1.10, supply of transport in these countries is relatively limited. Economic expansion, however, especially if it results in significant growth in some larger countries, could lead to substantial demands for car ownership and the need for major new infrastructure initiative. As can be seen from the table the link between per capita income and vehicle ownership is a positive one. It will also mean that there will increased strains on the environment, both within these countries and in terms of global effects such as emissions of greenhouse gases.

Table 1.10
Car ownership in low income and industrialised countries (1986)

Country	GNP per Capita ($US)	Cars per Capita	Commercial Vehicles ('000)
Burkina Faso	150	0.0020	14.0
Bangladesh	160	0.0005	35.0
Mali	180	0.0020	7.5
Burma	200	0.0016	45.0
Tanzania	250	0.0020	50.0
India	290	0.0015	1000.0
Kenya	300	0.0060	110.0
Pakistan	350	0.0049	183.2
Sri Lanka	400	0.0093	132.0
Indonesia	490	0.0063	1133.3
Morocco	590	0.0242	202.6
Thailand	810	0.0109	824.0
Cameroon	910	0.0083	65.0
Paraguay	1000	0.0161	30.2
Columbia	1230	0.0290	391.4
Brazil	1810	0.0723	2100.0
Mexico	1860	0.0648	2250.0
Uruguay	1900	0.0667	100.0
Hungary	2020	0.1452	189.1
Argentina	2330	0.1257	1434.7
Algeria	2370	0.0324	458.0

A significant feature of most low-income countries in recent years has been the secular drift of population into urban areas. Historically, the growth of car ownership in the largest cities in Third World countries was already of the order of 7–15 per cent in the decade 1960 to 1970. Added to this, the actual cost of transport in these cities has risen significantly with households spending 5–10 per cent of their income on transport, and in some cases 15 per cent, and city governments spending 15–25 per cent of their annual budgets on transport investments and operations. Looking forward, the situation in the urban areas of the developing world is inevitably going to get worse. The mid-1980s saw eight of the largest cities in the world with populations of over 10 million located in low-income countries. Predictions are that this number will have doubled by the end of the century while an 18 further agglomerations in the developing world will have populations of between 5 and 10 million. A major difficulty is that the growth of urbanisation and the level of motor car ownership and use are closely linked. While this is partly due to the concentration of wealth in the urban areas it is also entwined with the geographical spread which accompanies urbanisation and the resultant increase in the average journey lengths. Comparing Nairobi and Mexico City, for example, shows average trip lengths of between 1.5 to 2.8 miles for the former while those for Mexico City, which is much larger, are between 3.5 and 6.0 miles. Public transport is much less efficient at serving a spatially dispersed market and hence the automobile is used more often. How to plan and cater for the inevitable expansion in traffic as urbanisation continues in these countries will be a mounting problem for transport economist.

1.5   The framework of the book
The remainder of the book is concerned with the application of economic theory to the transport sector. Unlike other books which often concentrate on particular modes of transport, such as the railways or shipping, or specific sectors such as the nationalised transport industries, one of the main aims of this book is to show that many problems in transport are common to all modes (albeit with minor variations). Consequently, the approach is to show how economic theory may be applied to improve the overall efficiency of the transport sector; examples are, therefore, drawn from all forms of transport. Also while it is unavoidable, not to say desirable, that official transport policy must be implicitly incorporated in the analysis, this is not a book explicitly about transport policy. It is felt useful, on occasions, to give brief details of institutional arrangements since they can influence the type of economic analysis to apply (for example, a thumb-nail sketch of the historical and institutional framework of urban transport planning is included for this purpose), but, again, this is primarily for contextual reasons. The final chapter is concerned with policy and institutions and in particular with the matter of the economic regulation of transport markets.

At the theoretical level the discussion is couched in terms of verbal and diagrammatic analysis. Mathematical expressions are not shunned but equations are included rather as references, permitting readers to look up practical working models should they subsequently wish to undertake their own empirical investigations. There are virtually no mathematical derivations, but important equations are 'talked around' and the reader should find no difficulty in following the book even if his/her mathematical education has been neglected. Those interested in mathematical extensions of the arguments on specific topics are referred to the major references set out at the end of each chapter. An understanding of basic microeconomic theory is assumed and, while a knowledge of intermediate economic theory would be helpful, most of the theory does not go beyond that found in a standard introductory economics text.

The book begins by looking at the role of transport in the national economy and its interaction with other sectors of the economy, especially the land market. This interaction is often neglected in the literature but is central to understanding the role of transport in society. This is followed by a related chapter concerned with the benefits of transport and methods of measuring these benefits, drawing particularly upon the tools of welfare economics. While Chapters 2 and 3 are essentially demand-orientated, the two following chapters are concerned with cost and supply aspects (costs here being seen both in terms of conventional financial cost problems and, also, in terms of wider external costs). The accountancy costs of running transport are now recognised as offering too narrow a picture of the overall social costs associated with the movement of goods and persons.

The remaining chapters concentrate on optimising the size and use made of the transport sector both in the short term and in the longer term. Methods of pricing are reviewed in the context of the particular nature of transport activities with, once again, emphasis being directed to the wider social dimension as well as to narrow commercial criteria. Chapter 7, in particular, looks at methods of optimising the environmental effects of transport on society in general.

Longer-term planning and investment decisions are considered in some detail. This is because of both the complexities of the issues involved and the size of the potential resource wastage if the wrong decision is taken. The sheer costs involved are also enormous, particularly where major pieces of new infrastructure are under consideration – for example, a Third London Airport or a Channel Tunnel. The long working life of projects means that it is important to be able to forecast the future demands likely to be placed on the infrastructure, and consequently, in Chapter 9, some space is devoted to economic demand forecasting techniques. The emphasis is, once again, focused on the economic assumptions involved rather than the econometric and estimation problems which may be encountered.

The final chapters of the book take a much broader view of transport, considering both the role that transport policy may play in general economic development – within the UK and in less developed countries - and the influence that official transport policy exercises over the sector. The latter discussion is particularly concerned with the relative merits of central coordination and direction of transport *vis-à-vis* the use of the market mechanisms and competitive processes.

While each chapter is extensively referenced throughout to permit readers to follow up specific points in more detail should they wish, it has also been thought useful to mention a few key references and some indication of further reading at the end of each chapter. These references are annotated and are really designed to help student readers. The intention is that they should be references to material which is relatively accessible to most readers rather than obscure reports, working papers, etc. which are often extremely difficult for those outside official circles or the academic sphere to obtain. The lists of key references are kept short so that the main items are immediately apparent to those interested.

1.6 Further reading and references
The official *Transport Statistics, Great Britain* (UK Department of Transport, annual) published annually is an extremely useful source of up-to-date information on trends in United Kingdom transport. The United Nations *Statistical Yearbook* (United Nations, annual) offers wide-ranging, but rather less reliable, data on developments in world transport. A useful source of historical data for Great Britain is Munby and Watson (1978), which is an invaluable reference work. Due (1982) contains details of the main post-World War II developments in transport economics to the 1980s while Winston (1985) offers a concise overview of the theoretical underpinnings of modern transport economics. Small (1992) is an

extremely good analysis of urban transport economics for those with a specific interest in this field.

References

Alexander, K.J.W. (1975), 'Some economic problems of the transport industry', *Chartered Institute of Transport Journal,* 36, 306–308.

Baur, P. (1971), *Dissent on Development,* London, Weidenfeld and Nicolson.

Due, J.F. (1982), 'Major recent contributions to the literature of transport economics: a review article', *Quarterly Review of Economics and Business,* 22, 6–28.

Gwilliam, K.J. (1980), Review of *Transport Economics, Economic Journal,* 90, 677–8.

HM Treasury (1990), *Public Expenditure Analysis to 1993–4,* CM 1520, London, HMSO.

Meyer, J.R., Peck, M.J., Stenason, J., and Zwick, C. (1959), *The Economics of Competition in the Transportation Industries,* Cambridge, Mass., Harvard University Press.

Munby, D.L. and Watson, A.H. (1978), *Inland Transport Statistics Great Britain 1900–1970,* Oxford, Oxford University Press.

O'Connor, A.M. (1965), *Railways and Development in Uganda,* Nairobi, Oxford University Press for the East African Institute of Social Research.

Rakowski, J.P. (1976), *Transport Economics: A Guide to Information Sources,* Detroit, Gale Research Co.

Small, K.A. (1992), *Urban Transport Economics,* Chur, Harwood.

Thompson, M. (1974), *Modern Transport Economics,* Harmondsworth, Penguin.

UK Department of Transport (annual), *Transport Statistics, Great Britain,* London, HMSO.

United Nations (annual), *Statistical Yearbook,* New York, UN.

Winston, C. (1985), 'Conceptual developments in the economics of transportation: an interpretive survey', *Journal of Economic Literature,* 23, 57–94.

2   Movement, Transport and Location

2.1   The desire for movement

Robert Louis Stevenson once said, 'For my part, I travel not to anywhere, but to go. I travel for travel's sake. The great affair is to move.' (from *Travels with a Donkey*). He is very much in the minority; few people travel for the sheer joy of it, although some modes of transport do arouse feelings of excitement, romance or sentiment. There are also, of course, people who take touring holidays each year where sight-seeing from a bus or car is an integral part of the enjoyment. Most individuals, though, travel because they wish to benefit from the social, recreational, educational, employment and other opportunities which become accessible with movement. Similarly, freight transport opens up opportunities for greater efficiency in production and permits extensive geographical specialisation with the accompanying benefits of increased division of labour. More simply, transport permits the spatial disadvantages of separation to be reduced.

In more detail, Thomson (1974) provides a helpful classification of seven main reasons why people in the modern world desire to transport either themselves or their property:

(1)   The heterogeneity of the earth's surface means that no one part of it is capable of providing all the products people wish for. An acceptable bundle of such goods can only be obtained by either moving around collecting them or having them brought to you.

(2)   The continuation of modern society and the high levels of material well-being rely upon a degree of productive specialisation. Industry requires a multiplicity of diverse inputs which must be collected from wide-ranging sources and also, to permit the necessary level of specialisation, extensive market areas must be tapped and served.

(3)   In addition to specialisation, high quality transport permits the exploitation of other major economies of scale. There are essentially technical economies associated with high levels of output and include automation, bulk handling, research and development activities, mass marketing, purpose-built equipment, etc.

(4)   Transport has always served a political and military role. Internally, a country seeks good transport both to permit more effective defence of its borders and to improve the political cohesion of the nation. The Romans were certainly well aware of this and most of their road building was to this end. Externally, good transport permits a country to dominate any colonial or subservient provinces, while more aggressive states require transport to

pursue their expansionist policies. Politically, the ownership of expensive, modern transport infrastructure (especially aircraft or mercantile marine) is also treated as a symbol of power and status. In most developed countries the scale of transport required to meet strict needs normally exceeds that required to meet political or military criteria although individual components of a transport system (for example, specific roads or airports) may be provided explicitly for non-economic reasons.

(5)   Without transport, social relationships and contacts are normally very restricted. Transport permits social intercourse, and with it may come a greater understanding of the problems and attitudes of various geographically distant groups. In the developed world the enhancement of social understanding brought about by increased international travel is well recognised, but in many less developed countries the introduction of much more basic transport technology can have profound effects upon the social relationships between inhabitants of formerly isolated towns and villages which are, by Western standards, very close together.

(6)   Modern transport has widened cultural opportunities, permitting people to examine the artistic treasures of other countries and to explore their own national heritage. It also allows for the staging of international exhibitions, sports spectaculars, concerts, parades and fairs which stimulate new trends and innovations in the cultural and sporting spheres.

(7)   Transport is desired to permit people to live and work apart; specifically it permits the geographical separation of employment from leisure. It increases the life-style options open to people, giving them a choice among residential locations away from cities but involving a heavy commitment to travel, or ones much closer to the main employment centre but involving short commuting journeys. Transport, quite simply, widens the locational choices open to households.

What becomes apparent from this listing is the close link between location decisions (of both individuals and firms) and the transport system. It is this link we now turn to.

2.2   The 'chicken or egg' problem

If one takes very broad statistics, then there is unquestionably a link between mobility and affluence. This is, for example, fairly clear from Table 2.1 which presents some of the findings contained in Owen (1987) regarding levels of per capita GDP across a range of countries and the transport mobility (expressed as a combination of such things passenger miles per annum of automobile, rail and domestic air travel, miles of railway, number of lorries and so on) enjoyed by those living in these countries. While the correlation is apparent what is less clear is the direction of causation involved. Does high income lead to or result from higher levels of mobility? The answer is not immediately apparent.

At another level, in the previous chapter it was suggested that one of the reasons for the increased interest in transport economics from the late 1960s was the recognition of the important link between transport and land-use patterns (especially those relating to urban location). The effects of changes in the transport system on land-use tend to be long-term (hence they are often called 'activity shifts') but, given the longevity of much transport infrastructure, such interactions must to some extent concern transport policy-makers. The changes that occur in land-use will also, in turn, by altering the nature and size of the local residential population and industrial base, exert an enormous influence on future transport demand. A major new suburban underground railways system, for example, will immediately attract some travellers away from other modes of transport in addition to encouraging trips to be made by former non-travellers. In the longer term, sites near the underground termini will become desirable while those further away will appear relatively less attractive. There will, therefore, be important implications for residential and employment location patterns. Additionally, changing location and trip-making patterns will alter car ownership decisions.

Table 2.1
Mobility across countries

	GNP per capita	Travel mobility	Freight mobility
Switzerland	139	104	81
Sweden	119	96	151
USA	106	160	260
Netherlands	101	83	42
France	100	100	100
Canada	95	114	374
Australia	91	107	335
Japan	87	96	94
UK	63	78	47
Italy	53	86	49
Spain	43	54	44
Venezuela	31	24	36
Yugoslavia	24	32	55
Brazil	18	18	23
Mexico	15	14	42
Colombia	11	6	47
Nigeria	6	5	5
Egypt	5	5	13
Pakistan	2	3	10
China	2	3	16
India	2	5	26
Bangladesh	1	2	3

Source: extracted from Owen (1987)

While these interactions are now fully recognised, it is practicably difficult to construct a comprehensive theory which fully reflects all the linkages. The problem is further compounded by the fact that transport and land-use changes are on-going modifications to the spatial economy. There are continual cycles of cause and effect, and it is impossible to decide upon a point where it is sensible to break into this continuum of change. Consequently, from a pragmatic standpoint one has to make a rather careful judgement whether to treat land use as influenced by transport or vice versa. To some extent the final decision must rest with the questions being considered. Urban and regional scientists tend to treat transport as the influential variable because the focus of attention here is on the spatial dimension. Questions are posed, for example, in terms of why do certain population densities occur or why do specific urban economies interact. In contrast, transport economics usually accepts a given land-use pattern and looks at methods of providing efficient transport services within this constraint. Questions centre, for instance, on problems of aligning routes or controlling traffic flows.

An example of this latter approach which reveals both the methodology of conventional transport economics, but also highlights some of the difficulties in the modelling of urban decision-making, was developed by Kain (1964). This econometric study, looking specifically at public transport subsidies and calibrated using information from a 1953 survey of 40,000 households in Detroit, adopts four steps in its argument:

(1)   Workers initially select a residential density in which to live depending upon their income, their preference for a specific plot size and the price of residential land.

(2)   Once a location has been selected the decision to purchase a car is treated as dependent upon the local residential density, family income, public transport availability and the composition of the worker's family.

(3)   The decision whether to use public transport for the journey to work, besides depending upon the previous decisions regarding location and car ownership, is thought to be influenced by the quality of local public transport, and the demands of non–working members of the household to make use of the car (if one is owned).

(4)   Finally the length of journeys is treated as dependent both on previous decisions of the worker and on the price of residential land adjacent to workplaces.

The implied chain of decisions is, therefore, unidirectional and of the following form:

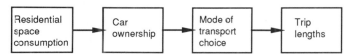

While Kain was clearly aware of the feedbacks from transport to land use, for a variety of statistical and theoretical reasons he could not adequately reflect them in his model. Besides not allowing for the longer-term feedbacks from travel behaviour to land use, the sequence takes no account of the influence of public transport quality on the car ownership decision (see Button *et al.*, 1982), or the length of journeys on the longer-term provision of public transport. What the sequence does do, however, is to permit Kain to examine the case for subsidising public transport *within* the current urban land-use framework. The assumptions of the sequential type of framework used by Kain are analogous to the standard *ceteris paribus* assumptions of conventional partial equilibrium microeconomics; they suffer from the same limitations but do provide boundaries within which useful analysis can be conducted.

The majority of this book is concerned exclusively with the transport sector and with short-run travel decisions. It assumes implicitly, therefore, that the causal link runs from land use to transport and, generally, that land-use is predetermined. It seems inappropriate, however, not to give some brief overview of the approach adopted by spatial scientists; not to do so would in effect ignore the part played by transport in both shaping land-use patterns and determining the size of the market areas served by various industries. In the remainder of this chapter, therefore, we present a brief introductory outline of modern location theory, concentrating primarily on that aspect of theory which gives a central role to transport. The theory is supplemented by some discussion of the applied work which offers quantification of the important role played by transport in this field. Later in the book (in Chapter 10) the subject of transport and locational interaction is touched upon again in the context of economic development.

2.3 Transport and industrial location

The earliest economic theories of industrial location argued that transport plays a key role in decisions concerning where industrial activities will be located. As we have seen, provision of good transport permits producers to be separated from both their sources of new materials and also their eventual customers. Weber (1929) developed an early model for mobile plant with transport costs determining the location of manufacturing industry. In Figure 2.1 all potential customers are located at A_1 while the two raw materials required by manufacturing industry are located respectively at A_2 and A_3. The ds represent actual distances between the points of raw material supply and final demand. It is assumed that all other factors of production are freely available at all potential production sites and that, topographically, all activities are located on a uniform plain. Transport costs are assumed proportional with respect to both distance covered and weight of goods carried. The location of a manufacturing plant will therefore depend on the relative pulls of the various material locations and the market. The problem is then one of finding the site, Z, for manufacture which minimises total costs, in other words the location which minimises T where:

$$T = a_1 r_{A_1} + a_2 r_{A_2} + a_3 r_{A_3} \tag{2.1}$$

a_1 is the physical amount of the final goods consumed at A_1;
a_2 is the physical amount of the raw material available at A_2 required to produce a_1 of the final good;
a_3 is the physical amount of the raw material available at A_3 required to produce a_1 of the final good; and
r_{A_1}, r_{A_2} and r_{A_3} are the distances from the respective sites A_1, A_2 and A_3 respectively.

It is easily seen that if any two of a_1, a_2, a_3 are exceeded by the third, then the location of production is determined at the site associated with this third variable (for example, if $a_2 > (a_1 + a_3)$, then production of the final commodity should be at site A_2). If no location is dominant, then graphical methods can be used to find the least-cost site. A second triangle is drawn with sides proportional to a_1, a_2 and a_3 and the three angles measured. We denote the angle opposite the a_1 side by α_1 that opposite a_2 as α_2 and finally that opposite a_3 as α_3. These angles then form the basis for erecting similar triangles around the original locational triangle (see Figure 2.1). Circles are drawn which touch the points of each triangle and the optimal production site Z is then found at the location where all three circles intersect (if Z is found to be outside of the original locational triangle, then it is simple to prove that one of the corner solutions, A_1, A_2, or A_3 is preferable.) This location minimises transport costs as defined in equation 2.1.

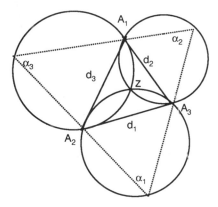

Figure 2.1
Weber's model of industrial location

This simple analysis implicitly assumes that transport costs are linearly related to distance, but there is ample evidence that there are often considerable diseconomies associated with short hauls and with partially full loads. While Weber originally suggested that one could adjust the sides of the locational triangle to capture this, the situation requires rather more complicated modifications. The difficulty is that in these circumstances location and transport costs are codetermined; without knowledge of the final location (that is, Z) it is impossible to assess the magnitude, if any, of economies of long-haul transport. There is a suggestion, however, that other things being equal, tapered transport rates (that is, when the rate per mile declines with distance) tend, in some circumstances, to draw industry to either the source of raw materials or the market for final products.

Suppose that only one raw material is needed to produce the final product (or that the range of raw materials required are located at a single point) and this is to be found at A in Figure 2.2. Further, there is no loss of weight in the manufacturing process required to produce the final product which will eventually be sold at M. Either the transport system offers a through service from A to M costing £10 per ton or alternatively there are services from A to the intermediate site B costing £6 per ton and one from B to M also costing £6 per ton. Since we assume no weight loss in production the cost-conscious manufacturer is clearly indifferent between A and M but would not select site B (because $(AB + BA) > AM$ in cost terms).

To relax the assumption of no weight loss in manufacturing does not remove the disadvantage suffered by B relative to A which is now preferable to location M. (It is possible in this situation for B to be preferred to M if a location at A is impracticable for technical or planning reasons, but this would depend upon the relative importance of the taper *vis-à-vis* the weight loss in manufacture.) Weight loss will only influence the choice between A and M, and this may even be true if different rates are charged not simply by haul length but also by type of commodity. Even if it is more expensive per ton to carry the final product it may still be preferable to locate production facilities at the material source rather than the final market. In the USA, for example, the meat-packing industry of the last century was gradually drawn westwards to the main source of beef (initially to Chicago and then to Omaha and Kansas City) even though rail rates per ton mile favoured transport of live animals rather than carcasses. The simple fact was that the dressed meat of a steer weighs only 54 per cent of the live animal weight; hence locations near the raw material were favoured.

Figure 2.2
The effects of tapered rates on industrial location

Of course, firms do not in general locate in isolation from one another. Lösch (1954) demonstrated that with all firms facing identical production and transport cost schedules, and confronted by a spatially uniform total market, the market would be divided out so that each firm would serve a hexagonal market area. The equilibrium number of firms, and the area served by each, would be determined by transport costs. The existence of a number of different, but interdependents product markets would, in the Löschian model, tend to encourage concentrations of firms at particular locations.

Discussion of the details of these locational and other models is beyond the scope of this book (although some references for further reading are mentioned at the end of the chapter), but it should be becoming increasingly apparent that transport costs have increasingly been recognised to be only one of many factors which influence industrial location. The factors influencing location include (in addition to transport considerations) market structure, demand elasticities, external economies of geographical concentration, expectations of future market changes and processing costs. Greenhutt (1963) suggests that in practice transport costs only become of major importance if freight costs form a large proportion of total costs or differ significantly among potential locations.

While theoretical models of industrial location offer useful insights into the role transport plays, its actual relevance in the real world requires detailed empirical study. If we follow Greenhutt's argument, in many cases transport costs are such a small component of overall production costs that it appears to be more costly to acquire the information necessary to find the least-cost location than to suffer the inefficiencies of a sub-optimal situation. (Cook's (1967) study, for example, of industrial location in the Black Country of the Midlands found that many firms were totally ignorant of their transport costs.) One can attempt to isolate such transport cost-insensitive industries by looking at the relative importance of transport costs in their overall costs of production. Table 2.1 offers some estimates of the percentage of the value of net output for a variety of US industries attributable to transport costs (Edwards, 1970, provides a similar list for the UK). It seems reasonable to conclude from this table that, *ceteris paribus,* industries such as leather goods, instruments, printing, etc. are going to be less influenced in their locational choices by transport considerations than chemicals, lumber, furniture, etc. In particular, production of raw materials such as coal-mining, chalk, clay, sand and gravel extraction represent nodal solutions in the Weberian triangle, with production at the raw material source. (In the US it is often suggested that Gary, Indiana, was chosen specifically by US Steel to minimise transport costs.)

Table 2. 2
Transport costs for selected US industries as a percentage of net output (1982)

Industry	Inbound and outbound transport costs (% of production price)
	Low
Leather and leather products	3
Electrical and electronic machinery	4
Printing and publishing	4
Apparel and other textiles	4
Instruments	4
Machinery excluding electrical instruments	5
Tobacco manufacturers	5
	Medium
Rubber and plastic products	7
Transportation equipment	8
Miscellaneous manufacturing	8
Fabricated metal products	8
Textile mill products	8
Primary metal industries	9
Paper and allied products	11
	High
Furniture and fixtures	12
Food and kindred products	13
Chemicals	14
Lumber and wood products	18
Petroleum products	24
Stone, clay and glass products	27

Source: Anderson (1983).

Changes in industrial structure over the past thirty years, and especially the movement away from basic industries to manufactures and services, suggest that transport is experiencing a diminishing influence over location decisions at least at the inter-regional level. Further, the existence of comprehensive transport and communications networks in virtually all industrialised countries suggests that proximity to good transport is much easier to achieve now than in the past. These factors contribute to the picture that emerged when Gudgin (1978) looked at the 1968 Census of Production: he found 'that almost three-quarters of British industry incurs total transport costs at levels of less than 3 per cent of the value of gross output. In 95 per cent of industry, by value of production, the transport costs are less than 5 per cent of total costs.' This finding has recently been reaffirmed by Diamond and Spence (1989) in a study of 190 manufacturing and service industries in the UK which found that most firms reported transport costs of between 3 and 6 per cent of production costs. Interestingly, at 9.9 per cent, transport costs represented a considerably higher proportion of costs in the service sector than for manufacturing firms (4.7 per cent).

As Gwilliam (1979) has pointed out, however, cost statistics may be giving a slightly distorted impression of the influence of transport factors. In particular, while transport costs may form only a relatively small portion of output costs in many sectors they may, nevertheless, have significant influence on profits. Chisholm (1971), for instance, suggests that transport costs may have represented as much as 25 per cent of profits in manufacturing industry during the 1960s. Additionally, while transport costs may, on average, be low for some industries they may vary considerably among areas. Edwards (1975) suggests that there existed a range of about 20 per cent in transport costs of manufacturing industry by region in 1963. It should also be remembered that simple cost estimates may disguise variations in other attributes of transport (speed, regularity, etc.) which can influence decision-makers. Reliable inter-urban transport, good international transport links and high quality local transport (necessary to retain scarce skilled labour) are, for instance particularly important for modern high-technology industry (Button, 1987).

Survey evidence, questioning industrialists about the motivations underlying their locational or re-locational decisions also provides some guide to the importance of transport considerations. There are obvious difficulties in using such results – for example, the sample may be unrepresentative, respondents offer answers which they hope may further their individual interests, while others offer *ex post* rationalisations of their actions – but some information may be gleaned from them.

Some years ago, for example, the UK Trade and Industry Sub-committee of the House of Commons Expenditure Committee (1973), when seeking information about the effectiveness of regional economic policies, was told by five of the seventeen major industrial firms interviewed that transport costs were a specific disadvantage for locations in developed areas. While accepting this as objective comment, it is important to note not simply the relatively small number of firms concerned but also their particular nature – for example, three were car manufacturers and one a large steel tube mill. These were large firms engaged in the production of bulky products whose per unit transport costs were likely to be high. The Armitage Committee (UK Department of Transport, 1980) supported this line and concluded that 'When industry and commerce make decisions about the location of factories or their systems of distribution, it is often less important to reduce transport costs than to reduce other costs such as those of stockholding or to take advantage of the grants for setting up factories in assisted areas.' Such a view is consistent with that of Cameron and Clark (1966), who in their study of 71 firms which located in Assisted Areas found that accessibility to main markets was only ranked third as a locational factor (behind the availability of trained labour and local authority co-operation) while local goods transport facilities were listed fifth and accessibility to main suppliers ranked sixth.

One factor which emerges from these studies, and has limited support in econometric work, is that during the post-war phase of full employment and strengthened land-use controls, access to markets and raw material supplies was often overshadowed in locational decisions by the availability of scarce skilled labour and factory space (for example, see UK Trade and Industry Sub-committee

of the House of Commons Expenditure Committee, 1973). International confirmation of this position is found in the West German context where in a survey of
newly located plants conducted in 1971, Fischer (1971) found that accessibility to
motorways ranked only fourth in the list of locational criteria.

More localised studies suggest that good passenger transport facilities may
influence industrial location rather more than the quality of long-distance or of
freight transport. In retailing and some other activities this argument is further
extended to embrace firms' desires to be accessible to customers. The importance
of local transport is, for instance, seen in a study of factors affecting location
choices of high technology firms in Pennsylvania. Allen and Robertson (1983)
found that while proximity to market, proximity to family and commuting
distance came first, second and fourth respectively in terms of factors influencing
firms, regional surface transport and proximity to an airport came only thirteenth
and sixteenth respectively. This confirms the emphasis that has been placed upon
the ready availability of trained workers. It is certainly clear from a number of
surveys (as shown, for instance, in Table 2.3 which reports the results of a study
of 104 US plants) that the availability of suitable labour is a key factor in location
choices of both high technology and more traditional industries. There is also
evidence that local transport can be influential in attracting or retaining such
labour. Transport and transport-related considerations would seem, therefore, to
still be very relevant in the location decisions of modern industries although the
specific transport attributes of importance may have changed somewhat over the
years.

Table 2.3
Factors influencing the location of high-technology and other types of plants

Rank	High-technology plants	Other plants
1	Labour	Labour
2	Transport availability	Market access
3	Quality of life	Transport availability
4	Market access	Materials access
5	Utilities	Utilities
6	Site characteristics	Regulatory practice
7	Communications characteristics	Quality of life
8	Business climate	Business climate
9	Taxes	Site characteristics
10	Development organisations	Taxes

Source: Stafford (1983)

In addition to the appreciation that transport is often not the dominant factor in
locational choice, there is now the increasing view amongst economists that firms
are not always motivated by notions of cost minimisation. Hence, even if one can
isolate the factors of interest to firms it is not certain that they should be treated
within a cost-minimising framework. In many cases provided a site offers, *ceteris
paribus,* a location where transport costs are below some threshold, it is considered acceptable. In other cases, the first acceptable location encountered is
adopted rather than a protracted search pursued (Townroe, 1971). The influences
of social setting and amenities on those who make the decisions about location,

and on the staffs whose preferences they have to consider are highlighted in this context by Eversley (1965). Firms often, therefore, adopt 'satisficing' policies in site selection rather than attempting to profit or revenue maximise or cost minimise. Under these conditions the exact role played by transport costs becomes almost impossible to define, but it seems likely that once a location has been chosen, a major rise in transport costs would be necessary to overcome the basic inertia which would seem to accompany such a managerial objective.

2.4 Output, market area and transport costs

Transport costs are not only instrumental in influencing where firms locate, but they also play an important role in determining the market area served by each firm. Transport costs, given the place of industrial location, can determine the total quantity of goods sold and their price and the spatial distribution of this output. Much of the early work looking at market areas was conducted by Lösch (1954) but here we focus on a specific transport orientated model which was devised by van Es and Ruijgrok (1974). The simple model treats transport demand as derived from the demand for the final product and assumes all supply and demand curves to be linear. For expositional ease the relevant functions are treated in a manner running counter to economic convention; specifically price is treated as dependent upon demand rather than vice versa. Initially our firm which produces a homogeneous product supplies a single customer who is located some distance from its predetermined site. Hence we have,

$$P^s = a_0 + a_1 Q^s + P^t \qquad (2.2a)$$
$$P^d = b_0 - b_1 Q^d \qquad (2.2b)$$
$$Q^d = Q^s \qquad (2.2c)$$
$$P^d = P^s \qquad (2.2d)$$

where:
P^s is the supply price of the commodity;
P^d is the demand price of the commodity;
Q^s is the quantity of the commodity supplied;
Q^d is the quantity of the commodity demanded; and
P^t is a constant transport cost per unit carried to the customer and treated as a cost borne by the supplier.

Manipulation and combination of these equations yields the profit-maximising supply, Q^e, that is,

$$Q^e = \frac{b_0 - a_0}{a_1 + b_1} - \frac{P^t}{a_1 + b_1} \qquad (2.3)$$

It is immediately clear that transport costs exert a negative influence on the quantity the profit-maximising firm ought to supply, that is, if $P^t = 0$, then the equilibrium output would rise by $\frac{P^t}{a_1 + b_1}$. Further we can derive the equilibrium price (P^e) which should be charged to the customer:

$$P^e = \frac{a_1 b_0 - a_0 b_1}{a_1 + b_1} + \frac{b_1 P^t}{a_1 + b_1} \qquad (2.4)$$

Here we see that the transport cost component increases the equilibrium price by $\frac{b_1 P^t}{a_1+b_1}$. The effect of this, together with the effects of transport costs on Q^e, are illustrated graphically in Figure 2.3. The vertical axis shows the final price per unit paid by the customer and the horizontal axis the quantity of goods sold. The introduction of the transport cost element to the diagram has the effect of pushing the supply curve up from $P^s (P^t = 0)$ to $P^s(P^t > 0)$. It is evident that transport cost rises will push up final prices and reduce the quantity sold. The exact impact depends not only upon the magnitude of P^t but also the elasticities of supply and demand – greater inelasticity increases the influence on price exerted by transport cost considerations.

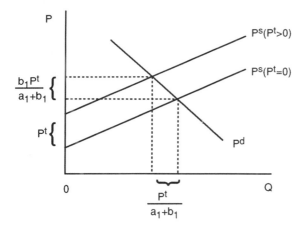

Figure 2.3
The effect of transport costs on price and ouput

To estimate the market area served when potential customers are spread evenly around the production site we will initially assume identical individuals are located at equal distances along a straight road from the site of the supplier. The customers will be confronted by prices which are composed of a fixed factory price reflecting production costs and a variable transport cost dependent upon the distance they live from the production site. Since each customer – by assumption – exhibits a similar demand response it is, therefore, the transport component which determines the amount each will buy. At the edge of the firm's market area, the amount supplied to the marginal customer vanishes to zero (this will be when $P^t = b_0 - a_0$). If j customers are served before this limit is reached, then from equation 2.3, we can see that the total sales of the firm (Q^T) will amount to:

$$Q^T = \sum_j Q_j^e = j\left[\frac{b_0-a_0}{a_1+b_1}\right] - \left[\sum_j P_j^e\right]\left[\frac{1}{a_1+b_1}\right] \qquad (2.5)$$

where Q_j^e represents sales to customer j.

This approach can be extended to show the entire geographical area served by the firm. In Figure 2.4 the vertical axis represents the quantity supplied to each customer, on the assumption that the customers are evenly spread over the plane. The amount sold to a customer falls from very high levels $Q^e = \dfrac{b_0 - a_0}{a_1 + b_1}$ immediately adjacent to the site of supply – where transport costs are zero - and falls to zero when transport costs become excessive. The total amount sold can be measured by calculating the volume of the cone, that is:

$$D = b\pi \int_0^R (P + T) \, T \, \mathrm{d}\,T \tag{2.6}$$

where:
D is total demand as a function of free on board price net of mill price P;
b is twice the population density of a square in which it costs 1 money unit to ship 1 unit of the commodity along one side;
$d = f\,(P + T)$ is an individual demand as a function of the price of the commodity at the place of consumption;
P is f.o.b. net mill price of the commodity;
T is freight cost per unit from the factory to the consumer; and
R is the maximum possible transport cost.

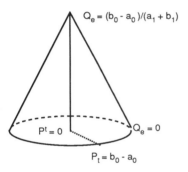

Figure 2.4
The influence of transport costs on market area

While this type of approach (relating the sales, prices and market area of production to transport costs) is obvious theoretically, interestingly it does rely upon many abstractions from reality for its internal consistency. As with many theories, some of the assumptions associated with the model outline above may be relaxed: it is possible for example to allow for variations in population density, for heterogeneity in consumer tastes, and non-perfectly elastic supply conditions – but this does tend to add complexity to the analysis. The general impression conveyed, however, is always the same, namely that transport costs are key in determining the size of geographical market served by a firm and the total volume of its sales. Further, one situation where the effects of transport improvements may have a magnified effect on the market area is when the producing industry is capable of exploiting manufacturing scale economies. This is not a novel idea and, indeed, it was recognised over two centuries ago by Adam Smith (1776).

An aspect of market area analysis which has gained in importance in recent years relates less to the area served by a producing unit and rather more to the area served by warehouses. Changes in transport technology and information systems combined with the increased importance of high-value, low-weight manufactures in the economy has brought forth new physical distribution systems (McKinnon, 1989). The traditional model (Figure 2.5) assumed a trade-off between warehousing and transport with the costs of operating warehouses rising with their number but transport costs falling assuming a constant throughput of goods. The optimal number of warehouses would be determined by minimising the combined costs of warehousing and transport (that is, Q_W). Recent modifications have incorporated the costs of holding inventories into the calculations which, in the simplest of terms, argue that variations in the costs of holding inventories follows the 'square root law'. This law effectively says that safety and cycle inventory requirements are related to the square root of the number of warehouses in the system. Hence, moving from a system of ten depots to an entirely centralised system would reduce inventory requirements by 68 per cent. This provides justification for companies reducing the number of warehouses and with it the market area served by each.

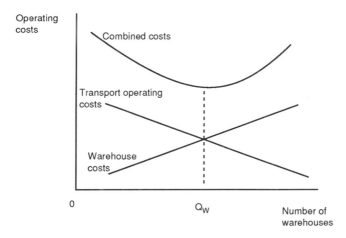

Figure 2.5
Trade-off in transport and warehouse operating costs

2.5   Urban transport and land values
The previous sections have been concerned with the interaction between transport and the physical, spatial economy but little has been said regarding the way in which transport quality can affect land values. Location, to date, has tended to be viewed in terms of where a firm would locate and the area which would be served. Little has been said about the distribution of land among alternative uses either within one sector, such as manufacturing, or among sectors, notably between industrial and residential use. Early work on this problem can be traced back to von Thünen's (1826) land rent model which attempted to explain

differences in agricultural land rent. He argued that concentric zones of crop specialisation would develop around the central market; the key feature of the model being that land rent differentials over homogeneous space are determined entirely by transport cost savings. While the nineteenth century agrarian economy provided the inspiration for 'bid-rent curve' analysis, it is in the context of twentieth-century urban development that it has been most fully developed.

Haig (1926) was the first to apply von Thünen's argument in the urban context arguing that, 'Site rents and transportation costs are vitally connected through their relationship to the friction of space. Transportation is the means of reducing that friction, at the cost of time and money. Site rentals are charges which can be made for sites where accessibility may be had with comparatively low transport-ation costs.' People who are prepared to pay the highest price for improved transport provision (that is, out-bid rivals) will enjoy the most accessible locations. This approach is clearly dependent upon some very stringent assumptions which need to be spelt out before we proceed further. We focus initially upon the residential location of households. The city under review is seen as a featureless plain with all production, recreational and retailing activities concentrated at a single urban core (the CBD). The population is homogeneous with respect to family size, income, housing demands, etc., but while building costs are invariate to location, transport costs rise with distance from the CBD. With these assumptions, the sum of transport costs plus site rents is constant across the entire city (that is, if we take a ray out from the CBD to the perimeter of the city and concentrate exclusively on household decisions we have the situation depicted in Figure 2.6. Total site rent in the city may be estimated as the volume of the inverted cone centred on the CBD).

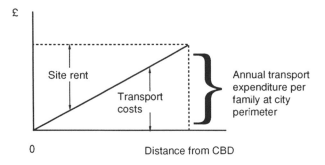

Figure 2.6
The site rent/transport cost trade off

An improvement in the transport system will result in a fall in land values at each location and an outward expansion of the city – the extent of this outward expansion being dependent upon the elasticity of demand for transport services. If the demand for transport is perfectly inelastic then the boundary of the city remains unchanged. If *AB* in Figure 2.7 is the initial rent gradient then, with a perfectly inelastic demand for transport services the result of, say, uniformly lower public transport fares is to shift the gradient to *A'B*. The city's perimeter remains at *B*. With a degree of elasticity, however, the reduced transport cost will encourage longer distance travel to work and recreational activities and the eventual rent gradient is likely to settle at a position such as *A"B"* and the city's boundary to extend out to *B"*. It should be remembered that this simple model assumes that transport costs vary linearly with distance from the CBD and that individuals are identical. If this is not the case then, as Mohring (1961) has pointed out, the precise relation between transport cost and location patterns would be obtained simultaneously rather than sequentially as above. Further, the change in relative site rentals may also result in households wishing to own different size plots of land; this complication is incorporated by allowing for some elasticity in the demand for quantities of land (see Alcaly, 1976).

This model of urban location, which was subsequently greatly refined in a classic paper by Alonso (1964), extends beyond the simple consideration of residential land rent. The priorities of households differ and there is clearly competition in a free-market land economy among the demands of industry, commerce and various classes of households for different sites. In general, there are so called 'agglomeration economies' to be enjoyed by industry and commerce from locating both close to each other and at the city core – they present an identifiable geographical entity (for example, medicine in Harley Street, tailoring in Savile Row, etc.), can be easily served by specialised suppliers, provide customers with a comprehensive range of services, etc. Consequently, given the potentially higher revenue associated with a core location, business tends to bid highly for central sites. Poorer people who cannot afford high transport fares and place a relatively low priority on large sites are willing to bid higher rents for inner area locations, while the wealthy will be more inclined to bid a higher rent for suburban locations.

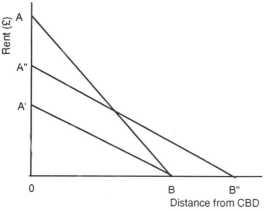

Figure 2.7
The site rent/transport cost trade off

Figure 2.7 shows in its upper half the bid-rent curves for three groups of urban land user: business, poor households and wealthy households. We see, in this very simple example, that business will outbid both classes of household for sites near the urban centre (that is, the CBD will extend from 0 to *B*), poorer households will locate adjacent to the CBD (that is, from *B* to *P*) while the wealthy will outbid the other groups for sites at the edge of the city (that is, from *P* to *W*). Traced out into a plane and rotated (as in the lower half of Figure 2.8) a concentric pattern of land use emerges. The actual boundary *jklm* is the revealed rent function for the city on the basis that land is allocated to the highest bidder. Clearly this is rather a stylised picture of urban land use and rents (Chapter 10 provides some further refinements), but it does offer some insight into the influence transport can have on intra-urban location patterns. Quite simply, high-transport-cost activities, *ceteris paribus,* will be located at a close distance to the CBD and low-transport-cost activities will take locations further away.

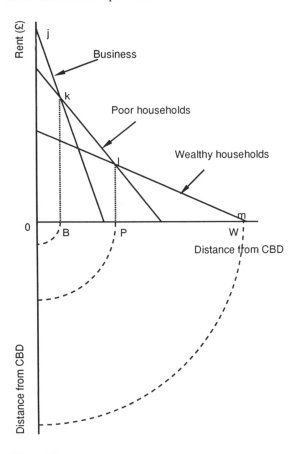

Figure 2.8
Rent-bid curves and concentric urban land use

Changes in transport costs may affect the amount of land taken up by various activities. The introduction of improved public transport with extremely low fares, for example, may well increase the willingness of poorer households to bid for locations further from the CBD and consequently the central ring of land use, as we see in Figure 2.9A, may both widen and, more probably, move outwards. Damm *et al.* (1980) found that the construction of the Washington Metro, with its cheap, good quality service, increased the willingness of people to pay for land parcels near metro stations. In the urban centre retailers were even more willing to offer high rents for sites near metro services. Alternatively the construction of an extensive urban road network is likely to improve the access offered to car-owning, wealthy households, shifting their rent-bid curve upwards and to the right (Figure 2.9B). The ring of land occupied by this group will thus be extended out beyond the original city boundaries (that is, from W to W'). Evans (1973), for instance, specifically attributes the 'flight to the suburbs' to 'the large-scale construction of urban motorways which increases commuting speeds and comfort for the commuter' and argues that the only way to get higher income groups back into the central area is to 'Make the transport system slow, cheap and uncomfortable, and not fast, comfortable and expensive.'

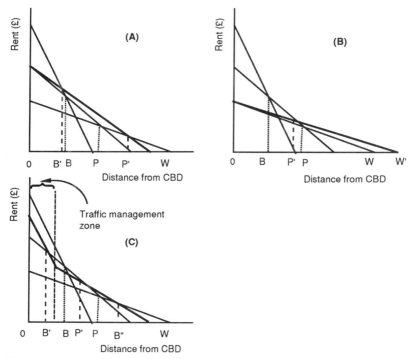

Figure 2.9
The impact of changing transport provision on urban land use

Another possibility is that a strict traffic management policy may be introduced in the city centre. Although the exact effect of such a policy depends upon its detailed design we will assume for the sake of illustration that this discourages shoppers, etc. from using the CBD. This will reduce the willingness of business to bid for a central site, but it will increase the bidding by business for outer locations. In Figure 2.9C the final result is that the CBD contracts (to OB') while a sub-centre of business activity emerges, as $P'B''$ in the diagram. Out-of-town shopping centres and commercial centres are obvious manifestations of this type of development.

Of course, the real world is a little more complicated than these examples suggest; for example we have treated the city in isolation, ignored variations in the geography of the area, assumed away any land-use planning agency, and treated locational change as instantaneous, but it becomes apparent that any attempt at formulating an urban transport policy or any advance in transport engineering will have important implications for urban form.

2.6   Transport and urban wage rates

Not only do transport costs influence urban land-use patterns, but they are also instrumental in determining spatial variations in urban wage rates. As Moses (1962) has pointed out, 'the wage differential, positive or negative, a worker is willing to accept is completely determined by the structure of money transport costs.' We will assume that all employment is either concentrated at the city centre or else spread evenly over the surrounding, mainly residential, area. All households are assumed initially to be in equilibrium, all enjoying the same level of welfare. Moreover, all workers are paid identical wages, work the same hours and undertake the same number of commuting trips. Initially then, net monies after work-trip outlays will vary among workers according to the nature of their intra-urban transport costs and the distance of their homes from the CBD. Variations in land values with distance from CBD, as we saw in the previous section, act as an adjustment mechanism to ensure uniformity of welfare. People living away from the urban core will pay more in transport costs, but their land rentals will be correspondingly lower.

In this simple world, however, a worker could improve his well-being by giving up his job at the CBD (and thus saving commuting costs) and work at one of the jobs which are spread evenly over the urban area and which is near his home. He would be willing to accept a lower income in this situation; indeed, he would be willing to sacrifice his wage rate down to the point where it is cut by as much as the commuting costs that are saved. Thus there will be an equilibrium wage at locations nearer home than the CBD which will be lower than the core wage.

The result of this type of approach is the development of an urban wage gradient the shape of which is determined by commuting cost factors. In Figure 2.10 OW is the wage paid at the urban centre, of this *WA'* is the travel cost between the boundary of the city, *A* and the CBD. *OA'* is the wage rate required to keep an employee living at *A* in his current occupation if he worked at (or very near) home. The worker living at *A* is, therefore, indifferent between commuting to the CBD and earning OW and working at home and earning *OA'*. The *WW'* curve traces out the wage rates at which a worker living at *A* would have to be paid to make him indifferent between working at home and at any intermediate site between *A* and the CBD. (It also shows the wage rates at which people living between *A* and the CBD will be indifferent between working at home and at the core.)

If we introduce the notion of some secondary employment concentration, say at *L*, then reverse commuting may develop. If this sub-centre requires labour which it cannot attract from households to the right of *L* it will need to compensate workers who travel out from areas between *L* and the CBD. Since the transport system tends to be less costly, in overall terms of money, time and comfort factors (see Chapter 4) for reverse commuting, the reverse commuting wage gradient is likely to be less steep than the commuting wage gradient. The main influence on reverse commuting costs *vis-à-vis* those for commuters are the generally lower levels of traffic congestion away from the CBD.

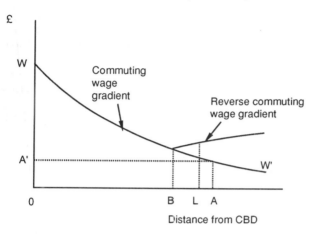

Figure 2.10
Transport costs and wages

Just how does the wage gradient theory stand up to empirical investigation? Quite clearly the spread of national wage agreements, combined with imperfections in the land and transport markets (for example, public transport subsidies and the growth in company cars), makes any exact testing of the theory difficult. American evidence from New York (Segal, 1960) found wages to be higher in suburban counties than at the CBD and, even after allowing for variations in industrial structure, no wage gradient emerged. However, Rees and Schultz (1970) in their study of Chicago found a 'strong positive association of wages with distance travelled to work', but the wage gradient for blue-collar workers had its peak in the area of heavy industrial concentration (the south-west of the city) and sloped downwards towards the north-west. In Britain, Evans (1973) suggests that while a wage gradient can be discerned for Greater London there is little conclusive evidence of one elsewhere. Indeed, in provincial cities, clerical wages are often almost uniform across metropolitan areas. Clerical wages were, however, found to be higher in the City and the West End of London than in the suburbs.

Although these findings are not conclusive, it is clear that the evidence supporting the wage-gradient theory is at least balanced by that rejecting it. The problems are that the studies to date fail to allow for the multiplicity of factors other than transport which affect wage levels. We have already mentioned some of the problems – notably imperfections in certain markets – but to these we must add the tendency for employers to compensate workers for high transport costs by unrecorded payments (free meals, shorter working hours, more flexible time-keeping, etc.). Additionally, in some cities there are unrecorded advantages of working in the city centre (better out-of-work and shopping facilities, increased career potential, etc.). The studies do not, therefore, refute the idea that transport costs influence urban wage patterns, but rather, the situation is more complex than the simple wage gradient theory suggests.

2.7 Further reading and references

Vickerman (1980) offers one of the few attempts to integrate transport, housing and industry within a comprehensive framework. Useful extensions of the conventional partial equilibrium approach to transport and land use are contained in the following which look at the interaction from the position of regional and urban economics; Richardson (1978), Alcaly (1976) and O'Sullivan (1981). For a more mathematical approach, Richardson (1977) considers the importance of transport in the so-called 'New Urban Economics'. Button and Gillingwater (1983) provide an edited set of papers which, amongst other things, provide a number of case studies looking at transport–location interaction. The latter also provides some useful insights into the relationship between urban transport and land values although the potential reader should be forewarned of the mathematical approach employed. Evans (1973) is the most complete work on transport and residential decisions while Thall (1987) offers a rigorous examination of the link between transport and land rents. It is also extremely readable with extensive references. Readers interested in up-to-date empirical studies of the role of transport in industrial location might usefully glance through the contents pages of journals such as *Regional Studies* and *Urban Studies*.

References

Alcaly, R.E. (1976), 'Transportation and urban land values: a review of the theoretical literature', *Land Economics*, 52, 42-53.

Allen, D.N. and Robertson, G.E. (1983), *Silicon, Sensors and Software: Listening to Advanced Technology Enterprises in Pennsylvania*, Institute of Public Administration, Pennsylvania State University.

Alonso, W. (1964), *Location and Land Use*, Cambridge, Mass., Harvard University Press.

Anderson, D.L. (1983), 'Your company's logistic management: an asset or a liability?', *Transportation Review*, (winter), 111–25.

Button, K.J. (1987), 'High-technology companies: an examination of their transport needs', *Progress in Planning*, 29, 79–146.

Button, K.J. and Gillingwater, D. (eds)(1983), *Transport, Location and Spatial Policy*, Aldershot, Gower.

Button, K.J., Pearman, A.D. and Fowkes A.S. (1982), *Car Ownership Modelling and Forecasting*, Aldershot, Gower Press.

Cameron, G.C. and Clark, B.D. (1966), *Industrial Movement and the Regional Problem*, University of Glasgow Occasional Paper No.6.

Chisholm, M. (1971), 'Freight transport costs, industrial location and regional development', in M. Chisholm and G. Manners (eds), *Spatial Policy Problems of the British Economy*, Cambridge, Cambridge University Press.

Cook, W.R. (1967), 'Transport decisions of certain firms in the Black Country', *Journal of Transport Economics and Policy*, 1, 344–56.

Damm, D., Lerman, S.R., Lerner-Lam, E. and Young J. (1980), 'Response of urban real estate values in anticipation of Washington Metro', *Journal of Transport Economics and Policy*, 14, 315–36.

Diamond, D. and Spence, N. (1989), *Infrastructure and Industrial Costs in British Industry*, London, HMSO.

Edwards, S.L. (1970), 'Transport costs in British industry', *Journal of Transport Economics and Policy*, 4, 65–83.

Edwards, S.L. (1975), 'Regional variations in freight costs', *Journal of Transport Economics and Policy*, 9, 115–26.

Evans, A.W. (1973), *The Economics of Residential Location*, London, Macmillan.

Eversley, D.E.S. (1965), 'Social and psychological factors in the determination of industrial location', in T. Wilson (ed), *Papers on Regional Development*, Oxford, Blackwell.

Fischer, L. (1971), *Die Berucksichtignung Raumordnungs Politiseler Zeilsetviengen in de Verkehrsplanung*, Berlin.

Greenhutt, M. (1963), *Microeconomics and the Space Economy*, Chicago, Scott-Foresman.

Gudgin, G. (1978), *Industrial Location Processes and Regional Employment Growth*, Farnborough, Saxon House.

Gwilliam, K.M. (1979), 'Transport infrastructure investments and regional development', in J.K. Bowers (ed.), *Inflation, Development and Integration – Essays in Honour of A.J. Brown*, Leeds, Leeds University Press.

Haig, R.M. (1926), 'Towards an understanding of the Metropolis', *Quarterly Journal of Economics*, 40, 179–208.

Kain, J.F. (1964), 'A contribution to the urban transportation debate: an economic model of urban residential and travel behaviour', *Review of Economics and Statistics*, 47, 55–64.

Lösch, A. (1954), *The Economics of Location*, New Haven, Conn., Yale University Press.

McKinnon, A.C. (1989), *Physical Distribution Systems*, London, Routledge.

Mohring, H. (1961), 'Land values and the measurement of highway benefits', *Journal of Political Economy*, 69, 236–49.

Moses, L.N. (1962), 'Towards a theory of intraurban wage differentials and their influence on travel behaviour', *Papers of the Regional Science Association*, 9, 53–63.

O'Sullivan, P. (1981), *Geographical Economics*, Harmondsworth, Penguin.

Owen, W. (1987), *Transport and World Development*, London, Hutchinson.

Rees, A. and Shultz, G.P. (1970), *Workers and Wages in an Urban Labour Market*, Chicago, Chicago University Press.

Richardson, H.W. (1977), *The New Urban Economics and Alternatives*, London, Pion.

Richardson, H.W. (1978), *Urban Economics*, Hinsdale, Dryden.

Segal, M. (1960), *Wages in the Metropolis*, Cambridge, Mass., Harvard University Press.

Smith, A. (1776), *The Wealth of Nations*, Harmondsworth, Penguin edition, 1970.

Stafford, H.A. (1983), *The Effects of Environmental Regulations on Industrial Location*, Working Paper, University of Cincinnati.

Thall, G. (1987), *Land Use and Urban Form: The Consumption Theory of Land Rent*, New York, Methuen.

Thomson, J.M. (1974), *Modern Transport Economics*, Harmondsworth, Penguin.

Townroe, P.M. (1971), *Industrial Location Decisions: A Study in Management Behaviour*, Centre for Urban and Regional Studies, University of Birmingham.

UK Department of Transport (1980), *Report of the Inquiry into Lorries, People and the Environment*, London, HMSO.

UK Trade and Industry Sub-committee of the House of Commons Expenditure Committee (1973), *Regional Development Incentives Report*, House of Commons Paper 85, London, HMSO.

van Es, J. and Ruijgrok, C.J. (1974), 'Modal choice in freight transport', in E.J. Visser (ed.), *Transport Decisions in an Age of Uncertainty*, The Hague, Martinus Nijhoff.

Vickerman, R.W. (1980), *Spatial Economic Behaviour*, London, Macmillan.

von Thünen, J.H. (1826), *Der Isoline Staat in Beziehung auf Nationale-Konomie und Landwirkschaft*, Stuttgart, Gustav Fischer, 1966 reprint.

Weber, A. (1929), *Theory of the Location of Industry*, Chicago, Chicago University Press.

3   The Demand for Transport

3.1   The demand for transport

Chapter 2 looked at the interrelationship between land-use patterns and transport; it thus offered some insights into a few of the factors influencing the demand for transport services. In this chapter the factors which influence demand for transport are considered in more detail. In particular, the previous chapter laid stress on the derived nature of the demand for the vast majority of transport services, and it is this feature of demand which explains another characteristic of the transport market.

One of the most pronounced characteristics of the demand for transport, for instance, is its regular fluctuation over time. In urban areas, the demand for road space and public transport services is markedly higher in the early morning and late afternoon than during the rest of the day; in the inter-urban context the demand for passenger transport fluctuates regularly over a year with high seasonal peaks, while with international freight transport (especially shipping) there are long-term cycles in demand. This tendency for peaks and troughs in the demand for transport is a reflection of fluctuations in the demand for the final products made accessible by transport services. In general, people wish to go on holiday in the summer; hence the seasonal peak in the demand for coach, rail and air services, while business finds it helpful to operate standard hours (that is, from 'nine-to-five') with the consequential concentration of commuter traffic. Longer-term fluctuations in the demand for shipping services reflect the state of business cycles in the trading nations – at the nadir of such cycles demand slumps, at the zenith it is extremely buoyant.

Despite these regular fluctuations, it has been suggested (for example, by Thomson, 1974) that over time, and in another sense, there has been a remarkable stability in the demand for travel, with households, for example, on average making roughly the same number of trips during a day albeit for different purposes or by different modes. There may be more leisure travel, but there are fewer work trips and greater use is now made of air transport and the motor-car at the expense of walking and cycling. It is suggested that this situation reflects the obvious fact that there is a limit to the time people have available for travel, especially if they are to enjoy the fruits of the activities at the final destinations.

More recent work on travel time budgets indicates that the situation is more complicated than this and that the constancy suggested above should be subjected to a much closer inspection. In the United Kingdom, for example, there is ample empirical evidence (see Gunn, 1981) that average travel times have increased steadily over the past quarter of a century. Explanations are difficult to find but one suggestion is that this is the result of rising incomes and that the constant time budget implied by Thomson only holds for *each in*come group. Thus people are moved from low income groups with low travel time budgets to higher income groups with associated higher travel time budgets. Some time ago, Goodwin (1973) showed that at the aggregate level time expenditure on travel per head increases roughly proportionally to income. Such findings emphasise the importance of time as well as conventional variables in travel demand analysis and, as we see in the following chapter, considerable emphasis is placed upon the role that time costs play in transport decision-making.

Given this rather general, aggregate background it is now relevant to look in much more detail at the actual influences and motivations which affect travel and transport-related demand. It seems appropriate to begin by considering the simple demand function.

3.2   The factors which influence travel demand

It is generally considered that the demand for a commodity (D_a) is influenced by its price (P_a), the prices of other goods ($P_1, P_2 .... P_u$) and the level of income (Y):

$$D_a = f(P_a P_1, P_2, ... P_u, Y) \tag{3.1}$$

While this simple framework holds for transport, as for all other goods and services, there are refinements and detail which need to be highlighted if one is to gain an understanding of the way the transport market operates. The individual terms in the above are, in fact, not simple variables but rather represent complex compounds of several interacting factors. Price, for instance, is not simply the fare paid but must embrace all the other costs involved in obtaining the transport service (of which 'time costs', as we noted above, are generally held the most important), while it may not be total income which influences travel demand by individuals but rather income in excess of some threshold subsistence level. Further, there is the need to be very clear on what exactly it is which is being demanded: is it a trip *per se* or is it something more specific than this, for example, a bus trip or a journey over a particular route? Quandt and Baumol (1966) have gone so far as to suggest that it is not transport at all which is being demanded but rather a bundle of transport services. (We look at this idea more fully in the context of forecasting in Chapter 9.)

These types of problems and issues are clearly difficulties which cannot be entirely circumvented in a general discussion of the influences affecting transport demand, but they should be borne in mind as we move on to look in more detail at some of the items contained in the demand function set out as equation 3.1.

The price of the transport service

As has been suggested above, the price of transport embraces considerably more than the simple money costs paid out in fares or haulage fees. In transport modelling and quantitative work these other components of price (that is, time costs, waiting, insecurity, etc.) may be combined to form a generalised cost index of the type we discuss in Chapter 4, but here we concentrate on money prices and, in particular, on the sensitivity of transport users to the price of transport services.

Generalisations are obviously difficult, especially across all modes of transport, but in many cases it seems clear that price changes within certain limits have relatively little effect on the quantity of travel or transport services demanded. The demand for cargo shipping is, for example, very inelastic, in part because of the lack of close substitutes for shipping services, in part because of the inelastic nature of the demand for the raw materials frequently carried, and in part because of the relatively small importance of freight rates in the final selling price of cargoes.

Studies of urban public transport in the 1970s covering a variety of countries also indicate relatively low price elasticities with a direct fare elasticity of around –0.3 being considered normal. Smith and MacIntosh (1974) looking at British municipal bus undertakings, for instance, produce figures ranging from –0.21 to –0.61, but the majority fall at the lower end of the spectrum. McGillivany's (1970) suggestion of a figure of around –0.2 for bus trips in San Francisco and Lave's (1970) finding of a direct fare elasticity of –0.11 for transit trips in Chicago imply the fare elasticity in the United States may be slightly lower than in the UK. In Canada an elasticity of –0.33 has for some time been used as a rule of thumb by operators. More recent studies, mainly from the 1980s, surveyed by Goodwin (1992) tend to produce similar figures to Smith and MacIntosh although highlighting the fact that the short term elasticities found in 'before and after' studies of fare change are in the order of a third of the size of longer term elasticities covering a reaction time in excess of five years. Something of a rogue result, however, was obtained in the econometric study of bus and underground use in London during the late 1980s by Gilbert and Jalilian (1991) – see Table 3.1 – which suggests long run elasticities exceeding unity for buses and approaching unity for the underground; rail demand elasticity at the more 'normal' low value.

Table 3.1
Estimated long-run price elasticities

		Prices		
	Bus	*Underground*	*British Rail*	*Non-travel*
Bus	–1.318	0.897	0.193	0.229
Underground	0.356	–0.688	0.211	0.120

Source: Gilbert and Jalilian (1991)

The effect of price change on private car transport must be divided between the effect on vehicle ownership and that specifically on vehicle use. Most UK studies of car ownership indicate an elasticity of about –0.3 with respect to vehicle price and –0.1 with respect to petrol price (Mogridge, 1978). American empirical work suggests a rather higher sensitivity (the Chase Econometrics Associates (1974) model, for example, implies a -0.88 purchase price elasticity and a –0.82 fuel price elasticity), but responsiveness is still very low. For car use, all the evidence suggests an extremely low fuel price elasticity in the short term (see Table 3.2) which may be attributed to changing patterns of household expenditure between vehicle ownership and use and people's perception of motoring costs. Early findings were brought together by Bendtsen (1980) in a series of international comparisons. He finds that petrol price elasticity of demand for car use to be –0.08 in Australia for the period from 1955 to 1976; –0.07 in Britain for 1973/4; –0.08 in Denmark for 1973/4 and –0.12 for 1979/80, and –0.05 in the USA for the period from 1968 to 1975. A slightly greater degree of sensitivity is observed in seven studies covering the UK, US and Australia examined more recently by Oum *et al.* (1992) which yield car usage elasticities in the range –0.09 to –0.52.

Table 3.2
Traffic elasticities with respect to petrol price (expressed as absolute values)

| | Explicit | | Ambiguous |
	Short run	Long run	
Time series	–0.16	–0.33	–0.46
	(0.08, 4.00)	(0.10, 4.00)	(0.40, 5.00)
Cross section	....	0.29	–0.50
		(0.06, 2)	(n.a., 1)

Note: Figures in parenthesis indicate one standard deviation and the number of quoted elasticities.
Source: Goodwin (1992)

If we move to the other extreme of the transport market and look at airline operations the evidence is that demand is slightly less elastic (Table 3.3) with long-term demand (estimated from cross-sectional data) emerging as elastic. What these coefficients, and indeed, those cited above relating to other modes often disguise are quite significant differences in the elasticities for different groups of traveller and between individual services. Table 3.4, for instance, presents the results of an investigation of air travel across the North Atlantic conducted by Mutti and Mural (1977). The general impression is of price inelasticity but there is obvious variability between routes. Examinations of internal air traffic within the United States, however, produce much more varied results. Brown and Watkins (1968) and Gronau (1970) show a remarkable degree of consistency by producing price elasticities of –0.85 and –0.75 respectively but Jung and Fujii (1976) came to a somewhat different conclusion, namely, 'The empirical evidence suggests that demand for air travel for distances under 500 miles in the south east and south central portions of the US is price elastic.'

The difficulty with many statistics on demand sensitivity is, therefore, that they are elasticities averaged over several groups. In fact, the price elasticity of transport, as with the price elasticity of other goods, should ideally be set in a specific context. In the case of transport four broad types of classification are important.

(1) Trip purpose. There is an abundance of evidence that the fare elasticity for certain types of trips is much higher than others. Business travel demand in particular seems to be relatively more insensitive to changes in transport price than other forms of trip. Kraft and Domenich (1970) found that public transport work trips exhibited a fare elasticity of –0.17 in Boston (USA) compared with –0.32 for shopping trips. These figures conform closely to those found by London Transport in this country. If we focus on the work that has looked at air traffic, Mutti and Mural (1977) attribute part of the variation they found in fare responsiveness on the North Atlantic to the fact that 'we expect personal travel to be more price elastic than business travel'. Straszheim (1978) subsequently provides confirmation of this view and isolates elasticities for different types of service. In particular he concludes, 'First class fares can be raised and will increase total revenue ... The demand elasticity for standard economy service is about unity, and highest

for peak period travel ... The demand for discount and promotional fares is highly price elastic....'. Oum *et al.* (1986) came to identical conclusions when looking at more recent North American data. Quite clearly, therefore, it is dangerous to attempt to analyse transport demand without considering the specific type of trip being undertaken.

Table 3.3
Demand elasticities of air passenger travel (expressed as absolute values)*

	Time series	*Cross-section*	*Others[†]*
Leisure travel	0.40-1.98, 1.92	1.52	1.40-3.30, 2.20-4.60
Business travel	0.65	1.15	0.90
Mixed or unknown	0.82, 0.91, 0.31-1.81 1.12-1.28, 1.48	0.76-0.84, 1.39, 1.63 1.85, 2.83-4.51	0.53-1.00, 1.80-1.90

* Based on 16 studies.
[†] Includes studies with unknown data sources
Source: Oum *et al.* (1992)

Table 3.4
Demand elasticities for air travel on the North Atlantic 1964–74 by country (expressed as absolute values)

Market	*Income elasticity*	*Fare elasticity*
United States	2.15	–0.99
United Kingdom	4.38	–0.40
Netherlands	1.77	–0.28
Italy	2.00	–0.72
Germany	2.71	–0.19
France	2.03	–0.14
Total	1.89	–0.89

Source: Mutti and Mural (1977)

(2) The methods of charging. Users of different forms of transport (or, sometimes, different services of the same mode) are often confronted with entirely different methods of payment. Consequently, their perception of the price of a journey may differ from the actual monies expended. Sherman (1967), for example, has suggested that motorists perceive very little of the true overall price of these trips because they base decisions on a limited concept of short-run marginal cost. As Harrison and Quarmby (1969) put it in a predecimal summary of the situation, 'Including fuel, oil, maintenance, tyres and mile-dependent depreciation, most private cars show a marginal cost of between 4d and 7d a mile. Various empirical methods indicate "perceived" costs of between 2d and 4d a mile (in the period 1966-9).' Users of public transport, on the other hand, are usually made much more aware of the costs of their trip-making by the requirement to purchase a

ticket, usually prior to beginning their journeys. Nevertheless, given the range of season tickets (which permit bulk-buying of journeys over a specific *route)* and 'travel card' facilities (which permit bulk-buying of journeys over a specified *network),* the distinction is not a firm one. The empirical findings are also not very helpful. White's (1981) review of the empirical information available on travel cards, for example, points to a much lower price elasticity for travel card systems than for conventional single ticket cash payment systems.

(3) The time period under consideration. As with other purchasing decisions, people confronted with a change in transport price may act rather differently in the ultra-short run, the short run and the long run. Immediate reaction, as graphically illustrated by Goodwin (1992) in his survey of elasticities, in the ultra short term, to a public transport fare rise may be dramatic, with people, almost on principle, making far less use of services, but over a longer period they may soften and their resolve weaken with the result that the longer-run elasticity is much lower than ultra short-term observations would suggest. The ultra short-term elasticity may, therefore, be extremely high but short-lived. This type of situation may be less common than is sometimes thought and, indeed, the reverse response may result in the slightly longer period. In the short term, for example, people may appear relatively unresponsive to a price change either because they do not consider it a permanent change or because technical constraints limit their immediate actions. The demand for private car transport following the dramatic rise in oil prices in the 1970s provides an illustration of this latter type of phenomenon. The situation is well summarised by Mogridge (1978):

> We have seen in the effects of the oil crisis a very clear demonstration that the short-run effects of price are not at all the same as in the long-run. In the short run, people try to continue doing what they were doing before; in the long run they adjust their behaviour. In the short run, the price elasticity of petrol is low, 0.1; in the long run it is taken up by an adjustment in car size.

Similarly, when considering the effect of general rises on commuter travel costs, the necessity of having to make journeys to work is likely to result in minimal changes in travel patterns in the short term but over a longer period relocations of either residence or employment may produce a more dramatic effect. This implies that one must take care when assessing elasticity coefficients, and it is useful to remember that cross-sectional studies tend to offer estimates of long-run elasticity while time-series studies reflect short-term responses.

(4) The absolute level of the price change. Elasticities are generally found to increase the longer the journey under consideration. This should not be seen simply as a function of distance but rather a reflection of the absolute magnitude of, say, a 10 per cent rise on a £5 fare compared with that on a £500 fare. It is also true that longer journeys are made less frequently, and thus people gather information about prices in a different way. Additionally, they often tend to involve leisure rather than business travel; this suggests that distance may be picking up variations in trip purpose. In the air transport market, for example, DeVany (1974) found that price elasticity rose from -0.97 for a 440 mile trip in the USA to -1.13 for a 830 mile trip. For similar journeys Ippolito (1981) found the respective elasticities to be -0.525 and -1.0.

While it is important to treat elasticities with care because of these type of aggregation issue, there is a further reason for counselling caution when considering such parameters. There are a number of statistical methods employed to calculate elasticities and these can influence the values obtained. In some instances these difference are related to the time span of the elasticity being studies; some techniques being mainly used for short term elasticity estimation while others are more suited to cross-sections and thus long-term elasticity calculations. The intention here is not to go into the technicalities of the various modelling frameworks, although some discussion of this is to be found in Chapter 9, but rather to highlight what seem to be the two main trends. First, if aggregate data are used, for instance looking at demand for an entire railway, then, although it is far from universally true, elasticities *tend* to be higher than from 'discrete choice' type models using data at the individual traveller level. Second, even within a particular modelling framework (be it involving the use of aggregate data or disaggregate data) the exact mathematical form of the equation used influences the elasticity calculated. Table 3.5 provides some general guidance to these effects with respect to estimated elasticities of demand for rail freight transport.

Table 3.5
Demand elasticities for rail freight transport (expressed as absolute values)

Commodities	Log-linear	Aggregate logit	Translog	Discrete choice*
Aggregate commodities	1.52 0.34–1.06	0.25–0.35, 0.83	0.09–0.29, 0.60	n.a.
Chemicals	n.a.	0.66	0.69	2.25
Fabricated metal products	n.a.	1.57	2.16	n.a.
Food products	0.02, 1.18	1.36	2.58, 1.04	n.a.
Iron & steel products	n.a.	n.a.	2.54, 1.20	0.02
Machinery	n.a.	0.16–1.73	2.27–3.50	0.61
Paper, plastic & rubber products	0.67	0.87	1.85	0.17–0.09
Petroleum products	n.a.	n.a.	0.99	0.53
Stone, clay & glass products	n.a.	2.03	n.a.	0.56
Transport equipment	n.a.	n.a.	0.92–1.08	2.68
Wood & wood products	0.05	0.76	1.97, 0.58	0.08

* Disaggregate data
Source: Oum *et al.* (1992)

Income levels
While there is ample evidence that transport is a normal good in the sense that more is demanded at higher levels of income, this generalisation does not apply to all modes of transport nor to all situations. As was seen in the data set out in Table 1.10 income exerts a positive influence over car ownership decisions (a point returned to in section 3.6), but this in turn has produced an inverse relationship with public transport use. As incomes have risen and, with them, car ownership has become more widespread, public transport has in many situations proved to be an inferior good. Gwilliam and Mackie (1975) suggest that the long-run elasticity of demand with respect to income is of the order −0.4 to −1.0 for urban public transport trip-making in the United Kingdom. Gwilliam and Mackie argue that although car ownership rises with income and hence some trips are diverted from public transport there is still a limited off-setting effect inasmuch as wealthier households make more trips in total.

The income elasticity of demand for many other modes of transport is seen to be relatively high. Table 3.1 has already revealed elasticities in the range 1.77 to 4.38 for North Atlantic air travel, while Taplin (1980) suggests a figure of the order of 2.1 for vacation air trips overseas from Australia. By its nature air travel is a high-cost activity (the total costs involved are high even where mileage rates are low) so that income elasticities of this level are to be expected.

As with price, income changes exert somewhat different pressures on transport demand in the long run compared with the short. In general, it may be argued, a fall in income will produce a relatively dramatic fall in the level of demand, but as people readjust their expenditure patterns in the long term the elasticity is likely to be much lower. Looking at the responsiveness of car-ownership levels to income changes, British and US studies suggest a short-term income elasticity of between 2.0 and 4.5 while in the long run it appears to fall to around 1.5 (see Button *et al.,* 1982, for a survey). However, as with price elasticities, the relationships between long- and short-term effects are not completely clear cut. Reza and Spiro (1979), for example, produce an estimate of 0.6 for the short-run income elasticity of demand for petrol rising to 1.44 in the long run. If one assumes that petrol consumption is a proxy for trip-making, then one could attempt to justify this in terms of a slow reaction to changing financial circumstances – a reluctance, for example, to accept immediately the consequences of a fall in income. In fact, the situation is likely to be more complex than this since the long run may embrace changes in technology, and possibly locations, that alter the fuel consumption–trip-making relationship. Thus these figures may still be consistent with the initial hypothesis regarding the relative size of short- and long-run income elasticities of demand for *travel.*

There is a growing literature on the possibility of a constant travel income budget akin to the travel time budget mentioned in section 3.1 (see Gunn, 1981) with households tending to spend a fixed proportion of their income on transport. Zahavi (1977), for example, when examining data from a wide sample of urban transport users, noticed that the proportion of disposable income spent on cars by car-owning households at any income level appears to be approximately constant at a given moment of time. (UK data suggests a proportion of around 15.5 per cent - slightly larger for low incomes – for the period 1971–75.) The evidence for bus transport is less clear, but Mogridge (1978) suggests that while the proportion of disposable household income spent on bus travel seems to rise with income, a constant proportion still emerges if adjustments are made for the number of people in each household. In the longer term there is evidence at the aggregate level that over the past 25 years or so there has been a steady increase in the overall proportion of income or disposable income allocated to travel in the UK. (This contrasts to a more or less constant proportion in Canada and the United States.) This may, though, be explained in terms of rising income levels but constant proportional travel budgets within each income group. The general conclusion about the idea that some overall budget mechanism governs individual travel decisions, however, must be that, to date, the evidence available still leaves many questions unanswered and the theory is still largely unproved.

The price of other transport services
The demand for any particular transport service is likely to be influenced by the actions of competitive and complementary suppliers. (Strictly speaking, it is also influenced by prices in all other markets operating in the economy but, with the possible exceptions of the land market, which was discussed in Chapter 2, and

electronic communications, the importance of these is less great.) We have already touched upon the importance of motoring costs *vis-à-vis* the demand for public transport services and more is said on this topic later in the chapter. Moreover, there are the cross-price effects between modes of public transport. Table 3.6 presents the results from a number of different studies looking at elasticities of demand (both own fare and cross-fare) for transport in Greater London during the period 1970–75. The variation in results generally reflects the adoption of alternative estimation procedures and time-lag allowances. One of the more interesting points is the almost total insensitivity of the demand for urban car use to the fare levels of both bus and rail public transport modes. This fact, which has been observed in virtually all studies of urban public transport, is the main reason that attempts by city transport authorities to reduce or contain car travel by subsiding public transport fares have, in the main, proved unsuccessful.

Table 3.6
Greater London estimated Monday-Friday fare elasticities (1970–75)

		With respect to	
Study	*Elasticity of*	*Bus*	*Rail*
Fairhurst and			
Morris (1975)	Bus	–0.60	0.25
	Rail	0.25	–0.40
Glaister (1976)	Bus	–0.56	0.30
	Rail	1.11	–1.00
Collings, Rigby			
and Welsby (1977)	Bus	–0.405	n.a.
Lewis (1978)	Peak road traffic	0.025	0.056

Source: Glaister and Lewis (1978) which contains full references to the studies cited.

Table 3.5 suggests that there is likely to be more switching of demand between public transport modes as a result of one changing its fare structure than between that mode and private transport. More recent work on cross elasticities between public transport modes (see again Table 3.1), however, has thrown up somewhat different results with the indication, in particular, that bus travel in London is more sensitive to underground fares – this may reflect the capacity problems the latter was suffering in the late 1980s.

In other transport markets the cross-elasticity of demand may be higher, both between operators of the same mode of transport and between modes themselves. Recently, price reduction in non-conference shipping lines has attracted considerable traffic away from the cartel carriers. Similarly, scheduled airlines have experienced a contraction of demand as reduced–rate operators have entered the market.

Evidence on the cross-price elasticity of complementary transport services, such as feeder links to longer distance trunk hauls, is scant. The expansion of the motorway network has, by reducing motorway travel costs, certainly increased the demand for certain feeder roads while at the same time reducing it or competing routes. The exact implications of such network effects are much more difficult to trace out than changes in modal split but, in practical terms, are important features of the transport system.

Tastes

One of the items which influences equation 3.1 and not mentioned to date, but which is often included in elementary discussion of demand, is the 'catch-all' variable, tastes. While there may be circumstances when such a term could and, indeed, should be included in the demand function, in general, tastes are more likely to influence the actual *form* of the demand equation. Consequently, a change in tastes may be seen to affect the relationships between demand and the explanatory variables rather than result in some movement along a demand curve following the pattern of an established relationship.

The economic meaning of 'tastes' is seldom made clear, but in practice it seems to embrace all influences on demand not covered by the previous headings. Over time tastes in transport certainly have changed. Burrell (1972), for instance, has emphasised the increased car orientation of society in private transport while in freight transport the changing structure of the national economy (especially the switch from basic heavy industry to light industry producing high value, low weight products) has shifted the emphasis from price to other aspects of transport service. Both of these changes must to some extent be related to rising standards of living. With more wealth and greater free time there is likely to be an enhanced desire to benefit from the greater freedom and flexibility offered by private transport. A change in location patterns is also possible with larger residential plots away from urban centres now becoming attractive.

Another aspect of 'taste' concerns inertia and asymmetry in decision-making (Goodwin, 1977; Banister, 1978). This has two implications. First, there may be discontinuities in the demand curve for transport, or at least parts of the demand curve reflect almost total insensitivity to price changes, as a result of habit and inertia on the part of individuals and firms. It may be explained in some cases quite simply by the fact that there are costs involved in seeking out information about alternatives and continuing as before is thus the rational response until more major price changes occur. Second, there may be cases where responses are not symmetrical; a ratchet effect exists whereby the reaction to a price fall is not the same as the reaction to an identical price rise. Limited empirical work has been done on such 'path dependencies' although Blase (1980) did find evidence of asymmetries in travel behaviour in the context of fuel price variation and, more recently (Table 3.7), Dargay (1993) has provided further support for this across a number of national studies.

Table 3.7
Long-run price elasticities of fuel consumption

	Reversible model	Irreversible model	
	Price rises and falls	Price rise	Price fall
France	−0.96	−0.80	−0.45
Germany	−0.33	−0.44	−0.02
UK	−0.40	−1.50	−0.10
US	−0.46	−0.67	−0.31

Source: Dargay (1993)

Rather more effort has been put into the question of service quality. It is noticeable, for example, from empirical studies that public transport demand is sensitive to changes in service quality, especially to any reduction in the speed or frequency of services. Again this fact reflects the decreased importance attached to the purely monetary dimension. Market research in the West Midlands, for example, revealed that only 27.1 per cent of people felt that keeping fares down would be the greatest improvement to local public transport; the remainder looked for service quality improvements, for example, 14.6 per cent for greater reliability, 10.4 per cent for higher frequency, 10.4 per cent for more bus shelters, 10.0 per cent for cleaner vehicles, etc. (see Isaac, 1979).

An extensive survey by Lago *et al.* (1981) examined a wide range of international studies concerned with urban public transport service elasticities. The general conclusion that services will generate less than proportional increases in passenger and revenue (that is, $E_s < 1$) would seem to contradict the above findings but this may be misleading. To begin with the survey looks at a number of service quality attributes in isolation rather than at a package of service features. It also admits that many of the services sought by potential public transport users are qualitative rather than quantitative and, hence, are not amenable to the types of analysis reviewed. The survey also highlights the fact that service quality is far more important when the initial level of service is poor; the general elasticities found for peak period ridership, for instance, are much lower than those for the off-peak. The evidence presented suggests that service headway is one of the more important service variables; the studies examined indicates an elasticity of the order of –0.42 compared with, for example, –0.29 for in-vehicle bus travel time.

Table 3.8
Service features consignors require from road hauliers (%)

Factor	Local	Intraregional	Trunk
Vehicle suitability	43	45	69
Quick delivery	29	36	2
Prompt collection	10	12	14
'Good reputation'	15	5	1
Access to handling facilities	8	4	-
Condition of vehicles	-	-	8

Source: Price Commission (1978)

The available evidence suggests that today low price is also no longer the dominant determinant of freight modal choice. In a survey conducted in the UK by the Price Commission (1978), for instance, it was found that only in 52 per cent of cases did consignors elect to use the cheapest road haulage operator available for local trips, 77 per cent for intraregional trips and 64 per cent for trunk-hauls. Many were so unconcerned about finding the lowest price that competitive quotations were not sought. The answers given to the Price Commission in a more recent survey are reproduced in Table 3.8. The emphasis placed upon vehicle suitability is seen to reflect customer concern about such factors as weather protection, systems for securing loads and compatibility of vehicle with product. These are concerns unlikely to have been of paramount importance when heavy industry dominated the economy but are of much more concern for the more modern, high-technology firms (Button, 1988). These firms are increasingly turning to 'just-in-time' production methods whereby inventories are kept to a minimum. To optimise such processes reliability of supply is vital and companies are willing to pay the additional financial costs which this may entail (Schneider, 1985).

To some extent extending from this, many industrialists prefer to use their own vehicle fleets rather than engage public hauliers despite considerable cost disadvantages. The reasons for this utilisation of high-cost transport are similar to those used by other consignors who select between hauliers (see Table 3.9). Once again it is service quality which dominates the decision process, consignors seeking reliability, control and speed in preference to a low price. Of course, this should not be interpreted to mean that price is of no consequence but rather that its importance has diminished over time as the nature of industrial production has changed.

Table 3.9
Reasons for the maintenance and use of an own-account fleet

Factor	Score
Reliability	14.9
Control	13.0
Customer relations	9.4
Speed of delivery	9.2
Flexibility	7.8
Costs v. prices	7.4
Ability of 'own account' to meet timing constraints	6.6
Price is subordinate to service considerations	6.5
Specialised capability	5.5
Speed of response	5.1
Adaptability	3.6
Consistency	3.5
Avoidance of damage or contamination	3.4
Security	2.6
Other (not financial)	1.1
Other (financial)	0.5
	100.0

Source: UK Department of Transport (1979)

3.3   The notion of a 'need' for transport

The demand function indicates what people would buy given a particular budget constraint, but it is often argued that allocation of resources on this basis results in inequalities and unfairness because of differences in household income or other circumstances. There are, thus, some advocates of the idea that transport services, or at least some of them, should be allocated according to 'need' rather than effective demand. The concept of need is seldom defined (or at best rather imprecisely so, see Williams, 1974), but seems to be closely concerned with the notion of merit goods - that is, needs 'considered so meritorious that their satisfaction is provided for through the public budget over and above what is provided for through the market and paid for by private buyers' (Musgrave, 1959). The idea is that just as everyone in a civilised society is entitled to expect a certain standard of education, medical cover, etc., so they are entitled to enjoy a certain minimum standard of transport provision.

One can point to a number of transport policy initiatives over time which are based upon this idea. The 1930 Road Traffic Act in the UK, for example, introduced, besides other things, road service licences into the bus industry which embraced the notion of *public need*. The Traffic Commissioners interpreted this to mean the provision of a comprehensive network of services for an area irrespective of the effective demand for specific routes. Licences were granted on this basis and operators cross-subsidised the unremunerative services with revenue from the more profitable ones. More explicit were the social service grants given to the railways under the 1968 Transport Act whereby 222 services were subsidised for social reasons, once again despite deficit effective demand for their services. Additionally, the government has, for many years, provided both capital and operating cost subsidies to assist the shipping and air services to the remoter islands of Scotland. The subsidies given by local authorities to bus services, both urban and rural, under the 1985 Transport Act are also meant to ensure that transport services meet the needs of the local community. There has also been a considerable growth of dial-a-ride systems in London and other cities, initially seen as an alternative to conventional public transport but since the mid-1970s as meeting the needs of the elderly and handicapped (Sutton, 1987). In a different context, the 1978 Airline Deregulation Act in the USA provided subsidies for services to small communities (the Essential Air Service Program) and the 1987 National Transportation Act in Canada provided explicitly for subsidies to 'essential' air services in the northern part of the country.

This notion of need rather than effective demand raises two important issues. Firstly, exactly what is the nature of 'need' in reality, and secondly, if one accepts that the concept has some operational meaning, how can it be incorporated into economic analysis? We look at these two questions in turn.

The need for adequate transport provision stems from the idea that people should have access to an acceptable range of facilities (Stanley and Farrington, 1981). It is, therefore, essentially a 'normative' concept. Transport is seen as exerting a major influence on the quality of the lives of people and a certain minimum quality should be ensured. The UK policy document *Transport Policy* (UK Department of Transport, 1977) emphasised this view of mobility: 'The social needs for transport also rank high – the needs of people to have access to their work, shops, recreation and the range of activities on which civilised society depends.' Defining the exact level of mobility in this context is difficult, but it is helpful to look at the groups who, for one reason or another, seem in need of transport services in addition to those that would be forthcoming in the market.

The most obvious group is the poor who cannot afford transport. Transport expenditure forms a substantial part of a household budget and, consequently, those on the lowest income must make fewer trips, shorter trips or trips on inferior modes of transport. A major problem is that as income levels rise, in general, there is a tendency towards higher car ownership leaving only depleted and expensive public transport facilities for those at the lower end of the income distribution. A household with a car tends, for instance, to make on average about 300 fewer bus journeys a year than comparable households without a car. But there are also wider issues, in that this change in the transport sector has implications for population distribution. In particular, higher car ownership in rural areas, and the resultant reduction in the *demand* for local public transport, has put pressure on rural bus and rail services. Between 1970 and 1974 the National Bus Company, which is responsible for most rural stage services in England and Wales, reduced its bus kilometres by 7 per cent. This, in turn, has been seen as one of the causes of rural depopulation. The question then arises as to whether society, in general, needs a balance between urban and rural society.

While inadequate income poses one problem, there are other groups in society that are often felt to need assistance. The old, infirm and children are obvious examples where irrespective of income, effective demand may be felt an inadequate basis upon which to allocate transport resources. The available evidence suggests that only about 10 per cent of households in the aged or disabled category have private transport at hand. Even when a household does own a car (or has one made available through employment agreements) there are still members of it who may be deemed in need of additional transport. A study of mobility by Hillman *et al.* (1973), for instance, found that 70 per cent of young married women in the outer metropolitan area of London had no car available for their everyday use – even 30 per cent of those qualified to drive were in this position. There are arguments, therefore, that these groups are in need of adequate and inexpensive public transport services (or special transport provision in the case of the disabled) and that the normal market mechanism is inadequate in this respect. Despite the comparatively limited availability of special transport services to cater for these forms of need, Bailey (1977) estimated that in 1977 some 35 million such trips were made in the UK.

If one accepts the notion that need is, in certain contexts, the relevant concept rather than effective demand, then, for practical purposes, this idea requires integration into more standard positive economic theory. (It should perhaps be noted that many people do not accept the idea of 'need' as an allocative device but advocate tackling problems of low income or disadvantage at their source through measures such as direct income transfers, but this is an issue outside our present discussion.) Perhaps the simplest method of reconciling the difficulty is to treat the monies paid out by government and other agencies in subsidies to social transport services, as the effective demand of *society* for the services. One can then perceive the situation as analogous to that of conventional consumer theory. Just as effective demand reflects the desire of an individual to purchase a particular service so government's response to need reflects society's desire to purchase particular transport services for certain of its members.

3.4 The valuation of travel time savings

The importance of travel time in transport economics should by now be apparent. While the action of travel involves some time costs, it is perhaps more useful to consider travel time in a chapter on demand and benefits rather than costs. This is because travel or transport time savings are normally considered to be a major component of any scheme designed to improve transport efficiency. As we see in Table 3.10 time savings form the major component of inter-urban road investment benefits – a situation also found in most fields of passenger transport. For reasons of comparability with other forms of benefit, a vast amount of energy has gone into devising methods of placing money values on such benefits.

Two quite distinct methodologies have been developed for time evaluation, the distinction being made between time saved in the course of employment and time saved during non-work travel (including commuter trips when fixed working hours are involved). The distinction is drawn because work time involves lorry drivers, seamen, pilots, etc. not simply in giving up leisure but also in incurring some actual disutility from the work undertaken. Hence, if they could do the same amount of work in less time these people would be able to enjoy more leisure and also suffer less disutility (or the employer must pay them more to encourage a continuation of the same work hours with a higher output). Savings in non-work time do not, by definition, reduce the disutility associated with work and, consequently, although more leisure may be enjoyed, they are likely to be valued below work travel-time savings.

Table 3.10
Benefits from an average road improvement scheme

Benefit	(%)
Accident savings	20
Vehicle operating cost savings	0
Working time savings	
Car	26
Light goods vehicles	11
Heavy goods vehicles	11
Buses	3
Non-work time savings	
Car	23
Buses	6
Total	100

Source: UK Department of the Environment (1976, Vol. 2)

The valuation of work travel time (which embraces all journeys made when travellers are earning their living) is made simpler if we accept the traditional economic idea that workers are paid according to the value of their marginal revenue product. On this basis, the amount employers pay workers must be sufficient to compensate them for the marginal time and disutility associated with doing the job. Thus it becomes possible to equate the value of a marginal saving in work travel time with the marginal wage rate (plus related social payments and overheads). An alternative way of arriving at this cost savings approach is by reflecting upon the opportunity costs involved – as Benjamin Franklin once said, 'Remember that time is money.' Time savings at work permit a greater output to be produced within a given time period which, again drawing on the marginal productivity theory of wage determination, will be reflected in the marginal wages paid. Official UK policy is to value work travel time savings as the national average wage for the class of transport user concerned plus the associated costs of social insurance paid by the employer and a premium added to reflect overheads.

A major problem with the wage equivalence approach is that it assumes employees consider the disutility of travel during work to be the same as the disutility of other aspects of their work which they may be required to undertake if travel time is reduced. In many instances workers may consider the travel much less arduous than these alternative tasks. This implies that savings in work-time travel should, in such cases, be valued at less than the wage rate plus additions. Also some people may view travel time as highly productive – many rail and air travellers, for instance, certainly work on their journeys – suggesting that reduced travel time would not significantly alter output. Even time spent in car travel can be used to complete mental tasks – for example Fowkes *et al.* (1986) found that about 3 per cent of business travel time by car was spent working. The wage rate ceases to be a useful measure of work travel time savings in such cases.

While labour economics provides a useful foothold to obtain values of work travel time, rather more empiricism is required in the evaluation of non-work travel time. The behavioural approach involves using revealed preferences to consider trade-off situations which reflect the willingness of travellers to pay in order to save time. In other words, if a person chooses to pay X pence to save Y minutes then he is revealing an implicit value of time equal to at least X/Y pence per minute. Empirical studies attempting to value non-work travel time have looked at a number of different trade-off situations (Waters, 1992 offer a survey), notably when travellers have a choice among:

(1) route;
(2) mode of travel;
(3) speed of travel (by a given mode over a given route);
(4) location of home and work; and
(5) destination of travel.

The standard approach in these trade-off studies is to employ a simple equation of the general form:

$$P_1 = \frac{e^y}{(1+e^y)} \text{ where } y = \alpha_0 + \alpha_1 (t_1 - t_2) + \alpha_2 (c_1 - c_2) \tag{3.2}$$

where P_1 = probability of choosing mode (route, etc.) 1;
          y = choice of mode (route, etc.); takes value of 1 for mode (route, etc.) 1 and 0 for mode (route, etc.) 2;
          e = exponential constant
          t_i = door-to-door travel time by the ith mode (route, etc.); i = 1, 2;
          c_i = door-to-door travel cost by the ith mode (route, etc.); i = 1, 2;
          α_1, α_2 and α_3 = constants to be estimated.

A value of time is then inferred by looking at changes in the dependent variable which result from a unit change in either the time or the cost difference. Strictly it may be found as the ratio α_1/α_2 in equation 3.2.

Many of the early studies of non-work travel time concentrated on urban commuter trips because there was pressure at the time to provide information for cost-benefit analysis of urban transport investment plans. In consequence, mode and route choice evaluation techniques were developed to a high level of mathematical sophistication. Early work by Beesley (1965) specifically employed discriminant analysis to examine the journey to work mode choices of employees at the UK Ministry of Transport during 1965/6. This technique essentially finds the trade-off value of time that minimises the number of misallocations of commuters to alternative modes. Beesley found that commuter trip time savings were valued at between 30 and 50 per cent of the gross personal income of the commuters. One of the main problems with this pioneering study is that it failed to isolate on-vehicle travel time from the other components of journey time (for example, waiting and walking time). The defect was subsequently remedied in a larger study of mode choice in Leeds undertaken by Quarmby (1967) which embraced seven variables including walking and waiting time as well as on-vehicle time. The findings indicate that savings in walking and waiting times are valued at between two and three times savings in on-vehicle time. Table 3.11 provides details of the non-work time values which have been revealed in these and subsequent studies.

Table 3.11
Computation of estimated values of travel time savings

Study	Country	Value of time as % of wage rate	Trip purpose	Mode
Beesley (1965)	UK	33–50	Commuting	Auto
Quarmby (1967)	UK	20–25	Commuting	Auto, Transit
Stopher (1968)	UK	21–32	Commuting	Auto, Transit
Oort (1969)	USA	33	Commuting	Auto
Thomas & Thompson (1970)	USA	86	Interurban	Auto
Lee & Dalvi (1971)	UK	30	Commuting	Bus
		40	Commuting	Auto
Wabe (1971)	UK	43	Commuting	Auto, Subway
Talvitte (1972)	USA	12–14	Commuting	Auto, Transit
Hensher & Hotchkiss (1974)	Australia	2.70	Commuting	Hydrofoil, Ferry
Kraft & Kraft (1974)	USA	38	Interurban	Bus
McDonald (1975)	USA	45–78	Commuting	Auto, Transit
Ghosh et al (1975)	UK	73	Interurban	Auto
Guttman (1975)	USA	63	Leisure	Auto
		145	Commuting	Auto
Hensher (1977)	Australia	39	Commuting	Auto
		35	Leisure	Auto
Nelson (1977)	USA	33	Commuting	Auto
Hauer & Greenough (1982)	Canada	67–101	Commuting	Subway
Edmonds (1983)	Japan	42–49	Commuting	Auto, Bus, Rail
Deacon & Sonstelie (1985)	USA	52–254	Leisure	Auto
Hensher & Truong (1985)	Australia	105	Commuting	Auto, Transit
Guttman & Menashe (1986)	Israel	59	Commuting	Auto, Bus
Fowkes (1986)	UK	27–59	Commuting	Rail, Coach
Hau (1986)	USA	46	Commuting	Auto, Bus
Chui & McFarland (1987)	USA	82	Interurban	Auto
Mohring et al (1987)	Singapore	60–129	Commuting	Bus
Cole Sherman (1990)	Canada	93–170	Commuting	Auto
		116–165	Leisure	Auto

Source: Waters (1992) which contains full references to studies cited.

Stated preference techniques, whereby hypothetical questions are posed to travellers to gain information about trade-offs they would be willing to make have become more common in recent years. A pioneering example was that of Lee and Dalvi (1969) who used questionnaires, rather than looking at actual choices, to discover the level of fare increase required before passengers switched from one mode of public transport to an alternative. Interestingly, in Manchester it was found that on-vehicle time, walking time and waiting time were not separately important and travellers did not distinguish among them. Overall it was estimated that non-work travel time was being valued at 15–45 per cent of hourly income.

While most urban studies have tended to focus on mode choice decisions, the evaluation of non-work inter-urban travel time has tended to concentrate rather more on route and speed choice situations - although imperfections in travellers' knowledge of the latter make speed choice trade-offs suspect. Pioneering work on route choice by Claffey *et al.* (1961) looked at choices made between tolled and free roads in the USA and attempted to allow for differing accident rates and levels of driver discomfort when assessing the time/money cost trade-offs. Mathematical weakness limits the value of this specific model but subsequent reworking suggests time differences are unimportant in route choices of this type. Thomas (1967), again using USA data, conducted a study on a similar basis and here time differences did appear significant and he estimates that non-work travel time appeared to be valued at between 40 and 83 per cent of average income. Dawson and Everall (1972), using a further modification and looking at route choices of motorists travelling between Rome and Caserta and between Milan and Modena, where autostrada offered alternatives to ordinary trunk roads, found that observed trade-offs indicate that commuting and other non-work travel time was valued at about 75 per cent of the average wage rate.

It is clear from the selection of studies cited above that non-work time savings are, indeed, valued below the wage rate, but it is equally clear that the actual values obtained from the behavioural studies are extremely sensitive to the assumptions made and the estimation technique employed. Hensher (1979) goes further and, in particular, points to the rather strong assumptions that are implicit in the not uncommon practice of taking time values obtained from, say, a mode choice study and employing them in route or speed choice situations. He also questions whether enough consideration is given to the composition of time savings beyond the in-vehicle/waiting time split and, in particular, to preferences between constant journey speed (with a lower average) and faster, variable speeds (with a higher average). There is also the common practical problem that it is difficult to separate the influence of comfort and convenience factors from travel time savings.

In Britain the UK Department of Transport and its predecessors have since the 1960s recommended standard values of time for transport analysis purposes (see Table 3.12). The use of standard figures is to encourage uniformity in investment appraisal. While the work-travel time figures are open to only minor criticisms (and even quite major errors here would seem unlikely to distort decisions), the use of standard non-work travel time values has met with more serious criticism.

Empirically, non-work travel time values have generally been shown to be correlated with income level (Heggie, 1976) being one of the few exceptions), but on occasions an *average* value across all income levels has been used for policy formulation purposes. The argument supporting this 'equity' value is that if time values were directly varied with income this would tend to bias project selection towards projects favouring the higher income groups. In evaluation, the travel time savings of such groups would automatically be weighted more heavily than those of the less well-off. The Leitch Committee in the UK, however, rejected this line of argument because it is not consistent with the way other aspects of transport investment are evaluated. Since the overall distributional effects of transport investment may be treated more directly in the appraisal process (see Chapter 9), the notion of 'equity' values was rejected in favour of income-based time evaluations.

Even if generally acceptable values of travel time could be obtained there are still difficulties associated with using them. One of the major problems is that some projects can result in a small number of large time savings while others pro-duce a multitude of extremely small savings. The problem becomes one of decid-ing whether sixty one-minute savings are as valuable as (or more valuable than) one saving of an hour's duration. It could be argued that travellers, especially over longer routes, tend not to perceive small time savings or cannot utilise such time savings (see Tipping, 1968). If this is so it would tend to make urban transport schemes appear less attractive *vis-à-vis* inter-urban ones because the main benefits of urban improvements have been small time savings spread over thousands of commuters. One suggestion is that a zero value should be adopted for small travel time savings with a positive value only being employed once a threshold level of saving has been reached (say ten minutes). This ignores the fact that small time savings may, in some circumstances, be combined with existing periods of free or idle time to permit substantial increases in output or in leisure enjoyment. Further, if there are non-linearities in the value of travel time this would imply that widely used trade-off methods of time evaluation based upon *average* time savings must be giving biased estimates of the value of travel time. The debate over the handling of small travel time savings is unlikely to be resolved easily.

Table 3.12
Official UK values of time for transport investment appraisal purposes (pence per hour)

Time category	1975	1976	1989
Working time			
Car driver	331	379	849.7
Car passenger	287	332	705.3
Rail passenger	357	407	1006.1
Bus passenger	168	196	701.2
Underground passenger	313	360	1050.0
Heavy goods vehicle occupant	155	178	622.5
Light goods vehicle occupant	139	158	660.8
Bus driver	166	191	647.6
Bus conductor	158	182	n.a.
Leisure time			
In-vehicle time	35	36	207.5*
Walking and waiting time	70	72	

* Standard appraisal value for all non-working travel time
Source: UK Department of the Environment (1976), UK Department of Transport (1978) and *COBA 9 Manual*.

Transport studies in less developed countries tend to adopt the convention that while work travel time savings should be given a monetary value based upon the cost-savings approach (although the wage rate is generally modified to allow for imperfections in the local labour market), savings in non-work travel time – especially in rural areas – are given a zero value (Howe, 1976). The justification for this is that the prime objective of improving transport infrastructure in the third world is to assist in economic growth and thus the emphasis should be exclusively concentrated on economically productive schemes – leisure time is not seen as 'productive'. Thomas (1979) has pointed to a serious anomaly, however, when this argument is carried into practice. While non-work travel time savings in rural areas are ignored, savings in vehicle operating costs for such travel is not. Not only is this inconsistent but it also has important distributional implications because the main beneficiaries of low operating costs are almost invariably high income car owners.

3.5   The demand for car ownership

Car ownership in Great Britain has risen considerably since the First World War with only brief halts during periods of major military conflict and occasional decelerations in the trend during periods of macroeconomic depression (see Table 3.13). This upward trend is not unique to Britain but is also to be found in all other countries irrespective of their state of economic development or the nature of their political institutions. The upward trend in car ownership is the result of both the considerable benefits which accompany car availability (notably improved access and greater flexibility of travel) and the long-term increases in income enjoyed by virtually all countries since the Second World War. The 'demonstration effect' has tended to accelerate the process in less developed countries as attempts are made to emulate the consumption patterns of more affluent states.

Table 3.13
Car ownership growth in Great Britain

Year	Cars and vans (thousands)	Cars and vans per capita
1930	1056	0.023
1935	1477	0.032
1940	1423	0.030
1945	1487	0.031
1950	2258	0.045
1955	3526	0.071
1960	5526	0.108
1965	8917	0.169
1970	11515	0.213
1975	13747	0.252
1980*	14772	0.277
1985*	16454	0.320
1990*	19742	0.374

*Not strictly comparable because of changes in data collection method
Source: *Transport Statistics in Great Britain* (various years)

Considerable effort has been focused on exploring both the rate of increase in vehicle ownership and reasons why this should differ between countries and between areas within a single country. Information on the underlying demand functions is sought in Great Britain for a variety of reasons. Car manufacturers need to know the nature of changing demands for new vehicles, both within the country and within their export markets, and to be able to forecast likely changes in the type of vehicles which are wanted. While work in this area often sheds some useful light on the workings of the car market, it is only of limited use to transport economists (see Button *et al.*, 1982). By contrast, central government is generally more interested in the aggregate number of vehicles in the country, mainly for road planning purposes, but also, to a lesser extent, to assist the Treasury in its fiscal duties. Regional variations, which can be quite pronounced (Table 3.14), are also of interest for strategic planning purposes.

Table 3.14
Regional variations in household car ownership patterns in the UK (1988)

| Region | *Percentage of households with regular use of* | | |
	No car	*One car only*	*Two or more cars*
England	34	44	22
North	46	41	13
Yorkshire & Humberside	43	41	16
East Midlands	31	46	22
East Anglia	27	48	25
South East	30	44	26
Greater London	40	43	17
Rest of South East	24	45	31
South West	25	49	26
West Midlands	35	43	22
North West	39	42	20
Wales	32	50	17
Scotland	47	39	14
Northern Ireland	40	44	16

Source: *Transport Statistics Great Britain* (1992)

The theory underlying much of the early forecasting work in this area is closely akin to the management theory of a 'product life' cycle, where a product has a predetermined sales pattern almost independent of traditional economic forces, although taste and costs are not altogether absent from the model. The logistic curve fitting model developed by the Transport Research Laboratory (then the Road Research Laboratory and subsequently the Transport and Road Research Laboratory over the period), in its basic form, treats per capita vehicle ownership as a function of time (Figure 3.1) with the ownership level following a symmetric, sigmoid growth path through time until an eventual saturation level is approached (Tanner, 1978). Broadly, it is argued that long-term growth in ownership follows a predictable diffusion process. Initially, high production costs and unfamiliarity will keep sales low, but after a period, if the product is successful, economies of scale on the supply side coupled with bandwagon effects on the demand side would result in the take-off of a comparatively rapid diffusion process. Finally, there is a tailing-off as the market becomes saturated and everyone wishing to own a car does so.

The TRL extrapolative approach provided relatively good forecasts in the 1960s, but it has tended to be less reliable in more recent years (see Table 3.15) and to suffer from a tendency towards over-prediction. While some of the difficulties may be associated with problems of estimating key parameters such as the ultimate saturation level, or with the correct configuration of the growth curve – in later work a power function replaced the logistic – at least one school of thought rejects the underlying extrapolative philosophy as inadequate (Bates *et al.,* 1978). In particular, it is argued, car ownership forecasting should be based upon explicit economic variables such as income and vehicle prices rather than 'proxy' variables such as time. The TRL forecasting framework has attempted to meet this criticism by incorporating economic variables, but both a time trend is still retained and the income and vehicle operating cost elasticities are not estimated internally within the model but derived from 'external' sources. The demand model developed by Bates and others, as part of a larger Regional Highway Traffic Model (RHTM), in contrast is based entirely upon 'causal' variables and all the relevant elasticities are estimated directly within the forecasting model.

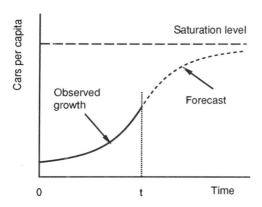

Figure 3.1
The logistic growth curve approach to car ownership forecasting

At the national level the RHTM relates car ownership per household (expressed mathematically in logit form) to household income. The data used is not the time series registration statistics employed by the TRL but rather a series of cross-sectional sets of statistics obtained from annual Family Expenditure Surveys and other sources. For forecasting purposes it is necessary to be able to predict reliably the level and distribution of future income. Additionally, it is recognised that changes in motoring costs will influence ownership levels, so rather than deflate changes in money income over time by changes in retail prices to obtain a real income prediction, money income is deflated by an index of anticipated motoring cost changes to give a projection of 'car purchasing income'. Simply, it is assumed that a £1 rise in income will have the same positive effect on car ownership as a £1 fall in car prices. The approach also concentrates on the probability of households having a certain level of vehicle ownership rather than, as with the TRL model, on forecasting the national average ownership level; this conforms more closely to other recent trends in transport demand forecasting (see Chapter 8). At present the TRL and RHTM approaches to forecasting car ownership have in a sense been combined; while economic variables are the main driving force along the lines of the RHTM, the addition of number of driving licences effectively acts as a time trend surrogate.

Table 3.15
Comparison of actual car ownership and TRL forecasts

Year of publication	Base year for calculation	Forecast annual growth in cars per capita 1975 ÷ Actual annual growth in cars per capita 1975	Forecast car pool 1975 ÷ Actual car pool 1975
1962	1960	1.14	1.13
1965	1964	1.57	1.57
1967	1966	1.67	1.68
1969	1968	1.84	1.84
1970	1969	1.66	1.66
1972	1971	1.62	1.58

Source: Button *et al.* (1980)

Differences in the geographical demand for car ownership interest transport planners both because they need to be able to forecast future demand for links in the local road network and because, where ownership is low, social commitments may require that alternative public transport is provided. At the national level there are quite marked differences in ownership levels, as we saw in Table 3.14. The nation can broadly be divided into three regions: the South-west, South-east and East Anglia have a high propensity for car ownership, the West Midlands, Wales and East Midlands form a middle grouping, while the North-west, Yorkshire and Humberside, the North and Scotland have the lowest incidence of car ownership. This general trend towards lower car ownership levels as one moves north has been observed in many studies of the car market but no really satisfactory explanation of the phenomenon exists. It has been observed, however, that if the regions are broken down by their constituent counties then those with low car ownership tend to incorporate substantial urban concentrations and many have a major industrial component in their economies. This association of urban concentration with low car ownership is also found at the local level and in Table 3.16, which looks at the situation in West Yorkshire, a clear trichotomy emerges among household car ownership levels in urban, suburban and rural areas even after allowing for variations in income levels.

It seems likely that these spatial variations at the local level may, once allowance has been made for differing income and demographic factors, be explained in terms of the quality of local transport services. Good, uncongested roads combined with poor public transport increases the demand. *ceteris paribus,* for private car ownership. Regional econometric studies of car ownership have attempted to reflect this cost of transport effect by incorporating variables such as residential density in their models (it being argued that a densely populated area is normally well served by public transport while motoring is adversely affected by the higher levels of traffic congestion). More sophisticated local models have shown the frequency of public transport services to influence car ownership rates (Fairhurst, 1975). In West Yorkshire it has been found that car ownership rises as the generalised cost of public transport trips increases (Button *et al.*, 1982). If these studies are correct then there is some evidence that the long-term growth in car ownership may be contained by improving public transport services although from a policy point of view the overall cost of such actions needs to be fully assessed.

Table 3. 16
Household car ownership in West Yorkshire in 1975 (UK)

Area				Household income				
	Less than £1041	*£1041-£2080*	*£2081-£3120*	*£3121-£4160*	*£4161-£5200*	*£5201-£6240*	*£6241-£7800*	*More than £7800*
Urban	0.07	0.25	0.55	0.68	0.84	0.95	1.16	1.47
Dormitory	0.15	0.53	0.80	1.03	1.41	1.65	1.50	2.07
Small town and rural	0.07	0.34	0.69	0.91	1.03	1.38	1.48	1.83

Source: Button *et al.* (1982)

3.6   Further reading and references
Readers interested in the influence of different variables on transport demand, especially demand elasticities, see Goodwin (1992) and Oum *et al.* (1992). Discussion of 'need' is usually rather imprecise but Banister *et al* (1984) offer a useful and more detailed assessment of many of the analytical problems. Sharp (1981) provides a detailed examination of the economics of time, Bruzelius (1979) a review of the theoretical literature while Waters (1992) provides a comprehensive survey of the empirical literature. The problems of evaluating travel time savings in low-income coutries is examined in Button and Pearman (1984). Hensher (1979) offers a much more rigorous critique, focusing specifically on the inappropriate use that is made of values obtained by empirical means. A detailed account of the development of national car ownership forecasts is provided by Tanner (1978) although the treatment of disaggregate modelling techniques is rather thin. Button *et al.* (1982) provides a more comprehensive overview and critique, with a specific emphasis on the economic content of car ownership forecasting. It also contains a considerable list of further, technical references.

References
Bailey, J. (1977), 'Voluntary and social services transport in Birmingham, Redditch and Bromsgrove', *Transport and Road Research Laboratory Report*, 467.
Banister, D. (1978), 'The influence of habit formation on modal choice – a heuristic model', *Transportation*, 7, 19–33.
Banister, D., Bould, M. and Warren, G. (1984), 'Towards needs-based transport planning', *Traffic Engineering and Control*, 25, 372–5.
Bates, J.J., Gunn, H. F. and Roberts, M. (1978), *A disaggregate Model of Household Car Ownership*, Department of the Environment and Transport Research Report 20, London, HMSO.
Beesley, M.E. (1965), 'The value of time spent in travelling: some new evidence', *Economica*, 32, 174–85.
Bendtsen, P.H. (1980), 'The influence of price of petrol and of cars on the amount of automobile traffic', *International Journal of Transport Economics*, 7, 207–13.
Blase, J.H. (1980), 'Hysterisis in travel demand', *Transportation Planning and Technology*, 6, 109–16.

Brown, S. and Watkins, W. (1968), 'The demand for air travel: a regression study of time-series and cross-sectional data in the US domestic marke', *Highway Research Record*, 213, 21–34.

Bruzelius, N. (1979), *The Value of Travel Time*, London, Croom Helm

Burrell, J. (1972), 'Recent developments in car ownership forecasting', in *Urban Traffic Model Research*, London, Planning and Transport Research and Computation (PTRC).

Button, K.J. (1988), 'High-technology companies: an examination of their transport needs', *Progress in Planning*, 29, 81–146.

Button, K.J. and Pearman, A.D. (1984), 'The value of time in road investment appraisal in less developed countries', *International Journal of Transport Economics*, 11, 135–48.

Button, K.J., Fowkes A.S. and Pearman, A.D. (1980), 'Disaggregate and aggregate car ownership forecasting methods in Great Britain', *Transportation Research*, 14A, 263–73.

Button, K.J., Pearman, A.D. and Fowkes, A.S. (1982), *Car Ownership Modelling and Forecasting*, Farnborough, Gower Press.

Chase Econometrics Associates (1974), *The Effect of Tax and Regulatory Alternatives on Car Sales and Gasoline Consumption*, NTIS Report No. PB-234622.

Claffey, P.J., St Clair, C. and Welder, N. (1961), 'Characteristics of passenger car travel on toll roads and comparable free roads', *Highway Research Bulletin*, no. 306.

Dargay, J.M. (1993), 'Demand elasticities: a comment', *Journal of Transport Economics and Policy*, 27, 87–90.

Dawson, R.F.F. and Everall, P.F. (1972), 'The value of motorists' time: a study in Italy', *Transport and Road Research Laboratory Report*, LR. 426.

DeVany, A.S. (1974), 'The revealed value of time in air travel', *Review of Economics and Statistics*, 56, 77–82.

Fairhurst, H.M. (1975), 'The influence of public transport on car ownership in London', *Journal of Transport Economics and Policy*, 9, 193–208.

Fowkes, A., Marks, P. and Nash, C. (1986), 'The value of business travel time savings', Working Paper 214, Institute for Transport Studies, University of Leeds.

Gilbert, C.L. and Jalilian, H. (1991), 'The demand for travelcards on London Regional Transport', *Journal of Transport Economics and Policy*, 25, 3–30.

Glaister, S. and Lewis, D. (1978), 'An integrated fares policy for transport in London', *Journal of Public Economics*, 9, 341–55.

Goodwin, P.B. (1973), 'Time, distance and cost of travel by different modes', *Proceedings of the 5th University Transport Study Group Annual Conference*.

Goodwin, P.B. (1977), 'Habit and hysteresis in mode choice', *Urban Studies*, 14, 95–8.

Goodwin, P.B. (1992), 'A review of new demand elasticities with special reference to short and long run effects of price changes', *Journal of Transport Economics and Policy*, 26, 155–170.

Gronau, R. (1970), *The Value of Time in Passenger Transportation: The Demand for Air Travel*, New York, Columbia University Press.

Gunn, H.F. (1981), 'Travel budgets - a review of evidence and modelling implications', *Transportation Research*, 15A, 7–23.

Gwilliam, K.M. and Mackie, P.J. (1975), *Economics and Transport Policy*, London, Allen & Unwin.

Harrison, A.J. and Quarmby, D.A. (1969), 'The value of time in transport planning: a review', in *Report of the Sixth Round Table on Transport Economics*, European Conference of Ministers of Transport, Paris.

Heggie, I. (1976), 'A diagnostic survey of urban journey to work behaviour', in Heggie, I. (ed), *Modal Choice and the Value of Travel Time*, Oxford, Clarendon Press.

Hensher, D.A. (1979), 'Formulating an urban passenger transport policy: a re-appraisal of some elements', *Australian Economic Papers*, 18, 119–30.

Hillman, M., Henderson, I. and Whatley, A. (1973), *Personal Mobility and Transport Policy*, PEP Broadsheet 542, London.

Howe, J.D.G.F. (1976), 'Valuing time savings in developing countries', *Journal of Transport Economics and Policy*, 10, 113–25.

Ippolito, R.A. (1981), 'Estimating airline demand with quality of service variables', *Journal of Transport Economics and Policy*, 15, 7–15.

Isaac, J.K. (1979), 'Price and quality in road passenger transport', *Journal of the Chartered Institute of Transport*, 38, 359–61.

Jung, J.M. and Fujii, E.T. (1976), 'The price elasticity of demand for air travel - some new evidence', *Journal of Transport Economics and Policy*, 10, 257–62.

Kraft, G. and Domenich, T.A. (1970), *Free Transit*, Lexington, D.C. Heath.

Lago, A.M., Mayworm, P. and McEnroe, J.M. (1981), 'Transit service elasticities – evidence from demonstration and demand models', *Journal of Transport Economics and Policy*, 15, 99–119.

Lave, C.A. (1970), 'The demand for urban mass transportation', *Review of Economics and Statistics*, 52, 320-3.

Lee, N. and Dalvi, M.Q. (1969), 'Variations in the value of travel time', *Manchester School*, 37, 213–36.

McGillivany, R.G. (1970), 'Demand and choice models of modal split', *Journal of Transport Economics and Policy*, 4, 192–207.

Mogridge, M.J.H. (1978), 'The effect of the oil crisis on the growth in the ownership and use of cars', *Transportation*, 7, 45–65.

Musgrave, R.A. (1959), *The Theory of Public Finance*, New York, McGraw-Hill.

Mutti, J. and Mural, Y. (1977), 'Airline travel on the North Atlantic', *Journal of Transport Economics and Policy*, 11, 45_53.

Oum, T.H., Gillen, D.W. and Noble, S.E. (1986), 'Demand for fare class and pricing in airline markets', *Logistics and Transportation Review*, 22, 195_222.

Oum, T.H., Waters, W.G. and Yong, J.-S. (1992), 'Concepts of price elasticities of transport demand and recent empirical evidence', *Journal of Transport Economics and Policy*, 26, 139–54.

Price Commission (1978), *The Road Haulage Industry*, House of Commons Paper HC 698, London, HMSO.

Quandt, R.E. and Baumol, W.J. (1966), 'The demand for abstract transport modes, theory and measurement', *Journal of Regional Science*, 6, 13–26.

Quarmby, D.A. (1967), 'Choice of travel mode for the journey to work: some findings', *Journal of Transport Economics and Policy*, 1, 273–314.

Reza, A.M. and Spiro, M.H. (1979), 'The demand for passenger car transport services and for gasoline', *Journal of Transport Economics and Policy*, 13, 304–19.

Schneider, L.M. (1985), 'New era in transportation strategy', *Harvard Business Review*, 63 (March/April), 118–26.

Sharp, C. (1981), *The Economics of Time*, London, Routledge.

Sherman, R. (1967), 'A private ownership bias in transit choice', *American Economic Review*, 77, 1211–17.

Smith, M.G. and McIntosh, P.T. (1974), 'Fares elasticity: interpretation and estimation', in *Symposium on Public Transport Fare Structure*, Transport and Road Research Laboratory Report, SR37UC, Crowthorne.

Stanley, P.A. and Farrington, J.H. (1981), 'The need for rural public transport: a constraints-based case study', *Tijdschrift voor Economische en Societe Geografie*, 72, 62–80.

Straszheim, M.R. (1978), 'Airline demand functions on the North Atlantic and their pricing implications', *Journal of Transport Economics and Policy*, 12, 179–95.

Sutton, J.C. (1987), 'Transport innovation and passenger needs - changing perspectives on the role of dial-a-ride systems', *Transport Reviews*, 7, 167–82.

Tanner, J.C. (1978), 'Long-term forecasting of vehicle ownership and road traffic', *Journal of the Royal Statistical Society*, 141A, 14–63.

Taplin, J.H.E. (1980), 'A coherence approach to estimates of price elasticities in the vacation travel market', *Journal of Transport Economics and Policy*, 14, 19–35.

Thomas, S. (1979), 'Non-working time savings in developing countries', Journal *of Transport Economics and Policy*, 13, 335–7.

Thomas, T. C. (1967), *The Value of Time for Passenger Cars: An Experimental Study of Commuters' Values*, Washington, US Bureau of Public Roads.

Thomson, J.M. (1974), *Modern Transport Economics*, Harmondsworth, Penguin.

Tipping, D. (1968), 'Time savings in transport studies', *Economic Journal*, 78, 843–54.

UK Department of the Environment (1976), *Transport Policy - A Consultative Document* (2 vols.), London, HMSO.

UK Department of Transport (1977), *Transport Policy*, Cmnd 6836, London, HMSO.

UK Department of Transport (1978), *Report of the Advisory Committee on Trunk Road Assessment* (Leitch Committee), London, HMSO.

UK Department of Transport (1979), *Road Haulage Operators Licensing (Report of the Independent Committee of Enquiry into Road Haulage Operators' Licensing)*, London, HMSO.

Waters, W.G. (1992), 'Values of travel time savings used in road project evaluation: a cross-country/jurisdiction comparison', *Australian Transport Research Forum*, Canberra, Bureau of Transport and Communications Economics.

White, P.R. (1981), '"Travelcard" tickets in urban public transport', *Journal of Transport Economics and Policy*, 15, 17–34.

Williams, A. (1974), '"Need" as a demand concept (with special reference to health)', in A.J. Culyer (ed.), *Economic Policies and Social Goals*, London, Martin Robertson.

Zahavi, Y. (1977), 'Equilibrium between travel, demand, system supply and urban structure', in E.J. Visser (ed.), *Transport Decisions in an Age of Uncertainty*, The Hague, Martinus Nijhoff.

4   The Direct Costs of Transport

4.1   The supply of transport

Elementary economic theory tells us that, in most circumstances, supply is a positive function of price. The nature of the relationship is heavily influenced by the costs involved. This and the following chapter look at the various costs associated with supplying transport services and, in particular, at the relationships between the resources required to provide these services and the types of output finally 'consumed' by travellers and freight consignors. This chapter is specifically concerned with the production functions perceived by the providers of transport, which relate the various factor inputs to the final services offered, and with the financial costs of these factor inputs.

The chapter differs from the following one in that it only deals with *direct costs* as borne by the supplying agency. These are normally, but not always, financial costs which are incurred as the result of purchasing factor services in the market (that is, the wages of labour, the interest on capital, the price of fuel, etc.). There is one very important exception, however, namely the actual cost of the travellers' or consignors' own inputs. Transport is special (but not unique) in that the actual person being transported has to contribute his own time inputs and, when private motor transport is involved, his personal energies, skills and expertise. The opportunity costs of this time and the utilisation of acquired skills will, therefore, directly enter the production function for trip-making. The external costs we move on to consider in the following chapter, although representing genuine resource costs, do *not* directly influence the decisions of transport suppliers in their provision of transport services. In brief, therefore, this chapter is exclusively concerned with the perceived or reaction costs which influence the supply of transport services. It should be pointed out, however, that the separation of direct and external costs is something of an expositional device and that in practice this distinction is becoming increasingly blurred as official policies attempt to make transport agencies fully cognisant of the full resource implications of their actions.

The importance of the distinction between those costs that enter the supplier's production function and those that do not is clearly reflected in an example drawn from Hicks (1975) concerning freight transhipment facilities. The objective of transhipment or consignment consolidation is to reduce costs by transhipping goods at some point between their origin and destination so that greater vehicle utilisation is achieved. The Post Office provides the classic example where large consignments of letters destined for a single city are collected together at a single sorting office and subsequently dispatched for final delivery in smaller consignments. Many large companies do this but perhaps the most obvious examples are freight forwarders in shipping and aviation. Transhipment may be from one type of vehicle to a different mode (for example, rail to road) or between different vehicles of the same mode. By being able to use large purpose-built vehicles for the trunk haul stage of the operation but small delivery vans for the final distribution to customers the transport undertaking reduces its line-haul and delivery costs. Because the degree of transhipment is closely related to average payload – greater consolidation inevitably increasing the average payload – we can see in Figure 4.1 that line-haul costs will fall with consolidation until the maximum physical or legal average payload is reached. If only haulage costs were to be considered this would represent the optimal payload, but there are also the resources costs involved with consolidation itself – the provision of depots, handling staff, administrative costs, etc. These terminal costs are likely to rise with the level of transhipment. Consequently, the transport operator when considering transhipment and looking at his costs will feel the optimal level of consolidation would imply an average payload of L_t in the diagram.

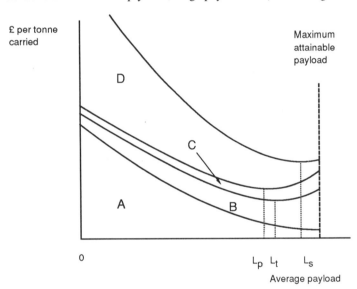

Figure 4.1
Freight consolidation costs (represented cumulatively)

So far we have only looked at the terminal and movement costs confronting the transporter; however, the final customer awaiting delivery will also have costs which vary with transhipment levels. The greater the amount of consolidation, and the higher the final average payload, the fewer the number of deliveries that will be needed. Longer frequencies between deliveries push up the costs of stockholding for customers and the overall level of inventories held. Thus the time costs of increased consolidation rise with average payload suggesting that, overall, final recipients of goods would prefer a level of consolidation consistent with an average payload of L_s in Figure 4. 1. There is a clear distinction, therefore, between the *direct* costs influencing the transporter's optimum and those affecting the final customer. Additionally, there are also wider *external costs* influencing those not directly concerned with transport operations; these include those affected by vehicle noise or fumes or who have their own travel disrupted by freight vehicles. Generally, increased consolidation and higher payloads will reduce these costs, because fewer trips are needed to transport the same volume of goods, and consolidation generally means less environmentally intrusive vehicles can be used in sensitive areas. Hence, from society's point of view, the optimal level of consolidation in the diagram is when all costs are minimised, that is, at point L_p.

In this chapter, and in the freight context, we would only be concerned with the first two categories of cost although where a transport undertaking is operating 'own account' services, carrying its own goods, the time element also becomes relevant. In the passenger transport context since, by definition, one is operating an 'own account' service (even when using public transport) the time element is relevant. The introduction of externalities into the overall production function is left to the following chapter.

4.2   Fixed and variable costs

Direct costs can be divided in a number of ways but two are particularly relevant to transport, namely distinctions according to variability over time and distinctions among the parties responsible for elements of cost. The first of these distinctions is discussed in this section. In the long run, or so the introductory texts tell us, all costs are variable, but the long run is itself an imprecise concept (even a tautology) and the ability to vary costs over time differs among modes of transport. The long run in the context of a seaport is, for instance, very different from that in road haulage or the bus industry. Port infrastructure is extremely long-lived, specific, indivisible and extremely expensive. It is, in reality, impossible to consider the standard question associated with long-run costs – namely, 'what is the cheapest way of providing a given capacity in the long run?' – when talking of time horizons twenty, thirty or even fifty years hence. Road haulage is different, capital costs are lower, physical durability less, and there is always the prospect of varying the use, within limits, of the vehicle fleet. Lorries are, unlike ports, mobile both among a range of potential employers and among a range of locations.

The nature of many costs, therefore, means that they may be considered fixed in the short term: there are temporal indivisibilities. The period under consideration will, as we have seen, differ among transport sectors, but it will also differ within a single transport undertaking. Railway operators owning track and rolling stock offer a useful illustration of this. A railway service involves using a large number of factor services, many of these being highly specific and each with its own physical life-span. When it comes to considering line closures the essential questions revolve around deciding exactly which costs are fixed. Figure 4.2 offers a general illustration of the main cost items associated with a rail service together with an appropriate, although not exact, indication of the physical life of existing equipment. In the very short period, since all other items have already been purchased (that is, they are fixed), the only savings the railways can make are in very variable costs, notably those attributable to labour, fuel and maintenance. However, if the railways are earning sufficient income to cover these costs then there is no justification for closing the line. After a period of about fifteen years, however, locomotives become due for replacement. Consequently locomotive costs become variable over a fifteen-year horizon and the managers must decide whether revenues justify replacement. Is fifteen years, therefore, the long run? The answer is probably 'no' because other factors have still longer lives, rolling stock lasting for 25 years and track and signalling for 45 years. (Earthworks effective have an infinite life and once constructed do not enter into further decision-making processes.) Further decisions regarding closure must, therefore, be made after 25 and 45 years even if the line earns sufficient revenue to cover its locomotive replacement needs. Consequently, the long run for railways, in this context, is anything up to forty years with, in the interim, a series of successive short-run cost calculations having to be made.

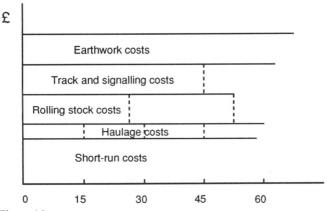

Figure 4.2
Railway costs

It should be quite apparent that the distinction between fixed and variable costs is a pragmatic device requiring a degree of judgement and common sense on the part of the decision-maker. In the short term – whatever that may be – some costs are clearly fixed resulting in a falling short-run average cost of use until capacity is reached. Figure 4.3, for instance, may be seen to illustrate the average cost of increased use of a ship ($SRAC_1$) which falls steeply until capacity is fully utilised. A second ship may then, if demand is sufficient, be brought into operation exhibiting a short-run average cost curve of $SRAC_2$. The fixed capacity constraint for each ship typifies that found in most modes of transport and tends to differ from the smooth, stereotypical, symmetrical U-shaped $SRAC$ curves often associated with manufacturing industry. The long-run curve is, following elementary economics, formed by the envelope of the short-run average cost curves.

In many sectors of the economy the long-run average cost curve is not horizontal, as in our illustration, but is often found to be downward sloping as a result of economies of scale. These economies may potentially take a variety of forms in transport and may be thought to vary according to the type of transport involved and the mode of operation being undertaken.

The standard method of examining for scale effects is to look at the cost elasticity with regard to output. Evidence presented in a survey of recent studies of rail, road haulage and aviation sectors in the USA (Winston, 1985) suggests that scale effects exist in some modes with respect to output but not in others. All studies examined, irrespective of the modelling framework used, indicate scale effects in rail freight transport but the empirical evidence is contradictory for road haulage although the more recent of the studies, employing state-of-the-art econometric techniques, suggest constant costs. Studies of US domestic aviation are almost unanimous that there are no scale effects, irrespective of how the cost function is specified. The more specific studies tend to consider particular features of transport industries, fleet size, infrastructure, etc. and these are looked at in turn.

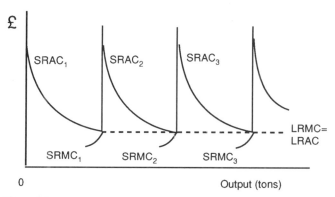

Figure 4.3
The long- and short-run costs of shipping

Economies from larger vehicle size
One approach is to look at costs with respect to size of vehicle or vessel. The classic example of this is in shipping where capacity (in terms of volume) increases much faster than surface area but this is also a feature of most other modes of freight transport. Thermal processes (such as engine size) also generally exhibit scale economies in all forms of transport and crew numbers do not increase proportionately with the size of mobile plant. Table 4.1 gives some indication of economies of scale in bulk carriers, but similar economies are also found in oil tankers. Such scale economies are not unique to shipping, but they are perhaps more pronounced in that mode. It should be said, however, that recent econometric work indicates that there are limits to such economies and that they may become exhausted for larger sized ships (Talley *et al.*, 1986.)

Evidence produced in the early 1970s by Edwards and Bayliss (1971), and depicted in Figure 4.4, suggest that there may be limits to the cost advantages of using extremely large road haulage vehicles. Diseconomies of scale appear to begin setting in after about 11 tonnes carrying capacity has been reached. Evidence from the Armitage Inquiry into heavy lorries (UK Department of Transport, 1980), however, indicates that there are still economies of scale to be enjoyed by using commercial road vehicles in excess of the 32.5 tonnes gross maximum weight permitted in 1980 (see Table 4.2).

While for engineering reasons economies of scale clearly do exist in utilising larger units of mobile plant – at least up to some point – it should be noted that it is often impossible to take advantage of them even when demand for transport services is high. In many instances there may be physical limitations associated with complementary inputs and, in particular, the associated infrastructure cannot

Table 4.1
Economies of scale in bulk carriers

Ship size (thousand dwt)	15	25	41	61	120	200
Index of size	100	167	267	432	793	1318
Capital cost index	100	140	197	291	457	641
Operating cost index (excluding fuel)	100	121	134	155	201	275
Seagoing fuel consumption index	100	155	230	353	578	843
Crew size	31	38	38	38	38	38

Source: Goss and Jones (1971)

always handle the larger vehicles (ports and airports pose specific problems in this context) while in others the consignments of traffic are small and can be more efficiently handled in smaller vehicles (see, for example, Jansson and Shneerson, 1978). Returning to our maritime example, large ships on liner routes often incur heavy costs as frequent landings and embarkation of individual consignments require rearrangements of the entire cargo. This is one reason why hub-and-spoke operations are gaining in importance – see Section 4.3.

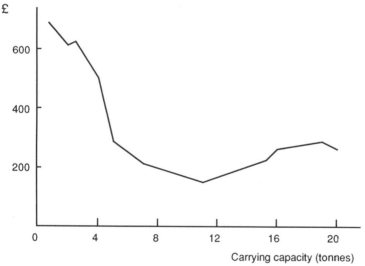

Figure 4.4
Cost variability with lorry size

Economies of scale in infrastructure provision
Transport demand is not spread evenly over space but tends to be concentrated on links between particular trip-generating and trip-attracting points, for example, journey to work trips are concentrated along links between residential and industrial estates; holiday air transport demand is highest between the main cities in the

UK and popular recreational resorts in Spain, Greece, etc. Thus, there is a tendency in transport, as we saw in Chapter 3, for demand to be concentrated on certain portions of the network and, *ipso facto*, certain parts of the static infrastructure. Technically this concentration of traffic is possible because of substantial scale economies in infrastructure provision.

Table 4.2
Estimated savings by increasing maximum lorry weight above 32.5 tonnes

35 tonnes, 4 axles	5–7%
38 tonnes, 5 axles	5–9%
40 tonnes, 5 axles	7–14%
42 tonnes, 5 axles	9–13%
44 tonnes, 6 axles	11–13%

Source: UK Department of Transport (1980)

Table 4.3
Economies of large port operations

	Vancouver	*Seattle*
Traffic (1973)	88000	377000
Number of berths	3	11
Wharfage	23.63	33.75
Handling and through port charge	81.27	40.00
Vessel service and facility charge	0	26.60
Tailgate loading	22.28	0
Total of port charges per container	127.18	95.35

Source: Heaver (1975)

An examination of the costs associated with handling container traffic in an average port (Vancouver) and a large port (Seattle) in Table 4.3 (which assumes the charges paid by container traffic reflect port costs) reveals the economies enjoyed from scale. It seems in port operations that a fourfold increase in size reduces costs by approximately one-quarter. Similarly, with internal transport, Tanner (1968) quotes the cost of four-lane motorways as being on average 78 per cent of those with six lanes. However, it should be said that evidence of scale economies in road provision is not altogether conclusive. The findings of Keeler and Small (1977), looking at 57 freeway segments in the San Francisco area, favour constant returns while Walters (1968), again employing US sources, finds evidence 'that there are increasing costs of (road) construction in urban areas'. The difficulty here, as with other forms of infrastructure costing, is to isolate comparable construction costs from those costs associated with specific locations. In terms of railways, the move from a single to a double-track system involves roughly a quadrupling of capacity by eliminating conflict between directions; that to quadruple track should more than double capacity by permitting segregation by speed. The estimated costs of these options (at 1967 prices) are seen in Table 4.4 and clearly they rise much less rapidly than the increase in potential capacities.

Economies from large fleet size

Larger fleets of vehicles may offer economies in maintenance, standardisation (or, in some cases, the availability of a mixed vehicle fleet to meet variable demand), easier crew scheduling, etc., although administrative problems and remoteness of decision-maker from customer may temper these advantages. Evidence on the existence of fleet economies of scale, however, is far from conclusive for all modes of transport and indeed there seems to be a gradual emergence of constant returns for many modes with limited scale economies in specialised forms of transport.

Table 4.4

Annual costs per mile of rail track (1967 prices)

| | | *Number of Tracks* | |
	1	*2*	*4*
Interest	£3020	£4260	£7900
Revenue of track			
and structure	£1400-2840	£1896-3442	£3422-4474
Signalling	£2600	£4030	£8060
Total	£7020-8460	£10190-11730	£19380-20430

Source: Foster and Joy (1967)

The picture regarding bus operations, for example, provides a rather confusing picture. The oft-cited statistical analysis by Lee and Steedman (1970), looking at the accounts of 44 UK municipal bus undertakings for 1966/7, suggests the notion of constant returns to scale, a situation agreeing with Williams's (1981) study of eleven American publicly owned operations. Wabe and Coles's (1975) examination of 66 UK operators, however, 'provides evidence that diseconomies of scale exist in the provision of bus services'. Koshal's (1970) work in India offers international support for the notion of constant returns in bus operations. The problem with most of these studies, however, is that they use econometric models which assume that the existence of scale effects do not extend over all levels of output. The 1980s witnessed the development of more 'flexible' model forms which allow for variation in scale effects as output changes – for example they allow for testing for a U-shaped cost curve. Button and O'Donnell (1985), applying such techniques to UK urban bus data, found that economies of scale do seem to exist up to a point, although diseconomies set in for the larger undertakings. This broadly conforms with both studies of Israeli bus fleets (Berechman, 1983) and for the US intercity bus industry (Williams and Hall, 1981).

Walters's (1968) work on UK road haulage produced evidence of constant returns, although the large number of owner-drivers working in this sector makes exact costing difficult. Regarding UK aviation the Edwards Committee (Board of Trade, 1969) found evidence of scale economies when there was fleet standardisation but generally concluded that the optimal size of fleet depends upon the task in hand. Looking at shipping, Tolifari *et al.* (1986) found evidence of scale effects in bulk fleets – see Figure, 4.5. The difficulty with empirical work

in this field, and in aviation, is the diversity of the market conditions which are
encountered and the support which is often forthcoming from government to
finance 'the nation's flag carrier'. As can be seen in Figure 4.5, the costs of a
fleet with traditional registry (in one of the major industrial states) tend to be
higher than when open registry (the adoption of a 'flag of convenience') is
favoured because of the standards demanded by the former. As we see below,
these scale effects also become rather clouded with the introduction of economies
of density.

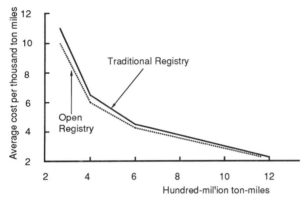

Source: Tolifari *et al*. (1986)

Figure 4.5
Economies of scale in bulk shipping

One indication of constant returns to fleet size is sometimes thought to be
diversity in the scale of operators in a sector of transport: large companies
competing directly against one or two vehicle firms suggesting that there is little
advantage in large fleets. Road haulage is possibly the most extreme example of
this phenomenon, as we see in Table 4.5, but throughout the whole of transport –
except

Table 4.5
UK public road hauliers by size of fleet (1977)

Fleet size	No. of operators	No of vehicles in fleets
1	25100	25100
2–5	14300	44400
6–20	5500	53700
21–100	1400	49500
over 100	100	16300
Total	46400	189000

Source: UK Department of Transport (1979)

for areas directly regulated by government – one finds large and small firms competing with each other. Differential managerial skills may permit some firms to grow larger than others but this does not imply technical economies of scale exist. They may also be supplying slightly different services, perhaps in qualitative terms which are not easy to quantify, and thus strict cost comparisons become difficult to make. Evidence of this type, therefore, may be capturing differential demands rather than any strict scale effect.

The variable costs of transport – those related to the rate of output – are generally considered to be dominated by labour and fuel items because these are thought highly flexible in the short term. Since infrastructure costs are relatively fixed, it is the cost of the mobile plant which is normally treated as marginal. Tables 4.6, 4.7 and 4.8 give some indication of the relative importance of these items in overall airline, road haulage and urban public transport operating costs.

Table 4.6
US and European air costs levels (1983)

| *Cost item* | *Passenger cost (US cents per seat kilometres)* | |
	Intra-Europe	*US domestic*
Crew	0.82	0.49
Fuel	1.33	1.09
Maintenance	0.68	0.41
Depreciation	0.39	0.30
Landing fees and *en route* charges	0.84	0.27
Station and ground	1.09	0.73
Passenger services	0.41	0.31
Ticketing, sales and promotion	1.53	0.71
Others	0.43	0.18
Total	7.52	4.49

Source: International Air Transport Association (1988)

It should perhaps be pointed out that even in the long term the costs of mobile plant are, in aggregate, likely to exceed those of infrastructure, but *individual* vehicle costs, in many cases, are relatively small. The costs of aircraft operations come within a sector with very high costs per unit of mobile plant while road haulage is a sector where the total operational costs per vehicle are low. The importance of both direct and indirect labour costs and fuel costs, however, is apparent at both ends of the spectrum.

The tables represent broad averages across many different types of operation but variable costs differ not simply with level of vehicle usage but also with the type of transport operation undertaken. Vehicles, for example, have an optimal speed above or below which fuel costs tend to rise steeply; consequently operations involving continually stopping and starting will, *ceteris paribus,* increase variable costs (Gyenes, 1980). Maintenance costs can also vary considerably with the type of terrain over which journeys are made. To some extent these variations may be offset by employing specialised vehicles whose variable cost profiles conform most closely to the type of operation undertaken. In the airline context there

Table 4.7
Expenditure by British public road hauliers (% of total costs in 1965)

Cost item	%
Fuel	16.5
Spares	4.4
Tyres	3.8
Other materials	0.7
Maintenance (inc. wages) and vehicle hire	8.9
Drivers' and attendants' wages	33.3
Licences and insurance (vehicles)	6.2
Depreciation (vehicle) and HP interest	10.2
Building depreciation and overheads, rates	7.7
Other staff wages	8.3

Source: Edwards and Bayliss (1971)

Table 4.8
Illustrative cost structures for urban public transport in Australia (percentages)

Cost component	Train	Tram	Bus
Crewing	14	49	48
Station manning /signalling	7	-	-
Maintenance	32	23	22
Fuel	5	3	9
Administrative/other	9	9	9
Capital related expenses	23	16	12

Source: Kinnear (1988)

Table 4.9
Road haulage running and standing costs per mile in 1977 (£s)

Cost	Fleet size	Bulk tankers	Tipping	Smalls & parcels	Long distance	Other general	Other sectors	All sectors
Running	100+	0.20	-	0.12	0.15	0.21	0.14	0.18
Standing	100+	0.27	-	0.30	0.18	0.31	0.42	0.28
Running	21–100	0.17	0.13	0.12	0.15	0.16	0.16	0.15
Standing	21–100	0.22	0.19	0.28	0.16	0.22	0.26	0.21
Running	1–20	0.19	0.15	0.12	0.13	0.12	0.16	0.14
Standing	1–20	0.31	0.12	0.19	0.19	0.14	0.25	0.18

Source: Price Commission (1978)

exists a whole range of different aircraft designed to meet the needs of different operational patterns – airbuses for short-haul, large-volume traffic, wide-bodied jumbos for long range operations, etc. Equally, Table 4.9 gives some indication of the running and standing costs of different forms of operation in the UK road haulage sector. While these figures are not strictly variable and fixed costs, they do convey a general impression of how costs vary, even within sectors, with the type of transport operation performed.

The cost profiles also vary with the type of firm controlling the operations. Evidence from statistical studies of US urban public transit systems, for instance, suggest that public ownership can lead to higher costs of provision (Pucher and Markstedt, 1983). Wallis (1980), in his study of urban bus operations in major Australian cities, gives some reasons why private operators enjoy lower costs in certain areas than their publicly owned counterparts:

• greater flexibility and efficiency in use of labour;
• relatively small proportions of maintenance and administrative costs;
• lower basic rates of pay; and
• lower wage/salary on-costs (taxes, pensions, etc.).

While in part cost variations may be explained in terms of either the size of the operator or the type of operation undertaken, cost differences may also reflect alternative operational objectives. There is ample evidence that large national airlines often employ high-cost modern equipment to enhance their image. But even at the level of local public transport, similar indications of X-inefficiency exists. Teal *et al.* (1980), for example, cite instances of local authorities preferring to operate their own paratransport system rather than make use of established private operators despite demonstrably higher costs.

Labour costs, although flexible, are usually much less variable than fuel costs. This is not simply because of imperfections in the labour market (for example, fixed working hours, union agreements on redundancies, training costs, etc.) which often make it difficult to increase or reduce the size of the labour force – even in the sense of dividing up public transport crews to conform with daily peaks in travel demand – but also because of the nature of many types of transport operation. Once a particular form of transport operation has been decided upon, and capital invested, there are high labour costs associated with maintaining and servicing this equipment irrespective of the traffic carried. Further, once an undertaking is committed to a scheduled service, labour becomes a fixed cost in providing this service.

One of the major problems in this latter context is the technologically unprogressive nature of many forms of transport operations which makes it difficult to substitute one factor input for another as their relative prices change. In the case of the mercantile marine it has proved possible to substitute fixed for variable factors (notably capital for labour) as labour costs have risen but this is much less easy in areas such as public transport provision. It is difficult to see how the basic operations of taxi-cabs, for example, could be retained with a substantial reduction in labour input. Attempts to reduce labour costs in the urban public transport sphere by introducing one-man operated vehicles has had some limited effect on costs (Brown and Nash, 1972, estimated a 13.7 per cent cost saving and Lee and Steedman, 1970, a cost reduction of about 20 per cent), but this should be seen as a once-for-all step rather than the prospect of continual factor substitution.

4.3   Economies of scope, density and experience
In recent years it has become increasingly appreciated that while economies of scale in its strictest form may be of considerable importance in many transport activities, there are instances where it is not simply the pure size of the undertaking or activity which is the prime determinant of cost variation. A number of other factors are of particular importance in the transport context.

Many transport undertakings provide a variety of outputs. Taking aviation as an example, at the most basic level these may be scheduled and charter services in the aviation context but in more detail there is the matter of outward and return services and, at a more detailed level still, each particular flight may be viewed as a specific product. The economic question then becomes one of deciding whether there are cost savings in one supplier producing this range of services rather than there being a number of suppliers each specialising. Where there are cost economies from multi-product production then economies of scope are said to exist. Just as with conventional scale effects, it is possible for economies of scope to exist at some levels of output but not at others. As a city expands, for example, there may exist economies of scope in bus service provision favouring a monopoly supplier but as it gets larger and demand rises so these economies may disappear and a number of much smaller operators prove more cost effective.

There are also instances where there are cost economies from serving larger markets – it effectively allows the more intensive use of capital. Again aviation provides an example of these so-called economies of density where larger markets enable higher load factors to be enjoyed and hence lower unit cost per passenger.

The coming together of these economies of scope and of density has been characterised by the adoption of 'hub-and-spoke' operations (Brown, 1991). While US domestic aviation is the most cited example of this phenomena, with all the main airlines basing their services on radial flights from a limited number of hubs it is also appearing in shipping – with traffic into Europe coming by large ships to a small number of large ports to be distributed to other ports by smaller vessels - and in some spheres of bus operators – such as the importance of Victoria Coach Station in London as the hub for long distance inter-city bus services in the UK.

Figure 4.4 offers an indication of the cost advantages of hub-and-spoke operations. Assume that there are a number of small cities and three large centres, A, B and C. An airline operating between the small centres will attempt to reduce costs by providing a network of the general type set out in the diagram. It will provide few (in our case no) flights between the small centres but will force travellers to fly via the large links. Hence a passenger will not be able to fly w=>x but must go w=>A=>x. In some cases two links may be involved (such as w =>A=>B=>z for someone wishing to travel from w to z). By adopting such a service pattern the load factor from w to A is increased, indeed further economies can be attained if larger aircraft become viable. These savings stem from the range of services offered, rather than the pure size of the airline. Of course, not all services are generally hub-and-spoke – there may be direct services between hubs (such as A=>C in the diagram) both to meet the needs of that specific market but also because density effects are enjoyed as travellers using this link in a hub-and-spoke fashion also make use of the 'direct' service (here, for example, travellers w =>C; w =>v and A=>v would be drawn into the market).

A further recent development is the appreciation that there is a 'learning-by-doing' element in many activities which can reduce costs. These economies of experience tend to be under-researched in the transport sphere but technically exist when unit costs decline as more is produced or as a supplier stays in a market for an extended period of time. In the UK, for instance, it has been argued that these experience effects may have been advantageous to National Express in the period following the deregulation of the inter-city bus network after 1980. It was the incumbent supplier and enjoyed, along with other things, considerable experience in the market which enabled it to dominate newcomers (Button, 1989).

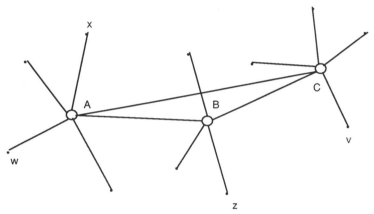

Figure 4.6
Economies of a hub-and-spoke network

4.4   Specific, joint and common costs

When dividing out costs, according to the groups of services produced, it is often useful to allocate responsibility to specific users or consignors. While the fixed/variable cost dichotomy poses problems about the relevant time period to consider, cost responsibility raises issues of the traceability of costs. Some costs are very specific and can, therefore, be allocated quite easily – the stevedore costs of loading and unloading a particular cargo onto and off a ship is a case in point. In other cases a degree of averaging may be necessary but, nevertheless, costs can generally be traced to specific groups of classes of user. But there is also a whole range of other costs that may be either 'joint' or 'common' to a number of users and are difficult to trace directly to any specific group. It is sometimes said that fixed costs may generally be treated as joint or common while variable costs may be treated as specific but this is too simplistic. Many variable costs are, in practice, joint (for example, the fuel costs incurred in moving a train in one direction and bringing it back are joint to both movements) or common (for example, the basic maintenance costs of retaining a freight and passenger rail link) while certain fixed costs are clearly specific (for example, the capital costs of freight wagons have no connection with passenger demand).

Strictly, joint costs exist when the provision of a specific service necessarily entails the output of some other service. Jointness is a technical feature and exists at all points in time, that is, both before as well as after any investment decisions are made. Return trips (or 'back-hauls'), where the supply of transport services in one direction automatically implies the provision of a return service, are the classic examples in transport economics. The fact that true joint products are produced in *fixed* proportions means there can be no variability in costs making it logically impossible to specify the cost of, say, an outward journey when only the overall cost of the round trip is known. Joint costs are, consequently, non-traceable. This further implies that joint costs can only be escaped jointly, with services in both directions being withdrawn together.

In a market situation joint costs pose few problems in practice (Mohring, 1976). If there is a competitive road haulage service offering a round trip between A and B and back again each week using M trucks then equilibrium rates would soon emerge for each service (that is, from A to B and from B to A). Although there are specific delivery, terminal, pick-up costs, etc., little difference exists between the costs of running the lorries fully loaded or empty and hence prices would be primarily influenced by the differences in the demand in each direction. In the short term the combined revenues from the A to B and the B to A services may not be sufficient to cover joint costs but in such a situation the number of trucks offered would soon fall below *M*, increasing the price of trips in both directions until joint costs are recovered. Excess revenue above joint costs would have the opposite effect. The key point is that differences exist in the demands for the out and return services and that different prices should be charged for each in equilibrium. Consequently, knowledge of the relevant demand elasticities together with that of joint cost permits the problems of traceability to be avoided. We return to consider this problem in more detail in our discussion of pricing in Chapter 6.

Common costs are similar to joint costs, in that they are incurred as the result of providing services to a range of users, but differ in that the use of resources to provide one service does not *unavoidably* result in the production of a different one. The classic example of common costs in transport is the provision of track facilities. A road may be used in common by lorries and cars but the withdrawal of rights for hauliers still leaves costs to be borne by motorists. With several classes of user it is often possible to trace certain components of cost to those responsible but there is still usually a large proportion which is untraceable. We now turn to look at some attempts that have been made to allocate common track costs across different categories of traffic.

4.5   Problems of common cost allocation – the road and rail track cases

The allocation of common track costs among users poses particular practical problems in transport and deserves specific attention. The road network in the UK is the responsibility of local and central government. Users, since the effective abolition of the Road Fund in 1937 and its legal death in 1955, make no direct, hypothecated payments to use the network – save for a small number of toll bridges – but do pay considerable sums to government each year in the form of fuel tax, value added tax, car tax and vehicle excise duty. When deciding upon the desirability of making a road journey, potential users are to some extent influenced by these taxes. Attempts have, therefore, been made, on the grounds of economic efficiency, to allocate accurately the public costs of road provision (both the construction and maintenance of the track) to users. The EC, for example, now wishes members to ensure that all road users pay at least their allocated short-run marginal costs of track provision and that the full long-term cost is recovered in total.

There are problems of deciding exactly what constitutes the total cost of road track provision in any period – for example, should the maintenance costs be estimated in the same way as depreciation in nationalised industries or simply considered as they are incurred and what exactly constitutes the capital cost of any one year?

National comparisons of annual expenditures against tax revenue (Table 4.10) suggest that most governments of industrial countries recover from road users more than is spent on road provision. It may be felt that the UK ratio is low and should be brought into line with other states but this is only justified if the overall economic, demographic and geographic features of the countries are the same and other countries are themselves behaving optimally. There is also certainly no reason why, as some have advocated, the ratio should approximate to unity. Part of the revenue raised from road users must be considered as a 'pure' tax in the same way that there are taxes on other expenditures. Also there are social costs associated with road transport (see Chapter 5) and motoring taxes may, in part, be seen as a method, albeit a very imperfect one, of making road users aware of such costs. Additionally if prices in other sectors of the economy deviate from costs, there are sound economic reasons for this to be also the policy on roads (see Chapter 6).

Table 4.10
Revenue/cost ratios associated with road use in selected industrial countries

Country	Road taxes as % of road expenditures*
Netherlands	434
Great Britain	335
New Zealand	235
Sweden	230
Denmark	214
Germany	148
Australia	113
Switzerland	107
Austria	80
Japan	80
United States	63

* Methods of estimating expenditure vary between countries
Source: Organisation for Economic Cooperation and Development (1987)

While there is no sound reason why expenditure should match revenue in aggregate, it may still be desirable for each class of road vehicle to more or less cover its allocated track costs – this is the view, for example, of the EC. Allocation of track costs to vehicle categories is, therefore, still important. The difficulty is that roads provide a common service to a variety of modes of transport (cyclists, motor cars, light vans, heavy lorries, buses, etc.) and the exact apportionment of marginal costs is, therefore, far from easy. The method of allocation favoured by the UK Department of Transport is based upon a refined version of an approach pioneered in the *Road Track Costs* study (UK Ministry of Transport, 1968) which crudely attempts to allocate long-run marginal costs (LRMCs) to different classes of road users.

The calculations are done for the four standard categories of road, motorway, trunk, principle and other. Of total capital expenditure (made up of the average expenditure over the previous year, the current year and the forecast for the following year), 15 per cent is allocated directly to heavy goods vehicles according to their maximum vehicle weight times the kilometres run, on the grounds that they necessitate higher engineering design standards. The remaining 85 per cent is allocated out on passenger car unit (pcu) kilometres (pcu being an estimate of the amount of road required to accommodate a vehicle expressed in terms of car equivalents), on the argument that capital expenditure is determined by changes required in the physical capacity of the network. Current maintenance expenditures are allocated according to a series of *ad hoc* calculations that attempt to relate the various component items (such as resurfacing, grass cutting, lighting, road markings, traffic signs, drainage, etc.) to different vehicle characteristics, namely their size, number of standard axles (high axle loadings doing considerable damage to road surfaces) and the use made of roads. The criteria used to decide how costs are affected by the vehicle characteristics are based upon 'expert advice from traffic engineers and research scientists'. Special items such as policing and car parks are treated separately.

Table 4.11 compares the cost allocations with revenues for different broad categories of road user. All classes cover their allocated cost, a situation which is also common in many other industrialised countries. A similar picture is seen within vehicle classes. For example, while all sizes of heavy goods vehicle pay tax in excess of the public road costs attributable to them, there is considerable variation in the revenue/cost ratio and large vehicles with a small number of axles tend to have the lowest ratios. This may be particularly undesirable if these large vehicles are also responsible for generating a high level of external costs.

Table 4.11
Allocated taxation/revenue ratios by vehicle type in the UK (1989)

Vehicle class	Tax to cost ratios
Cars/light vans/taxis	3.4:1
Motorcycles	2.3:1
Buses and coaches	1.1:1
Goods vehicles over 1.525	
Tonnes unladen:	
Not over 3.5 tonnes GVW	3.1:1
Over 3.5 tonnes GVW	1.3:1
Other vehicles	2.4:1
All vehicles	2.6:1

Source: UK Department of Transport (1989)

The UK Department of Transport's method of cost attribution has come under some criticism. At one level, Button (1979) has suggested that the detailed allocation within the Department's framework is biased against heavy goods vehicles because of (i) the excessive emphasis on vehicle weight in the allocation of capital costs when much of the network's design is determined by vehicle speed; (ii) the implied assumption in the calculation that the network is of optimal size;

(iii) the rather dubious nature of pcus as a measure of road capacity; and (iv) the relevance of the 'standard axle' measure used in the calculations. In particular, there is evidence that there may be an element of double counting when estimating heavy goods vehicle costs. Cars are accredited with a small allocation of road maintenance costs, but this is only possible because of the high engineering standards of roads required to carry heavy goods traffic. Hence, heavy goods vehicles are allocated both the additional costs of high design standards and the bulk of maintenance costs whereas with lower design specifications, suitable for cars only, cars would be allocated much higher maintenance costs.

This last point has been examined in some detail in a US study of that country's road investment and pricing policy (Small *et al.*, 1989). The evidence produced is that under the US regime, where certain federal road taxation revenue is directly hypothecated to road building and maintenance, the amount of investment has historically been sub-optimal resulting in pavements which are, from an economic prospect, too thin. The result is the need for high maintenance and reconstruction outlays relatively soon after a road is opened. The economic evidence is that if higher taxes had been introduced initially and higher standard roads constructed then subsequent taxation to finance maintenance would, on average, have been much lower than it inevitably will have to be if the network is not to deteriorate. The actual structure of the taxation should also have been adjusted to more closely correspond to the damage associated with various classes of user. Table 4.12 provides data on actual taxation, the taxation needed in the near future to maintain the current road system and what it would have been if optimal taxation and investment policies had been adopted.

Table 4.12
Examples of actual and optimal road vehicle taxation in the USA

Vehicle	Taxes (cents per mile)		
	Current	*Marginal cost existing roads*	*Marginal cost improved roads*
2-axle single unit			
26000lbs	2.5	9.2	3.6
33000lbs	3.0	23.8	9.3
5-axle tractor-trailer			
33000lbs	4.0	1.2	0.5
80000lbs	7.2	41.3	16.2

Source: Based on data in Small *et al.* (1989)

At a more fundamental level, Nash (1979) suggests that the traditional road track cost approach is really asking the wrong question and that track cost allocation should be along altogether different lines. He suggests the way ahead is to adopt a sequential approach where greater emphasis is placed upon differing demand elasticities among road users. Specifically he advises:

(1)   Forecast traffic growth rates by vehicle type using alternative assumptions about future taxation levels and structures.
(2)   Estimate the full costs of catering for different traffic growth rates.

(3)   Identify the level and structure of taxes at which the revenue obtained from an incremental slice of traffic matches incremental costs both for traffic as a whole and for individual traffic types.

(4)   To the extent that the resulting taxes fall short of government revenue requirements, raise taxes on vehicle classes along second-best lines (that is, according to demand elasticities).

Such calculations obviously place greater demands on informational sources but they do offer a rather more realistic basis for track cost allocation and pricing consistent with principles adopted elsewhere in the transport sector.

Railway track allocation is done in a slightly different context because the railways, unlike the roads case, have traditionally been responsible in most countries for providing both track and rolling stock. Even in countries such as Sweden where track is now separated from operations, the need to directly charge operators their costs makes the situation somewhat different to most roads. In the UK, the necessity for devising a method of allocation stems not simply from designs for internal efficiency but also to permit the allocation of common fixed costs between those services that are operated on commercial criteria (for example, intercity services) and those that are operated on social criteria (for example, commuter services) and are given central government subsidies.

One of the difficulties with railway operations is that common costs (which must include signalling, termini, etc. in addition to track) form a very substantial part of total cost. Normal commercial practice would be to use a 'cost-plus' method of pricing so that each customer would pay a rate covering his specific costs plus contribution to overheads. Provided this results in all costs being recovered in aggregate the problem of common cost allocation is not a serious issue. Unfortunately, for the reasons mentioned above, plus the difficulty of devising a sufficiently sensitive price discrimination regime given the diversity of services offered (see Chapter 6), the railways have found it important to be able to allocate their track costs.

A major difficulty in this area is that the railway's 'jargon' does not conform to conventional economic definitions. The railways talk of 'direct costs' and 'indirect costs' but the former (which embraces haulage costs, maintenance, marshalling, booking, insurance, collection and delivery by road) is clearly different from the economic notion of short-run escapable costs (and may or may not exceed them). As the Select Committee on Nationalised Industries (1960) said, 'The direct costs ascertained by traffic costing methods are not the same thing as short run marginal costs. Nor do they correspond with the savings that would flow immediately from the discontinuance of a small part of railway activities.' Equally, indirect costs, as defined by the railways (that is, track, signalling and general administration) are not sufficiently fixed costs which are common to all traffic. While certain costs (for example, those of earthworks) are invariant with traffic it is often possible to allocate track and signalling costs to particular services according to causation. The type and density of traffic determine whether a single track route is operated with no signalling or a multi-track, multiple-aspect signalling system is provided. Joy (1964) showed how these costs can vary with the quality of service – an express Category A service on double track with twelve trains a day cost £8250 per mile per annum in track costs (at 1961 prices); a less frequent, Category B service, £7250; heavily used non-express Category C services, £6250; and slow, Category D services, £3500. It is possible with poorer quality services to have more basic signalling and lower track maintenance standards. Further there are quite significant differences associated with the costs of track used exclusively for passenger services and that used only for freight. The *Beeching Report* (British Railways Board, 1963) found that a single track maintained to passenger standards costs at least £3500 per mile per annum but if it were only required to conform to freight standards it would cost £2000 per mile per annum, and it has been argued this could be reduced further (Joy, 1973).

The improvement in costing in the UK came about in part because of the 1968 Transport Act and the introduction of social service subsidies for specific routes – the system required 'identification and costing of those services and facilities whose cost should properly be borne or aided by the community' . The common costs were allocated according to the 'Cooper Brothers' formula (which it should be noted was essentially an average, rather than marginal, cost type of framework) which endorsed the idea of allocating track costs on the basis of gross ton miles and signalling costs on the basis of train miles. With homogeneous traffic flows evenly spread this is reasonable but with mixed traffic and peaks in use the allocation technique is unlikely to match causation with costs.

British Rail moved in the late 1970s to a system of 'contribution accounting' which entailed breaking down revenue and costs into some 700 major sub-sectors (or 'profit centres'). These profit centres – which are composed of single traffic flows, groups of flows or specific passenger services – are defined so that resources allocated to them can be specifically identified with a minimum of controversy. Even so not all common costs could be so allocated and thus British Rail accounts revealed the surplus of revenue over directly attributed expenses which are a 'contribution' to the indirect costs. The sum of all avoidable costs recovered may not cover all business costs, however, and a 'basic facility cost' is likely to remain. British Rail argue, though, that this approach, given the high proportion of indirect costs, 'ensures a high level of certainty in profit assessment' (see Dodgson, 1984, for further comment on these rail costs issues).

The problems of allocating costs common to several services is, therefore, seen to be a difficult one. Economic principles advocate the notion of seeking avoidable costs associated with specific users and then allocating these accordingly. The problem is in defining the base from which to begin the series of allocations – in the case of roads are they mainly designed for cars with lorries imposing additional costs or are they there to provide a quality of service with the faster car traffic necessitating higher engineering standards? We have seen that it is possible to allocate many items on an avoidable cost basis although practical application may necessitate a high degree of averaging.

4.6 Transport user costs and the notion of generalised costs

From the traveller's point of view, or that of a consignor of freight, a multiplicity of factors influence decisions. In particular, travellers take notice of the time it takes to make a trip and the money costs involved and, frequently, also the quality of the service offered. Consignors are concerned not simply with the financial costs of carriage but also the speed, reliability and time-tabling of the service. The demand for transport is not, therefore, simply dependent upon financial costs but rather on the overall opportunity costs involved. Transport is not unique in this, but it does differ from other services in that money costs may only form a relatively small part of overall costs. In terms of decision-making, the money cost of a trip may have minimal influence over whether it is undertaken or the transport mode preferred; a fact which may explain the considerable use of private motor cars even when 'cheaper' alternative modes are available (Sherman, 1967).

User costs are also, according to Mohring (1976), important in the urban public transport context for another reason. He argues that in the context of very frequent public transport in cities the main scale economy effects are associated with saving in passengers' time. These economies exist when the service is such that people do not arrive at a stop intending to catch a particular scheduled bus but rather know that headways are so close that at any time the wait will be short. If say the average headway is ten minutes then the average wait, assuming random arrivals of passengers, will be five minutes. A reduction of headway to five minutes will reduce the average wait to two and a half minutes. Increased output of bus services, therefore, reduces average waiting time and thus the users, cost of travelling by bus.

In analysing transport demand or when forecasting future consumer response it is often possible to assess responses to the individual components of overall cost, that is money costs, time costs, inconvenience costs and so on. In some situations, however, it has proved useful to have a composite measure. This may be true in situations where multi-dimensional cost functions are unwieldy or when a simple unidimensional measure, by focusing attention on general trends in cost, permits a clearer understanding of changes in the demand for transport services. A pragmatic device to reduce the wide range of costs involved in travel is to employ a single index expressing 'generalised cost'.

The generalised cost of a trip is expressed as a single, usually monetary, measure combining, generally in linear form, most of the important but disparate costs which form the overall opportunity costs of the trip. On occasions a generalised time cost measure may replace the financial index (Goodwin, 1974). The characteristic of generalised cost is, therefore, that it reduces all cost items to a single index and this index may then be used in the same way as money costs are in standard economic analysis. Simply, generalised costs can be defined as:

$$G = g(C_1, C_2, C_3, \ldots C_n) \tag{4.1}$$

where G is generalised cost and $C_1, C_2, C_3, \ldots$ are the various time, money and other costs of travel. This permits the demand for trips to be expressed as a function of a single variable (that is, $Q_D = f(G)$). While in simple indices, generalised cost is formed as a linear combination of time and money (or distance) costs in most applied analysis the time and money components are divided into a number of elements (for example, walking time, waiting time, on-vehicle time, etc.). This results in an expression of the general form:

$$G = \sum_i M_i + \sum_j T_j \tag{4.2}$$

where the M_i are the actual money costs of a journey (for example, fare or petrol costs), T_j are the time costs (for instance, on-vehicle time, waiting time) and t_j are the monetary values of the various time components (these were discussed in detail in Chapter 3).

For expositional ease, the specific form of the generalised cost function used in the South-east Lancashire, North-east Cheshire (SELNEC) transport study conducted in the late 1960s (Wilson *et al.*, 1969) provides a useful illustration of actual application. The generalised cost index used in the combined trip distribution–modal split element of the analysis (see Chapter 8) was of the form:

$$G_{ij}^K = a_1 t_{ij}^k + a_2 e_{ij}^K + a_3 d_{ij}^K + p_j^K + \zeta^K \tag{4.3}$$

where: G_{ij}^K is the generalised cost of travel by mode K between points i and j;

          t_{ij}^k is the travel time from i to j by mode K (in minutes);

          e_{ij}^K is the excess time (for example, waiting time for public transport) for the journey from i to j (in minutes);

          d_{ij}^K is the distance from i to j which acts as a surrogate for the variable money costs of trips (which are assumed proportional to distance);

          p_j^K is the terminal cost (for example, parking charges) at j (in pence);

          ζ^K is a modal penalty reflecting the discomfort and lesser convenience associated with public transport journeys; and

          a_1, a_2 *and* a_3 are parameters which, since p_j^K and ζ^K have unit coefficients, value other cost items in monetary terms.

An important issue is how these costs should be treated in analysis of transport decisions. Economics is concerned with costs which influence behaviour in the short term and with those which affect long-term decisions. In the short term, people may well only perceive a limited range of costs or not fully appreciate the full magnitude of some cost items. Nevertheless, it is this set of costs which influences their immediate actions. The problem of perception is generally associated with the external costs which travellers generate by ignoring their actions (see Chapter 5) but here we are concerned with the misperception of the costs they bear themselves.

People misperceive the costs of their journeys (or of moving goods) for a number of reasons:

(1)   The money or time cost may be so small that it is not worth taking into account.
(2)   Certain variable costs may be regarded wrongly as fixed costs; included here would be the tendency for car users only to take account of petrol costs of journeys and ignore depreciation of the vehicle and its maintenance.
(3)   Users may be unaware of the connection between a particular action and the costs to which it gives rise, for example, a fast driver may be unaware of the additional fuel costs he incurs.
(4)   Habit can make regular trip-makers unaware of changing cost conditions over time even if they were fully cognisant of the full resource costs of their actions at some earlier point in time. This is more likely to be a problem encountered by car users than public transport travellers who face regular ticket purchases.

While the final three reasons for misperception result from poor or inadequate information, the first represents a departure from the conventional economic idea of maximising behaviour. While this latter subject poses interesting theoretical questions, reasons (2)–(4) are likely to be of greater quantitative importance for transport economists. Lack of good information is likely to result in different

travel behaviour to that anticipated in full information situations. Whereas perceived generalised costs offer a basis for travel behaviour analysis, it is actual
resource costs which are appropriate for investment decision-taking. Where
people accurately perceive the costs of their travel there is no difference between
the perceived and resource generalised cost. Where there is misperception,
however, resource costs, being the full opportunity cost of trip-making, will
exceed the perceived costs and this may result in over-investment in transport
facilities if adjustments are not made. (Of course, we are still ignoring external
costs such as pollution but these complicate rather than change the argument.)

The social welfare gains associated with an investment should be assessed by
comparing the resource costs with the benefits generated; the difficulty is that the
actual traffic levels using the facility depend upon perceived costs. In Figure 4.7
we have a linear demand curve for use of a road with an initial perceived generalised cost of usage equal to p^1. A widening of the road speeds traffic, causing the
perceived generalised cost to fall to p^2. If, however, the actual resource costs of
trip-making along the road are f, and p for the respective pre- and post-
investment situations, then there will be 'deadweight' welfare 'losses' generated
at both the t^1 and t^2 traffic levels. (At the pre-investment traffic flow, t_i, this loss is
equal to area c and at the post-investment flow, t^2, it is h.) If no account is taken
of this, however, the apparent consumer surplus gain from the road widening is
equal to $(d + e + f + g)$. In fact, since the genuine resource costs are measured by
f^1 and f^2, the investment will result in a net benefit of $(b + c + d + e - h)$. The area
$(b + e + d)$ represents a straight resource cost saving under the demand curve by
reducing the resource costs of travel, while $(c - h)$ reflects the change in
deadweight welfare loss between the two traffic flow situations. Neuberger (1971)
has generalised this calculation to take account of the effects of policies which
alter costs and travel patterns over a network of roads.

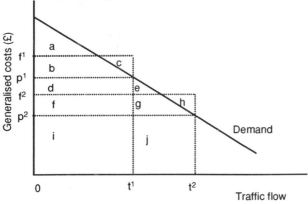

Figure 4.7
Welfare gains from a cost reduction with misperceived transport costs

The adoption of a single index idea of transport costs has permitted significant
advances in transport forecasting and project appraisal to be made. This does not
mean, however, that the concept is not without its critics nor that other advances
have not been made by those choosing to ignore its existence. First, the inherent

constraints implicit in aggregation of different elements of cost, in particular the aggregating of the various cost components into a unique index, restricts the separate elasticities of demand with respect to *each* individual cost component (Grey, 1978). One ends up with an elasticity with respect to generalised costs but cannot, for example, assess the specific effect of a reduction in travel time costs. Second, there is concern about the long-term stability of money as the numerator. Because income rises over time, it is argued, the utility of money will fall relative to other items, especially time which is fixed in quantity. McIntosh and Quarmby (1972), therefore, argued that time should be used as the basis of measurement and the operational concept should be generalised time costs. Additionally, time is equally distributed (in the sense that everyone has 24 hours in a day) which circumvents some of the distributional difficulties of using money values of travel cost components. Third, even if the basic notion of generalised cost is accepted there are critics who oppose the use of a 'universal' index for application throughout a country, for example of the form McIntosh and Quarmby (1972) put forward for the UK some years ago. A difficulty is that there is little evidence to support the universality of any weighting scheme employed. Although the use of official time valuations and formulae ensure consistency in *approach,* they may lead to inconsistencies in *results* if the overall index is only accurate in certain sets of circumstances.

Generalised cost is, despite these criticisms, a useful tool in helping us to understand, in broad terms, how variations in travel cost can influence travel behaviour. Above all, it is an extremely useful pedagogic aid which can help policy-makers articulate their ideas and plans to a more general audience. It also serves as a pragmatic device for assisting in certain types of modelling and decision-making where otherwise, as Searle (1978) points out, no information would be forthcoming at all. In this context the index is likely to be an imperfect instrument but, when used with sufficient circumspection, it can yield useful insights into the possible effects of alternative transport policies.

4.7 Further reading and references

Walters (1965) provides a useful theoretical examination of the more technical issues involved in separating short- from long-run transport costs; it is also non-mathematical in its approach. Waters's (1985) study of railway costing offers insights into the practical problems of applying these principles. At the operational level, Joy's (1973) study of the history of British Rail during the post-war period, offers a unique examination of the difficulties in apportioning costs as seen through the eyes of a former chief economist on the Railways Board. Berechman and Giuliano's (1985) review of econometric work on scale effects in bus operations contains both a careful assessment of measuring problems and good coverage of recent findings. *The Road Track Cost Report* (UK Ministry of Transport, 1968) still provides interesting reading for those interested in the practical problems of finding a workable method of allocating track cost to users, and Small *et al.* (1989) is an interesting study of how the general approach to road finances could be improved. Grey's (1978) paper on generalised costs, although now somewhat dated, contains both a more detailed description of the theory behind the concept and an account of its uses besides being a carefully argued, stimulating and clearly presented criticism of generalised cost as a tool in transport economics.

References

Berechman, J. (1983), 'Costs, economies of scale and factor demand in road transport', *Journal of Transport Economics and Policy*, 17, 7–24.

Berechman, J. and Giuliano, G. (1985), 'Economies of scale in bus transit: a review of concepts and evidence', *Transportation*, 12, 313–32.

Board of Trade (1969), *British Air Transport in the Seventies*, Cmnd 4018, London, HMSO.

British Railways Board (1963), *The Reshaping of British Railways*, London, HMSO.

Brown, J.H. (1991), 'An economic model of airline hubbing-and-spoking', *Logistics and Transportation Review*, 27, 225–40.

Brown, R.H. and Nash, C.A. (1972), 'Cost savings from one-man operations of buses', *Journal of Transport Economics and Policy*, 6, 281–4.

Button, K.J. (1979), 'Heavy goods vehicle taxation in the United Kingdom', *Transportation*, 8, 389–408.

Button, K.J. (1989), 'Contestability in the UK bus industry, and experience goods and economies of experience', in J. Dodgson and N. Topham (eds), *Bus Deregulation and Privatisation: An International Perspective*, Aldershot, Gower.

Button, K.J. and O'Donnell, K.J. (1985), 'An examination of the cost structures associated with providing urban bus services in Britain', *Scottish Journal of Political Economy*, 32, 67–81.

Dodgson, J.S. (1984), 'Railway costs and closures', *Journal of Transport Economics and Policy*, 18, 219–236.

Edwards, S.L. and Bayliss, B.T. (1971), *Operating Costs in Road Freight Transport*, London, Department of the Environment.

Foster, C.D. and Joy, S. (1967), 'Railway track costs in Britain', in *Development of Railway Traffic Engineering*, London, Institution of Civil Engineers.

Goodwin, P.B. (1974), 'Generalised time and the problem of equity in transport studies', *Transportation*, 3, 1–24.

Goss, R.O. and Jones, C.D. (1971), *The Economics of Size in Dry Bulk Carriers*, London, Government Economic Service Occasional Paper 2.

Grey, A. (1978), 'The generalised cost dilemma', *Transportation*, 7, 261–80.

Gyenes, L. (1980), 'Assessing the effect of traffic congestion on motor vehicle fuel consumption', *Transport and Road Research Laboratory Report 613*.

Heaver, T.D. (1975), *The Routing of Canadian Container Traffic Through Vancouver and Seattle* , Vancouver, WESTMAC.

Hicks, S.K. (1975), 'Urban goods movement: a political economist's viewpoint', in K.W. Ogden and S.K. Hicks (eds), *Goods Movement and Goods Vehicles in Urban Areas*, Melbourne, Commonwealth Bureau of Roads.

International Air Transport Association (1984), *International Air Fares in Europe*, Geneva, IATA

Jansson, J.0. and Shneerson, D. (1978), 'Economics of scale of general cargo ships', *Review of Economics and Statistics*, 45, 287–93.

Joy, S. (1964), 'British Railways track costs', *Journal of Industrial Economics*, 13, 74–89.

Joy, S. (1973), *The Train that Ran Away*, London, Ian Allan.

Keeler, T.E. and Small, K.A. (1977), 'Optimal peak-load pricing investment and service levels on urban express-ways', *Journal of Political Economy*, 85, 1–25.

Kinnear, R. (1988), 'Financial realities: cost trends and productivity', *Transport Reviews*, 8, 341–350.

Koshal, R.K. (1970), 'Economies of scale in bus transport II: Some Indian experience', *Journal of Transport Economics and Policy*, 4, 29–36.

Lee, N. and Steedman, I.W. (1970), 'Economies of scale in bus transport I: Some British municipal results', *Journal of Transport Economics and Policy*, 4, 15–28.

McIntosh, P.T. and Quarmby, D.A. (1972), 'Generalised costs and the estimation of movement costs and benefits in transport planning', *Highway Research Record*, 383, 11–23.

Mohring, H. (1976), *Transportation Economics,* Cambridge, Mass., Ballinger.

Nash, C.A. (1979), 'The track costs issue – a comment', *Journal of Transport Economics and Policy,* 14, 113–16.

Neuberger, H.L.I. (1971), 'Perceived costs', *Environment and Planning,* 3, 369–76.

Oldfield, R. (1974), 'Elasticities of demand for travel', *Transport and Road Research Laboratory, Supplementary Report 116 UC.*

Organisation for Economic Cooperation and Development (1987), *Toll Financing and Private Sector Involvement in Road Infrastructure,* Paris, OECD.

Price Commission (1978), *The Road Haulage Industry,* House of Commons Paper HC 698. London, HMSO.

Pucher, J. and Markstedt, A. (1983), 'Consequences of public ownership and subsidies for mass transit: evidence from case studies and regression analysis', *Transportation,* 11, 323–45.

Searle, G. (1978), 'Comment – generalised cost: fool's gold or useful currency?', *Transportation,* 7, 297–9.

Sherman, R. (1967), 'A private ownership bias in transit choice', *American Economic Review,* 77, 1211–17.

Small, K.A., Winston, C. and Evans, C.A. (1989), *Road Works: A New Highway Pricing and Investment Policy,* Washington, Brookings Institution.

Talley, W.K., Agarwal, V.B. and Breakfield, J.W. (1986), 'Economies of density of ocean tanker ships', *Journal of Transport Economics and Policy,* 20, 91–9.

Tanner, J.C. (1968), 'An economic comparison of motorways with 2 or 3 lanes in each direction', *Road and Research Laboratory Report, LR.203.*

Teal, R.F., Marks, J.V. and Goodhue, R. (1980), 'Subsidised shared-ride taxi service', *Paper Presented to the Transportation Research Board.*

Tolifari, S., Button, K.J. and Pitfield, D. (1986), 'Shipping costs and the controversy over open registry', *Journal of Industrial Economics,* 34, 409–427.

UK Department of Transport (1979), *Road Haulage Operators' Licensing (Report of the Independent Committee of Enquiry into Road Haulage Operators Licensing),* London, HMSO.

UK Department of Transport (1980), *Report of the Inquiry into Lorries, People and the Environment,* London, HMSO.

UK Department of Transport (1989), *The Allocation of Road Track Costs 1989/90,* London, Department of Transport.

UK House of Commons Select Committee on Nationalised Industries (1960), *Report: British Railways,* London, HMSO.

UK Ministry of Transport (1968), *Road Track Costs,* London, HMSO.

Wabe, J.S. and Coles, O.B. (1975), 'The peak and off-peak demand for bus transport: a cross-sectional analysis of British municipal operations', *Applied Economics,* 7, 25–30.

Wallis, I.P. (1980), 'Private bus operations in urban areas – their economics and role', *Traffic Engineering and Control,* 22, 605–10.

Walters, A. A. (1965), 'The long and the short of transport', *Bulletin of the Oxford Institute of Economics and Statistics,* 27, 97–101.

Walters, A.A. (1968), *The Economics of Road User Charges,* Baltimore, Johns Hopkins Press.

Waters, W.G. (1985), 'Rail cost analysis', in Button, K.J. and Pitfield, D.E. (eds), *International Railway Economics,* Aldershot, Gower.

Williams, M. (1981), 'The economic justification for local bus transport subsidies', *International Journal of Transport Economics,* 8, 79–88.

Williams, M. and Hall, C. (1981), 'Returns to scale in the United States intercity bus industry', *Regional Science and Urban Economics,* 11, 573–84.

Wilson, A.G., Hawkins, H.F., Hill, G.J. and Wagon, D.J. (1969), 'Calibration and testing of the SELNEC transport model', *Regional Studies,* 3, 337–50.

Winston, C. (1985), 'Conceptual developments in the economics of transportation: an interpretive survey', *Journal of Economic Literature*, 23, 57–94.

5   The External Costs of Transport

5.1   What is an externality?

Chapter 4 was concerned with showing the types of financial costs confronting transport users. It is quite clear from our everyday experience, however, that there are other costs associated with transport that are not directly borne by those generating them. Air travellers impose noise costs on those living below aircraft flight paths, road travellers inflict dirt and vibration on those living adjacent to major trunk routes while, at the same time, impeding the progress of pedestrians in towns. Maritime transports frequently pollute bathing beaches with their oil discharges. These are external costs generated by transport users and inflicted on the non-travelling public. Formally, externalities exist when the activities of one group (either consumers or producers) affect the welfare of another group without any payment or compensation being made. They may be thought of as relationships other than those between a buyer and a seller, and do not normally fall within the 'measuring rod of money'. There are also external benefits as well as costs although these are generally thought less important in the transport sector. The fact that wide streets, for example, act as fire breaks, in addition to serving as transport arteries, may be thought of as an external benefit associated with urban motorways.

A vast theoretical literature has grown up over the last fifty years refining the rather complicated concept of external costs. While much of the detail of this work has a greater or lesser importance in a transport context there are two major distinctions which need to be highlighted.

The distinction between pecuniary and technological externalities

The formal difference between these two categories of externality is that when the latter effects occur in production (or consumption) they must appear in the production (or utility) function while this is not the case with pecuniary externalities. Pecuniary effects occur when, say, a firm's costs are affected by price changes induced by other firms' actions in buying and selling factors of production. An example can help to clarify this. A new motorway may block or destroy a pleasant view formerly enjoyed by the resident of an area. The fact that this directly enters the resident's utility function means it is a technological externality. If this new motorway also takes business away from a local garage and transfers it to a motorway service station, then the reduced income suffered by the garage proprietor is a pecuniary externality since the effect is indirect, namely through changes in the prices charged by the two undertakings.

   The distinction is a fine one, particularly since in practice both forms of externality usually occur simultaneously, but it is an important one. Technological externalities are real resource costs which strictly should be taken into account in decision-making if optimal efficiency is to be ensured. Pecuniary externalities do not involve resource costs in an aggregate sense but they do normally have important distributional implications (for example, in our motorway example the service station gains while the garage loses). The fact that there may be pecuniary externalities associated with a project does not reduce the total net benefit but rather reveals that there are adjustments in the economy which influence who is to enjoy the gains and who is to suffer the costs. The distinction between technological and pecuniary externalities is, therefore, important in the appraisal of public sector transport investment where one is concerned with the incidence of the costs and benefits in addition to their overall level (see Chapter 8).

The distinction between pollution and congestion
Conventional welfare economics distinguishes between a variety of externality categories according to the different types of agent involved. Rothenberg (1970) offers a simple dichotomy which is possibly of more use in the transport context than some of the more complicated categorisations. He distinguishes between two forms of what he calls 'generic congestion'. The underlying idea is that externalities result from attempts by different agents to share a common service which is not provided in discrete units earmarked for each (that is, it has 'public good' characteristics). The presence of other users already affects the quality of service which is rendered to each. Generic congestion may be divided into:

   Pure pollution 'The essence of pollution ... is that there are some other users who do abuse the medium – the polluters – while others are relatively passive victims of such abuse – the public – Jet planes make the noise, housewives are forced to submit to it.'
   Pure congestion 'If highway traffic is the classic example of congestion, then the central inter-personal distributive fact about it is that all users are using the medium (the public good) in much the same way, each is damaging service quality for both others and himself, and the ratio of self:other damage is approximately the same for all users... The whole user group loses homogeneously by their self-imposed interaction.'

   The remainder of this chapter focuses in turn on these two types of externality and on the extent to which they can be associated with transport activities. Initially, we look at the pure pollution generated by the movement of goods and the journeys of people and then turn to consider the economics of traffic congestion.

5.2   Transport and the environment
Transport pollutes the environment in three broad ways. First, it imposes many local environmental costs on those living, working or taking recreation near major pieces of transport infrastructure. These include such factors as noise, visual intrusion, local air pollution (for example, particulates, lead and carbon monoxide) and the disposal of obsolete vehicles. A major problem here is that, unlike many other forms of environmental intrusion, it is generally difficult to move transport facilities away from sensitive areas simply because users demand easy access and close proximity to roads and to public transport terminals. Second, there are transboundary effects such as emissions which contribute to acid rain (such as

NOₓ) and maritime spillage which have impacts some distance from the transport activities themselves. Finally, there is the contribution of transport to the global environmental problems of global warming (such as emissions of CO_2) and to upper level ozone depletion (in particular CFCs). Some indication of the contribution of transport to these problems in industrialised nations is set out in Table 5.1.

Table 5.1
Transport's contribution to major environmental problems

	North America	OECD Europe	Japan	OECD States
		Air		
	Total transport emissions as % of total emissions			
Nitrogen oxides (NO_x)	47	51	39	48
Carbon monoxide (CO)	71	81	na	75
Sulphur oxides (SO_x)	4	3	9	3
Particulates	14	8	na	13
Hydrocarbons (HC)	39	45	na	40
		Noise		
	Population exposed to road traffic noise over 65dBA			
	19 million	53 million	36 million	110 million

Many environmentalist groups argue for substantial reductions or total elimination of these adverse environmental effects but this ignores the cost associated with removing such nuisances. While some people suffer from the environmental intrusion associated with transport, others clearly benefit from being able to travel more freely or move goods more cheaply. In almost all cases environmental improvements would reduce the net benefits enjoyed by transport users. Economists tend, therefore, to think in terms of optimising the level of pollution rather than 'purifying' the environment entirely.

If we look at Figure 5.1 we see plotted on the vertical axis the money value of the costs and benefits of reducing the noxious fumes emitted by motor cars and, on the horizontal, the environmental improvements that accompany a reduction in such fumes. The marginal costs of reducing the emissions are likely to rise quite steeply. While more sophisticated filters may be fitted and fuel subjected to more extensive refining, both become increasingly costly to apply as the toxicity of the exhaust is reduced. Additionally, they reduce the efficiency of vehicles and may, in the case of improved refining, impose higher levels of pollution on those living around refineries. The marginal benefits of 'cleaner' road vehicles, in contrast, are likely to fall with successive improvements. The public is likely to be relatively less conscious of lower levels of emission and be aware that many of the seriously toxic materials (for example, lead) are likely to be amongst the first to be removed in the clean-up programme. Consequently, the marginal cost and revenue curves

96 — Chapter 5

associated with improved emission quality are likely to be of the form seen in Figure 5.1. There is quite clearly an optimal level of improvement (that is, OE_1) beyond which the marginal costs of further emission reductions exceed the marginal benefits. If the clean-up programme reduced emissions to the point where further reductions would yield no additional benefit (that is, exhaust fumes would be considered 'pure' although this may not mean zero toxicity if individuals' perceptions are faulty), then the situation is not optimal. Improvements beyond OE_1 to OE_2, in fact, result in a net welfare loss equal to the shaded area ABC in the diagram.

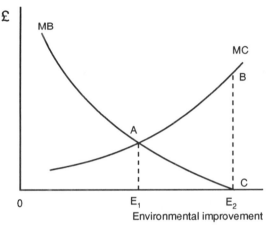

Figure 5.1
The optimal environmental improvement

Consequently, when talking about the excessive environmental harm caused by various forms of transport it is important to remember that this is an excess above the optimal level of pollution, not above zero pollution or some perceived 'pure' environment. We return to this topic and methods of attaining the optimum in Chapter 7.

5.3 The valuation of externalities
In order to compare the external costs and benefits of transport with other features of transport it is often found useful to convert such costs and benefits into monetary terms. This is no easy task but economists have developed a number of procedures which, at least in the case of some externalities, do provide reasonable guidance to the value of these external effects (Button, 1993). In recent years the level of sophistication used in this process has risen considerably and only a very brief outline of some, the more common techniques is set out here.

Precedents
Consistency over time is the prime reason for suggesting that historical precedents could be used as a means of valuing certain aspects of the environment. Precedents in this context are legal rulings on compensation for inflicting environmental damage. While having some superficial attractions, the procedure has severe limitations.

The main applications have been in terms of valuing injury and death in transport accidents although there are instances of transport suppliers, and especially shipping companies, having to compensate for spillage of toxic pollutants. This is because precedents exist only where there are established rights and these extend to very few environmental attributes. Even without this practical limitation, the usefulness of the techniques is restricted by the nature of most legal systems. They normally apply to the need for victims (including relatives of people killed) of the incident to be cared for during the remainder of their lives. Consequently, where the environmental damage causes death the 'cost' to the deceased is not considered. Equally, damage to flora and fauna is generally outside of the scope of legal rulings on compensation. Finally, where evidence has been produced looking at legal precedence it tends to show little by way of a consistent pattern.

Averting behaviour
Many adverse environmental consequences of transport can be ameliorated by insulation. Noise nuisance can be reduced by double-glazing windows, the adverse effects of air pollution by installing air conditioning and accident risk by the adoption of safer engineering design standards for transport infrastructure and the vehicles which use it. A widely deployed technique for assessing the costs of environmental damage is to equate them with the cost of avoidance.

The main problem is the difficulty of isolating specific expenditures for environmental reasons from the implicit joint expenditure on other benefits accompanying, for example, double-glazing (such as, reduced heating bills, etc.) or air conditioning (for example, a cooler room temperature). Noise insulation is also only partial in that it does not offer protection when in the garden or when windows are open. More fundamentally, there are questions about the optimality of the level of avoidance adopted. In terms of safety, for example, the aviation industry provides an extremely safe product but only at a tremendous cost. In terms of potential lives saved each is implicitly valued more highly than, say, a life saved on the roads where the per capita safety expenditure is much lower.

Revealed preference: hedonic prices
There are circumstances where consumers of environmental resources, through their actions, implicitly reveal the values that they place on them. They make trade-offs involving sacrificing some monetary benefits to limit the use of environmental resources or gain some environmental benefit. The classic case is the willingness of people to pay to live away from noisy airports or roads or to pay a premium for a hotel room away from a busy street.

The underlying theory can be discussed in terms of Figure 5.2 which plots the welfare enjoyed by an individual at various levels of wealth. The diminishing marginal utility of money gives, for example, the trade-off curve *I* for an individual living in a quiet, rural setting. The construction of an airport adjacent to the house imposes measurable noise costs on this person and, for every level of wealth, this pulls the trade-off curve down, that is, it becomes *II*. If the person was initially at a point *A* on *I* then the imposition of the noise will reduce welfare to level *B*. To get him back to his original welfare level, compensation of *BC* would be needed, this being sufficient to move him around *II* until the original level of welfare is restored.

This approach assumes, however, that there is a finite level of compensation which satisfies the individual. If, however, one starts at an initial position $A^\dagger$ then it is not altogether clear this is so. (This type of problem essentially arose in the late 1960s when researchers were trying to value the noise costs of aviation at alternative sites for a third London airport – eventually an arbitrary value was adopted for some individuals.) Second, the onus of the technique as described above is on compensation. One would normally get a different value by taking the amount required to be paid by the individual to bribe the authorities not to construct the airport (that is, that necessary to get back to the higher trade-off curve *I* at the new level of welfare *B*).

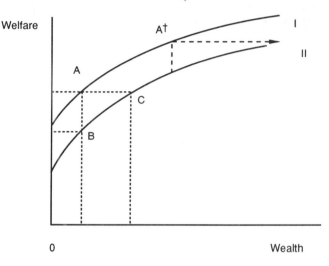

Figure 5.2
The basic trade-off model

In practical terms revealed preference techniques normally require sophisticated econometric analysis. The is because most goods involve a variety of attributes of which environmental elements represent only a sub-set. In consequence, the normal approach is to use an *hedonic price index* which puts values on the diverse attributes of the good being examined (for example, the various features of houses in the noise case mentioned above). The specifications of individual models differ, indeed one of the problems with hedonic indices is that of model specification, but whatever form they take they seek to isolate the 'price' of each characteristic in the equation. This leads on to a further problem. It is necessary to have a substantial amount of information on the determinants of, in our example, housing selection processes just to gain an insight into the value of one environmental influence. It is also important that the characteristics used are the ones perceived to be important to house occupiers and buyers. It is not the actual set of characteristics which determine hedonic prices but rather the characteristics as seen by those active in the housing market.

Travel-cost method
New transport infrastructure can destroy recreation sites such as parks and fishing facilities which have been provided at a zero price. People, however, travel to such locations to make use of the natural amenities and thus incur a measurable

travel cost both in terms of time and money. Use can be made of this information to gain some idea of the value of such facilities. This is a special case of the more general revealed preference approach.

Figure 5.3 offers guidance to the simplest travel-cost approach. Surveys find that the number of visits to, say, a park from an origin A amounts to X_a and from B to X_b. Further, the actual average generalised travel costs (that is, including travel time costs) for these trips amount to P_a and P_b respectively from the two origins. A succession of further surveys looking at other origins enables the distance decay function to be derived. From this the consumer surplus derived from visiting the park and enjoyed by an individual living in A is seen to be area $(A+B)$. Total surplus for those originating from A is then found by multiplying $(A+B)$ by the number of trip-makers originating from there. Similar calculations can be carried out for each origin to get the aggregate surplus.

The main application of the technique is in evaluating specific types of environmental impact but is of less use where there are a number of environmental factors involved and one wishes to evaluate them individually. Perhaps a bigger problem, however, is the need to specify the generalised cost function which itself should include a monetary value of travel time. While, as we have seen, the work on the value of travel time is extensive, the subject is itself at least as controversial as that in the field of environmental evaluation.

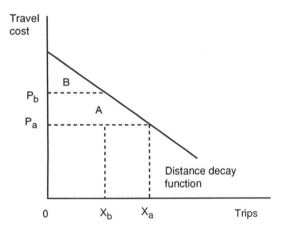

Figure 5.3
The basic travel-cost method

Stated preference
Stated preference techniques (often called contingency valuations in the environmental literature) do not involve attempting to place values on environmental costs by observing actual trade-offs but rather seek to elicit information on the trade-offs individuals *would* make when confronted with particular situations. The most widespread approach is that of asking, through questionnaires and surveys, a relevant group of individuals either what compensation they would need to keep them at their current level of welfare if some pre-defined transport-induced environmental degradation took place or, alternatively, what amount

would they be willing to pay to prevent this occurrence . The questions are set in an institutional context (for example, to make it clear what methods of finance are involved) and, so as to provide a market framework, the questioner initiates the process by suggesting an opening 'bid' to which the respondent reacts. The questions need to be couched carefully to ensure that the hypothetical trade-offs are clear and that the potential problems with the techniques are minimised.

Inevitably questions arise as to the extent the information gained through a stated preference approaches that which would emerge if an actual market existed. Strict comparisons are not possible, since, by definition no actual market exists, but comparisons with other techniques can, at least, give some indication of consistency. In their analysis of a number of case studies (which were not transport specific) where stated preference techniques were deployed alongside other methods of evaluation, Pearce and Turner (1990) found that there was a 're-assuring' degree of overlap in the findings reported. Differences do, however, still exist and it is difficult to decide whether this reflects variations in the quality of individual studies or is a reflection of the usefulness of differing techniques.

One of the main problems in using the above set of procedures is that they do not all have the same theoretical underpinnings and this makes comparisons of results difficult. Is it valid, for example, to compare a value for noise pollution derived from an averting study with a value of air pollution derived from a stated preference study? There are obvious problems nevertheless Quinet (1990) has tried to use the best information available to give a general, minimum estimate of the monetary costs of the damage transport imposes on the environments of industrialised countries (see Table 5.2). The figures are seen as conservative because they cover only some of the damage done by transport (see Section 5.4) and because only lower estimates for each form of social cost considered are used in the calculations.

Table 5. 2
The costs of traffic congestion and environmental damage to society

Environmental problem	Costs	
	Road	Other modes
Noise	0.10%	0.01%
Pollution	0.40%	
Accidents	2.00%	
Time	6.80%	1.70%
User expenditure (including infrastructure management)	9.00%	3.00%
Total	18.30%	4.71%

Source: Quinet (1990)

5.4   The magnitude of the environmental problem
Table 5.2 offers some very broad indications of the costs of transport on the environment; most policy formulation, however, requires rather more micro analysis. For example, Figure 5.1 presented hypothetical marginal cost and benefit curves associated with reducing motor vehicle exhaust emissions but in order to make

practical use of these concepts it is first necessary to measure physically the levels of pollution and then to put a monetary value on the units of pollution generated. This section looks at the measurement problem and also considers some of the ways in which pollution has been evaluated in practice. Also some attempt is made to assess the economic importance of various forms of transport-associated environmental effects. These topics embrace many complex issues and have been subjected to major research efforts. The coverage presented here is, by necessity, limited and a much fuller account of work in this field is contained in Organisation for Economic Cooperation and Development (1988) and Button (1993).

Noise

A survey conducted by Market and Opinion Research in 1972 found that 12 per cent of respondents thought that excessive noise was one of the three or four most serious problems in Britain. More recently, in pre-unified Germany Frenking (1988) found 65 per cent of the population were adversely affected by road traffic noise, with 25 per cent seriously affected – by way of comparison this represented twice the problem of noise from neighbours and three times the problem from industrial noise. It is an especial nuisance in urban areas, in towns that suffer from a lot of through traffic (for example, located astride major trunk arteries, such as rail lines, motorways, etc.) and at locations around transport terminals, such as airports, bus stations, car parks. It should also be remembered that noise is not just generated by traffic but extremely high levels of noise are also often associated with the construction of transport infrastructure – up to levels of 110dB when piles are being driven.

It has been estimated (see again Table 5.1) that about 110 million people in the industrial world are exposed to road traffic noise levels of more than 65 dB(A), a level considered unacceptable in OECD countries. While consistent data is somewhat sparse, there is also ample evidence that there are, in large part because of the nature of national land-use patterns but also because of differing national legal structures, quite considerable differences between countries in terms of the populations affected by transport-related noise. Equally it is difficult, because of data limitations, to discern exact trends in population exposure to high noise levels. International comparisons provide tentative evidence of a decline in numbers suffering from serious noise problems (that is, over 65dB(A)) in some countries but a rise in others, but there does seem to be a pattern of significantly increasing numbers of people falling into the 'grey area' of intermediate noise nuisance of between 55 and 65dB(65) (Organisation for Economic Cooperation and Development, 1991).

Noise has several different effects on health and well-being. It affects activities such as communication (speaking, listening to radio and TV) and sleep. These effects further induce psychological and physiological disorders such as stress, tiredness and sleep disturbance. Noise can also contribute to cardiovascular disease and, at high and prolonged exposure, hearing loss.

In practical terms there are, however, problems in measuring noise nuisance. First, noise nuisance depends upon both the intensity and the frequency of the noise. The 'A' weighted decibel scale (dB(A)) attempts to allow for this by offering a measure based on a weighted avenge of decibel readings where the weights reflect the level of unpleasantness caused by different frequencies and the decibels reflect the actual intensity of the noise. (While this measure is used in most transport-related work, a slightly different set of weights is employed in the perceived noise scale *(PNdB)* used in the measurement of aircraft noise). The dB(A) scale is logarithmic and Table 5.3 gives some example of dB(A) measured peak noise of different forms of transport relative to other sources of noise.

Table 5.3
The relative noise generated by different forms of transport

Noise source	dB(A)
Jet aircraft on the ground	130
Noise under the flight path of a supersonic aircraft within 5 miles of take-off	125
Pop group	110–125
Noise under the night path of heavy jet within 5 miles of take-off	115
Riveting machine in sheet metal shop	115
House near airport	100
Heavy lorry	88–92
Train	90–92
Sports car	80–82
Large car	77–83
Major road with heavy traffic	63–75
Residential road with local traffic only	56–65
Quiet bedroom	30
Sound proofed broadcasting studio	20

Source: Sharp and Jennings, 1976

The dB(A) scale is sometimes prefixed by a term such as L_{10} which means that it relates to a specific proportion of time (that is, L_{10} refers to the 10 per cent peak noise level). On some occasions decibel measures have been combined with other indicators of noise annoyance in a composite index. The Noise and Numbers Index (NNI) developed for the economic appraisal of the Third London Airport, for example, combined the average peak level of noise at an airport (measured in PNdBs) with an indicator of the daily number of aircraft heard. The logarithmic nature of the NNI means that a one unit increase in the index represents a greater increase in noise nuisance, the higher the existing level of the index.

A scale against which noise nuisances may be measured does not, in itself, offer an economist trying to optimise noise emitted by transport much assistance – he needs to be able to place a monetary value on the noise so that the opportunity costs of different policies may be assessed. There are several ways in which noise has been evaluated.

The Commission on the Third London Airport (1971) considered changes in property values with higher noise levels. A number of surveys were conducted at the existing Heathrow and Gatwick airports seeking both the actual sale prices of properties at different distances from the airports and estate agents' estimates. While the Third London Airport method is useful it does present some difficulties. In particular, house prices vary for many different reasons and not simply because of the noise levels inflicted upon them. House prices around Gatwick, for example, tended for a variety of reasons to be higher than Heathrow, which explains the greater fall in house values with respect to noise levels in the former. This does not in itself invalidate the house valuation technique but it does suggest that values obtained by employing it should be used with circumspection and, more specifically, that a value for noise nuisance derived using it in one area may be inappropriate for transport studies elsewhere without adjustment. Indeed, as we see in Table 5.4 there has been some variation in the values derived in subsequent studies which have used similar techniques.

Table 5.4
Estimate impact on house prices of a change in noise levels

Location	Impact of one unit change in Leq
United States	
North Virginia	0.15
Tidewater	0.14
North Springfield	0.18–0.50
Towson	0.54
Washington	0.88
Kingsgate	0.48
North King County	0.3
Spokane	0.08
Chicago	0.65
Canada	
Toronto	1.05
Switzerland	
Basle	1.26

Note: Equivalent continuous sound level (Leq) equals a level of constant sound (in dB(A)s) which would have the same sound energy over a given period as the measured fluctuating sound under consideration.
Source: Pearce and Turner (1990)

Atmospheric pollution
Transport is a source of many harmful gases In relative terms transport is one of the major contributors of these atmospheric pollutants. Further, it is worth emphasising that while in some respects the environmental damage done by transport is increasing, in others there are reductions. In the Netherlands, for example, nitrogen oxides and particulates emissions have grown rapidly in recent years but there has been a modest decline in hydrocarbon emissions and, in absolute terms, in sulphur dioxides.

It is also worth remembering that exhaust fumes have a time and a spatial coverage. There is a time gap as the impacts move from one level to another. Figure 5.4 offers a broad picture of what happens. At the higher levels, the original impacts are connected to many other effects and systems, which are not exclusively related to transport. A potent cocktail of transport- and non-transport-related emissions, therefore, often exists. For ease of exposition, however, we deal with each of the main pollutants separately. The discussions below provide some indication of both these long- and short-term implications, as well as the nature of the spatial coverage, when this is particularly relevant.

Fuel additive emissions. To enhance engine performance, additives are added to fuels. While some are relatively benign in their environmental effects others have caused increasing concern over time. The organic lead compounds added to gasoline as an anti-knock agent, especially when used by automobiles in confined urban spaces, have been singled out for particular attention. Lead is a metallic element that can be retained in the body in the forms of its compounds and can have an adverse affect on the mental development of children and affect the kidney, liver and reproductive system.

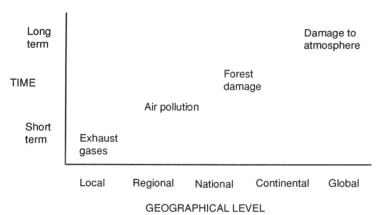

Figure 5.4
The time and spatial coverage of exhaust gases

   In industrialised nations, transport is the single largest source of lead emissions with some 50 per cent of Pb associated with transport but the figure can approach 100 percent in confined urban spaces. However, the tightening of maximum lead content in gasoline laws (for example, in the UK's case from 0.84 grams per litre to 0.40 per litre in 1981 and a further reduction to 0.15 grams per litre in 1985) and the fostering of increasing use of lead-free gasoline through fiscal measures has caused major changes in recent years.

Particulate matters. These embrace fine solids or liquid particles found in the air or in emissions such as dust, smoke or smog. Sources include the fine asbestos and other particles stemming from wear and tear of tyres and brakes as well as matter resulting from engine, and especially diesel engine, combustion. Transport is the major source of particulate emissions in many industrialised countries including the UK. Particulate matter may be toxic in itself or carry toxic (including carcinogenic) trace substances absorbed into its surfaces. It also imposes costs on physical structures, for example, in terms of the need to clean and repaint buildings.

Carbon dioxide emissions. The environmental concern here is in relation to carbon dioxide's possible climatic impact, for example, it is generally viewed by scientists as a major contributor to the greenhouse effect and consequential global warming. CO_2 emissions result from the combustion of fossil fuels. The contribution of CO_2 to the atmosphere varies considerably between countries but the industrialised countries as a whole are responsible for about 80 per cent of the total. Estimates suggest that about 15 per cent of the world's total man-made emissions of CO_2 is generated by motor vehicles and in some OECD countries the figure may reach 40 per cent. In the UK while transport is currently responsible for about 16 per cent of emissions, it is the fastest growing source and 98 per cent of this is associated with road transport – see Table 5.5.

Since CO_2 is a natural constituent of air (although only about 0.03 percent) it is not strictly a pollutant. Additionally, excess amounts of the gas have no detrimental effect on personal health. The problem is that there is mounting, although some would argue not yet conclusive, evidence that high levels of the CO_2 in the atmosphere, by preventing heat from escaping from the planet, will lead to global climate changes.

Table 5.5
CO_2 emission sources in the UK

Source	1978	1983	1988	Change 78–88(%)
Domestic	23	23	24	4.4
Power stations	58	52	52	–10.3
Refineries	5	5	5	0.0
Other industry	50	38	37	–26.0
Transport	23	24	31	34.8
Other	12	10	9	–25.0
Total	171	152	158	–7.6

The issue is not really one about the merits of the greenhouse effect *per se* (without it estimates suggest the global average temperature would fall to about –19°C), but rather about the desirability of the effects changes in its intensity will have. The exact geographical impacts of global warming and their timing are difficult to predict and the long-term economic consequences even harder to foretell. The types of problems which are feared, however, include: a rise in the sea level as a result of thermal expansion of the sea and the melting of land ice; changes of climatic zones, for example, of desert regions and regions affected by tropical storms; detrimental effects on water resources in many areas; and problems of adapting agricultural production.

Nitrogen oxide emissions. These pose particular difficulties when combined with other air pollutants or in areas where residents already suffer ill-health. In the latter case they can lead to respiratory difficulties and extended exposure can result in oedema or emphysema. At the transboundary level, NO_X emissions converted to nitric acid and combined with SO_2, form a significant component of 'acid rain' (or acid deposition) which has serious detrimental effects on ecosystems, for example, damage to fish stocks and deforestation. About 50 per cent of NO_X emissions stem from the transport sector, and the rest from the energy and industrial sectors, although in many countries their output is falling. In the UK it is the fastest growing source of emissions, rising by about 2 per cent per annum.

Carbon monoxide emissions. CO can have detrimental effects on health because it interferes with the absorption of oxygen by red blood cells. This may lead to increased morbidity and adversely affects fertility and there is evidence that it affects worker productivity. CO is especially a problem in urban areas where synergistic effects with other pollutants means it contributes to photochemical smog and surface ozone (O_3). Concentrations of O_3 at lower levels have implications for the respiratory system. CO emissions result from incomplete combustion and some 90 per cent of all CO emissions originate from the transport sector and about 80 per cent is associated with automobile use. The figure reaches 100 per cent in the centre of many built-up areas. Additionally, in countries such as the UK if the trends of the 1980s continue then emissions will grow by about 2 per cent per annum in the future.

Sulphur dioxide emissions. Emissions of this colourless but strong-smelling gas can result in bronchitis and other diseases of the respiratory system and they are the major contributor to 'acid rain'. Transport is directly responsible for about 5 percent of total SO_2 emissions with diesel fuel containing more SO_2 per litre than gasoline. What is more important, coal-fired electricity generation is a major source of this gas and thus there are further transport implications both for electric rail transport and the manufacture of transport vehicles.

Volatile organic compounds. These comprise a wide variety of hydrocarbons and other substances (for example, methane, ethylene oxide, formaldehyde, phenol, phosgene, benzene, carbon tetrachloride, chlorofluorocarbons and polychlorinated biphenyls). They generally result from incomplete combustion of fossil fuels, although evaporated gasoline from fuel tanks and the carburettor is increasingly contributing to releases of aromatic HCs such as benzene.

When combined with NO_x in sunlight, hydrocarbons and some VOCs can generate low-level ozone – the main component of photochemical smog. Besides producing respiratory problems and causing eye irritations, some of the compounds are suspected of being carcinogenic and possibly mutagens or teratogens (which can result in congenital malformations). Excluding methane, emissions of which largely stem from agricultural sources, about half of VOC emissions in industrialised countries are generally associated with road traffic and the proportion, with the exception of the US, tends to be rising. About 30 per cent of all HC emissions are directly related to transport.

Accidents

Transport is a dangerous activity. These accidents can concern not just those involved in transport itself but also third parties. The dangers inherent in the transport of dangerous and toxic substances are, in fact, increasing this latter problem. From a purely statistical perspective this is mainly seen in relation to road transport where there are, on a day-to-day basis, many fatal and serious accidents. Less frequent, but from a public perceptions perspective, more alarming because of the degree of potential severity associated with each incident, are rail, maritime and aviation disasters.

Some indication of the order of magnitude of the risks involved in transport is the fact that road accidents cost some 48,800 lives in the US and 7,967 lives in West Germany during 1987 and 10,961 in France during 1986 while in the UK 5,052 people were killed on the roads in 1988 with a further 63,000 seriously injured. In Italy, between 7,076 and 9,308 people were killed in 1986 (the number depending upon whether deaths are measured at times of accidents or a week later) and 213,159 injured.

It should be pointed out, however, that in many developed countries the number of fatal road accidents is decreasing – for example, the figure for the UK is the lowest since 1954 and that cited for Germany for 1987 should be compared with 19,139 in 1970. In the US, despite many more road accidents (which rose from 16 million in 1970 to 18.8 million in 1984) the number of fatalities and injuries has declined. This is not, however, the situation in many low-income countries where, as private transport is expanding, the number of fatalities continues to rise. The increased amounts of hazardous waste transported in recent years, and the associated problem of spillage, is also adding to the risks borne by third parties throughout the world.

If one considers the accident rates by mode then road transport incidents dominate the statistics although, because of variations in modal split between countries, there are national variations in their relative importance. Some indication of the different accident rates by mode and over time for the US is, for example, given in Table 5.6. Interpretation of such data does, however, pose some problems. In particular, there is the point of comparison against which numbers of accidents should be set. Commercial aviation is, from a statistical perspective, generally cited as the safest mode of transport but this may not be the case viewed in terms of time exposure.

Valuing the external accident costs of transport poses a particular problem. Accident risks are partly internalised within transport in the sense that individuals can insure themselves. However, many travellers have no insurance or, where it has been taken up, it is on the basis of a misperception of the risks involved. There are also third-party risks involved in the possibility of accidents during the transporting of dangerous goods or toxic waste. Attempts to devise methods for valuing accident risk have a long history, especially with regard to fatal accidents.

The methods of valuation currently in use, however, still differ between countries. Some adopt cost avoidance calculations, others use lost production/consumption-type techniques but the use of revealed and stated preference methods is becoming more widespread. The lost production (or *ex post*) method essentially asks what output the economy forgoes if, for example, someone is killed in a road accident – essentially a discounted calculation of the difference between what that person could have been expected to produce over the rest of his life and what he could have been expected to consume. The obvious problem is that a pensioner's death would be accorded a positive value with such a procedure! The lost consumption (or *ex ante*) method avoids this problem by assuming that the individual would gain utility by not dying and thus does not net out lost consumption, the ability to enjoy this consumption acting as proxy for the welfare of remaining alive.

There is still no universally accepted value for accident prevention. For example, values of £0.5 million, DM1,240 million and $2–$7 million per life preserved by safer transport are now being used for policy-making in the UK, the states of the pre-unified FRG and the USA respectively. Academic studies also show some variability in their results. A review of studies in the US, UK and Sweden using mainly stated preference methods (Jones-Lee, 1990) concludes that the most reliable estimates from such studies give a distribution of values of life in 1989 with a median of $1.1 million and a mean of $3.4 million.

Of course, not all accidents are fatal and, in many cases, only motor vehicles are damaged. In the pre-unified FRG, values are placed on reduced incidence of serious accidents (DM56,000 each) and on material damage (DM25,000 per accident). In the USA, data for 1980 suggests that property-only damage accidents cost some $21.71 billion.

Table 5.6
Transport accidents in the USA by mode

	Motor vehicles* (thousands)	Rail†	Commercial aviation	Waterborne§
Deaths				
1970	52.6	765	....	....
1975	44.5	575	221	243
1980	51.1	584	143	206
1981	49.3	556	132	154
1982	43.9	512	320	223
1983	42.6	498	89	289
1984	44.3	598	102	113
1985	43.8	454	638	69
Injuries				
1970	2000	21327	....	....
1975	1800	54306	109	97
1980	2000	62246	74	176
1981	1900	53003	82	141
1982	1700	37638	98	271
1983	1600	32196	49	209
1984	1700	35660	67	134
1985	1700	31617	73	57

*   Data on deaths are from US National Highway Traffic Safety Administration and are based on 30-day definition.
†   Deaths exclude fatalities in railroad–highway grade crossing accidents.
§   Covers accidents involving loss of life or injury causing a person's incapacity for more than three days.
Source: US Department of Transportation

While reservations must be expressed over the method of valuing lost life (in terms of lost production), and some of the other forms of accident damage, these types of figures can also be aggregated to give national overall costs of accidents – for example, this has been estimated as being 33 billion francs for France in 1986 and $57.2 billion in the USA in 1980.

Visual intrusion
Transport infrastructure and mobile plant is frequently visually intrusive and often far from aesthetically pleasing. The problem is measuring the effect. Some attempts have been made to assess the intrusion of motorways on the landscape by looking at the percentage of the skyline obscured (for example, Clamp, 1976), but this approach only considers one dimension of a multi-faceted problem. In particular, transport infrastructure must be viewed in the context of its surroundings – a new motorway located in formerly unspoilt countryside is likely to be viewed differently from one that blots out an unsightly waste tip. Design is also impor-

tant. Also it should be remembered that vehicles are as intrusive as infrastructure and large lorries or buses are, for example, often totally out of place in unspoilt villages or 'historic towns'. Whether it is the actual size of vehicles which is alarming or simply the level of traffic flow is difficult to disentangle.

A newer problem is that caused by the eyesores created by the difficulties of disposing of the old hardware of transport. The problem not only embraces disused infrastructure of road, rail and maritime transport but also increasingly the vehicles themselves. In the Netherlands, for instance, some 450,000 cars are scrapped each year but of the 750,000 tones of waste generated only 450,000 tons is recycled leaving metals, oily products, paint, plastics and other materials to be dumped.

Vibrations
Low flying commercial aircraft, heavy goods vehicles and railway wagons create vibrations which can affect buildings. Again *useful* measures are elusive. While it is known, for example, that groundborne vibration is related to axle loads, it has proved impossible to relate this effectively to any measure of structural damage. The evidence suggests, however, that the physical damage caused may be less than is sometimes claimed. Improved engineering techniques have reduced the damage caused by road transport and much of the damage formerly thought 'caused' by heavy lorries is more likely to have simply been 'triggered' by them. As Whiffen and Leonard (1971) point out, 'Attention can be drawn to vibration by the rattling of doors, windows, lids of ornaments, mirrors, etc... The association of these audible and visible signs with the possibility of damage to the building results in exaggerated complaints about vibration, even though, in fact, there may be no risk of damage.' Vibrations may still be a cost in an economic sense, however, even if there is no structural damage to buildings. Martin (1978) found that 8 per cent of the population are considerably bothered by vibrations from road traffic, but his suggestion that this could be measured cardinally by looking at the spectra of emitted low-frequency noise has yet to be attempted.

Community severance
Roads, railways, canals and other transport arteries often present major physical (and sometimes psychological) barriers to human contact. An urban motorway can cut a local community in two, inhibiting the retention of long-established social ties and, on occasions, making it difficult for people to benefit from recreational and employment opportunities on the other side of the barrier. Although it may be possible to obtain estimates of pedestrian delays and reassignments resulting from the impedance, suppressed trips are much harder to identify. Quantification of community severance is not, therefore, an immediate prospect. As the *Jefferson Report* (UK Department of Transport, 1977) stated, 'the overall conclusion is that no acceptable way is seen of extending the assessment of severance beyond an individual examination of some of the perceived effects except, perhaps, by means of subjective statements in appropriate cases'.

5.5 Introduction to traffic congestion
The demand for transport is not constant over time. In large cities there are regular peaks in commuter travel while on holiday routes, both within the country and to overseas destinations, there are seasonal peaks in demand. Transport infrastructure, although flexible in the long run, has a finite capacity at any given period of time. One cannot, for example, expand and contract the size of an airport terminal

to meet seasonal fluctuations in demand. When users of a particular facility begin to interfere with other users because the capacity of the infrastructure is limited, then congestion externalities arise. Of course, some degree of congestion is almost unavoidable if facilities are not to stand idle most of the time, but the question is just how much congestion is desirable. Since people accept some level of congestion but resent excessive congestion, because of the time and inconvenience costs imposed, there is some implied notion of an optimal level of congestion.

One should add, with reference to the previous section, that congestion does not only impose costs on the road user in terms of wasted time and fuel (the *pure congestion cost*) but the stopping and starting it entails can also worsen atmospheric and other forms of pollution – see Table 5.7. The problem is particularly acute with local forms of pollution because road traffic congestion, in particular, tends to be focused in areas where people work and live.

Table 5.7
Atmospheric pollution caused by different stages in the driving cycle

Pollutants	Composition of exhaust gases (parts per million)			
	Idling	*Accelerating*	*Cruising*	*Decelerating*
Gasoline engines				
Carbon monoxide	69000	29000	27000	39000
Hydrocarbons	5300	1600	1000	10000
Nitrogen oxides	30	1020	650	20
Aldehydes	30	20	10	290
Diesel engines				
Carbon monoxide	trace	1000	trace	trace
Hydrocarbons	400	200	100	300
Nitrogen oxides	60	350	240	30
Aldehydes	10	20	10	30

Source: Organisation for Economic Cooperation and Development (1983)

Road traffic poses some of the greatest congestion problems and also offers a useful basis of analysis. The economic costs of road congestion can be calculated using the engineering concept of the speed–flow relationship. If we take a straight one-way street and consider traffic flows along it over a period of time at different speed levels then the relationship between speed and flow would appear as in Figure 5.5. Flow is dependent upon both the number of vehicles entering a road and the speed of traffic. Hence, at low volumes of traffic, when vehicle impedance is zero, high speeds are possible, constrained only by the capability of the vehicle and legal speed limits, but as the number of vehicles trying to enter the road increases so they interact with existing traffic and slow one another down. As more traffic enters the road, speed falls but, up to a point, flow will continue to rise because the effect of additional vehicle number outweighs the reduction in average speed. This is the normal flow situation.

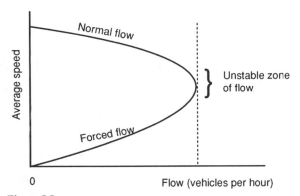

Figure 5.5
The speed-flow relationship

At the point where increased traffic volume ceases to offset the reduced speed the road's 'capacity' is reached at the maximum flow. (This is the road's *engineering* capacity and differs from the economic capacity which is defined as that flow at which the costs of extending the capacity are outweighed by the benefits of doing so.) Absence of perfect information means that motorists often continue to try and enter the road beyond this volume causing further drops in speed and resulting in the speed–flow relationship turning back on itself. These levels of flow are known as forced flows. There is often a degree of 'learning from experience' which can improve the quality of decision-making and in practice, without any intervention, flows would settle around the zone of instability during rush hour periods. A cross-sectional study of the main urban centres (see Table 5.8) suggests that this zone of instability occurs at speeds of about 18 kmph.

Table 5.8
Traffic speeds in selected cities

City	Year	Population (million)	City centre traffic speed (kmph) Peak hour	Off peak
New York	1970	13.3	16.0	26.0
Detroit	1970	4.0	17.7	-
Salt Lake City	1970	0.9	27.0	-
London	1971	7.4	20.6	20.3
Birmingham	1965	1.1	22.1	-
Leeds	1965	0.5	18.0	
Paris	1970	6.4	16.9	-
Athens	1971	2.7	15.5	24.0
Copenhagen	1967	1.7	14.5	-
Stockholm	1969	1.3	18.0	-
Calcutta	1971	7.5	11–16	19.0
Singapore	1972	2.2	21.0	-

Source: Adapted from Thomson, 1977

The actual form of the speed–flow relationship and the engineering capacity of any individual road will depend upon a number of factors. Clearly, the physical characteristics of the road (its width, the number of lanes, etc.) is of central importance – these may be seen as the long-term influences. Short-term factors include the form of traffic management and control schemes in operation (traffic lights, roundabouts, etc.). Finally, the type and age of vehicles combined with their distribution may influence capacity.

A fairly typical set of speed–flow relationships which illustrate these points are, for example, offered by Neutze (1963) in his study of Sydney's arterial road system. Information obtained from over 400 locations on main roads in the city was used in the exercise, the results of which are seen in Figure 5.6. As one might expect, the capacity of six-lane roads exceeds that of either two- or four-lane roads, although at most traffic densities the speed is slightly higher on the two- rather than the four-lane roads. The explanation for this is that traffic management policies slow down flows of the four-lane roads because road-side parking is permitted and thus the capacity of curbside lanes is severely restricted, and they also tend to pass through more densely populated areas with more restrictive traffic management controls.

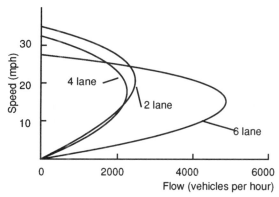

Figure 5.6
Speed–flow relationships on different road types in Sydney

The speed–flow relationship provides a key supply-side input into the analysis but it is road space which is actually demanded. The type of theoretical framework which can link the two elements is described by Evans (1992) although a somewhat less complete exposition is to be found in Else (1981). The density function, the number of vehicles on a road at any one time, is important in this analysis.

In Figure 5.7, element B shows the standard speed–flow relationship with the maximum flow depicted as F_{max}. This is traced round to the travel cost-flow diagram in element C. People essentially demand to join a road and this demand to join enter a road is seen as the demand curve, D, in element A of Figure 5.7. This diagram also depicts the relationship between travel cost and traffic density – the MC being the rising marginal cost of congestion each additional motorist imposes on others using the road. The curve rises as the number of vehicles increases. The S curve represents the cost of joining the road as seen by the additional motorist – in effect his cost of trip making ignoring the consequences of his actions for the others on the road.

The curves in element C of the diagram, concerned with travel cost-flow relationships, are derived from elements A and B. The *s* curve is the average cost curve relating to congestion in a simple interaction model (see below) and the *mc* curve is the associated marginal curve. These relate directly back to the speed-flow relationship. Generalised costs (see Chapter 4) provide the vital link between physical traffic flows and cost. Broadly, faster travel in urban areas means cheaper travel in terms of generalised costs – vehicles are used more effectively and travel times are reduced. The S curve in Figure 5.7 represents the average generalised cost of trip-making at different levels of traffic flow. It is a reverse of the speed-flow curve seen in Figure 5.5 with the positively sloped portion corresponding to the negatively sloped section of the speed-flow curve – this stems from the inverse relationship between speed and generalised cost. The *mc* curve is the associated marginal curve which takes into account the congestion costs the additional user places on the existing traffic flow. The *d* curve is a derived demand curve reflecting the way in which the desired traffic flow changes as the cost of travel changes because the number of vehicles put on the road changes.

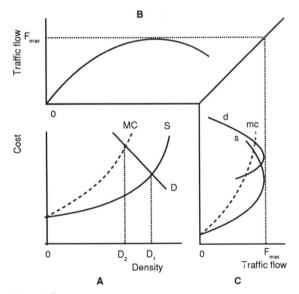

Figure 5.7
The speed–flow relationship and the demand for road space

The actual traffic density which will emerge is where the demand for road space equals the average cost (*S*) of joining the road – D_1. This exceeds the optimal level, where road users take account of the impedance they impose on others, which is where *MC* is equated with demand. Moving across to the flow diagram, which is much more frequently found in the academic literature, the optimal traffic flow is where the *mc* curve intersects the derived demand curve.

5.6   The economic costs of congestion

Most analysis of congestion focuses purely on segment C of Figure 5.7. It is usually presented in the form set out in Figure 5.8, with the *AC* curve representing he average cost of congestion at each level of traffic flow, and the *MC* curve the cost of additional traffic to existing flow. The optimal flow is, as we have seen above, where *MC* and demand are equated (F_o) while the actual flow, because road users ignore the congestion that they impose on others, tends to be F_a. A further interpretation can be placed on the *AC* and *MC* curves. The curves reflect the average and marginal generalised costs associated with different flows – they show all the time and money costs borne by road users when trip-making. In this sense they may be seen as representing 'social costs' in the limited sense that they are the costs to the *society of road users*. However, any individual user entering the road will only consider the costs he personally bears. He will, in most circumstances, either be unaware of or unwilling to consider the external, congestion, costs he imposes on the other road users. Consequently, the individual motorist will only consider the average costs experienced by road users and take no account of the congestive impact of his trip on other vehicles. It is frequently argued that the *MC* curve, therefore, relates to the marginal *social* cost for *the new trip-maker and existing road users* of an addition to the traffic flow while the *AC* curve is equivalent to the marginal *private cost* curve – that is, the additional cost borne and perceived by the *new trip-maker* alone. The difference between the AC and *MC* curves at any traffic flow reflects the economic costs of congestion at that flow.

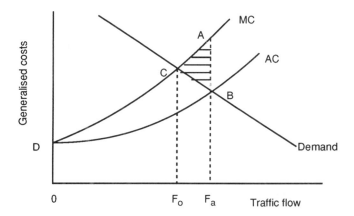

Figure 5.8
The deadweight-loss of excessive traffic congestion

   It is often important from a policy perspective to gain some idea of the actual costs associated with excessive congestion. From a social point of view the actual flow, F_a, is excessive because the F_ath motorist is only enjoying a benefit of F_aB but imposing costs of F_aA. The additional traffic beyond the optimal level F_0 can be seen to be generating costs of F_oCBF_a, but only enjoying a benefit of F_oCBF_a– a deadweight welfare loss of (*ABC*) is apparent. A traffic flow lower than F_o is also sub-optimal because the potential consumer surplus gains from trip-making are not being fully exploited. Of course, this does mean that even at the optimal traffic flow there are still congestion costs, the area between the MC and AC curves up to traffic flow F_o, but these are more than off-set by the benefits enjoyed by those using the road.

While the work on congestion costs is extensive, estimating the overall costs associated with excessive congestion is not simple. Work looking at the money value of lost travel time has a long pedigree – information on such costs is of commercial value to public transport suppliers who may trade off faster services against higher fares. The exact cost depends upon the mix of traffic and the reason trips are being made. Periodically crude estimates, of the type produced by the UK's Confederation of British Industry in 1988, are made of the total costs of time wasted in congestion (about £15 billion per year for commercial traffic) but these tend to suffer from major theoretical and measurement problems. In the CBI case the calculations were based on scaling up the responses to a small survey of distribution companies which were asked to assess the costs traffic congestion was imposing on their operations. Besides the small size of the sample and the inherent dangers of aggregation, there was no effort to define a base-line level of optimal congestion as a basis for comparison nor was there any effort to net out the costs that the distributors were imposing on others but not paying for.

Table 5.9
Estimated congestion costs by road type in the UK

Road type	Marginal cost (pence per km)
Motorway	0.26
Unban central peak	36.97
Urban central off-peak	29.23
Non-central peak	15.86
Non-central off-peak	8.74
Small town peak	6.89
Small town off-peak	4.20
Other urban	0.08
Rural dual carriageway	0.07
Other trunk and principal	0.19
Other rural	0.05

Source: Newbery (1990)

A more rigorous approach is to consider the opportunity cost of lost travel time (see Chapter 3). Using the figures adopted by the UK Department of Transport when appraising road schemes, Newbery (1990) produced value of marginal congestion costs by road type in the UK (Table 5.9). These show the costs imposed by an additional vehicle joining the traffic stream. Aggregation gives an estimated annual congestion cost in the UK of about £12,750 million for 1989–90. Recent work in the USA has attempted, using traffic modelling techniques, to put a monetary value (in terms of travel time and excess fuel costs) on congestion for 39 urban areas (Hanks and Lomax, 1990). This produced values in the range from $5,240 million per annum for Los Angeles to $290 million for Minneapolis-St Paul. The city with the highest congestion cost per registered vehicle was Washington at £920 per annum.

5.7   Some refinements on the basic model

The analysis of congestion set out above is based upon a very simple modelling framework: a linear road, no junctions, homogeneous traffic and equally skilful drivers. In practice, as we would expect from our discussion of the speed-flow relationship, the total cost function varies with the details of the transport system under consideration. Also, considerable traffic congestion stems from 'incidents' such as accidents, road repair and breakdowns which do not fit comfortably into the simple framework.

Vickrey (1969) distinguishes five separate types of congestion relevant in this rather more complex world. While these are couched in terms of road congestion, they are equally applicable to most other modes of transport – one can quite simply substitute airlane or waterway for roads. The types of congestion are:

(1)   *Simple interaction* This occurs at comparatively low levels of traffic flow where the number of mobile units is small. Delays are minimal and usually result from slow and careful driving on the part of users who wish to avoid accidents. Total delay tends to vary as the square of the volume of traffic, so that each additional motorist causes a delay to *each other* road user roughly equal to that which he himself suffers. This is essentially the type of congestion we have been concerned with above.

(2)   *Multiple interaction* This occurs at higher levels of traffic flow where, although the road capacity is not reached, an additional vehicle causes considerably more impedance to each other vehicle than with simple interaction. Empirical evidence suggests that for every minute the marginal user is delayed, other vehicles each suffer a delay of three to five minutes.

(3)   *Bottleneck situations* These occur when a particular stretch of a road (or other piece of transport infrastructure) is of more limited capacity than either the preceding or subsequent links in the network. If the flow is below that of the capacity of the bottleneck then either simple or multiple interaction may occur, but once the capacity is reached, and in particular if this is sustained for any length of time, then queues develop. An exceptionally high level of congestion is then likely to arise.

(4)   *Triggerneck situations* When a bottleneck situation results in queues of traffic, these may impede the general flow of traffic even for those not wishing to use the section of road with limited capacity. At the extreme, congestion may become so severe that the traffic comes to a complete standstill and can only flow again after some vehicles have backed up.

(5)   *Network and control congestion* The efforts of traffic engineers and managers (by the introduction of different traffic control devices) may reduce congestion costs at certain times of the day or, for example, in the case of bus lanes, for specific types of traffic but increase them at other times or for other modes. This results from the general bluntness of most traffic control schemes which may help solve major problems but do, at times, create other, albeit usually less significant, difficulties. This type of congestion was not fully appreciated in the United Kingdom until the mid 1970s and had

earlier led to excessively high estimates of urban congestion costs. Previously it was assumed that congestion tended to be of the simple or multiple interactive kind but as the discussion paper on *Transport Policy* (UK Department of the Environment, 1976) said, 'Once account is taken of the limitations placed upon urban traffic speeds by factors such as the incidence of traffic lights and the multi-purpose nature of urban road networks, traffic speeds associated with even very low levels of congestion can be expected to be quite low – almost certainly below 20 mph in central areas.'

In addition to these five types of traffic congestion which can arise when the infrastructure is fixed, Vickrey also points to the more general problem of transport congestion in the economy as a whole. In the context of urban areas, roads in the United States take up 30 per cent or more of the land area of city centres, while in Western Europe the figure is between 15 per cent and 20 per cent and in third world countries about 10 per cent. The question then becomes one of whether in the *long term* the general welfare of urban society is being excessively reduced by too much transport infrastructure congesting city centres. The acceptance of this view makes it rather difficult to define meaningfully optimal levels of transport provision in the traditional welfare sense.

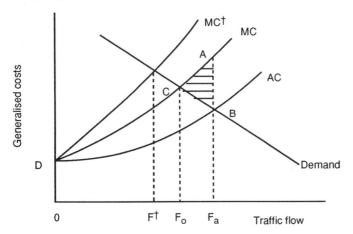

Figure 5.9
The problems of misperceived private costs

A further problem is that many travellers, and especially road users, have a very poor perception of their own private costs. Indeed, in the case of car users the perceived cost of many trips may only embrace the time involved. In such cases the perceived *AC*, while reflecting some of the costs to a motorist thinking of joining a traffic stream, is an inadequate basis for calculating the *MC* curve which embraces the congestion costs to other road users. The appropriate policy curve in these circumstances is *MC†* which is based upon the resource costs of making trips rather than just the perception of the additional user. As we see in

Figure 5.9, the implication of this is that congestion may well be somewhat higher than is sometimes estimated.

5.8   The economic value of congestion

Congestion, or to be more exact excessive congestion, has been shown to imply a 'dead-weight' welfare loss and to reduce the economic efficiency of any transport system. In recent years there has been some debate, however, about whether this welfare loss is compensated by other beneficial effects of congestion which are not immediately apparent in the standard, static, marginal cost type of analysis. These arguments tend to follow three broad lines, those focusing on issues centring on the distributional effect of congestion on different groups in society, those concerned with more straightforward efficiency problems and those which take other forms of cost into account.

The main costs imposed by traffic congestion are usually found to be time costs (although there may also be fuel and other components of generalised costs to be considered). Queuing up for the use of a transport facility and slowing down in its consumption takes up the user's time. Measures to reduce the demand, increase the supply, or the introduction of market prices to optimise congestion (all of which are discussed later in the book) impose some form of either financial or welfare loss which, although on very simple efficiency criteria must be lower than the congestion costs saved, still have to be borne by someone. Those who favour the retention of a high level of congestion as a method of allocating scarce transport facilities argue that, since in the short term time is evenly distributed to everyone – that is, there are 24 hours in every person's day – it is a more equitable method of allocation than many alternative techniques. If a traveller really wants to make a journey he would be willing (and able) to wait, whereas if a high, congestion-deterring, charge is levied his financial budget constraint may make it impossible to make the trip. While there seem to be some grounds for this type of argument if one accepts that transport is unique in requiring a substantial time input for its consumption (a proposition that is far from self-evident), in the longer term the wider distributional issue is probably more effectively tackled by direct income redistribution measures. There seems no reason, in the general case, for singling out transport rather than a number of other economic activities for this special treatment. In addition, even when goods have in the past been provided free of charge, there is empirical evidence that, despite the equal distribution of time, it is the rich who tend to obtain them and, *ipso facto,* a disproportionate share of the benefit (Barzel, 1974).

Moving to the second mitigating argument in favour of allocation by congestion we turn to efficiency considerations. Congestion is seen by some as a complementary method of allocating certain types of facility, supplementing rather than competing with other, usually monetary price, mechanisms (Smolensky *et al.*, 1971). The dead-weight loss associated with congestion may in some situations, it is claimed, be outweighed by other forms of welfare benefit. In some instances people, for example those on aircraft stacking at congested airports, may use time spent in queuing productively while, in others, the dead-weight loss associated with sub-optimally excessive congestion may be exceeded by the administrative or other costs of achieving optimal utilisation of the transport facility. As we see in Chapter 7 this has been one argument used against the introduction of sophisticated metering devices for urban road pricing. More generally, it is argued that, since transport users are far from homogeneous, different groups of users will value time differently and hence a system with both time-allocated and financially allocated facilities could well be optimal. If analogies are made with other forms of economic activity from retailing to car manufacturing then both money and time are used for allocation. For example, one can get fast, personal service at a small local store but prices are likely to be higher than at a large, possibly distant, supermarket where queuing is normal at checkouts. This sort of approach is in general use for some forms of transport, with many countries, for instance, having fast, tolled motorways running parallel to slow, free trunk roads. Also one can often choose between expensive, readily available air services or cheap stand-by facilities which often involve queuing or waiting for a flight. With a given distribution of income, this increased choice necessarily increases welfare which may, in turn, offset any, or at least part of, the dead-weight loss incurred on congested parts of the system. Essentially there is product differentiation taking place in response to variations in the opportunity cost of time among consumers.

The difficulty with this argument is that in many cases physical factors make it impossible to provide different types of transport service. In other cases, economies of scale are sufficient to make the provision of alternatives excessively wasteful. One approach, favoured by theoreticians, may be to decide upon the optimal flow, and only let that flow on to the road or facility at any one time leaving a queue of potential users waiting. The optimal flow in this sense being such that the length of the queue of traffic wishing to use the road would make the opportunity time cost of waiting equal to the money price at which the traffic flow is optimal. It is difficult to see how this could be put into practice on urban roads although it may be appropriate for making optimal use of facilities such as bridges or ferries where queuing is practicable. The information costs of estimating optimal queue lengths may also prove an insurmountable practical problem.

Finally, a high level of congestion may itself be optimal (even with the dead-weight losses it imposes and where neither of the former lines of argument are applicable) when other forms of cost are also considered. It may be, for example, that the transaction costs of moving from an over-congested to an optimally congested situation exceed the conventionally defined benefits of eliminating a dead-weight loss. The transition costs involved in removing an externality such as excessive congestion are of three broad types: the cost per unit of reducing the externality, initial lump sum costs of organisation, and information/enforcement costs of carrying the action through (Dahlman, 1979). To remove excessive congestion would, in virtually all cases, involve costs in one or more of these categories and it could well be that in many cases such transaction costs could be very high. A related point is that the actual reduction of congestion to the optimal level *for transport users* may mean spreading other forms of external cost (generally noise and air pollution) to a much wider group of non-users in the community. Raising landing fees at over-used major airports, for example, is likely to divert traffic elsewhere and place environmental costs on people living near other, formerly under-utilised airports. Congestion may in these circumstances, where the demand for transport concentrates the incidence of environmental costs on a relatively small group in the community, be felt to offer a more acceptable use of transport infrastructure than if congestion is reduced but this results in demand being spread geographically. This is more likely if the initial congestion is concentrated in relatively insensitive areas, but its reduction would increase the environmental nuisance experienced in residential or other sensitive locations.

5.9   Further reading and references

Pearce and Turner (1990) offer a detailed examination of environmental economics and, although it is not specifically aimed at transport economists, much of the material is still highly relevant. The Organisation for Economic Cooperation and Development (1988) provides a considerable amount of useful information on the environmental impacts of transport. For an overview of the economics of relevace to studying transport and the environment see Button (1993) while useful reading on the subject covering a range of international experiences are contained in Barde and Button (1990) and Banister and Button (1992). The evaluation of life has been subjected to considerable research in recent years and the resultant literature is voluminous. Perhaps the most accessible further reading in this area that also offers some rigorous questioning of conventional methodology is Jones-Lee (1990). Congestion is an equally well-researched topic with an extensive literature. Else (1981) and Evans (1992) provide some novel ideas but Walters (1961) is a classic paper which the careful reader may feel stands up well to recent attacks. The *Armitage Report* (UK Department of Transport, 1980) provides a useful and informative case study of the environmental costs associated with heavy lorries while the UK Department of Transport (1992) considers the problems of including these costs in transport investment appraisal.

References

Banister, D. and Button, K.J. (eds)(1992), *Transport, the Environment and Sustainable Development*, London, E. & F.N. Spon.

Barde, J.-Ph. and Button, K.J. (eds) (1990), *Transport Policy and the Environment: Six Case Studies*, London, Earthscan.

Barzel, Y. (1974), 'A theory of rationing by waiting', *Journal of Law and Economics*, 17, 73–95.

Button, K.J. (1993), *Transport, the Environment and Economic Policy*, Aldershot, Edward Elgar.

Clamp, P.E. (1976), 'Evaluation of the impact of roads on the visual amenity of rural areas', *Department of the Environment Research Report 7*.

Commission on the Third London Airport (1971), *Report*, London, HMSO.

Dahlman, C.J. (1979), 'The problem of externalities', *Journal of Law and Economics*, 22, 141–62.

Else, P.K. (1981), 'A reformation of the theory of optimal taxation',*Journal of Transport Economics and Policy*, 15, 217–32.

Evans, A.W. (1992), æRoad congestion: the diagramatic analysis', *Journal of Political Economy*, 100, 211–17.

Frenking, H. (1988), *Exchange of Information on Noise Abatement Policies. Case Study on Germany*, Report prepared for the Environmental Directorate of theOECD, Paris, OECD.

Hanks, J.W. and Lomax, T.J. (1990), *Roadway Congestion in Major Urbanised Areas 1982 to 1988*, College Station, Texas Transportation Institute.

Jones-Lee, M.W. (1990), 'The value of traffic safety', *Oxford Review of Economic Policy*, 6, 39–60.

Martin, D.J. (1978), 'Low frequency traffic noise and building vibration', *Transport and Road Research Laboratory Supplementary Report*, SR.429.

Neutze, G.M. (1963), 'The external diseconomies of growth in traffic', *Economic Record*, 39, 332–45.

Newbery, D.M. (1990), 'Pricing and congestion: economic principles relevant to road pricing', *Oxford Review of Economic Policy*, 6, 22–38.

Organisation for Economic Cooperation and Development (1983), *Effects of Traffic and Roads on the Environment in Urban Areas*, Paris, OECD.

Organisation for Economic Cooperation and Development (1988), *Transport and the Environment*, Paris, OECD.

Organisation for Economic Cooperation and Development (1991), *Fighting Noise*, Paris, OECD.

Pearce, D.W. and Turner, R.K. (1990), *Economics of Natural Resources and the Environment*, Hemel Hempstead, Harvester Wheatsheaf.

Quinet, E. (1990), *The Social Costs of Land Transport*, Environment Monograph N° 32, Paris, OECD.

Rothenberg, J. (1970), 'The economics of congestion and pollution: an integrated view', *American Economic Review, Papers and Proceedings*, 60, 114–21.

Sharp, C.H. (1966), 'Congestion and welfare: an examination of the case for a congestion tax', *Economic Journal*, 76, 806–17.

Sharp, C.H. and Jennings, A. (1976), *Transport and the Environment*, Leicester, Leicester University Press.

Smolensky, E., Tideman, T.N. and Nichols, D. (1971), 'The economic uses of congestion', *Papers of the Regional Science Associations*, 26, 37–52.

Thomson, J.M. (1977), *Great Cities and their Traffic*, London, Gollancz.

UK Department of the Environment (1976), *Transport Policy: A Consultation Document* (2 vols), London, HMSO.

UK Department of Transport (1980), *Report of the Inquiry into Lorries, People and the Environment*, London, HMSO.

UK Department of Transport (1992), *Assessing the Environmental Impact of Road Schemes, Report of the Standing Committee on Trunk Road Appraisal*, London, HMSO.

Vickrey, W. (1969), 'Congestion theory and transport investment', *American Economic Review (Papers and Proceedings)*, 59, 251–60.

Walters, A.A. (1961), 'The theory and measurement of private and social costs of highway congestion', *Economica*, 19, 676–9.

Whiffen, A.C. and Leonard, D.P. (1971), 'A survey of traffic induced vibrations', *Road Research Laboratory Report, LR.418*.

6   Pricing of Transport Services

6.1   The principles of pricing

Pricing is a method of resource allocation; there is no such thing as the 'right' price but rather there are optimal pricing strategies which permit specified goals to be obtained. The optimal price, for example, to achieve profit maximisation may differ from that needed to maximise welfare or ensure the highest sales revenue. In some cases there is no attempt to devise a price to maximise or minimise anything but rather prices are set that permit lower level objectives (for example, security, minimum market share, etc.) to be attained. Further, prices may be set to achieve certain objectives for the transport supplier in terms of *his* welfare (this is normally the case of private enterprise transport undertakings) while in other fields prices may be set to improve the welfare of *consumers* (as has been the case with some publicly owned transport undertakings). The distinction here is a fine one and many undertakings consider that the employment of the pricing mechanisms to achieve their objectives is automatically to the benefit of customers. One of the major problems in discussing pricing policies in practice is to decide what exactly the objective is. A good example is port pricing where there has been a blurring between the 'European' doctrine of setting prices to facilitate the economic growth of the port's hinterland and the 'Anglo-Saxon' approach which attempts to ensure that ports cover their costs and, where possible, make a profit irrespective of the effects on the wider local economy (see Bennathan and Walters, 1979).

This chapter looks at the appropriate pricing policies to adopt for transport undertakings with a variety of objectives and confronted by different market conditions. While the latter sections focus on criteria concerned with maximising the social benefits of transport, this section briefly reviews the prices likely to exist in situations where transport suppliers are interested in purely commercial criteria (defined here as the pursuit of their own self-interest).

Profit maximisation is the traditional motivation of private enterprise undertakings. The actual price level in this case depends upon the degree of competition in the market. Where competition is considerable then no single supplier has any control over price and must charge that determined by the interaction of supply and demand in the market as a whole (Adam Smith's 'invisible hand'). Within this perfectly competitive environment, it is impossible for any supplier to make super-normal profits in the long term because of the incentives such profits would have on new suppliers entering the market and increasing aggregate supply. Elementary economics tells us that in the long run price will be equated with the marginal (and average) costs of each supplier .

In contrast, a true monopoly supplier has no fear of new entrants increasing the aggregate supply of transport services and has the freedom *either* to set the price *or* to stipulate the level of service he is prepared to offer. The effective constraint on the monopolist is the countervailing power of demand which prevents the joint determination of both output and price. However, given the absence of competition and the degree of freedom enjoyed by the monopolist, it is almost certain that a profit-maximising price will result in charges above marginal and average cost (the only exception being the most unlikely situation of a perfectly elastic *market* demand curve). This is one reason why governments have tended to regulate the railways, ports and other transport undertakings with monopoly characteristics.

This simple description of textbook situations does, however, hide certain peculiarities which may arise in some transport markets. Since the actual unit of supply, the vehicle, is mobile it is possible for the transport market to appear to be essentially competitive but the individual suppliers to price as if they were monopolists or, at least, exercised some monopoly power. The unregulated urban taxi-cab market is an example of this (see Shreiber, 1975). In Figure 6.1 D_M is the market demand for taxi-cab 'rides' per hour in a market supplied solely by cruising taxi-cabs. The cost of taxi cruising activities is almost constant irrespective of whether a fare is carried or not and to stay in business the cab operator must charge fares which permit such costs to be recovered.

In the diagram, the iso-profit curve for a single operator indicates combinations of fare and ridership which allow a normal profit to be earned. It is constrained to a minimum fare (P_2) by the physical impossibility of carrying more than R_2 passengers an hour. Also, it is unlikely that a fare above P_2 would ever be feasible; potential users would simply not accept it. Further, for the market as a whole fares must exceed P_1 if taxi-cab services are to be offered but this should not be seen as the true long-term floor level of fares. Because potential customers are seldom positioned exactly where empty cabs are cruising, there must be an excess of rides offered *above* total demand if sufficient rides are to be supplied – this is indicated by the 'useful' rides curve. This lack of synchronisation means, in effect, that the 'rides offered curve' in Figure 6.1 is not a true supply curve since it is dependent upon demand conditions. At higher fares, the rides offered will increase but even at the intersection with the total demand curve (with R_3 rides offered) there will still be unsatisfied demand (Shreiber, 1977), that is, the amount of taxi rides *taken* is less than the amount demanded. This is because the taxis may not be at the same location as potential customers. Only if cabs were always exactly where they were wanted would demand always be satisfied. The demand will, in normal circumstances, only be fully satisfied at a price above the intersection – say P_O – because at this and higher prices the ratio between the amount of rides demanded and the amount offered will correspond to *the rate of occupancy*. This is so because the amount demanded is then assumed equal to the number of rides taken, and there are no frustrated passengers who give up waiting because they are unable to obtain a ride.

The actual fare level may be set at any point above P_1 but below P_2 hence the apparently perfect taxi-cab market does not have a unique price. However, there are reasons to suspect that the final price will be nearer P_1 than P_2 thus permitting the earning of supernormal profit by the cab operators. It also means that those who still wish to pay the fare and use taxi-cab services will have a good service provided for them – the rides offered being well in excess of those demanded – although the short waiting time and abundance of capacity is likely to be wasteful in resource utilisation. The tendency towards high fares is caused by the monopoly power enjoyed by any individual taxi at the point of hire. Unlike normal perfect markets, individual suppliers are not normally confronted with perfectly elastic demand schedules for their services but when hailed by a potential customer are virtual monopolists able to charge a high fare for their services. People seldom turn away a cab upon hearing the fare to hail another one – the low probability of a lower cab fare does not justify it. Once fares are at the higher level there is, therefore, no incentive for individual cabs to cut their fares because to customers they all appear alike and no additional business is attracted (that is, revenue for any cab acting differently will inevitably fall).

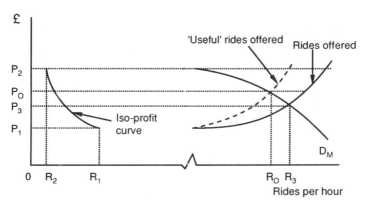

Figure 6.1
Taxi-cab fare determination

Of course, the cab market is somewhat more complicated than the simple model suggests (there are, for instance, cab ranks, and it may be possible to differentiate cabs by colour schemes etc.), but the fear that cabs could exploit local monopoly power of the type described and keep fares sub-optimally high is one reason why authorities in most major cities control fare levels. While this may be justified it is hard to see why at the same time most cities outside of the UK regulate the number of taxi-cabs operating within their domain; if fares are deemed optimal at P_O then rides offered will automatically adjust to R_O and there is no need for official regulation of capacity which can seriously distort the market (see, for instance, Beesley 1973).

While it is possible that the simple picture of perfectly competitive price determination is often complicated in the transport sector, it is equally true that the basic model of monopoly also on occasions needs modification. There are few if any natural monopolies in transport, there are normally competitive modes even if the one in question tends to be monopolistic in character. Also users of transport services often have the alternative of either changing their method of production (in the case of freight transport) or pattern of consumption (with passenger modes) so that transport is itself competitive with different forms of human activity. In some cases where these countervailing forces are weak or the introduction of competition would mean wasteful duplication of services, government may institutionalise a monopoly but by controlling price and other commercial aspects of its operations prevent the exploitation of customers. Much of the regulation initiated in a wide range of countries in the 1930s and 1940s, which is discussed in Chapter 11, was ostensibly introduced for this sort of reason.

The fear of potential competition, especially in the long term, tends to regulate the activities of essentially monopoly transport suppliers even when government intervention is minimal. The pricing policies pursued by liner conferences, when shippers combine to monopolise scheduled services between major ports, offers an illustration of this. Some discussion of detailed pricing of consignments by conferences is contained in Section 6.4; here we focus on the general principles. Sturmey (1975) argues that conferences do not price to maximise immediate profits but rather to maximise the present value of the flow of revenue from the market. The emphasis on revenue reflects the concern with market size while that on the present value shows that long-term objectives dominate short-run considerations. If, in Figure 6.2, the intention was to maximise profit in each market then price would be set, assuming the conference enjoyed a short-term monopoly position, at P_M with a monthly output of Q_M. If sales-revenue maximisation (subject to cost recovery) is the objective then price P_R is charged (expanding output to where the MC curve hits the horizontal would violate the break-even constraint).

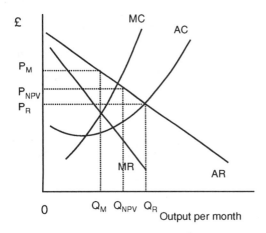

Figure 6.2
Pricing of shipping conference services

In practice, however, Sturmey argues that conference rates are found to be below P_M because the high short-term profits would encourage competition to enter the market; they are also unlikely to equal P_R because the conference looks beyond the immediate period although there is no *a priori* method of telling whether they will be above or below this level. The conference is likely to base its pricing policy on a relatively long time horizon – hypothesised by Sturmey to be the period over which the scale of productive enterprise is unchanged, but long enough to allow for additional capital equipment, which duplicates existing equipment, to be installed – although not long enough for all factors to be considered truly variable. The net revenue over this period, discounted to yield its current worth (see Chapter 8.2), is then seen as the key variable to maximise. The conference rate is, therefore, likely to be, say, at P_{NPV} in Figure 6.2 at which the maximum present value is obtained without attracting new entrants.

6.2   Marginal cost pricing

As was pointed out in the previous section, the pricing policy adopted by any transport undertaking depends upon its basic objectives. The traditional, classical economic assumption is that firms price so that profits are maximised. More recent variations on the theory of the firm suggests that many undertakings adopt prices that maximise sales revenues (Baumol, 1962) when in an expansive phase, or simply price to ensure that certain satisfactory levels of profit, security, market domination, etc. are achieved (Simon, 1959) when a defensive stance is adopted. Whatever the underlying operational objective, the theory of the firm assumes that the supplier is intent on maximising *his own* welfare, be this defined in terms of profits or higher-level objectives.

Welfare economics takes a rather wider view of pricing, looking upon price as a method of resource allocation which maximises social welfare rather than simply the welfare of the supplier. In some cases, since the good or service is actually provided by a public agency, this may be equated with maximising the suppliers' welfare. In other instances, controls or incentives may be applied to private companies so that their pricing policy is modified to maximise social rather than private welfare. This may take the form of restrictions on pricing flexibility, or the taxing and subsidising of firms so that their prices are socially optimal. Social optimality has a wide variety of meanings but in broad terms it means maximising the joint net social surplus (that is, the total revenue (*TR*) plus consumers' surplus (*CS*) generated by an undertaking minus the total cost (*TC*)). We can, therefore, define the objective of public policy as the maximisation of:

$$SW = TR + CS - TC \qquad\qquad\qquad (6.1)$$

Figure 6.3 takes the example of charging for rail freight capacity as an illustration of how the optimal price is arrived at. For expositional ease, assume that there are constant costs and that the railway undertaking is a monopoly. If it seeks to maximise its profits it will charge P_M, which in terms of equation 6.1 will produce total revenue of $P_M b Q_M 0$, consumer surplus of abP_M and total costs of $P_{MC} e Q_M 0$ resulting in a social welfare level of $abeP_{MC}$. While this may yield the maximum profit to the railway it is not, however, the price which maximises social surplus. That price is P_{MC}; the price at which marginal cost is equated with demand. At this price, the total revenue is $P_{MC} d Q_{MC} 0$, consumer surplus is adP_{MC} and total cost are $P_{MC} d Q_{MC} 0$ which gives a total social welfare which exceeds that associated with the profit maximising price by *bed*.

In other words, social welfare is maximised when price is equated to marginal cost. What marginal cost pricing does, in effect, is to result in transport services being provided up to the point where the benefit for the marginal unit is equated with the costs of providing that unit. The policy is a fairly well established one in economic theory and, indeed, formed the basis for UK public enterprise pricing from 1967. Traditional theory also tells us that such a condition prevails in the long term when perfect competition exists despite the fact that each firm is attempting to maximise its own profits. The ability to exercise any degree of monopoly power, however, permits a firm to price above marginal cost so that it can achieve additional profit at the expense of reduced output and at costs to the consumers. The price charged by a profit maximising monopolist will force some potential consumers to forgo consumption despite their willingness to pay for the costs of their activities. Indeed, it was the fear of monopoly exploitation that led to controls being imposed on railway pricing in the late nineteenth century and has led to the United States controlling rate fixing by shipping conferences operating from its ports.

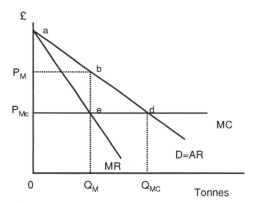

Figure 6.3
Marginal cost pricing

While it has been shown that social welfare is maximised by adopting marginal cost pricing, the exact definition of the appropriate marginal cost has been left vague. More specifically, there is the question of whether long-run *(LRMC)* or short-run marginal cost *(SRMC)* pricing is the more appropriate (short-run being when there is a fixed capacity which can be modified only in the long run). *SRMC* pricing has the advantage that it ensures existing capacity is used optimally but does not take account of capital and other fixed cost items. Wiseman (1957) was particularly concerned with this problem since, he argued, that the shorter the time period under consideration, the lower will appear the *SRMC* and, *ipso facto,* the price charged to users. This concern is misguided, however, because if there is fixed capacity, as is almost always the case with transport in the short term, a premium should be added to *SRMC* as an effective rationing device to contain excessive demand. Price is, after all, an allocative device.

Figure 6.4 shows the demand for a passenger railway service with capacity Q_I. The marginal cost of carrying each additional passenger is constant until the capacity of the system is reached whereupon the *SRMC* becomes infinite. If a price of P_I is charged then demand will exceed capacity by $Q'_d - Q_I$. In these circumstances, where demand will exceed absolute capacity using *SRMC* pricing policy, a mark-up to price level P'_I is appropriate to ration the available seats. The extra revenue thus generated in excess of *LRMC* provides an indication that it would be beneficial for the capacity of the railway service to be expanded. The optimal scale of service will, in fact, be offering capacity Q_2 where the price charged travellers is equated with *LRMC* (and the up-turn of $SRMC_2$ curve). We see, therefore, that the long-run optimum is where *P=LRMC=SRMC*. In some cases, (for example, airports or motorway systems), indivisibilities may make it impossible to provide exactly the optimal capacity Q_2 and a choice must then be made between a sub-optimally small system or a sub optimally large-one. Under such conditions decisions must be based upon weighing the full costs and benefits of the alternatives against one another.

6.3   Difficulties of 'second best' situations
The preceding analysis contained a number of implicit, as well as the stated, explicit assumptions. In particular, it assumed that all other prices in the economy are set equal to marginal cost. A variety of factors – some economic, others political or institutional – mean that in reality all other prices in the economy are not equal to marginal cost. The problem, again couched in terms of the railway example, then becomes one of deciding whether marginal cost pricing is, in these circumstances, appropriate in the railway context.

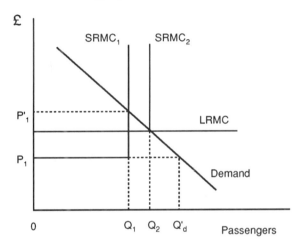

Figure 6.4
Short-run and long-run marginal cost pricing

For simplicity we assume that there is only bus and rail transport in the economy. Further, the bus sector is under monopoly control and fares are set above the marginal costs of providing services. The issue is then whether the railways should marginal cost price or adopt some alternative strategy which would maximise social welfare. In Figure 6.5, we have the production possibility curve for bus and rail services and, additionally, denote A as the traffic mix which would result in maximum social welfare; it is tangential to the highest attainable indifference curve. Extending the analysis of Figure 6.3, since this combination maximises social welfare, the two modes will be charging marginal costs at this point. Since, however, we have said that bus fares are above marginal cost $(P_{bus} > MC_{bus})$ the attainable position on the production possibility frontier with the actual price ration if rail adopts marginal cost pricing $(P_{rail} = MC_{rail})$ is B which is on a lower utility curve (U_2). The question then arises as to whether the railways by deviating from marginal cost pricing and adopting a 'second-best' pricing strategy can enhance total social welfare.

The simplest approach to the second-best in these conditions, as established by Lipsey and Lancaster (1956/7), is that rail should adopt fares which deviate by the *same proportion* from marginal costs as do those of bus. In other words it is possible to attain social welfare level U_1 by adopting prices which conform to:

$$\frac{P_{rail} - MC_{rail}}{MC_{rail}} = \frac{P_{bus} - MC_{bus}}{MC_{bus}} \qquad (6.2)$$

What this effectively does is to ensure that the two modes are comparable in terms of their relative attractiveness. In practice the calculations are more complex and Nilsson (1992) offers an illustration of how second-best prices could be determined for Sweden's freight rail services in conditions where road transport is not paying its full marginal costs. A general problem is that here we are only looking at transport but while the second-best rule will ensure the social optimal mix of transport use there may be problems with other prices in the economy. If they all remain set at marginal cost but both rail and bus are priced along second-best lines above marginal cost then transport will be relatively expensive when compared to other possible expenditures. Ideally, all prices should deviate by appropriate percentages from their marginal costs in these circumstances.

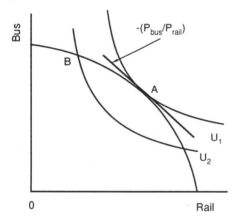

Figure 6.5
Second-best problems

Under some conditions the problem may not be serious and, from a purely pragmatic stance, it may be more efficient to charge marginal cost prices than to bear the costs of working out any optimal adjustments. In other cases, deviations from marginal cost principles elsewhere in the economy may be so remote that they have minimal influence on the demand for transport. Under such conditions, and assuming the distortions cannot be removed, Davis and Whinston (1967) demonstrate that piecemeal optimisation within separate sectors of the economy using marginal cost pricing is optimal. Mishan (1962) suggests that since in many cases people spend a fixed amount of their income upon transport, there is, therefore, only a very low cross-elasticity of demand between transport as a whole and other goods consumed in the economy. This situation means that the issue can be reduced to optimising the allocation of traffic between *forms of transport,* on a piecemeal basis, rather than have to consider the allocation of expenditure between a certain form of transport and all other goods. If, in our example, all competing forms of transport apply marginal cost pricing principles then these should also be adopted by the railway service.

While Mishan's empirical approach has a certain practical common-sense appeal for some forms of transport – such as inter-urban passenger transport – it has less applicability in the freight sector or in the context of international travel. Freight costs have a considerable bearing upon both final prices charged for products and the location of the manufacturing industry; these are the main reasons for the attempts to develop a Common Transport Policy within the European Community. If all other inputs to industry are priced above marginal cost because, say, of the monopoly power of suppliers, but transport is priced at marginal cost, then this could lead to an over-development, from the national efficiency point of view, of transport-intensive industry. (Although it is possible that the relatively 'cheap' transport could break the monopoly power of the suppliers of other inputs forcing them, in the long run, to price at marginal cost.) International air and sea transport has the complication that, except in certain well-defined areas, many nations consciously subsidise their 'flag bearers', enabling them to charge rates below *LRMC* and, on occasions, even below *SRMC*. Any single operator charging fares based on marginal cost in this situation would find himself unable to attract the optimal volume of traffic, and thus some deviation from the marginal cost principle may be necessary.

The existence of monopoly and other distorting influences in the economy has been shown to necessitate some variations to marginal cost pricing in certain transport sectors. The key to the degree to which prices should deviate from marginal cost is clearly the sign and magnitude of the cross-elasticities of demand between transport and other goods and services in the economy. The practical difficulty in many cases is not the derivation of the appropriate theoretical model but rather our inadequate knowledge of the size of the cross-elasticities. The evidence that is coming forward tends to be piecemeal. Additionally, most of the evidence is only related to intra-transport cross-elasticities with extremely few estimates of transport/other goods cross-elasticities.

6.4   Price discrimination and yield management

The adoption of marginal cost pricing can, in certain circumstances, result in an undertaking making a financial loss. The classic example of this is the decreasing cost industry where, because of high initial capital costs, the setting of charges equal to short-run marginal cost will result in a financial deficit. The railways are often cited as an example of an industry where marginal cost pricing may ensure optimal utilisation but leave the undertaking with a financial deficit. In Figure 6.6 the railways are assumed to be a monopoly supplier of freight services and, indeed, although it is not shown, if a monopoly profit maximising price were adopted then abnormal profits could be earned. The adoption of marginal cost pricing (P_{MC}), however, with the downward sloping *AC* and *MC* curves, at least over the relevant range, will result in a loss shown by the shaded area. A break-even situation could be attained by average cost pricing (that is, charging P_{AC}) but this would mean $Q_{MC} - Q_{AC}$ potential rail travellers, willing to pay the additional costs they impose, are priced off the service.

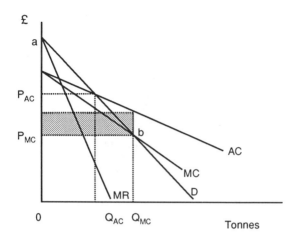

Figure 6.6
Second best, average cost pricing, with decreasing costs

Table 6.1
Revenue sources from road users in the EC

Country	Percentage revenue from		
	Fuel tax	Vehicle tax	Tolls
Belgium	76	24	-
Denmark	62	38	-
Germany	75	25	-
Greece	83	17	-
France	74	12	14
Irish Republic	92	8	-
Italy	82	7	11
Luxemburg	86	14	-
Netherlands	59	41	-
Portugal	93	7	-
United Kingdom	71	29	-

In these circumstances the adoption of marginal cost pricing is essentially a welfare decision and it is clear that if the undertaking does make a financial loss this is attributable to the pricing policy pursued rather than the incapacity of the service to be financially viable. The fixed costs of the service may be met in these cases by subsidy or by operating a 'club' system with potential users paying a fixed sum for the right to travel by rail and mileage rate (or some other 'cost'-related variable fee) to reflect use. It could be argued that the fixed rates of road vehicle taxation combined with fuel duties reflect a type of club arrangement but, if so, the system is extremely imperfect. At the very crudest level of analysis, the very considerable variation in the ratio of licence fee to fuel tax revenue shown in

Table 6.1 reveals diversities across EC countries which bear no relation to their relative expenditures on investment and maintenance. The UK, for example, spends about 55 per cent of its annual road budget on current (variable) costs.

Figure 6.7 illustrates a somewhat different situation, but one which does occur with certain forms of transport service. Here at no level of output does average revenue exceed average cost. It is impossible in this type of situation for costs to be recovered by charging a single price to all users even if monopoly pricing policies are adopted. In this case even a club arrangement is incapable of preventing the service from being unprofitable. There may be justifications for keeping the service operating with the losses financed through subsidies if there are wider benefits to be enjoyed outside of those generally linked to transport; the service may, for instance, have a strategic value or it may be deemed a 'merit good' which society ought to provide to enable isolated communities to continue in existence.

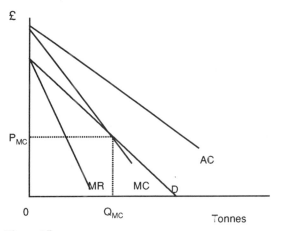

Figure 6.7
Decreasing costs with demand always inside the average cost curve

In the more conventional case, if subsidies are to be avoided, two-part tariffs are impractical and average cost pricing is deemed inappropriate then price discrimination can still be used to finance the service. Essentially, price discrimination involves charging 'what-the-user-will-bear' provided they cover their marginal costs. In other words it involves attempting to define the maximum amount each consumer or, more realistically, each identifiable group of customers, is willing to pay for the service. The demand curve reflects willingness of users to pay and a perfectly discriminating supplier will charge down this curve. In Figure 6.6 output would be fixed at the level comparable to simple marginal cost pricing (that is, Q_{MC}) but each user would pay a different price dependent upon demand. This would yield a total revenue of $0abQ_{MC}$ which may be compared with the total cost of providing the service, namely $0P_{MC}bQ_{MC}$. The costs are fully recovered and a profit of $P_{MC}ba$ is being earned. Of course, price discrimination does not always guarantee cost recovery, it depends on the revenue raised *vis-à-vis* the costs involved. One should also note that perfect price discrimination as described results in the marginal cost level of output; in fact it results in social welfare maximisation but with all of the benefits being derived by the provider of the transport service.

In many cases a transport undertaking itself provides a number of different types of service (for example, first- and second-class rail services) and is also under a remit to make a prescribed level of profit, or to break even, rather than to profit maximise. Given these conditions and assuming that the cross-elasticity of demand for the different service is negligible, Baumol and Bradford (1970) have demonstrated that the price of any services should be set equal to its short-run marginal cost plus a mark-up inversely proportionate to the service's price elasticity of demand (ε). Hence, where the demand for a service is highly inelastic a substantial addition should be added to marginal cost. Where the demand is perfectly elastic, short-run marginal cost pricing is applied. In this way revenue above *SRMC* can be obtained to meet the financial target without distorting the allocation of traffic between services. If cross-elasticities are not zero, then the simple rule must be modified to ensure that the relative quantities of goods sold correspond to the proportions which would occur if marginal cost pricing were applicable. The rule, for example, for substitutes is that optimal prices should be derived so that 'all output be reduced by the same proportion from the quantities which be demanded at prices equal to the corresponding marginal costs' (Baumol and Bradford, 1970). This is often called Ramsey Pricing after earlier work in the field by Ramsey (1927). Assuming the railways offer two products, express and commuter rail services, then they should, following this principle, price such that:

$$\frac{(P_{exp} - MC_{exp})}{P_{exp}} \varepsilon_{exp} = \frac{(P_{com} - MC_{com})}{P_{com}} \varepsilon_{com} \qquad (6.3)$$

It is not always possible for practical reasons to discriminate perfectly: the administrative costs of operating the system may be too high or exact knowledge of the demand curves unavailable. These, for example, are the reasons cited in the 1960s by British Rail for their reluctance to adopt more sophisticated costing and pricing policies – the diversity of services provided made it impracticable (Foster, 1975). In other cases it may be felt socially undesirable to charge 'what-the-user-will-bear' because of distributional consequences. Passengers with a low elasticity of demand may be from the poorer sections of the community and unable to transfer to alternative modes of transport. It may still be justified, even in these circumstances, to provide services even if not all costs are recovered by the operator providing that the *potential* revenue if discrimination were adopted exceeds the costs of the service. If this is the case, a subsidy is required to bring actual revenue up to potential revenue and, to some extent, the British government accepted this in the 1968 Transport Act when, for a period, it introduced specific social subsidies to maintain a number of railway services.

While price discrimination is relatively uncommon outside of the transport sector it is a familiar feature of pricing policy within it. Truelove (1992) provides an apt description of the current pricing practices of British Rail,

> The distinction between first and second class is further refined by the exclusion of discount fares from peak weekday and holiday trains, by the limited availability of old people's and students' discounts, and the reduction in supplement for travel in first class carriages at weekends, when leisure travel is heavy and business travel almost negligible.

Another well-documented example of price discrimination is provided by shipping conferences. These act as monopoly suppliers of regular liner services between major ports. The possibility of airline competition tends to increase the elasticity of demand for their services to carry high-price–low-volume goods while tramp shipping becomes competitive for low-price bulk cargoes. Consequently, one can hypothesise an inverted S-shaped demand curve for liner services over any route. Given the high capital costs associated with shipping, there is adequate evidence that, prior to the widespread use of containers, without price discrimination, most conference lines would become unprofitable. A detailed look at the Australia-Europe Conference by Zerby and Conlon (1978) produced a breakdown of rates which clearly shows the high degree of price discrimination exercised by these maritime cartels. Figure 6.8 reproduces their average revenues for each type of cargo carried in 1973/4 and it is clear that traced out this corresponds closely to the type of demand curve hypothesised. The low-value bulk cargoes (that is, ores and metals) are carried at (or sometimes below if ballast is required) the average incremental costs of loading and unloading. While the high-value products are carried at considerably higher rates, the tapering off in rates caused by potential competition from air transport is seen to be effective at the top of the price range.

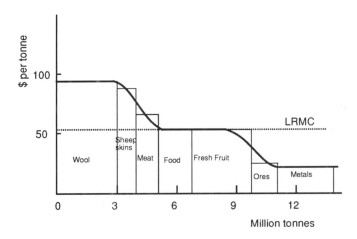

Figure 6.8
Average revenues from cargoes carried by the Australia-Europe conference (1973/4)

Price discrimination does not only permit suppliers to recover their costs, it also helps travellers and consignors in that services can be retained even if, in some cases, it is necessary to differentiate the quality of service provided as well as the fare charged. International air travel offers some examples of this type of situation where differential prices are charged over a route according to the specifications of the types of service the travellers are willing to pay for. The gradual breakdown of the International Air Transport Association's (IATA) system of regulating air fares across the Atlantic in the 1970s was accompanied by the introduction of cut-price services such as 'Skytrain', operated by Laker Airways

(Abe, 1979). No-frill flights were introduced at low fares with seat allocation dependent upon the willingness of potential passengers to queue – tickets could not be purchased until six hours prior to take-off. Subsequently this type of service has been modified and regular scheduled airlines now offer a variety of ticketing arrangements on their flights. A clear segmentation of the market had been recognised.

Figure 6.9 provides an illustration of the sort of situation which has emerged. If, for example, there are three different groups of potential travellers with separate demand curves D_1, D_2 and D_3, then three separate fares should be charged (P_1, P_2, P_3) to maximise the consumers' surplus enjoyed. P_1 is charged for the highest quality flight, equalling the marginal cost of service, with lower fares for poorer quality flights. On the surface it appears that ON_1 passengers will travel first class reaping a consumer surplus of ABP_1, and N_1N_2 passengers will pay P_2 for the slightly lower quality of service and enjoy consumers' surplus of HIG. This ignores the possibility that first-class travellers may switch to the poorer quality but cheaper services (that is, there may be some 'revenue dilution'). In fact, travellers N'_1N_1 could switch and increase their welfare. Similarly, N'_2N_2 passengers appear to be the probable number of customers for the poor quality service but again a further N'_2N_2 may be induced to join them by the lower fare. Whether people actually do take advantage of the possibility of switching to cheaper but less convenient forms of service is uncertain, but the availability of the range of services means the total *potential* consumer surplus (the shaded areas will exceed that generated if only a single price and service package were available.

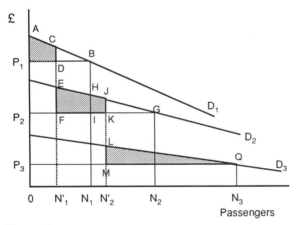

Figure 6.9
Price discrimination according to service quality

This type of practice is an integral part of what has become known as yield management. Essentially it is the ability of management to maximise the revenue from a pre-defined activity (e.g. a scheduled flight or sailing) by a combination of price discrimination and product differentiation. It has become a key element in, for example, the scheduled airline industry where the chief executive of one major operator, R.L. Crandall of American Airlines, stated, 'I believe that yield management is the single most important technical development in transportation management since we entered the era of airline deregulation in 1979' (cited in Smith *et al.*, 1992). The use of computer reservation systems by airlines enables an airline to adjust the fares offered on a given flight, the seats available at each fare and the preconditions for booking at any fare. The preconditions (combined with some relatively minor quality differentials inherent in first class, business and coach class areas of an aircraft) introduce product differentiation into the management equation while the various fares charged for what are, in many ways, very similar services represent the price discrimination element. The combinations offered and the adjustments made by an airline as the time of any flight departure approaches are designed to maximise the yield from the predetermined decision to offer that particular service. The technique is somewhat different to that of the classic economic model of price discrimination where management increases revenue by charging different groups of customers (differentiated by their price elasticities) different prices for the *same product*. The cost of serving each customer is, in the classic model, identical. There is, however, normally some qualitative or other form of product differentiation involved in yield management which implies cost differentials in the provision of services to customers. First-class air travel does cost an airline more than discount travel. Equally, however, the existence of economies of scope may mean that the supplier of a range of different services can keep unit costs lower than a number of suppliers each specialising. In overall resource terms, therefore, yield management may provide for the development a more efficient market structure.

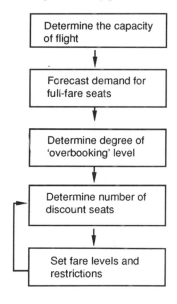

Figure 6.10
Stages in arriving at yield-maximising revenue in scheduled aviation

The set of decisions confronting industries practising successful yield management is often complex. The interactions and options available are too numerous for fare levels, fare structures, constraints and capacity distribution to be determined simultaneously. This leads to a further common feature of yield management, namely sequential decision-making. The form this takes varies between both sectors and firms within sectors but a broad indication of the decision sequence adopted by many airlines when considering a particular scheduled service is set out in Figure 6.10 (Smith *et al.*, 1992). In this case the nature of the technology does permit a degree of interaction between some of the stages (e.g. discount levels and allocation of seats to different fare classes) as the time of the flight approaches.

Price discrimination is not only by type of traffic or quality of service but may also be by length of journey. Friedman (1979) offers a classic example of such a policy in the context of long-haul/short-haul differentials on American railways. The practice of charging short-haul traffic a higher mileage rate on railways than long-haul, despite attempts to legislate to the contrary, was common in nineteenth-century America. Friedman's justification for this practice demonstrates that without it there may arise quite serious distortions in transport infrastructure provision.

As an example, suppose there is a railway link between three towns, *A, B* and *C* where *B* is located between the other two towns. There is also river transport (priced at marginal cost) available between *A* and *C* offering an identical service to the railway but offering no communication for town *B*. The fixed. sunk cost of the rail link is such that

$$C_{AC} = C_{AB} + C_{BC} \tag{6.4}$$

that is, the sunk cost of the line from *A* to *C* is the sum of the two component sublinks. Also, on the same basis, the variable cost is,

$$V_{AC} = V_{AB} + V_{BC} \tag{6.5}$$

Figure 6.11 shows the respective demand schedules for transport between the different pairs of towns. The railways may maximise their profits by charging down the demand curves D_{AB} and D_{BC}, where there is no competition from riverborne transport, to the point where marginal (that is, variable) cost is reached. Where competition does exist over the long route between *A* and *C*, the railways, to attract customers, will want to charge *at most* the rate offered by river transport (call this R_{AC}). The railways will, however, accept traffic at rates below R_{AC} but above the variable cost. The areas BAV_{AB}, CDV_{BC} and $R_{AC}EFV_{AC}$ show the revenues enjoyed by the railways on different links. If R_{AC} is lower than either the highest position of D_{AB} or D_{BC}, then there exists long-haul/short-haul discrimination in addition to discrimination within each type of traffic. In other words, *identical* goods with *identical* demand for transport schedules would be charged more per mile for a short haul than for a long haul.

The sum of the revenues in the diagram offers a measure of the social value of building and operating the *ABC* railway line. The aggregate producer surplus generated should be set against the fixed costs of provision, which together with calculations for *AB* and *AC* separately, indicate the long-term desirability of keeping the entire line open or only segments of it. Without long-haul/short-haul discrimination the railway would have either to give up some of its long-haul business or fail to capture some of the consumer surplus generated on short haul. Whatever the case, the railway's incentive to invest would be distorted and some economically desirable lines would not be operated.

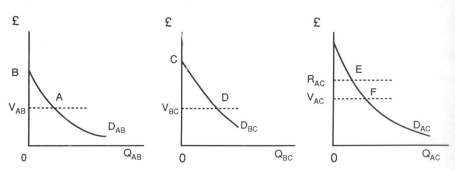

Figure 6.11
Railway revenues from discriminate pricing according to length of haul

6.5 Pricing with stochastic demand

Our discussion of price discrimination as a method of recovering costs has to date made the rather heroic assumption that the supplier of transport – be he shipowner, railway manager, airline operator or whatever – has perfect knowledge of the demand situation confronting him. In practice this is unrealistic. Most transport managers have, from past data and employing 'managerial intuition' some notion of the average level of demand for their services and some idea of how this demand fluctuates. (The specific problem of systematic and regular *known* peaks in demand is considered in the following section; here we concentrate on irregular fluctuations in demand of a stochastic nature.) They may, for instance, know that fluctuations are about 20 per cent of the average daily demand but have no way of telling whether tomorrow's demand will be, say, 7 per cent above the average or 14 per cent below it.

The introduction of this notion of 'stochastic' demand requires a slight modification to the marginal cost pricing approach (Turvey, 1975). The conventional arguments for discriminate pricing revolve around the idea that simple marginal cost pricing will, because of declining average cost, result in the supplier incurring a financial loss. Turvey's position is that the problem should be expressed in terms of the difficulties associated with matching the services supplied (usually vehicle journeys) with those which are demanded (usually passenger journeys) when a fixed timetable is operative. Approached from this way, the problem is seen as one of defining a price structure which will cover all relevant costs but which will, at the same time, ensure reasonable utilisation of the transport capacity available. Two broad approaches emerge. The first of these depends upon fairly reliable information about demand and its range of fluctuation while the second is reliant upon good information on all relevant costs. Here, we concentrate on the first approach and, in particular, the load factor for a service. If fares are fixed so high that the number of people wishing to use the service *never* exceeds the available capacity then, as a result of the fluctuating demand condition, there will frequently be substantial numbers of empty seats and resources will be wasted. Alternatively, if the fares are set so low that capacity is fully utilised all of the time then many people, who often have spent time queuing for the service, will, again because of demand fluctuations, find themselves unable to obtain a seat. Clearly, common sense suggests a compromise between these extremes which will meet the requirements of both supplier and potential traveller. Turvey's pragmatic solution is that operators should structure their fares so that on *average* a certain percentage of seats will remain empty.

To some extent this is the situation which developed with the introduction of 'Skytrain' – as discussed in the previous section – where passengers have even greater flexibility by being able, via the premium charged on normal scheduled services, to ensure themselves a seat if they wish or, at a lower fare, to risk disappointment. The situation is also evident on the streets of central London where parking meter fees are fixed so that on average 15 per cent of spaces are vacant although, of course, from experience we know that at times it is impossible to find a vacant parking space while at others they are in abundance. One might also point to the 'stand-by capacity' kept by British Rail until the 1968 Transport Act which, it was claimed, acted to cope with long-term fluctuations in demand for railway services.

To cover costs in this type of situation without recourse to either direct or cross-subsidisation it is likely that price discrimination is necessary. Any of four standard types of discrimination (that is, by (i) type of passenger, (ii) degree of comfort, (iii) regularity of use and/or (iv) seat availability) could be used for this purpose.

Where knowledge of demand fluctuations is less precise, then Turvey's (1975) second and rather more pragmatic approach may be applicable. Here fares can be determined by simply dividing available costs of the service by the passengers carried and the service only runs if such fares broadly correspond to those on the remainder of the transport system. Additional revenue may then be gained on an *ad hoc* basis by raising fares for those groups where willingness-to-pay exceeds the cost-based fare. The actual avoidable costs can be estimated, where there is uncertainty about initial traffic levels, using the following formula which for simplicity is couched in terms of a railway service:

$$\left[\left\{ \begin{array}{l} \text{Probability that marginal passenger} \\ \text{will necessitate an extra carriage} \end{array} \right\} \ \text{x} \ \ (\text{Cost of extra carriage}) \right]$$

$$+ \left[\left\{ \begin{array}{l} \text{Probability that marginal passenger} \\ \text{will necessitate an extra train} \end{array} \right\} \ \text{x} \ \ (\text{Cost of extra train}) \right]$$

Because this probability long-run marginal cost curve represents costs as an increasing function of the number of passengers and also since this is itself a decreasing function of the fare charged, there is likely to be a fare structure where such marginal costs are recovered.

Whether the fare is optimal, however, depends upon time-table flexibility; so far we have implicitly assumed a *given* time-table. The overall fare is set at the level of the marginal *social* cost of an extra passenger – in other words equal to the frustration and inconvenience he causes to other potential but disappointed travellers by occupying a scarce seat. The combination of time-table and fare that equates the marginal cost, so defined, with the marginal financial cost is thus an overall optimum. In practice, of course, imperfect knowledge of demand situations, plus the need to make time-tabling and pricing decisions simultaneously, makes it unlikely that such an overall optimum will be attained except by chance.

6.6 The problem of the peak

Most forms of transport, both freight and passenger, experience regular peaks in demand for their services. Urban public transport (upon which our attention is focused later) experiences peaks in demand during 'rush hours' each weekday morning and evening. Urban freight transport also has peaks in demand to match the needs and operating practices of customers. In London, for example, the majority of deliveries are made between 11.00 a.m. and noon while clear peaks are revealed for Newbury and Camberley in Table 6.2. Over a year, air, bus and rail services meet peaks in demand from holiday traffic during the summer months and over public holidays, while within a week there are marked differences between weekend and weekday demand levels. Over an even longer period, shipping is subjected to cyclical movements in demand as the world economy moves between booms and slumps.

Table 6.2
Urban freight deliveries in Newbury and Camberley

Time of arrival	Newbury	Camberley
07.30–07.59	3.1	0.8
08.00–08.59	12.3	8.5
09.00–09.59	12.7	11.2
10.00–10.59	12.1	15.3
11.00–11.59	15.5	16.4
12.00–12.59	12.3	9.4
13.00–13.59	11.9	11.2
14.00–14.59	8.4	11.7
15.00–15.59	7.1	7.6
16.00–16.59	4.2	4.3
17.00–17.30	0.4	1.7
Unknown		1.9

Source: Christie *el al.,* 1973

The difficulty in all these situations is to determine a pattern of prices which (i) ensures that transport infrastructure is used optimally, (ii) provides a guide to future investment policy, and (iii) ensures that all relevant costs are recovered. Unlike the previous section, we are concerned here with problems arising from *systematic* variations in demand, frequently over a relatively short time period during which adjustments cannot be made in capital equipment to ensure that price is always equated with long-run marginal cost. (The problem is essentially one of indivisibility in the time dimension of supply relative to demand and is, therefore, a particular form of the joint production problem.) Problems of this kind do occur in other sectors of the economy but transport (like electricity and some other forms of energy) cannot be stored to reconcile systematic changes in demand with smooth, even production. Reconciliation can only be through price.

Before proceeding to look at the peak-load pricing problem it is worth noting that there exists a parallel spatial/directional problem of joint costs in transport which can be treated in an identical way to that of the peak. This involves the question of deriving appropriate rates for front-hauls and back-hauls – a situation often found in the provision of unscheduled road haulage, or freight and shipping services. Basically there is a high demand for a service in one direction (the front haul) but a lower one for a return service (the back haul); that is, demand is unidirectional in nature whereas supply consists of round-trip journeys. This situation is directly analogous to the peak-load situation, with the front-haul being the spatial/directional equivalent of the peak, and simple substitution of words yields the appropriate analysis (see also Waters, 1980).

Perhaps the most widely discussed peaking problem involves urban public transport and particularly bus services. The size of most urban bus fleets is determined by the demand for public transport services during the morning and evening commuter rush hours. Typically over half the passengers carried during a day travel during the main peak periods. In Manchester, for example, 1090 buses were required to meet rush-hour demands in 1966 while only 400 were used during the midday period. Comparable figures for Birmingham Corporation Transport Department in 1969 were 1500 and 327 vehicles respectively. Bus road crews may also be considered as a joint cost since numbers are determined by peak demand. It is seldom possible to cover both daily peaks with one shift, hence either two shifts are required, or else split-shifts must be introduced usually involving inconvenience payments (often equal to the standard wage) being paid for time between peaks. The total wage bill for road staff, which amounts to about 50 per cent of total cost of most British bus operators, is, therefore, almost invariant with demand and may be treated as a joint cost of providing peak and non-peak services.

To determine optimal prices let us assume that during a twelve-hour period a bus operator is confronted by two different demand situations, each of six hours' duration. In Figure 6.12, D_1 is the low, off-peak demand situation and D_2 the peak level demand curve. The short-run marginal costs of operation (fuel and mileage dependent depreciation) are assumed constant at level Oa until the capacity of the bus fleet, which initially is assumed as fixed, is filled whereupon they become infinite. In the short term, with capacity fixed, the objective is to maximise social welfare by making optimal use of the fleet. In this case the off-peak and the peak demands should be priced at their respective *SRMC*. The fares should, therefore, be P_1 and P_2 at the off-peak and peak respectively with corresponding passenger numbers Q_{po} and Q_{no}.

Changes in capacity brought about by varying the fleet size do not influence short-run marginal costs except to the extent that the capacity constraint is pushed further to the right if vehicles are added and to the left if they are withdrawn. Long-run capacity costs (*LRMC*) are treated as constant at a level A. Since the capacity is joint to both sub-periods, changes in capacity should be determined by the combined demand of peak and off-peak periods, that is, the full cycle of activities (Hirschleifer, 1958). Consequently, it is D_{cycle} which is the relevant demand curve (because this represents the vertical summation of D_1 and D_2). Further, it is $LRMC_{cycle}$ which is the relevant long-term cost curve (because this represents the combination of the short-run costs in the two periods plus fixed costs; that is, $2a + A$). In essence the situation is analogous to that of a collective good. The optimum long-run capacity in the case illustrated, and assuming there are problems of indivisibilities, involves a contraction of capacity to OQ_O. The non-peak travellers will then pay P'_1, and peak travellers P'_2. Given the way the D_{cycle} and $LRMC_{cycle}$ curves are derived the combined revenues from off-peak and peak fares will be exactly equal to the costs involved. Also the off-peak fare now exceeds *SRMC* and capacity is fully utilised around the clock, the pricing differences reflecting differing strengths of demand. In summary, changes in capacity, because it is joint to both periods, now depend upon the sum of the differences between price and the capacity's operating costs per period relative to the cost of providing new capacity for the entire cycle (that is, investment is justified if $\{(P_1 - a) + (P_2 - a)\} > B$). It is relatively simple to extend the analysis to any number of sub-periods, which may be of unequal duration, by weighting the different periods according to their fractional importance in the entire cycle.

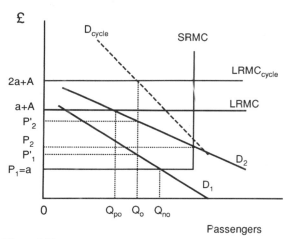

Figure 6.12
The optimal peak-pricing solution

In practice, the situation is often somewhat more complicated than that depicted, because passengers are not rigidly confined to either period but may switch trips between them if differential fares are levied. Unfortunately little empirical work has been conducted on this (Oum *et al.*, 1992) but it is quite possible that our implicit assumption that D_1 and D_2 are independent is often unrealistic and allowance needs to be made both for their own and also cross-elasticities. Also, of course, it may be necessary to take cognisance of interdependencies between the demand for urban bus travel as a whole and the possibilities of switching with private transport (Glaister, 1974).

While there is a firm economic basis for peak-load pricing, its implementation has been piecemeal to date. An early example was the pricing policy pursued in the Manchester-Salford area between the summers of 1970 and 1975 – see Tyson (1975) for details – and we also find British Rail excluding discount ticket holders from their peak services. It is employed at the major airports in the UK (Table 6.3, see Doganis, 1992, for more details) although the primary objective is to raise revenue for investment rather than as a strict short-term capacity rationing device. The charter airlines also practice peak-load pricing when setting their fares, in their case reflecting seasonal variations in demand patterns (Bishop and Thompson, 1992).

6.7   Transport subsidies, operational objectives and pricing
Many sectors of transport enjoy quite substantial levels of government subsidy. Table 6.4 provides some detail of the situation regarding rail and bus subsidies in

the UK while Table 6.5 offers a comparison of urban transport subsidies in Europe and the administrative structure underlying them. Subsidies complicate the pricing problem. To some extent the type of problem created depends upon the form of subsidy given. If a central or local government provides the subsidy for a specific service, then it may be seen as representing that government's demand for that service and treated alongside the demand of other customers; the service subsidies given by local authorities to specified bus services in the UK under the 1985 Transport Act may be categorised in this way as may many of the subsidies to franchised services in other European countries and in some US cities (Morlok, 1987). From a pricing/operational point of view such subsidies are relatively easily assimilated into standard economic models. This is particularly so in the UK case where the routes to be subsidised are put up for competitive tender; a process which is designed to ensure the minimum subsidy is paid for the designated service. Further, the evidence from London, and from similar systems in the USA, is that there are cost efficiency gains (after allowing for administrative and monitoring expenses) of about 20 per cent over more general subsidy arrangements.

Table 6.3
Landing fees at London's airports in 1991 (in £s)

Airport	Peak	Off-peak	Weighted average
Heathrow			
B 757	1680	658	844
Short 360	654	153	38
B 747	6259	747	3336
Gatwick			
B 757	1122	450	634
Short 360	444	111	211
B 747	4866	1867	2709
Stansted			
B 757	734	365	507
Short 360	123	71	88
B 747	3807	1806	2810

Note: A Boeing 757 seats 140 passengers and is a Stage III aircraft, and thus has a lower noise charge. The Shorts 360 seats 22 passengers. The Boeing 747 seats 270 passengers and is a Stage II aircraft which carriers a higher noise charge.

When lump sum subsidies are given to transport undertakings for general revenue purposes, however, problems arise in deciding upon the best methods of using the subsidy and the appropriate charge to levy on customers. In particular, it is difficult to devise pricing and operational objectives which ensure that management uses the fixed subsidies efficiently to attain the welfare objectives for which they are intended. A number of possible objectives have been cited as offering a way around this problem.

Table 6.4
Subsidies and grants for UK bus and rail services (£m)

	1971	1974	1979/80	1984/5	1987/8[1]	1989/90[1]
Rail[2]						
Local government	5	18	114	211	78	104
Central government	79	394	643	956	106	819
Bus						
Local government	15	122	410	902	673[3]	668[3]
Central government	31	55	133	128	150	174
Total	130	589	1300	2197	1907	1765
at 1985 prices	613	2089	2046	2281	1745	1572

[1]   Rail subsidies in 1987/8 and 1989/90 reflect transfer of responsibility for London transport from GLC to central government.
[2]   Includes London Transport rail services.
[3]   These figures include revenue support for bus services in London, despite the transfer of responsibility to central government.
Source: Else (1992)

Table 6.5
Level and nature of urban transport subsidies in Europe

Country	Type of operating subsidy	Revenue/cost ratio(£)	Regulatory system
Denmark	Network/route	55–56	Planned/franchised
Belgium	Network	30–40	Planned
Finland	Network	57–92	Planned
France	Network	53	Planned/franchised
Greece	Network	4–50	Planned
Ireland	Network	80–95	Planned
Israel	Network	66	Planned/franchised
Italy	Network	24–28	Planned
Netherlands	Network/route	28–40	Planned
Norway	Network/route	55–60	Planned/franchised
Portugal	Network/route	67	Planned/market
Spain	Network	70–90	Planned
Sweden	Network/route	39–48	Planned/franchised
Switzerland	Network	54–82	Planned
Turkey	Network		Planned
United Kingdom	Route		Market
West Germany	Network	54	Planned
Yugoslavia	Network		Planned

Source: Anderson (1992)

It has been argued that commercial criteria (with profit-maximising pricing) in this situation would lead to monopoly exploitation and be counter-productive in terms of the social objectives justifying the subsidy, while a social welfare maximising criterion (with marginal cost pricing) would break the link between costs, prices and output and lead to probable X-inefficiency: the provision of services at excessive costs (Nash, 1978). To circumvent these problems, and to provide clear pragmatic guidelines for lower-level management, London Transport attempted in the late 1970s to maximise passenger mileage subject to a budget constraint (that is, that costs are recovered after the fixed sum subsidy has been taken into account). Operationally, when the criterion is applied at the margin, this means:

> Reduce price as long as the increase in passenger mileage resulting exceeds the loss of revenue multiplied by the shadow price of public funds; increase bus mileage as long as the increase in passenger mileage resulting is greater than the net addition to the financial loss multiplied by the shadow price of public funds. (Nash, 1978)

The criterion, therefore, permits adjustments to the system operated so that costs are met (after allowing for the subsidy) and relatively junior management can assess the desirability of alternative courses of action. The criterion is, however, demonstrably inferior in theoretical terms to a pure marginal cost pricing strategy – price discrimination and cross-subsidisation may result which push fares on inelastic services above marginal operating costs so that revenue is available to finance services which exhibit a relatively high elasticity (and thus easily provide an increase in passenger miles). It is quite possible, therefore, for a service to be operated for which the level of demand is *never* high enough to permit price to cover marginal costs (Glaister and Collings, 1978).

It is possible, at the expense of complicating the criterion, to devise weighting schemes which can be attached to passenger miles on various routes to reflect their importance to the decision-maker and schemes do exist which yield the same results as marginal cost pricing. Whether it is justified to adopt such weights must be an empirical question, depending on the loss of welfare which may accompany the simple unweighted passenger miles maximisation approach relative to the administrative costs of implementation. Bos (1978) also points to the distributional implications of the criterion and suggests that positive distributional effects may justify a certain level of welfare loss although, again, the exact distributional effect cannot be determined by *a priori* argument. (Empirical evidence in London suggests, however, that the London Transport scheme did have desirable distributional implications.)

6.8 Further reading and references
A comprehensive, but rather difficult, account of the principles of marginal cost pricing is presented in Millward (1971, Chapters 7 and 8). This reference, while long-in-the-tooth, looks in more detail at both the long- and short-run pricing decision and also at specific difficulties associated, for example, with peaked demand. Ying (1992) concerns himself with the problems of calculating cost elasticities, and although technical, the paper highlights some important issues. Train (1991) provides a thorough look at the specific issue of pricing natural monopolies. Attempts to devise operational pricing rules for urban transport are reviewed both cogently and in depth by Nash (1978). This reference usefully contrasts the approaches to public transport pricing. Subsidies in transport are often alluded to in the literature but, despite their quantitative importance in the

real world, are seldom rigorously assessed. Else (1992) offers an up-to-date discussion of subsidies policy.

References

Abe, M.A. (1979), 'Skytrain: competitive pricing, quality of service and the deregulation of the airline industryÆ, *International Journal of Transport Economics*, 6, 41–47.

Anderson, B. (1992), 'Factors affecting European privatization and deregulation policies in local public transport: the evidence from Scandinavia', *Transportation Research*, 26A, 179–91.

Baumol, W.J. (1962), 'On the theory of the expansion of the firm', *American Economic Review*, 52, 1078–87

Baumol, W.J. and Bradford, D.F. (1970), 'Optimal departures from marginal cost pricing', *American Economic Review*, 60, 265–83.

Beesley, M. E. (I 973), 'Regulation of taxis', *Economic Journal*, 83, 150–72.

Bennathan, E. and Walters, A. (1979), *Port Pricing and Investment Policy for Developing Countries*, Oxford, Oxford University Press.

Bishop, M. and Thompson, D. (1992), 'Peak-load pricing in aviation: the case of charter air fares', *Journal of Transport Economics and Policy*, 26, 71–82.

Bos, D. (1978), 'Distribution effects of maximisation of passenger rules', *Journal of Transport Economics and Policy*, 12, 322–9.

Christie, A.W., Bartlett, R.S., Cundhill, M.A. and Prudhoe, J. (1973), 'Urban freight distribution: studies of operations in shopping streets at Newbury and Camberley', *Transport and Road Research Laboratory Report*, LR.603.

Davis, O.A. and Whinston, A.B. (1967), 'Piecemeal policy in the theory of second-best', *Review of Economic Studies*, 34, 323–31.

Doganis, R. (1992), *The Airport Business*, London, Routledge.

Else, P.K. (1992), 'Criteria for local transport subsidies', *Transport Reviews*, 12, 291–309.

Foster, C. D. (1975), *The Transport Problem*, London, Croom Helm.

Friedman, D.D. (1979), 'In defence of the long-haul/short-haul discrimination', *Bell Journal of Economics*, 10, 706–8.

Glaister, S. (1974), 'Generalised consumer surplus and public transport pricing', *Economic Journal*, 84, 849–67.

Glaister, S. and Collings, J.J. (1978), 'Maximisation of passenger miles in theory and practice', *Journal of Transport Economics and Policy*, 12, 304–21.

Hirschleifer, J. (1958), 'Peak loads and efficient pricing – comment', *Quarterly Journal of Economics*, 72, 451–62.

Lipsey, R.G. and Lancaster, K. (1956/7), 'The general theory of second best', *Review of Economic Studies*, 24, 11–32.

Millward, R. (1971), *Public Expenditure Economics*, Maidenhead, McGraw-Hill.

Mishan, E.J. (1962), 'Second-thoughts on second best', *Oxford Economic Papers*, 14, 205–17.

Morlok, E.K. (1987), 'Privatising bus transit: cost savings from competitive contracting', *Journal of the Transportation Research Forum*, 28, 72–81.

Nash, C.A. (1978), 'Management objectives, fares and service levels in bus transport', *Journal of Transport Economics and Policy*, 12, 70–85.

Nilsson, J.-E. (1992), 'Second-best problems in railway infrastructure pricing and investment', *Journal of Transport Economics and Policy*, 26, 245–259.

Oum, T.H., Waters, W.G. and Yong, J.S. (1992), 'Concepts of price elasticities of transport demand and recent empirical evidence', *Journal of Transport Economics and Policy*, 26, 139–54.

Ramsey, F. (1927), 'A contribution to the theory of taxation', *Economic Journal*, 37, 47–61.

Shreiber, C. (1975), 'The economic reasons for price and entry regulation of taxicabs', *Journal of Transport Economics and Policy*, 9, 268–79.

Shreiber, C. (1977), 'The economic reasons for price and entry regulation of taxicabs: reply', *Journal of Transport Economics and Policy*, 9, 298–304.

Simon, H.A. (1959), 'Theories of decision-making in economics and behavioural science', *American Economic Review*, 49, 253–83.

Smith, B.C., Leimkuhler, J.F. and Darrow, R.M. (1992), 'Yield management at American Airlines', *Interfaces*, 22, 8–31.

Sturmey, S.G. (1975), *Shipping Economics*, London, Macmillan.

Train, K.E. (1991), *Optimal Regulation: The Economic Theory of Natural Monopoly*, Cambridge, Mass., MIT Press.

Truelove, P. (1992), *Decision Making in Transport Planning*, London, Longman.

Turvey, R. (1975), 'A simple analysis of optimal fares on scheduled transport sources', *Economic Journal*, 85, 1–9.

Tyson, W.J. (1975), 'A study of the effect of different bus fares in Greater Manchester', *Chartered Institute of Transport Journal*, 37, 334–8.

Waters, W.G. (1980), 'Output dimensions and joint costs', *International Journal of Transport Economics*, 7, 17–35.

Wiseman, J. (1957), 'The theory of public utility price – an empty box', *Oxford Economic Papers (New Series)*, 9, 56–74.

Ying, J.S. (1992), 'On calculating cost elasticities', *Logistics and Transportation Review*, 28, 231–236.

Zerby, J.A. and Conlon, R.M. (1978), 'An analysis of capacity utilisation in liner shipping', *Journal of Transport Economics and Policy*, 12, 27–46.

7 Containing the External Costs of Transport

7.1 Introduction

Chapter 5 offered evidence of the magnitude and diversity of the external costs associated with transport. In this chapter we are concerned with methods of containing the externality problem and, if possible, optimising the environmental and congestion costs of transport. It should be emphasised at the outset that the focus on the external costs of transport, while glaring in the developed world, is much less intense in less wealthy countries. The affluence of the western world has transferred part of the desire from improving material living standards to that of improving (or retaining) environmental quality. The marginal utility of additional financial income, it is often argued, is, for the majority of people in the West, possibly of less value than a cleaner, quieter and safer environment in which to live. This is a comparatively recent phenomenon and books on transport economics written in the pre-war period gave scant attention to externalities. Although increasingly concerned with matters such as deforestation and soil erosion, most Third World countries still retain this comparative indifference to the environmental impacts of transport – their generally poor living standards and inadequate transport systems necessitate that effort be directed almost exclusively at improving material output. This is despite mounting environmental problems (Button, 1992).

We have seen in Figure 5.1 that ideally, externalities should be contained to the point where the costs of further reductions exceed the marginal social benefits ('pollution should be reduced to the point where the costs of doing so are covered by the benefits from the reduction in pollution', Royal Commission on Environmental Pollution, 1972). It should be re-emphasised that this is unlikely to mean zero pollution or zero congestion but rather optimal levels of external cost. To achieve this optimum a number of possibilities recommend themselves and the objective of this chapter is to evaluate the effectiveness of each.

A broad indication of the range of policies which can be applied to limiting the external costs of the motor vehicle are set out in Table 7.1. As can be seen, policies can broadly be divided between the market-based approaches and command-and-control measures, although in practices 'baskets' of instruments are usually employed. Further, the table reflects the ability to direct attention at various aspects of the problems and they can be aimed at the vehicle, the fuel used or at affecting the level and composition of traffic.

While it is useful at times, both for illustration and to retain a link between theory and policy, to refer to actual measures employed by transport authorities, the emphasis is on the direct economic implications of the alternative approaches rather than their political or social virtues. We begin by looking at the traditional 'Pigouvian solution', namely internalising external costs by charging those who generate them.

Table 7.1
Policy instruments to control environmental impacts of motor vehicles

	Market-based incentives		Command-and-control regulations	
	Direct	*Indirect*	*Direct*	*Indirect*
Vehicle	•Emissions fees	•Tradable permits •Differential vehicle taxation •Tax allowances for new vehicles	•Emissions standards	•Compulsory inspection and maintenance of emissions control systems •Mandatory use of low polluting vehicles •Compulsory scrappage of old vehicles
Fuel		•Differential fuel taxation •High fuel taxes	•Fuel composition •Phasing out of high polluting fuels	•Fuel economy standards •Speed limits
Traffic		•Congestion charges •Parking charges •Subsidies for less polluting modes	•Physical restraint of traffic •Designated routes	•Restraints on vehicle use • Bus lanes and other priorities

Source: Cabajo (1991)

7.2 The 'polluter–pays' principle

There is an inevitable problem with optimising externalities, as pointed out by Coase (1960) and this involves the perspective with which one looks at an externality. Coase argued that externalities could theoretically be removed by allocating environmental property rights either to polluters or those adversely affected and allowing trade to take place in those rights. There are clear practical problems of doing this, not least of which is that of policing the system, but the idea does pinpoint the symmetrical nature of externalities. Should those who suffer be protected or should those who benefit be compensated for desisting from their current transport activities? While from an efficiency perspective there is no clear answer, international agencies such as the Organisation for Economic Cooperation and Development have taken the line that morally those who pollute should pay for the excessive damage they cause the environment.

The idea is not a new one and the publication of Pigou's (1920) seminal work on *The Economics of Welfare* caused a large number of economists to examine the merits of adopting emissions charges. The idea is that the authorities take responsibility for the environment and charge users of the environment an appropriate price (or tax) for that use. Figure 7.1 provides an illustration of how such a charge would apply to transport. Without the internalisation of the external costs of traffic, let us say the noise of aircraft operating at an airport near a residential area, the traffic level would be at Q – the level which maximises the net private benefit to those using the airport. The noise would be at this level because the marginal net private benefit ($MNPB$) to the airport users falls with traffic until additional use offers no extra utility. (The $MNPB$ is simply the difference between the marginal private benefit and the marginal private cost of using the airport. Since increasing traffic can be expected to generate successively lower incremental private benefit, the curve will be negatively sloped.)This clearly exceeds the socially optimal traffic level Q^*, which is the point at which the $MNPB$ is equated with the marginal environmental costs (MEC) of the noise suffered by residents in the locality. To reduce traffic to this optimum a tax of t per unit of traffic would need to be imposed. This makes the aircraft operators aware of their social costs and stimulates them to treat ($MNPB{-}t$) as their relevant decision-making parameter.

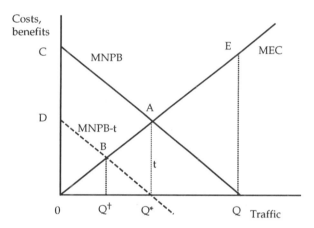

Figure 7.1
The idea of the Pigouvian tax

Such taxes, while not common, are increasingly being used in transport – the best-known example being the differential tax on leaded petrol which virtually all industrialised countries have adopted – Table 7.2.

While the basic concept is not difficult to appreciate it has been refined and argued over for the past seventy years. Perhaps the most important of these is the fact that it is the authorities who impose the Pigouvian tax who are the main beneficiaries. The airlines in our example lose. Those affected by the noise gain by some reduction in its level but are not freed entirely from it. The authorities gain revenues of $CDAQ^*$ by imposing the charge and the airlines suffer both this loss in terms of payments of the charge and the $MNPB$ previously enjoyed from the Q^*Q landings they no longer find viable, that is, a loss of Q^*AQ. From the residents' perspective, while the tax in Figure 7.1 will reduce activities to the level Q^*, and thus benefit them by $QEAQ^*$, they will still have to endure noise nuisance which is equal, in welfare terms, to OAQ^*.

Two important general points regarding the pricing approach however need to be made. First, in order to calculate the optimal pollution charge or price it is necessary to have reliable information about the *MEC* curve. As we have seen in Chapter 5, knowledge in this area is scant and although the use of, for example, hedonic house price indices may shed some light on the monetary importance of noise nuisance they are far from perfect. Additionally, evaluation of the marginal environmental costs of many other forms of pollution is, while improving with time, even less perfect should the principle be applied to externalities other than noise. Secondly, the revenue generated by the tax or price does not go directly to those affected by the noise nuisance that remains. (In terms of the criteria laid out later in Chapter 8, the policy does not result in a genuine Pareto improvement but rather a hypothetical one.) It is the government or local authority who enjoy a 'windfall' gain of *t* times *OQ** which may be used in compensation payments.

Table 7.2
Differential fuel taxation in EC countries (January 1990)

	Leaded Petrol		Unleaded petrol		Diesel	
	VAT(%)	Duty	VAT(%)	Duty	VAT(%)	Duty
Belgium	25.0	325	25.0	291	25.0	190.0
Denmark	22.0	424	22.0	343	22.0	223.0
Germany	14.0	321	14.0	281	14.0	218.0
Greece	36.0	198	36.0	152	6.0	4.0
Spain	12.0	331	12.0	316	12.0	190.0
France	18.6	448	18.6	397	18.6	231.0
Ireland	25.0	395	25.0	373	25.0	290.0
Italy	19.0	580	19.0	538	19.0	279.0
Luxembourg	12.0	234	6.0	140	12.0	101.0
Netherlands	18.5	346	18.5	342	18.5	158.0
Portugal	8.0	424	8.0	380	8.0	213.0
UK	15.0	277	15.0	240	15.0	234.0

At a rather more theoretical level, as we have indicated above, it is possible to question whether the 'polluter–pays' principle is being correctly applied in Figure 7.1 (Coase, 1960). We have implicitly assumed that the airport users should buy the right to create noise in the area, but this could be turned on its head, and the proposition presented that non-hauliers should buy the right to relative peace and quiet, that is, the hauliers should be *paid* a subsidy of *t* in the diagram to curtail their activities. The question is essentially a moral-legal one involving property rights although where there are actual administrative costs of introducing either prices or subsidies these should also be considered.

As Baumol and Oates (1975) have stressed, one of the problems of charging polluters is that information about the *MEC* curve is imperfect and that, even if some initially arbitrary price is charged, there is no indication of whether this is too high or too low. The usual 'trial and error' method of pricing used in industry is, therefore, not appropriate. Since information about the *MEC* curve is necessary for virtually all optimal containment of noise, irrespective of the method used, Baumol and Oates argue in favour of pricing on the grounds that it will cause less distortions than other policies. Their arguments have recently found favour with the Organisation for Economic Cooperation and Development (1975), who argue, 'The costs of these measures (to ensure that the environment is in an acceptable state) should be reflected in the cost of goods and services which cause pollution in production and/or consumption.' We extend our arguments to embrace two modes of transport, road haulage and railways, and in Figure 7.2 relate the marginal net private benefits associated with using each mode to the noise nuisance emitted. These curves are unknown to the authorities but it may be decided that it would be beneficial to do something about pollution rather than leave it at a high level. In these circumstances one may wish to reduce noise emissions by say 15 per cent and to use polluter charges to achieve this. Baumol and Oates (1975) demonstrate that a uniform charge on both road haulage and railway noise is the appropriate 'second-best' policy to pursue. In the figure the marginal abatement costs (MAC) of noise emissions for the two modes, road (A) and rail (B), are plotted out. These curves are not known with any degree of exactitude to policymakers. A mandatory reduction of 15 per cent for each mode would result in emissions being reduced to A and B for road haulage and rail respectively. While the desired objective has been satisfied, what one sees is that the MAC costs involved differ as between the modes – they are higher for road than for rail. It would be more cost-effective to reduce noise by a greater amount on the railways than on roads quite simply because it is cheaper per unit to cut emissions in the former. A noise emissions charge of P per unit per dB would automatically achieve the aimed for improvement because it would be more of an incentive to cut pollution where it is cheaper to do so (a level $B^{\dagger}$ for rail) and have smaller reductions where the costs of abatement are higher (to $A^{\dagger}$ road haulage).

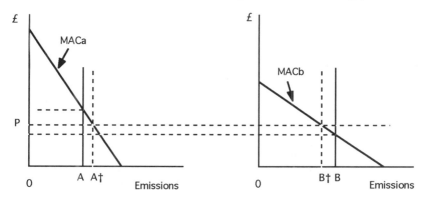

Figure 7.2
The advantage of fiscal instruments when there is uncertainty

The Baumol and Oates argument highlights the fact that if a particular standard is to be aimed for then the most efficient way of attaining it is by using fiscal instruments. One can see the particular importance of this in many transport contexts. Because of its very nature much transport activity is a mobile source of environmental intrusion but the domains in which it operates often differ in their sensitivity to its presence. Different airports, for example, because of their location and prevailing wind conditions impose different noise envelopes on their surrounding populations. The actual physical noise associated with any aircraft type may, therefore, impose different costs at different airports. To set a standard that all aircraft should reduce noise levels by a specified amount would thus be inefficient. A charge, on the other hand, which would bring about the same overall noise reduction would give the flexibility to airlines to use their quieter aircraft at locations where noise is a major nuisance and their older, noisier ones where the problem is less severe.

The 'polluter pays' principle tends to be favoured by many academics but it is not without its critics. Sharp (1979), for example, questions the distributional implications and argues that in some instances an environmental improvement may be obtained as efficiently by means of progressive taxation without the possible regressive effects of pollution charges. Essentially, the argument revolves around the fact that the benefits from any environmental improvement are closely related to income. A poor person would probably have a preference for no pollution charges (and *ipso facto* lower final money prices) than a wealthier person whose marginal utility of income is lower. Hence, from a distributional point of view, a subsidy of *t* in Figure 7.1 to the airport to suppress aircraft noise, financed from a progressive taxation system, will have the same environmental effect but none of the regressive features of the pollution charge.

While hardly common, pollution charges have been used in transport with some success. One clear illustration of where fiscal incentives (in this example, coupled with regulation) have proved particularly effective has been in reducing the levels of lead (Pb) pollution. Many countries have introduced significant tax differentials between leaded and unleaded gasoline but, equally, many have also initiated regulations regarding the fuels which can be sold. In particular, the banning of normal gasoline (providing the tank capacity for garages to stock unleaded fuel and leaving only the more expensive super) has effectively further reduced the real choice open to most automobile users in the Netherlands, Switzerland, the UK and Germany. The combined impact of these measures in the UK was a rise in vehicles using unleaded gasoline from 0.1 per cent of the car park in March 1988 to 25.9 percent in October 1989. Similarly, in the pre-unified FRG the percentage of automobiles using unleaded rose from 11 per cent in 1986 to 28 per cent in 1987.

7.3 Congestion charges

It is not only in the context of pollution that externality pricing has been advocated. One idea for optimising the level of congestion is to use the price mechanism to make travellers more fully aware of the impedance they impose upon one another. The idea is that motorists should pay for the additional congestion they create when entering a congested road or that aircraft should pay a premium to land at busy times of the day. In the case of road traffic, ideally, as with pollution charges, they should pay the actual road users affected but practically this is quite clearly impossible so the idea is that the relevant road authority or agency should be responsible for collecting the charges.

The optimal road price, as such a charge is called, reflects the difference between the marginal cost of trip-making and the average cost (as defined in Chapter 5). This means that in Figure 7.3, where we assume there is only the problem of simple interaction, the optimal road price per vehicle is *RP*, that is, the charge which equates the demand for road space with the *MC* curve. Road pricing generates a welfare gain of (*Pcde – abc*). This is because the traffic flow is reduced by (*Q–Q**) resulting in some motorists who are deterred from using the road, losing consumers' surplus of *abc* but, at the same time, the road authority collects revenues of *BP*de*. This revenue is not all a social benefit; a part of it (equal to *P*acP*) represents a transfer of consumers' surplus enjoyed by road users to the providing agency in the form of additional revenue. Providing the relevant section of the demand curve has a degree of elasticity then (*Pcde – abc*) must be positive and road pricing increases social surplus. It is important to note that it is the *providing agency* which directly benefits from the scheme, not road users. Of course, since it is either local or central government which collects the revenue, the monies raised *could* always be given back to motorists through some distributional mechanisms.

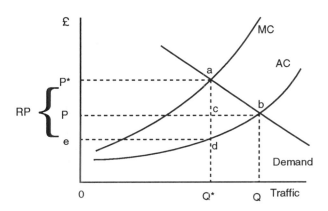

Figure 7.3
The optimal road price

The optimal level of road price has been the subject of much empirical work over the years and the results of some of the main studies are set out in Table 7.3. The number of desk-top studies has been considerable, and has been expanding in the early 1990s as governments in the UK and several other European countries, confronted with mounting congestion but constrained from expanding infrastructure by limited resources and considerable objections on environmental grounds, have begun to explore road pricing as a restraint strategy.

While the basic theory of road pricing is comparatively straightforward, its detailed implementation has been subject to debate. There several areas of controversy.

(1)   *The difficulty of devising a practical method of collection.* Congestion varies across urban areas but it is quite clearly impossible to make a separate charge for each segment of the road network. Some general attempt at this may be practicable in the long run if vehicles are fitted with automatically activated meters, charging rates that vary with traffic conditions, but then there arises the problem that motorists are only retrospectively made aware of the congestion costs of their trips. Such systems are also likely to prove expensive to install and administrate. Recent advances in 'smart-card' technology, however, indicate that these costs are now falling. Crude area licensing is cheaper and, since permits must be purchased before entering

specified urban zones, the full cost of a journey is made known to motorists before they enter congested streets – if they are still prepared to do so. The disadvantage of this simpler system is its insensitivity to changes in traffic conditions throughout the day.

Table 7.3
Estimates of the optimal road price

Study	Place	Road price at peak time (current prices)
Walters (1961)	Generic US Urban Expressway	$0.10–0.15/auto-mile
UK Ministry of Transport (1963)	Urban Areas in Great Britain	9d (old pence)/auto-mile
Greater London Council (1974)	Central London	£0.60/auto-day
Elliott (1975)	Los Angeles	$0.03–0.15/auto-mile
Kraus *et al.*(1976)	Twin-Cities Expressways, 1970	$0.03–0.15/auto-mile
Keeler and Small (1977)	Bay Area Expressways, 1972	$0.027–0.343/auto-mile
Dewees (1978)	Toronto, 1973	$0.04–0.38/auto-mile
Cheslow (1978)	Berkeley, 1977	$2.0/auto-trip
Spielberg (1978)	Madison, 1977	$1.0/auto-trip
Mohring (1979)	Twin-Cities	$0.66/auto-mile
Gomez-Ibanez and Fauth (1980)	Boston, 1975	$0.5–1.0/auto-mile
Viton (1980)	Bay Area Bridges, 1972	$0.154/auto-mile
Starrs and Starkie (1986)	Adelaide Arterial Roads 1982	A$0.025–0.22/auto-km
Cameron (1991)	Los Angeles Expressways	$0.15/auto-mile

Source: taken from Button (1984) and Morrison (1986) which contain full references to studies cited.

(2)   *The possibility of undesirable distribution repercussions.* With road pricing the use of roads depends upon the capabilities of potential users to pay the congestion charge. Whether this would result in undesirable regressive effects on social welfare is an empirical question. It is likely that public transport, which could move more freely, would provide a better service for the lower income groups which tend to patronise it. Also, the wealthy are likely to benefit from being able to 'buy' uncongested road space, a situation they value because of the importance they attach to time savings. In contrast, middle income groups could be forced to switch from private to public transport, a mode they consider inferior (Richardson, 1974). Interpersonal welfare comparisons of this type are difficult to make but it is possible, for example, that if some of the revenue from road pricing were directed towards further improvements in public transport (which may or may not mean heavily subsidised fares), then the adverse effects on the middle income group could be substantially reduced.

(3)   *There are difficulties in disposing of the revenues raised.* Sharp (1966) pointed out that the revenues from road pricing need to be reallocated with a degree of circumspection. While it has been suggested above that some of the money could be used, on distributional grounds, to improve public transport, strictly direct transfer payments to former road users are more efficient in achieving this objective. (Subsidies also pose problems for management in defining their operational objectives.) Direct transfers back to

former motorists, however, pose the problem that they are likely to use at least part of the money to 'buy-back' road space. An alternative method of compensating motorists adversely affected may be to use the road pricing revenues to construct more roads. Indeed, revenues from different areas offer a useful *general* guide to road building priorities. Despite this, investment decisions should be based upon a much wider range of criteria than simply the revenues raised from road pricing (see Chapter 9). Possibly a less controversial approach would be to treat the revenues as a pure tax income and to use them as part of general public expenditure, in this way wider problems of efficiency and distribution may be tackled. Goodwin (1989) has suggested that the pragmatic way around the problems would be to spread the revenue between more road expenditure, public transport investment and reductions in general taxation – the mix being initially equal but subsequently shaped by public debate.

(4)   *The impact on freight costs may prove inflationary if the road price is passed down to final consumers.* In fact, the inflationary impact is unlikely to be as great as some people suggest (Button, 1978). Urban transport costs only form a small part of final retail prices and, therefore, the imposition of road pricing is unlikely to have a significant effect on final prices. Additionally, since many of the costs of urban freight transport operations are time related, the reduced congestion which results from road pricing is likely to reduce substantially many costs of urban distribution and offset the financial cost of the road price. A desk study forming part of the Coventry Transportation Study confirms this.

(5)   *The demand functions for road use are more complex than the simple analysis suggests.* The analysis above has assumed that the demand for road space may be represented by a continuous function but in practice there may be kinks or discontinuities. Sharp (1966) implies that there may be no optimal road price because the demand situation is such that pricing would result in either too much traffic or too little depending upon the levy charged. This is a theoretical possibility. After all, the smooth curves used in basic analysis are only expositional aids, but, in fact, the actual form of the demand function is an empirical question which can only be resolved in the light of practical experience. There is, however, no *a priori* reason to suspect the demand for road space is *atypical* of demand curves in general.

(6)   *Road pricing is a first-best solution in a second-best world.* Marginal cost pricing of road space is only strictly optimal if all other goods in the economy are also marginal cost priced. However, since the overall demand for urban transport tends to be independent of the demand for other commodities providing that urban public transport pursues marginal cost pricing policies, no serious distortions within the transport sector should arise (see also Chapter 6).

Despite the theoretical speculation about the economic pros and cons of road pricing, practical implementations have been limited. Desk-top studies of possible schemes are being conducted in a number of British cities (most notably, Cambridge, Edinburgh and London) but political concern, combined with worries about distributional consequences, has discouraged implementation to date. One of the difficulties in the UK is the close economic interdependence of adjacent urban areas which makes the unilateral introduction of road pricing in one area extremely difficult. While there is only academic speculation about the probable effect of road pricing on British cities a limited number of road pricing experiments have been conducted elsewhere. Since May 1975, for example, Singapore has operated an area licensing system for rush hour traffic.

The Singapore scheme offers some practical evidence of the effects of congestion pricing (Behbehani *et al.,* 1984). The initial policy of simply charging for vehicles entering the centre of the city between 7.30 a.m. and 9.30 a.m. was found to be inadequate as traffic spread to either side of the licensing period and in August 1979 the period of licensing was extended to between 7.30 a.m. and 10.15 a.m. Later, an evening period of pricing was also brought in. The impact of the scheme was, nevertheless, impressive from its inception. There was an immediate reduction of 24,700 cars travelling during the peak period. Traffic speeds during the peak rose by about 22 per cent. While Table 7.4 indicates that there have been subsequent increases in traffic volume since 1975, these are considerably below the levels anticipated in the absence of road pricing. There was also some initial geographical spread of traffic to 'escape corridors' outside of the licensing area, but this was contained by adjusting traffic signals and other control measures on circumferential routes.

Table 7.4
The long-term effects of the Singapore Area Licensing Scheme

Time	Traffic March 1975	Traffic May 1976	Traffic May 1979	Traffic May 1983
Cars				
07.00–07.30	5384	5675	5723	6413
07.30–10.15	42790	10754	13181	15473
10.15–10.45	na	6459	5527	7069
All vehicles				
07.00–07.30	9800	10332	10596	11280
07.30–10.15	74014	35787	49606	57035
10.15–10.45	na	13441	15179	16490

Source: Behbehani *et al.* (1984)

The scheme was initially seen as part of a comprehensive package of measures embracing ring route designations and public transport, park-and-ride facilities. The latter proved singularly unsuccessful as commuters took to car pooling – since full cars were initially exempt from the licensing fee – rather than public transport. The minibuses forming the park-and-ride fleet were eventually diverted to other uses and the parking sites transformed into housing estates, tennis courts, etc. It was anticipated that the reduced morning traffic flow would be mirrored in the evening but evening peak hour traffic flow only declined by 3–4 per cent. This is because commuters diverting to escape corridors or travelling earlier in the morning had no incentive to do so at night while others engaging in car pooling were collected in the evening by other members of the family who, by adjusting their own daily routine, acted as chauffeurs after making trips into the city for shopping, recreation or other purposes. Road pricing, it appears, needs to be applied *directly* at times congestion occurs.

Cordon charges, although still far from widespread, are becoming increasingly common, with Bergen and Oslo being the most obvious examples. The motivation in most cases, however, is not strictly that of directly containing congestion but rather of revenue raising mainly for infrastructure building. Since a charge is levied in cordon schemes, however, it is almost inevitable that there will be some impact on travel behaviour and *ipso facto* they may have positive environmental implication. In some instances, such as Oslo (Solheim, 1990), an argument has also been advanced that since the revenue collected is to be used to construct ring road facilities, which in turn will ultimately reduce congestion, and to a lesser extent (some 10 per cent of revenue) fund public transport, there will be long-term positive secondary gains. Certainly, the indications from the scheme initiated in Bergen in 1986 (Larsen, 1988) are that cordons do impact in traffic flows crossing them. The Bergen scheme covers the period 6.00a.m. to 10.00p.m. hours each weekday, and consequently is not just confined to congested periods of the day, but it has induced a 6 to 7 per cent reduction in car traffic in the urban area.

There are two broad ways of implementing more sophisticated forms of electronic road pricing. The first uses automatic vehicle identification (AVI), which records centrally the congestion costs of individual trips for each vehicle. The second does not identify individual vehicles but deducts the cost of using congested roads from a stored value medium (similar to the current use of telephone cards) where the proprietor of the system is not able to establish who is using the facility. This latter approach, which might usefully be called non-smart-card technology, can be extended to the use of smart cards, similar to credit cards, which automatically debit the costs of trips directly from bank accounts or charges them to a credit card account (such as VISA).

There is very little practical experience of electronic road pricing. There has been experimentation with equipment and operational practices in Hong Kong (Dawson and Catling, 1986). On the operational side, the two-year experiment during the mid-1980s involved fitting over 2500 vehicles with AVIs together with the setting of electronic loops in the road surface at the edge of charge zones. When a vehicle crossed a boundary, a power loop energised its AVI which in turn sent a message, via inductive receiver loops, to a road-side recorder. What it did was to give some credence to the view expressed in the Smeed Report that metering devices could be 'developed into an efficient charging system' (UK Ministry of Transport, 1964). The technical and economic feasibility of the electronic road pricing system used was found to have achieved 99 per cent effectiveness and reliability against the criteria set it.

There are, however, practical difficulties with the Hong Kong style of road pricing, especially in terms of devising a mechanism enabling its phased introduction on a large scale and of road users having a poor idea of the road price they must pay in advance of making a trip.

The Netherlands has been particularly forward in advocating the adoption of such systems and recently, although now postponed, plans were drawn up to have electronic road pricing based on this technology operational in the west of the Netherlands (the Randstad) by the mid-1990s . The objectives were partly environmental as set out in the Second Transport Structure Plan and explicitly aimed at reducing the growth of car traffic. Political factors, however, watered down the extent to which electronic road pricing will actually be deployed and the plan has become little more than a scheme for automatic tolling for tunnels. Interest in electronic road pricing also has a long history in the UK and there is the possibility that Cambridge will adopt a form of it to combat its severe traffic congestion problems. The system proposed employs dedicated, non-smart cards from which the road-user charge is deducted.

While the Singapore scheme has shown that road pricing can reduce congestion successfully, the effect of any scheme seems rather more difficult to forecast than some advocates suggested. The actual details of this scheme are obviously tailored to the geography and political climate of Singapore and replication elsewhere may result in somewhat different effects. It is also questionable whether the actual prices charged are truly optimal or whether they are excessively high (Toh, 1977), acting as a method of revenue collection for the government as much as an instrument of microeconomic resource allocation. Quite clearly transport may be a legitimate field for pure indirect taxation but in assessing the effectiveness of a road pricing scheme it is important to isolate the price efficiency aspect from that of taxation *per se*.

Roads are not the only area where congestion pricing has been advocated. Walters (1976), for example, has argued that appropriate marginal cost pricing (including congestion charges) is 'no panacea for ailing or congested ports, but it does supply a useful set of principles to deploy in the discussion of port pricing policy'. Others have considered the benefits of its use at airports (Morrison and Winston, 1989). Focusing on ports, the general principles are identical to road pricing (a rigorous framework has been provided by Vanags, 1977), but in some circumstances the nature of the shipping industry may result in complications. In the road context there is a monopoly supplier adopting social pricing policies coupled with competition for road space amongst many, uncoordinated potential users. While the majority of ports conform to this type of market situation, in some instances the port authorities are confronted by a monopoly (or, more likely, a cartel) of shipping companies.

Figure 7.4 shows the demand curve for shipping (the demand for port services may be seen as proportional to this) in terms of total import and export traffic. The port is assumed to have constant marginal handling costs, OH, which are passed to the ship owners as port charges. The shipping companies, if competitive, would then charge these customers an additional amount, RH, to reflect their own average costs, to give a total shipping rate of OR. The AC of shipping will itself rise after a certain point as port congestion forces queuing to load and discharge. Since the AC curve does not reflect the true costs of increasing traffic the port authority should, on welfare economic grounds, levy a congestion charge of AB. Assuming there is no potential for modifying the types of ship in service or methods of cargo handling this will reduce the tonnage passing through the port from T_1 to the optimal level T_2. This is identical to the road-pricing case.

Suppose that instead of a competitive shipping market, the port was used exclusively by a closed liner conference. There are now two important differences. Firstly, the conference, being the sole operator, will bear the costs of congestion itself – the congestion costs are internalised. Secondly, the conference is likely to act as a monopolist (although, as we have seen in the previous chapter countervailing powers act as a limited constraint in practice) and be more concerned with the marginal revenue curve than with demand. Thus the ship owner will charge customers a rate of OS for his services which comprise (i) port fees, OH; (ii) his own costs, including that of congestion, HU; and (iii) economic, monopoly, rent, US. The tonnage passing through the port is now suboptimally small at OT_3.

Although one might argue that in this situation the optimal use of the port could, technically, in some situations, be achieved by *not* charging a congestion

toll and by *reducing* port fees below *OH* (see Bennathan and Walters, 1979), this
rather evades the real problem, namely the monopoly power of the shipping conference. Such a policy also places excessive power in the hands of the conference
when negotiating with port authorities the fees (and, *ipso facto,* the subsidy) to be
charged. The solution here is to tackle distortions at source, namely, in the shipping market, rather than maladjust port prices.

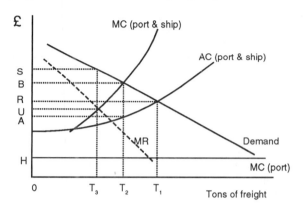

Figure 7.4
Port congestion pricing

7.4 Parking charges

In some cases, often for political reasons but also possibly because it is more cost
effective to operate, a parking charging policy may appear preferable to road pricing as a means of containing congestion externalities. This is particularly true if
much of the traffic is terminating in the area concerned. Again, while the most
extensive coverage of parking is in the context of urban car traffic, the principles
are equally valid for airports or seaports – for example, high standing charges for
aircraft at air terminals can stimulate changes in flight patterns and traffic concentrations.

A simple way to look at the role of parking fees (Verhoef *et al.*, 1992) is set in
Figure 7.5. Quadrant A has the marginal cost and average cost curves (where we
assume simple interaction congestion to be the only externality) but added to this
is the cost of parking (reflecting the opportunity costs of parking space and
assuming for simplicity that each individual's parking duration is identical). This
gives the combined costs curve of *TMC*. The optimal road price plus parking fee,
with regard to traffic density, then become *RP* in the diagram. We now take the
extreme case that for some reason the road price element of *RP* cannot be collected.

On the assumption that all vehicles paying appropriate prices which enter
during the study period will find parking, then we can draw the 45° line in
quadrant B of the diagram which relates traffic density to parking occupancy.
The parking fee for the period, *F*, required to achieve this is then mapped out in
quadrant C. This demand curve again assumes that willingness to pay the set fee
will guarantee a parking place; if this assumption is not valid because of

suboptimal capacity the analysis requires modification (see Douglas, 1975). The demand curve for parking places is derived from the difference between *Demand* and the *AC* in quadrant A. The parking fee here is acting as a rationing device and its size could be adjusted accordingly if a suboptimal road price were initiated at some later date.

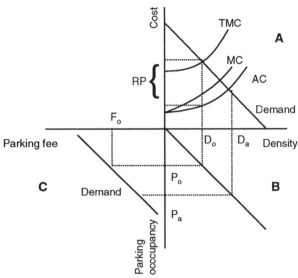

Figure 7.5
A simple analysis of parking charges

Parking policy has its own limitations. It obviously has little impact on through traffic and, indeed, by terminating stopping traffic, may actually encourage it in city centres. It also has distributional consequences. In particular, it bears more heavily on those making short journeys since the parking fee will form a relatively larger part of the overall costs of their trips compared to those driving a greater distance. The policy is also likely to be relatively insensitive to actual levels of congestion since it is acting on a complement to road use rather than road use itself. From a practical perspective, many parking places are privately owned (see Table 7.5) and hence direct control of prices is difficult for policy-makers although indirect measures, such as taxing land used for parking, provide a mechanism for tackling the problem (Higgins, 1992).

7.5 Emissions standards

Figure 7.1 indicates that external costs can be optimised by charging a pollution price of t. It is equally possible, however, that rather than operate the pricing mechanisms the desired output of OQ^* could be obtained by, for example, setting emissions standards limiting the noise generated by aircraft. In practice this has been the approach of the UK authorities with the establishment of 'noise abatement zones' and the controls embodied in a series of Road Traffic Acts which have, since 1973, laid down regulations regarding car silencers and exhausts. Noise standards were introduced at the manufacturing stage for new lorries in 1970 with limits of 91dB(A) for vehicles with engines over 200 hp and 89dB(A) for less powerful lorries while from March 1983 new vehicles coming into production had to meet more stringent requirements of 88dB(A) and 86dB(A) respectively. Supranational legislation has gained in importance recently with the EC setting vehicle noise limits (Vougias, 1992). The Civil Aviation Act 1971 lays down regulations about night movements over built-up areas and specifies overfly patterns for aircraft. The speed limits operative on roads are primarily designed to reduce accident risk – with some supplementary effects on fuel economy. The compulsory wearing of seat-belts in many countries is also to reduce accident costs. Similarly, the periodic testing of vehicles and the licensing of lorries, aircraft, etc. are to ensure that minimum safety and environmental standards are achieved. In many overseas countries the regulations are more stringent (for example, the removal of lead from petrol in the USA, and stricter annual checks on pollution emissions from internal combustion engines in New Jersey and Oregon) or take different forms (such as airbags in cars in the USA) but their intended effect is the same, to reduce the marginal environmental cost of transport.

Table 7.5
Distribution of city centre non-residential parking stock (%) in the UK (1976)

City	On-street	Public off-street	Private off-street
Bristol	21	19	60
Cambridge	16	24	60
Huddersfield	21	42	37
London	17	30	53
Nottingham	25	37	38
Oxford	26	16	58
Reading	22	56	22
Southampton	34	22	44
Wolverhampton	9	59	32

Source: Armitage (1977)

While all the above represent physical regulations to contain pollution they should strictly be divided between those controls that act directly to contain the externality (for example, noise emission legislation) and those that control transport in such a way as to reduce the external costs (for example, lorry routes and aircraft flight path regulations). The effects of these alternative broad sets of physical controls are not the same. Actual emission standards act directly to limit the external effects permitting other characteristics of operations to be adjusted freely. The operational regulations impose much more stringent controls, severely limiting the alternative courses of action open to the operator. With noise emissions standards for aircraft flying over an area, for instance, an airline can either conform and pay the costs of suppressing noise or avoid the area in question; with operational controls only the latter option is available. This point should be borne in mind during the more general discussion of physical controls which follows.

We return to the question of operational restrictions, traffic calming and vehicle routing in a more general context in Section 7.7.

While in the simple case illustrated in Figure 7.1 the effect of an optimal standard produces an identical level of road transport activity (and, *ipso facto,* environmental intrusion) to an optimal pollution charge, it can be argued that, with more realistic assumptions, the pricing approach offers a superior solution to the externality problem. Lowe and Lewis (1980) argue that even if full information permitted the alternative policies to be applied optimally, the standards/regulation approach can lead to excess capacity in airport provision. The argument is that while any airport would have to conform to the standard, the fact that there is no need actually to pay for the cost of remaining pollution (that is, area $0AQ^*$) may result in too many airports being constructed. While this type of problem is theoretically possible, it is most likely to occur in sectors such as road haulage or inter-urban bus services which are highly competitive and fragmented, and where the size of the industry depends mainly upon new entrants or firms leaving. It is less relevant to monopoly or oligopolistic modes of transport where movement into and out of the sector is less important.

When information about the exact shape of the *MEC* curve is poor, the use of standards is demonstrably less efficient than the Baumol–Oates charging approach seen in Figure 7.2. If, in order to achieve the 15 per cent reduction in transport noise used in our example, both road and rail were compelled to cut their noise emissions (that is, to $OA^\dagger$ and $OB^\dagger$ respectively), then it is clear from the diagram that the marginal net private benefits generated by the two modes are no longer equal (at the new emission levels, $MAC_a > MAC_b$) Consequently, social welfare could be improved by lowering the standard for road haulage and increasing it for rail. Unfortunately in the real world lack of perfect knowledge of the *MAC* curves means that the optimal differentiation of standards is likely to be impossible to define. Thus in this imperfect situation, the 'polluter-pays' principle is almost certainly going to prove superior to the use of emission standards.

It is probable that pollution pricing will prove more flexible than standards. While transport infrastructure may impose external costs of visual intrusion it is normally the mobile unit which generates the greatest external costs. Given the differing income levels and preference patterns in various parts of the country one could re-interpret the *MAC* curves in Figure 7.2 in terms of the marginal abatement associated with a single mode but operating in different parts of the country. In this case the uniform emissions charge would be both theoretically superior and, in addition, reduce the costs to transport undertakings of reducing their noise emissions. The imposition of different standards for each area means that operators must either ensure that vehicles moving between areas conform to the most stringent standards or have specific, variously suppressed vehicles designed to conform with local regulations. Both options are likely to be wasteful. With a charging regime, the operator can select a vehicle mix that minimises his overall costs of operation – vehicles may be suppressed or pay the emissions price *or* they may be subjected to a combination of the two.

Moving to a more dynamic situation, where technology is variable, Maler (1974) has suggested that pollution prices have important advantages over regulations for the encouragement of a rapid adoption of cleaner technologies. His argument rests upon the implicit assumption that transport suppliers, when confronted with either a pollution price or emissions standard, assume this price or standard to be fixed in the medium term irrespective of their individual action. Consequently they will always assess the benefits to themselves of adopting new

Chapter 7

operating methods or technologies against *existing* prices or standards. In Figure 7.6 we show the marginal private costs of reducing exhaust fumes for a road haulier confronted with the existing technology (MC_1) and with the new technology (MC_2). The MC_2 curve is inside MC_1 because it is cheaper to quieten vehicles with the new technology at all noise levels. On the assumption that the authorities have full information on *MEC* and can, therefore, define the optimal level of traffic noise we see that either a pollution charge of *OP* or a standard of *OC* will ideally be in force. If the pricing policy is pursued the haulier will find it financially worthwhile to quieten his vehicle by CD_1 (costing CD_1B) and pay *OCBP* in charges. With a standard he pays no pollution charges but it costs him CD_1B to conform to the noise regulation. However, if the new technology is available an individual haulier will perceive, *ceteris paribus,* the benefits of adopting it as D_2EBD_1 if there is a charging policy operative, that is, he will reduce his emissions with the new technology to OD_2 (costing AHD_2 and pay charges of *OPHA.* The incentive to adopt the alternative technology with the emissions standard is only *debc,* that is, the cost of conforming to the standard with the new technology rather than the old. Thus the pollution charging policy offers an incentive of the shaded area, *abe,* in excess of an emissions standard to move to the cleaner technology.

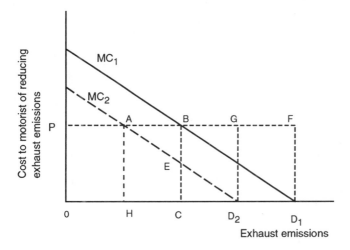

Figure 7.6
Pollution charges, emission standards and technical change

One possible option is a combined environmental tax/standards approach whereby all vehicles are obliged to meet a set standard and there is a scale of emissions-related 'fines' for vehicles which exceed this. If the standard were rigorous and well below the existing level of emissions (that is, consistent with the optimal level of pollution with the cleaner technology in our example above), then this would be as effective as the pricing approach and at the same time offer a firm target for vehicle operators to aim at. Such a tax/standards approach may, however, be particularly appealing at the vehicle manufacturing stage where new technology can most easily be injected into the transport sector.

7.6 Transport subsidies and the environment

An alternative to operating directly upon the transport undertaking generating externalities (either pollution or congestion) is to offer a carrot for transport users to switch to more socially desirable modes. This line of reasoning has been widely used as a partial justification for the large subsidies given to support the railways and urban transport services. In the UK, the Railways Act 1974, for example, permitted government grants of up to 50 per cent of the costs to be paid to British Rail customers for the installation of sidings and provision of rolling stock on the basis of an assessment of the environmental harm of the lorry movements which would be avoided if the investment concerned went ahead. The 1968 Transport Act initiated a system of centrally and locally financed public transport operating and capital subsidies (the latter of which has subsequently been abandoned) with the objective of containing the growth in private motor traffic in the large urban areas. In a perfectly competitive world there would be no justification for this type of policy but in a situation where marginal cost pricing is not universal and where political expedience leans against the introduction of measures such as road pricing, subsidies may offer a pragmatic second-best approach to the externality problem.

Where the cross-elasticity of demand between transport and other goods is negligible and the overall demand for transport is totally inelastic – a situation not unrealistic in the context of commuter travel in many large urban areas – the optimal subsidy to a zero externality generating transport mode will have the same effect on the use of an externality generating mode as pollution charges. In Figure 7.7, the total demand for transport, which is supplied by private cars and a light rapid transit system, is fixed. Cars have associated with their use external costs to the difference between the MPC_c and the MSC_c, the LRT system has no such externalities associated with its use (that is, $MSC_{LRT}=MPC_{LRT}$) and for simplicity we assume it is a constant cost form of transport. The free market outcome, where no cognisance is taken of externalities, will be a division of traffic at point $OQ^\dagger$ in the diagram. The optimal solution is a spit of Q^* which may be brought about by charging a pollution tax of the level indicated or alternatively subsidising the public transport mode by an identical amount. The modal split effects are the same.

If aggregate demand is not perfectly inelastic then the optimal subsidy is more difficult to define although it may still offer a second-best solution to the externality problem. Figure 7.8 shows the cost conditions for the externality generating mode (the car) with a demand curve for its services of D_c. It also shows the cost and demand for the public transport mode, *pt*. A subsidy for mode Y will cause D_c to shift to the left (say to D'_c), reducing the dead-weight welfare loss associated with the suboptimally high level of car usage. (Unless, however, the demand for car use is pushed so far left that it intersects the cost curves in some area where $MPC_c= MSC_c$ – a dead-weight loss will remain.) As with Figure 7.7 the subsidy itself will also result in some loss of welfare. The fall in the cost of car use as people switch to public transport will have the effect of pulling back the demand for the latter to D'_{pt} and thus reduce the amount actually needed to fund the optimal subsidy. The ultimate cost of the subsidy is sub times Q' which exceeds the area of net consumer surplus enjoyed at the subsidised fare level by *wxy*. If we denote the dead-weight loss saving associated with the reduced level of demand for car as *abcd* (that is, the area between MSC_c and MPC_c as D_c shifts to the left) then the optimal subsidy can be defined as that which maximises the difference between the gain from reducing the dead-weight loss of excessive congestion minus the efficiency cost of the subsidy. In the diagram, the subsidy which will maximise [(*abcd*) – (*wxy*)].

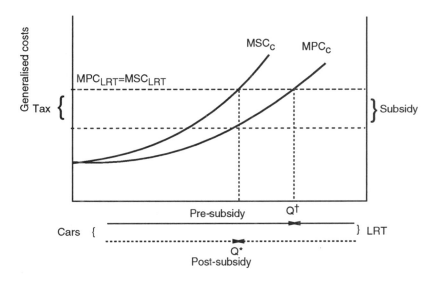

Figure 7.7
Optimal subsidy with fixed aggregate demand for travel

The practical difficulty with this approach is that the optimal subsidy may be extremely large and, theoretically, if the cross-elasticity of demand between modes is low, may even result in negative fares. The use of public transport subsidies in urban areas has been questioned for this very reason. In an early survey, Kemp (1973) found that in general the direct fare elasticity for urban public transport was low (–0.1 to –0.7), suggesting that substantial subsidies are necessary to attract passengers to public transport irrespective of whether they constitute new travellers or those diverted from private cars. Baum's (1973) work is even less optimistic, yielding fare elasticities in the range from –0.1 to –0.4 for Britain, the US and West Germany. The findings of these studies have been generally supported by more recent analysis of direct fare elasticities by Goodwin (1992) who in surveying 50 studies found that the short-term elasticity seems to be about –0.41 which rises to about –0.55 after four years and to –0.65 after a decade. He concludes,

> Thus in the short term, bus demand remains, as traditionally thought, inelastic enough to make revenue raising by fare increases an effective policy, but demand increases by fare reductions (for example to assist congestion) rather limited. But in the longer run the effectiveness of the first policy is reduced, and of the second is increased.

This problem is compounded by two further points. First, is the issue of the degree to which there may be leakage from subsidies into, for example, X-inefficiency in the management of the system. There are methods of tendering which, for example, are being used in the UK to minimise such losses but it is not altogether certain that they may not meet problems in the longer term as incumbent subsidised operators essentially enjoy economies of experience over potential new suppliers. Second, there is the question of the nature of the subsidy required. Fare subsidies, for example, may be of social importance in income distribution terms but often it is quality of service (that is, frequency, reliability, amenities, etc.) which is of more importance to commuters.

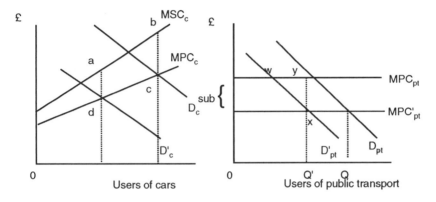

Figure 7.8
Optimal subsidy with elastic aggregate demand for travel

7.7   Protecting the sufferers

The strategies examined so far have relied upon either forcing the generator of externalities to change his production process or encouraging the adoption of a different method of operation. We have only touched upon the idea of insulating the public from environmental intrusion (that is, in the context of aircraft landing path controls and lorry routes). Insulation in the short term may be achieved either by directing traffic away from sensitive areas or by physically protecting people and property (for example, with double glazing for sound insulation) while in the longer term new investment permits a more efficient separation of transport from those sensitive to its wider impact (the main reason for the official rejection of the Roskill Commission's recommendations on the siting of a Third London Airport was that an inland site would be excessively damaging to the country's environment – see Chapter 8).

The *Armitage Report* (UK Department of Transport, 1980) goes as far as to recommend the establishment of 'Lorry Action Areas' to protect residents living in a limited number of areas but who suffer from the worst environmental effects of road freight transport. Specifically such areas would involve:

(1)   the installation of double glazing in houses, which would reduce considerably the major problem of noise in homes;
(2)   grants for repairs to houses physically damaged by lorries;
(3)   maintaining road surfaces to high standards, which would reduce vibrations;
(4)   minor road improvements to reduce accidents and to reduce noise, for example, by the use of noise absorbing road surfaces;

(5)   the building up of pavements or erection of bollards to reduce the problems of vehicles cutting corners and of damage to buildings through physical contact; and

(6)   in the worst cases of intense local nuisance by a specific generator of lorry traffic, compensation for discontinuance action taken by a planning authority in respect of a site with planning permission or existing use rights.

The difficulty with protective options, both long- and short-term, is that their effects are often much wider than simply protecting sensitive groups in the community and their overall cost may be considerable. Limiting the flight paths of aircraft can both increase the risk of accident (by forcing the adoption of less safe climbing and turning patterns) and increase the cost of operations (especially energy costs). Similarly, lorry routing both necessitates higher infrastructure costs and often leads to longer trip distances.

In the longer term it should, theoretically, be easier to design the spatial economy so that transport's effect on the environment is significantly lower. Many options are available (Foster and Mackie, 1970), including:

(1)   sterilisation of land between nuisance and dwellings;
(2)   use non-sensitive buildings (for example, light industry) as barriers between nuisance and sensitive areas;
(3)   design dwellings so that little-used rooms confront the nuisance rather than living rooms or bedrooms;
(4)   make use of self-protecting developments – for example patio style housing – to reduce intrusion.

Such designs obviously generate additional costs and only provide a partial solution to the environmental problem. Like most of the shorter-term protective measures they only ameliorate those aspects of environmental costs inflated while people are at home. Land-use planning may offer some limited protection at other times especially in the reduction of accident risk – but it is unlikely to separate completely transport from the non-traveller.

One should also perhaps include under protective measures the notion of traffic calming. This entails the use of such things as road humps, speed tables, raised junctions, reduced carriageway widths and 'changed road surfaces' both to slow traffic flows and to encourage the use of particular 'suitable' links in the network or alternative modes. Essentially the idea is to make streets more attractive and liveable. In Europe traffic calming has tended to come about as part of wider packages and has often been tied to legal speed limits of 30kph and, in the Netherlands, to a walking pace limit. The latter is part of the country's *Woonerven* – where road users have equal rights to road space. In the UK, traffic calming schemes have come about more as part of a policy to reduce urban traffic speed for safety reasons – about 70 per cent of schemes have this as a primary objective. Evidence from Germany suggests that serious casualties have fallen by up to 50 per cent in areas where it has been introduced, for example by 44 per cent in Heidelberg.

7.8   Some conclusions
The optimisation of the external effects of transport is a complicated matter. The previous sections have indicated the pros and cons of alternative courses of action, highlighting specifically the difficulties of putting theoretical solutions into

practice. One of the biggest problems which has only been touched upon in passing is that many externalities are interrelated and cannot adequately be handled in a partial framework. Many of the relationships are joint and a reduction of vehicle noise, for example, is often accompanied by less air pollution but this is not always so. Larger lorries, for example, may involve greater individual intrusion but at the same time fewer lorries are required. Road pricing may act to optimise urban traffic congestion but in doing so diverts traffic through areas sensitive to noise and vibration; a faster traffic flow is also likely to result in fewer but more serious accidents.

To date policies have been piecemeal, usually focusing on modes of transport rather than directly on transport externalities and, generally, with the explicit objective of reducing the effect of different modes rather than optimising them. This suggests that the social objective of government policy has been one of satisficing rather than optimising although it has been argued that the actual effect of some regulations has been excessive. Schwing *et al.* (1980) have, for instance, suggested that the US Clean Air Act of 1970 imposed car exhaust emission levels which were far too stringent, with a consequential welfare loss. Table 7.6 presents the results of their cost-benefit study. While the high benefit estimate suggests some welfare advantage from the Act, the underlying assumptions required to reach this conclusion are deemed very unrealistic. The optimal levels for the toxic exhaust emissions were estimated to be 0.73 per cent, 0.31 per cent and 0.82 per cent control for nitrogen oxides (NO_x), carbon monoxides (CO) and hydrocarbons (HC) respectively.

Table 7.6
The cost and benefit of the US Clean Air Act 1970

Benefit estimate	% Control level			Benefit (10^9)	Cost (10^9)	Net benefit (10^9)
	HC	CO	NO			
Low	0.98	0.97	0.94	9	65	− 56
Prime	0.98	0.97	0.94	34	65	− 31
High	0.98	0.97	0.94	102	65	37

Source: Schwing *et al.* (1980)

Piecemeal approaches were also studied from a different perspective by Crandall *et al.* (1986). They were concerned about the conflicts which arose in the USA between the setting of safety standards (by Highway Traffic Safety Administration), emissions standards (by Congress and administered by the Environmental Protection Agency) and fuel economy measures (set by Congress and administered by the Environmental Protection Agency). While static conflicts emerge as technically unavoidable (for example, the safety regulations initiated in the USA between 1968 and 1982 pushed average car weights up by 136lbs and increased fuel consumption by 3.5 per cent which conflicted with measures aimed at fuel efficiency and emissions controls), the dynamic effects of uncoordinated policies, for instance, slowing down replacement of older, less socially desirable cars was a serious administrative failure.

The acceptability of this type of work would be questioned by environmentalists in terms of both the items included in the cost-benefit calculations and the valuations placed upon them. The problem, common to most studies of environmental aspects of transport, is the inadequacy of knowledge both about the actual physical impact of the various external effects generated by transport and about the values society places upon them. Until some clear understanding of these matters is obtained it is difficult to see how the external effects of transport are likely to approach the optimal level.

7.9   Further reading and references

Road pricing is a well researched subject area but is still open to some controversy. Walters (1968) is still the seminal work on the subject and justifies continual re-reading. A well written and comprehensive review of the recent literature on road pricing is contained in Morrison (1986) while Chartered Institute of Transport (1990) offers a less technical introduction to the topic.. Singapore offers the only major application of road pricing and the reader is thoroughly recommended to read some of the references cited in the chapter, but should these be difficult to obtain, Behbehani, *et al* (1984) offers a good survey of the work. The *Armitage Report* (UK Department of Transport, 1980) provides some useful comment on the relative merits of different policies towards the externalities associated with heavy lorries. The paper by Foster (1974), although now nearly twenty years old, offers possibly the most thorough discussion of the different approaches to contain the specific externalities generated by urban traffic movement and extends the argument beyond the simple issue of economic efficiency. Button (1993) provides an up-dating of some of this material. Barde and Button (1990) offers case studies of national approaches to containing environmental problems and Banister and Button (1993) a collection of papers on the subject.

References

Armitage, G.S. (1977), 'Traffic restraint – a function parking control', *Proceedings of PTRC Summer Annual Meeting, Seminar L*, London, PTRC.

Banister, D. and Button, K.J. (eds)(1993), *Transport, the Environment and Sustainable Development* , London, Spon.

Barde, J.-P. and Button, K.J. (eds)(1990), *Transport Policy and the Environment: Six Case Studies*, London, Earthscan.

Baum, H.J. (1973), 'Free public transport', *Journal of Transport Economics and Policy,* 7, 3–19.

Baumol, W.J. and Oates, W.E. (1975), *The Theory of Environmental Policy: Externalities, Public Outlays and the Quality of Life,* New York, Prentice-Hall.

Behbehani, R., Pendakur, V.S. and Armstrong Wright, A.T. (1984), *Singapore Area Licensing Scheme: A Review of the Impact*, Washington: World Bank Water Supply and Urban Development Department.

Bennathan, E. and Walters, A.A. (1979), *Port Pricing and Investment Policy for Developing Countries,* Oxford, Oxford University Press

Button, K.J. (1978), 'A note on the road pricing of commercial traffic', *Transportation Planning and Technology*, 4, 175–8.

Button, K.J. (1984), 'Road pricing – an outsider's view of American experiences', *Transport Reviews*, 4, 73–98.

Button, K.J. (1992), 'Transport regulation and the environment in low income countries', *Utilities Policy*. 2, 248–57.

Button, K.J. (1993), *Transport, the Environment and Economic Policy*, Aldershot, Edward Elgar.

Cabajo, J. (1991), 'Accident and air pollution externalities in a system of road user charges', Informal Working Paper, Washington: World Bank.

Chartered Institute of Transport (1990), *Paying for Progress: A Report on Congestion and Road Pricing*, London, Chartered Institute of Transport.

Coase, R.H. (1960), 'The problem of social cost', *Journal of Law and Economics, 3,* 1–44.

Crandall, R.W., Grueenspecht, H.K., Keeler, T.E. and Lave, L.B. (1986), *Regulating the Automobile,* Washington, Brookings Institution.

Dawson, J.A.L. and Catling, I. (1986), 'Electronic road pricing in Hong Kong', *Transportation Research,* 20A, 129–34.

Douglas, R.W. (1975), 'A parking model – the effects of supply on demand', *American Economists,* 19, 85–6.

Foster, C.D. (1974), 'Transport and the environment' J.G. Rothenberg and I.G. Heggie (eds), *Transport and the Urban Environment,* London, Macmillan.

Foster, C.D. and Mackie, P.J. (1970), 'Noise: economic aspects of choice', *Urban Studies,* 7, 123–35.

Goodwin, P.B. (1989), 'The rule of three: a possible solution to the political problem of competing objectives for road pricing', *Traffic Engineering and Control,* 29, 495–7.

Goodwin, P.B. (1992), 'A review of new demand elasticities with special reference to short and long run effects of price changes', *Journal of Transport Economics and Policy,* 26, 155–63.

Higgins, T.J. (1992), 'Parking taxes, effectiveness, legality, and implementation, some general considerations', *Transportation,* 19, 221–30.

Kemp, M.A. (1973), 'Some evidence of transit demand elasticities', *Transportation,* 2. 25–52.

Larsen, O.I., (1988), 'The toll ring in Bergen Norway – the first year of operation', *Traffic Engineering and Control,* 22, 216–22.

Lowe, J. and Lewis, D. (1980), *The Economics of Environmental Management,* London, Philip Allan.

Maler, K.G. (1974), 'Environmental policies and the role of the economist in influencing public policy', in J.G. Rothenberg and I.G. Heggie (eds), *Transport and the Urban Environment,* London, Macmillan.

Morrison, S.A. (1986), 'A survey of road pricing', *Transportation Research,* 20A, 87–97.

Morrison, S.A. and Winston, C. (1989), 'Enhancing the performance of the deregulated air transportation system', *Brookings Papers on Economic Activity (Microeconomic Issue),* 61–112.

Organisation for Economic Cooperation and Development (1975), *The Polluter Pays Principle,* Paris, OECD.

Pigou, A. (1920), *The Economics of Welfare,* London, Macmillan.

Richardson, H.W. (1974), 'A note on the distributional effects of road pricing', *Journal of Transport Economics and Policy,* 8, 82–5.

Royal Commission on Environmental Pollution (1972), *First Report,* London, HMSO.

Schwing, R.C., Southworth, B.W., von Buseck, C.R. and Jackson, C.J. (1980), 'Benefit-cost analysis of automotive emission reductions', *Journal of Environmental Economics and Management,* 7, 44–64.

Sharp, C.H. (1966), 'Congestion and welfare: an examination of the case for a congestion tax', *Economic Journal,* 76, 806–17.

Sharp, C.H. (1979), 'The environmental impact of transport and the public interest', *Journal of Transport Economics and Policy,* 13, 88–101.

Solheim, T. (1990), 'The toll-ring in Oslo', paper presented to the Ecology and Transport Conference, Gothenburg.

Toh, R. (1977), 'Road congestion pricing: the Singapore experience', *Malayan Economic Review,* 22, 52–61.

UK Department of Transport (1980), *Report of the Inquiry into Lorries, People and the Environment* (Armitage Report), London, HMSO.

UK Ministry of Transport (1964), *Road Pricing: The Economic and Technical Possibilities,* London, HMSO.

Vanags, A.H. (1977), 'Maritime congestion: an economic analysis', in R.O. Goss (ed), *Advances in Maritime Economics,* Cambridge, Cambridge University Press.

Verhoef, E.T., Nijkamp, P. and Rietveld, P. (1992), 'De economie van parkeermanagement systemen', paper presented to Vervoersplanologisch Srewwek 1992, CVS, Delft.

Vouglas, S. (1992), 'Transport and environmental policy in the EC', *Transport Reviews*, 12, 219–36.

Walters, A.A. (1968), *The Economics of Road User Charges*, Baltimore, Johns Hopkins Press.

Walters, A.A. (1976) 'Marginal cost pricing in ports', *Logistics andTransportation Review*, 12, 99–105.

8 Investment Criteria - Private and Public Sector Analysis

8.1 The importance of infrastructure

The preceding chapters have been primarily concerned with making the best use of an existing transport network or fleet of vehicles. They have, therefore, principally focused on short-term problems involving the management, regulation and pricing of an established transport system. In particular, they were concerned with emphasising the central role of marginal cost pricing (including social costs) in encouraging the optimal utilisation of transport facilities. There is, however, a longer-term aspect to be considered, namely possible changes in the size or nature of the basic transport system by either investment or disinvestment. In the case of road haulage, airline and shipping operations, the commercial nature of decision-making bodies means that changes are normally analysed in terms of their financial repercussions. With road track, railways and port authorities, which in most countries are owned by public agencies, the provision of basic infrastructure is usually determined by looking at much wider considerations.

Before moving on to look at some of the key techniques employed in investment analysis, it is perhaps helpful to consider the actual scale of transport infrastructure which exists and to provide some factual information on variations in modal provision and technology. Table 8.1 provides relevant data for a large number of OECD countries and it is clear from this that road infrastructure provision far exceeds that of rail. The picture, however, is different in the former communist states which have extensive rail networks. When compared to OECD states, however, only a relatively small percentage of it is doubled tracked; for example, 23 per cent in both Bulgaria and Hungary and Poland and 15 per cent in Hungary compared to 63 per cent in the Netherlands, 69 per cent in the UK and 45 per cent in France. Taking another parameter, while there are considerable variations in the electrification of rail networks in industrialised countries, they all have more extensive systems than in the post-communist states. For example, of 31,000 kilometres of line, nearly 12,000 are currently electrified in the western states of pre-1990 Germany but out of 14,024 kilometres in the former East Germany only 3,475 kilometres are electrified and in Poland, of 26,545 kilometres only 6,296 are electrified.

While the capital stock of transport infrastructure is large, the evidence is that investment in transport, and especially rail transport, has tended to slow down in recent years and, in some cases, disinvestment may well have taken place. In the case of rail this manifested itself in a 4.1 per cent reduction in the total rail network of OECD countries between 1970 and 1985, although effective capacity may well have increased as electrification programmes were carried through.

There are also significant variations in the 1980s between countries (Table 8.2) in terms of the proportion of national resources which are invested in transport infrastructure. As can be seen this is not simply in terms of the modal division of expenditure but also in the absolute proportion going to transport as a whole.

Table 8.1
Transport infrastructure in industrialised countries (1988)

Country	Roads (motorways) thousand kilometres	Rail (electrified) thousand kilometres
Austria	12(1.2)	5.1(3.0)
Belgium	16(1.5)	3.7(2.0)
Denmark	70(0.6)	2.5(0.2)
Federal Republic of Germany	490(8.2)	31.0(12.0)
Finland	76(0.2)	5.9(1.5)
France	800(6.0)	35.0(11.0)
Greece	110(0.1)	2.5(-)
Irish Republic	92(0.1)	1.9(-)
Italy	300(5.9)	20.0(10.0)
Japan	1100(3.6)	n.a.
Netherlands	97(2.0)	2.8(1.8)
Norway	86(0.3)	4.2(2.4)
Portugal	50(0.2)	3.6(0.5)
Spain	220(2.1)	14.0(6.4)
Sweden	130(1.4)	12.0(7.5)
Switzerland	70(1.1)	5.1(5.1)
UK	370(2.9)	17.0(3.8)
USA	6300(960)	240.0(1.7)
Yugoslavia	140(0.7)	9.3(3.5)

Table 8.2
Investment in transport infrastructure in European countries

Country	Infrastructure investment as % of GDP	
	Road	Rail
Belgium	0.67	0.29
France	0.65	0.09
Germany	0.79	0.26
Italy	0.62	0.27
Spain	0.50	0.27
United Kingdom	0.40	0.09

8.2   Basic principles
Simple economic theory provides straightforward guidelines for investment decision-making; essentially they involve pricing and output decisions where the

constraints of a fixed production capacity (for example, a given fleet or rail network) cease to be binding. In Figure 8.1, for example, we consider a profit-maximising airline with a fleet exhibiting short-run average and marginal cost characteristics of $SRAC_1$ and $SRMC_1$ respectively, and confronted by the demand curve D (with marginal revenue MR). Ideally, a price P_1 will be set and seat-kilometres Q_1 offered. The long-run marginal cost ($LRMC$) is, however, below MR at this output and, with this size of fleet, gives an inducement to expand output in the long term by acquiring more capacity. Higher seat availability will force price down but, and this is important in the example, it may also make it more economical to increase the aircraft fleet size. In the diagram, and assuming throughout that profit maximising prices are charged, the fleet could be expanded to correspond to $SRAC_2$ and $SRMC_2$. Here the long-run optimum situation is achieved with marginal revenue equated to long-run and short-run costs and with profit maximisation resulting. If the firm were concerned with social rather than commercial profit maximisation criteria and adopted instead marginal cost pricing, then the $SRMC_3$ and $SRAC_3$ curves become relevant because with this objective function it is the setting of $D = LRMC = SRMC$ which is important. Greater capacity still is needed for this (hence the $SRMC_3$ and $SRAC_3$ curves) and optimal long-run output will be higher at Q_3 seat kilometres with fares lowered to P_3. At this price and output, social surplus is maximised although, since $P_3 < LRAC$, in the long run a financial loss will be made.

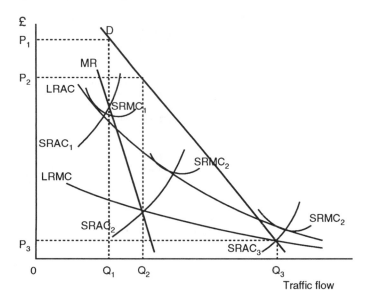

Figure 8.1
Optimal investment – profit maximisation and social surplus maximisation

The basic principles are simple and come straight from the elementary literature; the difficulty comes in the transport context in putting them into practice. In many cases investments are not divisible and, hence, the $LRAC$ and

LRMC curves are disjointed segments, or even points, which do not intersect with demand. This is an extremely common situation in transport and it does pose serious problems in many operational cases. It is not difficult, for example, to envisage routes where the available vehicles (be they planes, buses or whatever) are either too small or too large to be optimal and it is even more common in the case of infrastructure where, for instance, a two-lane motorway may be inadequate to cope with normal demand but a three-lane one is too capacious. Further, there is the problem of what exactly is meant by 'cost'. While we have treated the commercial and social criteria of profit maximisation and marginal cost pricing as amenable to presentation on one diagram, in practice most socially orientated undertakings look at a much wider range of costs (notably many of the externalities discussed in Chapter 5) when deciding upon investment than do those motivated by purely financial considerations. Coupled with this is the fact that the diagrammatic analysis assumes that, irrespective of the operational criteria, prices are optimal in the short term and thus can act as an aid and guideline to investment decision-making. Also, despite the sophistication of forecasting techniques (see Chapter 9) it is unlikely that the transport provider is completely aware of the exact form of the long-run demand curve confronting him. Indeed, the fluctuating nature of demand for transport (especially long-term cycles in demand associated with national and international economic conditions) means that it is rather more of a stochastic concept than a deterministic phenomenon as depicted.

Given all these difficulties, together with the general inadequacy of information enjoyed by most transport suppliers of their current levels of cost, let alone future costs, it is not surprising that investment analysis in transport has received considerable attention. The high costs and long-term implications of infrastructure investments in road and rail track, and sea- and airports has led to particular attention being directed at these areas. At the academic level they also pose particularly difficult questions because, in many cases, facilities are provided at prices unrelated to cost, or made freely available to users. Additionally, there are frequently widespread ramifications for transport users elsewhere or for the non-users living in surrounding areas.

8.3   Commercial and social approaches to investment

The administrative structure of transport in many countries means that most types of infrastructure are supplied with the intention of maximising economic efficiency – that is, they are appraised in terms of their social value assuming they are optimally utilised at marginal cost prices. There are clearly exceptions to this, however, where profit maximisation is seen as the primary objective. The distinction between the two approaches may be seen by contrasting the discounting approach used by large profit-orientated firms (and public corporations instructed to operate commercially) with the discounting approach of undertakings concerned with economic efficiency. (The discounting process is a simple weighting of different items of cost and income according to the time period at which they occur more distant items being given less emphasis in the calculations.) The commercial firm will, in the absence of a budget constraint, accept investments when the financial net present value is positive, that is,

$$NPV_f = \sum_{n=1}^{K} \left\{ \frac{P(R_n) - P(F_n)}{(1+i)^n} \right\} \tag{8.1}$$

where: NPV_f is the financial net present value;
      $P(R_n)$ is the probable social revenue that would be earned in year n from the investment;
      $P(F_{mn})$ is the probable financial cost of the investment in year n ;
      $(1+i)^n$ is the rate of interest reflecting the cost of capital to the undertaking; and
      K is the anticipated life of the investment;

A positive NPV_f, therefore, tells the businessman that it is worthwhile undertaking an initial investment – that is, it tells him that a movement from zero output in Figure 8.1 to output Q_1 with the associated short-run costs of $SRAC_1$ and $SRMC_1$ is commercially desirable and that a profit above both long- and short-run costs will be earned. A more normal case, where an expansion of operations is being considered involving some new capital outlay, requires the additional discounted profits from the investment to be compared with the additional discounted costs. If the resultant incremental NPV_f is positive then the investment is justified on profitability grounds. In terms of the diagram a movement down the *LRMC* curve to output level Q_1 with the short-run marginal costs of $SRMC_1$ would yield a positive *incremental NPV_f* but subsequent investment to take one down the *LRMC* curve to output Q_1 would not.

In contrast, economic efficiency is assessed using some form of cost-benefit analysis which, again in the absence of a budget constraint, suggests schemes with a positive social net present value should be undertaken where

$$NPV_s = \sum_{n=1}^{k} \sum_{m=1}^{j} \left\{ \frac{P(amBmn) - P(bmCmn)}{(1+r)^n} \right\}$$ (8.2)

where: NPV_s is the social net present value;
      $P(a_mB_{mn})$ is the probable social benefit to be enjoyed by individual m in year n as a result of the investment's completion. B_{ma} is given a weighting a_m to reflect society's welfare preference;
      $P(b_mC_{mn})$ is the probable social cost to be enjoyed by individual m in year n as a result of the investment's completion. C_{mn} is given a weighting b_m to reflect society's welfare preference;
      $(1+r)^n$ is the relative social weight attached to a cost or benefit occurring in a given year;
      k is the anticipated life of the investment; and
      j is the total number of individuals affected.

In terms of Figure 8.1, a positive NPV implies that the social surplus associated with an investment exceeds the discounted costs – that is, the demand curve at the final output is equal to or above the *LRMC* curve. An additional investment will be economically justified as long as the discounted value of incremental social benefit exceeds incremental costs. Contrasting this with the commercial criteria, the NPV_f associated with moving down the *LRMC* curve from output Q_2 to Q_3 is negative but the incremental NPV, would be calculated to be positive.

Not only is the cost-benefit type of analysis more comprehensive in terms of the items considered but it also redefines many of the items retained from commercial criteria. For example, the costs of imported raw materials used in a potential road construction project in a third world country would be valued at market prices if a commercial undertaking were responsible for road investment decisions. If a public body undertakes road investment using wider social criteria, then it would look beyond the immediate financial indicators and at the 'shadow' prices of imports so that the scarcity of foreign exchange and the limitations of adequate finance for imports is reflected in the decision-making. In some investments use is made of formerly unemployed factor services – for example, unemployed labour where the opportunity cost of employment in a transport scheme is really zero or the opportunity cost of the leisure they now forgo. A commercial concern would cost such inputs at the wages that have to be paid, but in a cost-benefit study they may not be considered a cost at all or, more probably, would be costed so that genuine resource costs are incorporated in the calculations.

A further very important distinction is that the social efficiency approach takes cognisance of the distributional effect of the investment (the a_m and b_m terms in equation 8.2). This is often difficult to do in reality although various schemes for weighting costs and benefits have been advanced by theoreticians (for example, McGuire and Gain, 1969). In practice there is a tendency to employ rather crude methods, often, as in the case of the Planning Balance Sheet approach used in several urban infrastructure investment appraisals (Lichfield and Chapman, 1968), involving the simple setting out in tabular form of the impacts of a scheme on the different user and non-user groups affected or, as with inter-urban road appraisal in the UK (UK Department of Transport, 1978), carrying out a partial CBA with no allowance for distributional effects and subjecting the results of this to further debate at public inquiry.

8.4 A consideration of the theory of cost-benefit analysis

While there are many complexities in undertaking commercial investment appraisal (for example, allowing for risk of unexpected changes in demand, deciding upon appropriate methods of raising capital, etc.), it is public sector transport investment which has attracted the greatest attention. The wide-ranging and long-term effects of most major changes in transport infrastructure necessitate the employment of sophisticated methods of project appraisal and of comprehensive techniques for decision-making. The underlying notion of cost-benefit analysis, which forms the explicit (and, on occasions, implicit) foundation for much of this work has already been alluded to in previous sections. While the algebra set down there suggests a comparatively simple set of standard calculations, the theoretical model is itself based upon a set of much more complex assumptions which makes the application a far more tortuous exercise than it might at first appear. Indeed, there is evidence that the optimism once felt for CBA as the panacea for all transport investment appraisal problems has gradually evaporated and the confidence felt in the strength of CBA calculations no longer exists.

This and the following sections attempt, in broad terms, to explain the CBA methodology and to point to recent innovations in theory and practice. The subject matter of CBA has now become so vast that the treatment here must, by necessity, be rather limited. We begin by looking at the basic welfare economics underlying the technique. This highlights some of the key assumptions upon which it is based.

The simple outline of CBA in the previous section emphasised the notion of selecting investments which maximise social surplus rather than just pecuniary returns. One of the major problems in this is that of interpersonal comparisons of welfare. Is it really possible to say social welfare has risen if one group becomes better off at the expense of another? This represents a common situation in transport where users tend to benefit at the expense of non-users. CBA attempts to circumvent this conceptual problem by making use of 'hypothetical compensation tests'. Strictly, since we only have a notion of the ordinal ranking of individuals' priorities, interpersonal welfare comparisons can only be made in very limited circumstances. The Pareto criterion, which underlies most modern welfare economics, states that an action can only definitely be said to be socially desirable if at least one agent benefits and *none* suffers diminution of welfare.

Diagramatically, in Figure 8.2(a) we have two individuals, x and y, who enjoy various levels of welfare recorded on the horizontal and vertical axis as U_x and U_y. If we have a finite collection of goods and services available (including transport services) together with a fixed level of costs, then the well-being of x and y will depend upon how these goods, services and costs are distributed between them. The utility possibility frontier I represents the maximum possible welfare they could enjoy given different distributions of the goods, services and costs. Initially, the goods etc. are distributed so that point A on the frontier is achieved (that is, x enjoys a utility of OX and y of OY). The goods, services and costs could be redistributed so that any other point on I could be obtained but no point outside of it. Suppose now a transport investment results in the bundle of goods, services and costs changing and that position B beyond frontier I is reached. This would be deemed a Pareto improvement because both x and y are better off. Indeed, any *ex post* position within the 90° zone marked would be Pareto-superior to A since, even on one of the limits, at least one person is better off while the other at worst retains his original utility level.

The strict Pareto criterion is of little use in practice – most transport schemes have either direct or indirect net adverse effects on some members of the community. The suggested method of allowing for this is to adopt a hypothetical Pareto criterion and decide whether after the investment it *would* be possible to redistribute the impacts in such a way that no one is worse off but there is still some residual gain to others. Whether such redistribution actually occurs is felt to be a normative issue and should be treated as within the domain of politics rather than economics. There are two broad approaches to the hypothetical compensation criteria. The first, initially advanced by Kaldor (1939), forms the basis for most CBA studies and suggests that a scheme is socially desirable if the beneficiaries could compensate the losers and still remain better off. In Figure 8.2(b), B is Kaldor-superior to A (although not strictly Pareto-superior) because B is on a new post-investment utility possibility frontier II which passes outside of A. Hence, the bundle of goods, services and costs which generate II could be redistributed from B to B' which is Pareto-superior to A.

Whether the government instigates a tax/subsidy scheme to cause such a movement along II is considered a political issue; Kaldor (in a discussion of the repeal of the nineteenth-century Corn Laws!) simply argues that it *could* be done. Hicks (1940) favours a similar approach but adopts *pre-investment* weights for his criteria. Specifically he argues for a project's acceptance if those who lose as a result of its implementation cannot bribe the gainers not to do it without becoming worse off themselves. In Figure 8.2(c), B is Hicks-superior to A because, with the *pre-investment* package of goods, services and costs which permitted frontier I to be attained, it is impossible for x (the loser) to bribe y (the beneficiary) not to support the investment. B is always above I and hence will be Pareto-superior to any point, such as A', which can be achieved by redistributing the pre-investment package.

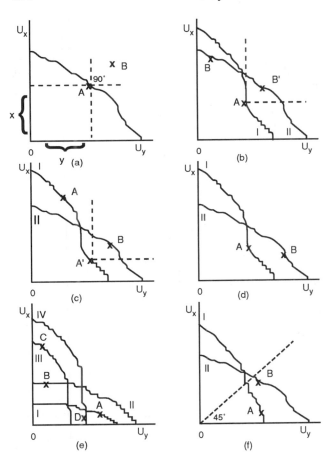

Figure 8.2
Compensation criteria

The problem with the Kaldor and Hicks approaches is that they may, in some circumstances, contradict one another. For example, in Figure 8.2(b) although *B* is Kaldor-superior to *A*, we can see that *A* is Hicks-superior to *B*. Further, even if one only used the Kaldor test and the investment was completed and position *B* attained, it then becomes possible to show that it is, again following the Kaldor criteria, socially beneficial to disinvest and return to *A*. (Similar types of problem exist in 8.2(c) with the Hicks test.) Samuelson (1961) argues that the problem will always exist as long as the pre- and post-investment utility possibility frontiers cross and that comparisons in such circumstances are invalid. This is an extremely restrictive view. As long as the two actual positions being compared are on the same side of any intersection of the frontiers then the two criteria give consistent assessments and there are no problems of 'reversibility' (Skitovsky, 1941). Figure 8.2(d), for instance, shows a situation where *B* meets both the Hicks and the Kaldor hypothetical compensation tests and may, therefore, be considered socially superior to *A*. There is also no question of advocating reversibility once the investment leading to *B* has been undertaken. Whether, in practice, transport analysts need to test for these problems is an empirical question which has, to date, been inadequately explored. At least one experienced economist in the CBA field suggests that the Skitovsky criteria may be violated on more occasions than is sometimes supposed (de V. Graaf, 1975).

A different problem may arise when appraising a series of piecemeal investments. It is possible because of the relative nature of consumer surplus – which underlies all these tests – for a series of small investments each to pass the Skitovsky test but for the eventual outcome to be socially inferior to the initial position (Gorman, 1955). In Figure 8.2(e), if we have an initial position of *A* on frontier I, then an investment which permits *B* to be reached satisfies the Skitovsky criterion (and, indeed, Samuelson's); further, a move from *B* to *C*, following additional investment, may be approved and, likewise, a subsequent move from *C* to *D*, which again meets the Skitovsky test. However, despite the fact we have seen that $A < B < C < D$ in terms of hypothetical compensation tests, it is clearly evident in Figure 8.2(e) that *A* is preferable, on Skitovsky grounds, to *D*. Each of the series of small changes appear desirable but the final, overall outcome leaves society worse off than before.

If this problem was only a theoretical curio there would be no need for concern, unfortunately this does not seem to be the case. Numerous examples of piecemeal decision-making leading to a subsequent diminution of social welfare can be cited in urban planning, but in the context of transport perhaps the most worrying problem concerns the growth in car use since the Second World War at the expense of urban public transport (Mishan, 1967). For simplicity, we take a concentric-shaped city with employment concentrated in the centre. The core is surrounded by a ring of residential estates. The analysis is short-term and assumes that this land-use pattern is fixed. It is now possible to define three phases:

Phase I   All commuters have only one mode of transport available to them and travel to work by means of public transport – taking 10 minutes – is the norm.

Phase II   One commuter (*X*) buys a car and drives to work taking 5 minutes, leaving the other travellers unaffected by his action and still taking 10 minutes to reach work by public transport.

Phase III   Many commuters, observing the advantage enjoyed by *X*, begin to buy and use cars which, with the resultant congestion generated, increase driving time to work to 15 minutes and, due to the impedance caused by the cars, slows public transport so that commuters using this mode now suffer a 25-minute journey. In the longer term, because of the technologically unprogressive nature of public transport, the service may be withdrawn (following the syndrome of few passengers – higher fares and poorer service – even fewer passengers etc., etc.) leaving a choice of car purchase or walking to work. The result is a 'prisoner's dilemma' type of situation where individually each commuter would prefer the original situation, rather than the new undesirable equilibrium, but cannot attain it by unilateral action.

The example illustrates the difficulties which may arise as the result of decisions based upon relative welfare measures: each commuter thought that he would benefit by investing in a car because he did not take cognisance of the whole set of decisions being made. Ideally, a CBA study should appraise all the systems or sequences of potential investments other than assess individual components of a programme of events. The urban planning process, discussed in Chapter 9, is an area where this is particularly relevant.

While most CBA studies of transport projects have concentrated on efficiency considerations, relying upon the hypothetical compensation criteria, it has been suggested by Little (1950) that some allowance for distributional impact should be incorporated. Specifically, it is argued that a project should only be accepted using the hypothetical type of criteria if the final outcome improves the income distribution. For example, in Figure 8.2(f), we assume that an improved income distribution means greater equality of welfare and thus corresponds to a movement closer to the 45° line depicted. Thus, *B*, on the post-investment policy frontier, is both Skitovsky-superior to *A* and also Little-superior because it is closer to the 45°, equal utility, line. It is important to note that it is the *actual* outcome which is being considered and not potential redistributed packages of the post-investment collection of goods, services and costs. As we see in section 8.5 there are several ways in which this distributional element may be incorporated within CBA studies.

8.5 Coping with network effects

The discussion above applies to all CBA applications but a particular difficulty of applying the technique to transport investment decisions is the need to incorporate adequately the wide-ranging effects a change in one part of the transport system has on the rest of the network. Most transport infrastructure forms a link in a much larger, interacting network and, consequently, changes in any one link tend to affect demand on competitive and complementary links. Although this sort of complexity exists for virtually all forms of transport, the problem of assessing the overall effect on road transport of improving a single link has, because of the dominance of this form of transport in modern society, attracted the majority of attention.

If there are two roads, one from *X* to *Y* and the other *X* to *Z*, where *Y* and *Z* are to some degree substitute destinations, then an improvement in route *XY* will affect three groups. We will assume for simplicity that all demand curves are linear and that the pre-investment traffic flows on *XY* and *XZ* are T_{xy} and $(T_{xz} + R)$ respectively. The three groups of users to consider are then:

(1)   Existing users who remain on their original routes (that is, T_{xy} and T_{xz}). These will enjoy a gain in consumers' surplus because those on route *XY* will now be using a higher quality facility while those on *XZ* will benefit from reductions in demand for this route as some former users switch to the improved *XY*. If this latter traffic which has diverted from *XZ* to *XY* is denoted as *R*, then the total benefit to those remaining loyal to their initial routes may be represented as:

$$T_{XY}(C_1 - C_2) + T_{xz}(D_1 - D_2)$$

where C_1, C_2, D_1, D_2 are the pre- and post-investment costs by roads *XY* and *XZ* respectively.

(2) Generated traffic consisting of people who did not previously travel (that is, G_{xy} and G_{xz}). On average (given the linear demand curves) each of these groups of new road users will benefit by half as much as existing, non-switching traffic. (Some will obviously be marginal trip-makers and only just gain by making a trip while others are intra-marginal and enjoy nearly as much additional consumer surplus as the non-switchers.) The total benefit of the investment to this group will thus be:

$$0.5 G_{xy} (C_1 - C_2) + 0.5 G_{xz} (D_1 - D_2)$$

(3) Diverted traffic which switches from route XZ to route XY as a consequence of the investment (that is, R). Obviously the switch, given the free choice situation open to travellers, must leave this group better off – they would not have switched otherwise – and the additional welfare they enjoy can be seen to equal half of the difference in benefit between the cost reductions on the two routes, that is,

$$R [(D_1 - D_2) + 0.5\{(C_1 - C_2) - (D_1 - D_2)\}]$$

which may be reduced to:

$$0.5 R \{(C_1 - C_2) + (D_1 - D_2)\}$$

The total benefit (TB) of the investment is the summation of these three elements namely:

$$TB = T_{xy} (C_1 - C_2) + T_{xz} (D_1 - D_2) + 0.5 G_{xy} ((C_1 - C_2) + 0.5 G_{xz} (D_1 - D_2) +$$
$$0.5R \{(C_1 - C_2) + (D_1 - D_2)\} \tag{8.3}$$

Figure 8.3 shows this diagramatically; Figure 8.3(a) representing the supply and demand situations on route XY and Figure 8.3(b) those on route XZ. On route XY we see that demand has increased the supply of road space but demand has declined because the relative generalised cost of using XZ changes as traffic diverts from it to the improved facility. Using the notation in the diagram, we know that $Q_{xy} = T_{xy}$ and that $Q'_{xy} = (T_{xy} + G_{xy} + R)$, therefore:

$$0.5 (Q_{xy} + Q'_{xy}) = (T_{xy} + 0.5 G_{xy} + 0.5R).$$

Similarly, since $Q_{xz} = (T_{xz} + R)$ and $Q'_{xz} = (T_{xz} + G_{xz})$, we know that;

$$0.5(Q_{xz} + Q'_{xz}) = (T_{xz} + 0.5 G_{xz} + 0.5R).$$

Substituting this into equation 8.3 we discover:

$$TB = 0.5(Q_{xz} + Q'_{xy}) (C_1 - C_2) + 0.5(Q_{xz} + Q'_{xz})(D_1 - D_2)$$

or more generally, this can be seen as the oft-cited 'rule of half',

$$TB = 0.5 \sum_{N} (Q_n + Q'_n) (C_n - C'_n) \tag{8.4}$$

This net benefit is equivalent to the shaded areas seen in Figure 8.3. The rule of half can be applied to all transport schemes that interact with other components of the transport system where demand curves are linear. (It must, however, be used with a degree of circumspection when routes are complementary, where demand for the non-improved links may shift to the right, but the broad principle applies.)

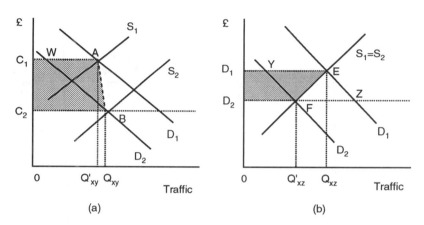

Figure 8.3
Social benefits over a transport network

The method of handling interdependencies outlined above was initially developed in the late 1960s as part of the London Transportation Study (LTS), but it does rely upon a rather strong implicit assumption that the income elasticities of demand for routes XY and XZ are equal (Foster and Neuburger, 1974). The problem is that there are many possible sequences in which the price changes on routes XY and XZ could follow; each would yield a different level of aggregate social welfare. For instance, if the chain of price changes is $(C_1, D_1) => (C_2, D_1)$ $=> (C_2, D_2)$ then the consumer surplus gain in the diagram would be $\{(C_1AXC_2) + (D_1YFD_2)\}$. But if the sequence is $(C_1, D_1) => (C_1, D_2) => (C_2, D_2)$ then the aggregate benefit would be $\{(C_1WBC_2) + (D_1EXD_2)\}$. The general measure set out in equation 8.3 assumes that the demand fluctuations are linear in their own prices and with respect to cross-price effects – if this is so then the measure would give identical results to both the sequences outlined above (which would themselves yield identical benefit estimates). Whether such assumptions are valid is debatable, but Foster and Neuburger argue that any deviation is unlikely to be of any practical significance in actual evaluation exercises. Certainly, given the other major difficulties of evaluation and measurement, the 'rule of half' provides a robust and useful guide to the user benefits of transport schemes.

8.6   CBA in practice and variations on the theme
Our attention, to this point, has focused on the theoretical ideas and concepts underlying CBA. We now turn to look more directly at its actual application in transport fields. The equation set out above (equation 8.2) gives a formal

mathematical definition of CBA, while Prest and Turvey (1965) give the verbal counterpart:

> CBA is a practical way of assessing the desirability of projects, where it is important to take a long view (in the sense of looking at repercussions in the further as well as the nearer future) and a wide view (in the sense of allowing for side effects of many kinds on many persons, industries, regions, etc.) – that is, it implies the enumeration and evaluation of all the relevant costs and benefits.

CBA has over the years formed the basis of investment appraisal of many major transport schemes in the UK (for example, the M1 motorway, the Victoria Line underground railway, the Channel Tunnel, London's system of ringway urban motorways and the siting of a Third London Airport) and elsewhere. It has also become a tool in more routine decision-making (for example, to assess railway social service subsidies in the late 1960s and as a component of inter-urban road investment appraisal in the form of COBA). The UK situation, however, is a particular case and there are quite important variations in the form of appraisal used to appraise transport projects in industrialised countries; some more comprehensive and others less so. Table 8.3 offers a broad overview of the differing nature of decision-making processes in a number of major European countries.

Table 8.3
The nature of transport infrastructure decision-making in European countries

Country	Systems approach	Master plan	Intermodal cooperation	Time horizon	Private financing
France	S	M	S	Long	M
Germany	M	W	M	Long	S
Italy	S	M	S	Short	S
Belgium	S	S	S	Short	S
Sweden	M	M	S	Medium	S
Denmark	M	M	M	Short	S
Norway	M	M	S	Medium	S
Finland	S	S	S	Medium	S
Switzerland	W	W	M	Long	S

S = Scarcely developed; M = Partially developed; W = Well developed

The Third London Airport Study (Commission on the Third London Airport, 1971) characterises the traditional textbook CBA approach although here, since it was assumed that a new facility was necessary anyway, the benefits were deemed virtually equal for all possible sites, that is, the question posed involved considering where and when an airport should be built – *not* whether. This meant that in some ways it became a social cost-effectiveness study – finding the site with the lowest social costs attached to it. The present values of the various cost and benefit items for each alternative discounted from 2006 to 1975 are given in Table 8.4. While the study team favoured Cublington as marginally superior to the other sites, subsequent Parliamentary debate overruled this in favour of

Foulness (that is, Maplin). Although even this revised proposal was later abandoned, the study proved useful in showing up some of the practical difficulties in conducting a CBA study of a scheme which has extremely wide-ranging and diverse impacts – many of them posing serious problems of evaluation.

Table 8.4
Social costs and benefits (£ millions) associated with alternative sites for a Third London Airport[a]

	Cublington	Foulness	Nuthampstead	Thurleigh
Capital costs				
Construction of airport	184.0	179.0	178.0	166.0
Airport services	14.3	9.8	14.5	11.6
Extension/closure of Luton Airport	– 1.3	10.0	– 1.3	– 1.3
Road and rail development	11.8	23.4	15.5	6.5
Relocation of defence and public scientific establishments	67.4	21.0	57.9	84.2
Loss of agricultural land	3.1	4.2	7.2	4.6
Impact on residential conditions	3.5	4.0	2.1	1.6
Impact on schools, hospitals, etc.	2.5	0.8	4.1	4.9
Other	3.5	0.5	6.7	10.2
Total	*288.8*	*252.7*	*284.7*	*288.3*
Current costs				
Aircraft movement costs	960.0	973.0	987.0	972.0
Passenger user costs	931.0	1041.0	895.0	931.0
Freight user costs	13.4	23.1	17.0	13.9
Airport services, operating costs	60.3	53.1	56.2	55.6
Travel costs to/from airport	26.2	26.5	24.4	25.4
Other	12.4	7.5	8.5	7.2
Total	*2003.3*	*2124.2*	*1988.1*	*2005.1*
Benefits (relative to Foulness)				
To common/diverted traffic (net of costs)	-		-	-
To generated traffic	44.0	-	27.0	42.0
Total (costs less differential benefits)	*2248.1*	*2376.9*	*2245.8*	*2251.4*

[a]The table is only a partial reflection of the results obtained and does not, for example, reflect the sensitivity analysis conducted.
Source: Commission on the Third London Airport (1971)

A less comprehensive approach than that devised by Roskill is the COBA computer programme (UK Department of Transport, 1989) which has been employed as part of the inter urban-road appraisal process in the UK from the 1960s, although, it should be emphasised, only as part of a more extensive procedure. The emphasis here has been rather more on consistency than on comprehensive coverage. The programme makes use of traffic forecasts derived from a standardised procedure and uses them to compare discounted monetary valuations of travel time changes, variations in vehicle operating costs and impacts on accident rates with the capital and maintenance costs of a project. While this provides an indication of the costs and benefits to traffic and the exchequer, additional information on third party effects, such as environmental impacts, have, until the early 1990s, been treated separately.

Despite the widespread adoption of CBA by the transport sector, there has been a gradual disillusionment with the all-embracing, stereotype appraisal implied by Prest and Turvey. This has manifested itself most strongly since the rejection of the Roskill Committee's recommendation regarding the siting of a Third London Airport and became particularly noticeable at public inquiries into new road proposals in the late 1970s and the early 1980s. While the criticisms of CBA as a method of socially evaluating transport investments have been extensive, they are perhaps most adequately summed up by Wildavsky (1966), 'Although cost-benefit analysis presumably results in efficiency by adding the most to national income, it is shot through with political and social value choices and surrounded by uncertainties and difficulties of computation.' A former Chairman of British Rail summarised the attitude evolving in the UK when he argued that there is a need for an approach that 'can be understood by ordinary intelligent people ... incorporates the methods of analysis developed by welfare economists over the last decade or so ... gets away from the naive position adopted by the early cost-benefit men which seemed to imply that every consideration could be perfectly weighted and that, therefore, there was a single best solution' (Parker, 1978).

The response of analysts to these dissatisfactions with mechanical CBA procedures have taken two broad lines. The first is an attempt to modify the original CBA framework (as exemplified by equation 8.2) so that some allowances are made for the major criticisms. In particular, greater effort has been put into evaluating the externality items included in a CBA account (see Chapter 5) and to placing more reliable values on time-saving attributes of schemes (see Chapter 3). Advances on this front have been more rapid in some countries than in others. Sweden, for example, uses a variety of techniques to enable a diverse range of effects, often expressed in monetary terms, to be brought into the appraisal process (Table 8.5). The position in the UK is that a more consistent process is taking rather longer to emerge although experimentation in embracing a limited number of environmental factors within the COBA framework began after the publication of a report by the Standing Advisory Committee on Trunk Road Appraisal (UK Department of Transport, 1992).

Additionally, techniques have been evolved that introduce allowances for the distributional effects of schemes – an area neglected in earlier work which concentrated on overall impact – and for the risk and uncertainty that the predicted cost and benefit streams will diverge from that forecast. Theoretically, distributional effects can be allowed for by weighting the costs and benefits according to the different groups affected. Unfortunately, it has been demonstrated at the theoretical level (Mishan, 1974) that in many investment situations the applications of such weights (which may, in particular, be based upon measures reflecting income tax liability) to cost and benefit items can still lead to the acceptance of projects which benefit the rich to the detriment of the poor. Consequently, there is a case for treating distributional considerations independently of efficiency.

Risk and uncertainty about probable outcomes pose even more difficult problems. With risks there is some knowledge about the likelihood of errors in forecasts and this can be incorporated in the analysis by indicating the range of

Table 8.5
Major components of the Swedish project analysis model for road investment

Traffic economy and road maintenance	*Environmental and land-use effects*	*Regional developments, etc.*
Traffic safety*[†]	Noise*[†]	Regional balance
Travel time*	Air pollution[†]	Effects for trade
Comfort	Barrier effects[†]	industry and tourism
Vehicle costs*	Water supply	
Maintenance*	Vibrations	
	Landscape/scenery	
	Nature conservation	
	Land development*	

* Effects evaluated in monetary terms based on willingness to pay
[†] Effects evaluated in monetary terms based on explicit public preferences

probable long-term effects of investment, together with an indication of the probabilities of different levels of costs and benefits occurring. Unfortunately, there is no such knowledge of possible error with uncertainty and consequently adjustments tend to be made according to intuition or 'skilled judgement'. With many transport projects, the costs of under-engineering are likely to be higher than those of comparable over-engineering (the 'premature' physical disintegration of the UK motorway system being a good example) and thus there is a tendency to over-react to the possibility of uncertain outcomes.

While these advances in traditional CBA techniques go some way towards meeting criticism of early studies in the field they tend to complicate the estimation and decision-making frameworks and, hence to move even further from the openness sought by Peter Parker and also the Leitch Committee on trunk road investment appraisal (UK Department of Transport, 1978). One offshoot of CBA which retains the notion of social welfare maximisation but also makes the CBA account accessible to the proverbial 'educated layman' is the Planning Balance Sheet (Lichfield and Chapman, 1968) which was initially devised and developed over a series of case studies to help urban planners. We discuss the PBS in more detail below.

The second response to the critics is to move entirely away from the notion of a social welfare maximisation CBA approach and to adopt a lower level, but possibly more operational and manageable, approach to investment appraisal. This, for example, is the approach which has increasingly been followed in France since the late 1960s (Quinet, 1993).

Broadly, it is argued that, like most large private companies, public transport undertakings have insufficient information about the stream of costs and benefits (including social items) associated with the different policy options open to them and should, therefore, attempt to meet broad minimum levels of achievement rather than to maximise net benefits. This notion of 'satisficing' fits in with the attitude of most mature industrial concerns towards managerial decision-making (Simon, 1959). Although this second type of response to the critics of CBA is, to date, still comparatively under-researched in the transport field, a number of multi-criteria investment appraisal techniques have been developed, often only at an abstract level, in related areas of study such as regional and national resource planning (Button, 1979).

The Planning Balance Sheet approach mentioned above, although firmly founded in the CBA tradition, offers a methodology which is sufficiently flexible to adaptation for both maximising and satisficing frameworks. It has two main merits; first it shifts the emphasis of analysis away from the total measure of net benefit to the distribution of the costs and benefits among affected groups and secondly, it circumvents many of the problems associated with expressing all costs and benefits in money terms.

The technique involves setting down, in tabular form, all of the pros and cons associated with alternative investment options. These socio-economic accounts are expressed in monetary values wherever possible but should this prove impracticable then physical values are used and, if quantification is not possible, ordinal indices or scales. The accounts are subdivided to show the effect of different schemes on the groups affected and this offers guidance to distributional implications. The accounts are compared with pre-determined planning goals (and these instrumental objectives may imply either maximisation or satisficing objectives) which are selected as reflective of community preferences. Alternative investment plans are ranked under each objective heading using ordinal ranking procedures and the ranks are then added together to produce a ranking of the investments with respect to the objectives taken as a whole.

A technique of this general kind met with approval from the Leitch Committee in the UK as a tool in inter-urban road investment appraisal. The Committee felt 'the right approach is through a comprehensive framework which embraces all the factors and groups of people involved in scheme assessment' (UK Department of Transport, 1978). The project impact matrix, as the Leitch Committee called their variation, sets out a 'general framework' of about eighty relevant measures of the effects of transport schemes. As with most PBS studies the final account produced was extensive but Table 8.6 provides a summary. The intention is to use such an account to make pair-wise comparisons between the magnitude of the effects associated with different investment alternatives or, where the problem is deciding upon a specific project in isolation, to compare them with some instrumental objectives.

The PBS type approach has, despite its attractions, some inherent limitations. In particular it depends upon crude ranking criteria and scaling methods. The selection of instrumental objectives is itself highly subjective and, although it does force the decision-taker to make his underlying value judgements explicit, it can result in some conflict between interested parties. There is also the danger that the subjectivity of these objectives and trade-offs is forgotten in the mass of data incorporated in the accounts. The PBS has the advantage over some of the more mechanical CBA approaches where numbers are simply fed into some computer program (such as COBA which was developed in the UK for trunk road investment appraisal) that the construction of the initial socio-economic account can often, in itself, be educational and shed considerable light on salient questions the decision-taker should be asking.

While PBS has been seen as an extension of CBA, it may also be viewed as a primitive form of a 'multi-criteria decision-making technique'. Multi-criteria decision making techniques fall into the second category of advances outlined above in that they are concerned more with the meeting of certain low-level aims than maximising social welfare. They involve weighting the different effects of an investment to reflect social priorities but the weights reflect the success at attaining certain objectives rather than maximising an output.

Table 8.6
The project impact matrix suggested by the Leitch Committee

Incidence group	Nature of effect	Number of measures	
		Financial	*Other*
Road users directly affected	Accident savings	1	3
	Comfort and convenience		1
	Time savings	6	
	Vehicle operating cost saving	5	
	Amenity		2
Non-road users directly affected	Demolition or disamenity to owners of residential commercial and industrial properties		22
	Demolition or disamenity to users of schools, churches, public open space		15
	Land-take, severance and disamenity to farmers		7
Those concerned with the intrinsic value of the area	Landscape, scientific and historical value	3 (plus verbal description)	
Those indirectly affected	Sterilisation of natural resources, land-use planning effects, effects on other transport operators		6 (plus verbal description)
Financial authority	Cost and financial benefits		7
Total		19	59

Source: Adapted from UK Department of Transport (1978)

A number of multi-criteria approaches have been devised, each attempting to achieve a multi-dimensional compromise between the wide diversity of goals and objectives which are embodied in any form of public choice (Nijkamp and van Delft, 1977). Approaches differ in their methods of presentation, the level of mathematical sophistication involved and the amount of data input required. Several of the techniques rely upon geometrical representation to produce multi-dimensional scalings while others involve a considerable degree of intuition. Of greatest practical value in transport are some of the weighting techniques of which there are numerous variations. Hill's (1968) goals achievement matrix, for example, offers an explicit treatment of various goals and applies a set of predetermined weights to them so that each option can be assessed in terms of goals achieved. To facilitate this, the goals are related to *physical measures* (for example, minimum traffic speeds, acceptable accident rates, reduced levels of specified toxic exhaust emissions, etc.) to reflect the extent to which they have been achieved. The final goals achievement account employs the weighted index of goal achievement to determine the preferred course of action.

The problem with all useful multi-criteria procedures is the derivation of weighting schemes which reflect the relative importance of physical 'goals' or "objective instruments' – seldom will a public sector transport scheme do all which is hoped for. The traditional CBA approach, albeit in a maximising context, avoids this problem by using monetary values as weights. While there is evidence that those actually responsible for decision-making in the publicly controlled sectors of transport favour movement towards multi-criteria appraisal techniques, the practical problems are unlikely to permit the widespread use of such approaches – beyond the project impact matrix type of analysis – in the near future.

These types of modification to the cost-benefit approach are likely to lead to a more consistent treatment of environmental effects but there is a more fundamental point about infrastructure provision. It has been argued (Wheaton, 1978) that the conventional cost-benefit analysis approach to appraisal, because of its inherent assumptions regarding pricing, can lead to over-investment in transport infrastructure and excessive transport use. In Figure 8.4 we show various combinations of prices charged for road use and, on the vertical, various levels (in money terms) of investment. There will be some optimal price-investment mix such as P^*/S^* which is optimal. This would be the socially efficient outcome if road users were charged optimal prices (embracing all external considerations) for their journeys.

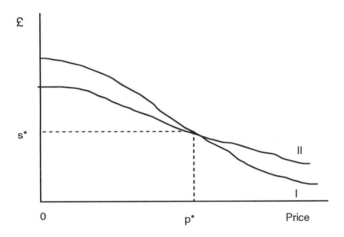

Figure 8.4
Second-best investment with sub-optimal congestion pricing

Suppose, however, that the price in effect does not fully reflect costs, then, since there would be a heavy demand for road use, the conventional cost-benefit analysis approach would imply that more investment than S^* is required. Curve *I* traces out the relevant optimal price-investment combinations which would emerge. In fact, the low price is generating demand beyond the optimal level and thus the overall amount of traffic on curve *I* at points to the left will be sub-optimally large. Wheaton argues, therefore, that investment should be limited along a

P/S curve such as *II*. The additional congestion occurring at any price below *P** because of the limited additional investment in capacity will in effect constrain traffic flows to the optimal level. The reasoning behind this conclusion is summarised by Wheaton in the following way:

> Such a reduction will increase congestion, and this helps to discourage the demand which has been 'artificially' induced by under pricing. It is important to remember that second-best investment does not call for building fewer road as the price of driving is lowered. That would result in 'excessive' congestion. Rather it requires accommodating less of the induced demand than would be met if a simple cost-benefit analysis were applied.

Applying this to the question of environmental policy, the relevance is mainly in terms of just how much investment in new infrastructure is economically justified when transport prices do not reflect true costs. The standard methodology tends to ignore the imperfections which exist in terms of transport users not paying for the full costs of their activities and thus to favour high levels of investment. Wheaton's analysis essentially implies that in these conditions where money prices are ineffective, second-best criteria determined by travellers' time costs (that is, congestion) can be used to limit travel to a level closer to the optimum. The actual conditions for achieving this second-best situation may, however, prove to be rather complex (Friedlaender, 1981). In terms of equity there may be a further argument in favour of such an approach in that time is allocated even across individuals. Practically, there are difficulties in working out the optimal second-best strategy and, in overall environmental terms, given the proportionately higher pollution, noise and other costs associated with congested roads, it is not altogether clear what the ultimate overall social outcome would be.

8.7   Comparability between appraisal techniques
If scarce investment funds are to be allocated to best effect within the overall transport sector and between it and the rest of the economy, it is clearly important that in some way comparisons are made between the potential effect of using funds in projects evaluated on commercial criteria and using them where social evaluation techniques such as CBA are employed.

Accepting that for institutional or administrative reasons there is no hope of a common method of assessment being employed in practice, then one possible method of comparing projects between sectors is to develop comparability criteria that reduce social and financial costs and benefits to a common denominator. Essentially a mathematical relationship between net social and net financial returns must be found. In certain, highly restrictive, situations this may prove to be feasible (Peaker, 1974). It is theoretically possible, under simplistic assumptions, to reduce everything to either a common financial or common social basis; we will assume, however, that we are assessing a potential investment aimed at improving an intercity rail service (where profit maximising levies are charged) and wish to convert the net reserves obtained into social welfare terms. Social welfare is assumed here to refer to social surplus (that is, combined consumer and producer surpluses) as is standard practice in welfare economics.

Figure 8.5 shows the demand curve for the existing rail service to be linear (D_1 with marginal revenue curve MR_1) and that the improvement will result in a parallel shift of this curve to D_2. The average and marginal costs of using the service are assumed constant irrespective of custom with $MC_1 (= AC_1)$ being the relevant curve prior to improvement and $MC_2 (= AC_2)$ being operative afterwards.

With these assumptions the demand curves are easily represented; D_1 as $p=a-kq$ and D_2 as $p=b-kq$ where p is price, q is the level of traffic flow and k is the slope of the parallel demand curves. With profit maximisation (that is, $MC = MR$) it is seen from Figure 8.4 that $q_1 = \frac{a-b}{2k}$ and $q_2 = \frac{b-f}{2k}$. Integrating under the relevant marginal revenue curves shows that the improved rail service would increase profits by {Area (bef)– Area (acd)}. This equals

$$0.5[b-f]q_2 - 0.5[a-b]q_1 = \frac{1}{4k}[(b-f)]^2 - (a-d)^2] \tag{8.5}$$

The increase in consumers' surplus associated with the improved rail service is obtained from integrating under the relevant demand curves but above price. In this case the integration yields Area (bhp_2) – Area (agp_1) which equals

$$0.5[b-p_2]q_2 - 0.5[a-p_1]q_1 = \frac{1}{8k}[(b-f)^2 - (a-d)^2] \tag{8.6}$$

Since total social surplus is composed of producers' surplus (that is, profit) plus consumers' surplus it is apparent from adding equation 8.5 to equation 8.6 (and then comparing back to equation 8.5) that the gain in social welfare as a result of the rail investment in this profit-maximising situation is 1.5 times the profit which would be earned. It seems possible, therefore, in the circumstances to be able to convert profits earned into a comparable social surplus by multiplying by 1.5.

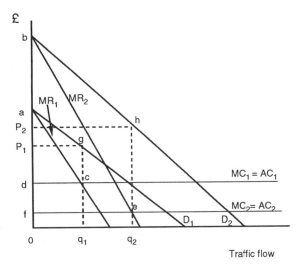

Figure 8.5
Comparability between commercial and social investment criteria

How useful is this conversion factor likely to be in practice? It is clear that it only applies to user costs and does not permit the inclusion of external factors, either in terms of pollution or congestion, which limits its usefulness in urban transport appraisal or for certain types of infrastructure, such as airports, which are particularly environmentally intrusive. Further, even within the strict confines of user-benefit analysis the conversion factor crucially depends upon a series of limiting assumptions. The factors which have been found to influence the ratio include (Harrison and Mackie, 1973):

(1)   the shape of the *MC* curve before and after the investment;
(2)   the shapes of the demand curves before and after the investment;
(3)   the extent of price discrimination;
(4)   the pricing policy actually pursued and the nature (if any) of its deviation from profit maximisation;
(5)   the consistency of the pricing policy employed as investment alters the cost and demand conditions;
(6)   the incidence of externalities including network effects; and
(7)   the extent to which revenue and benefit streams differ in their availability for reinvestment.

Given the sensitivity of the '1.5 rule' to these various factors, it can hardly be seen as a practicable method of introducing comparability into transport investment decision-making.

The comparability ratio approach assumes an investment is undertaken and then prices set to achieve some economic objective, usually profit maximisation. Financial returns are then compared to social returns. Starkie (1979) argues that a more practicable approach is to determine a common basis for pricing first and then adjust capacity accordingly. The basic idea stems from work on the railways by Joy (1964) which looked exclusively at freight investment, but Starkie generalises the approach to all forms of transport investment. It is assumed that the correct economic price for each mode is determined along the second-best pricing lines formalised by Baumol and Bradford (1970) and that investment (or disinvestment) should be adjusted until long-run marginal costs are equated with the revenues obtained. This means that prices are set to cover short-run marginal cost with a mark-up in proportion to the inverse of the price elasticity of demand for each mode. The mark-up then reflects 'what-the-user-will-bear' towards the cost of capacity provision (that is, consumer surplus above *SRMC*). If this mark-up, combined with the revenue covering *SRMC,* does not meet the full *LRMC* then capacity should be reduced until an equality is established. If such a pricing regime produces a surplus in excess of *LRMC* then, *ceteris paribus,* there is a case for expanding capacity.

The fundamental idea is that if sufficient price discrimination is applied then all potential consumers' surplus is transferred to the supplier and, *ipso facto,* net revenue can be equated with social surplus. Its main advance is the importance which it places on pricing and the recognition that in the long run it is possible to fine-tune investment at the margin. Such an approach obviously removes the need to conduct comparability studies but it has its limitations. The main difficulty is that while it may be possible in some areas to apply the discriminate pricing Starkie advocates - mainly those undertakings directly controlled by government – in other cases private provision of transport facilities makes it rather difficult to ensure that the Baumol–Bradford rules are being applied. Consequently, it is difficult to see how it could be decided what is the correct level of overall investment in the publicly owned sector of transport *vis-à-vis* the aggregate for the private sector. Because much public investment is assessed on social criteria and virtually all private-sector investment on commercial criteria, many of the problems of comparability remain. (This problem is avoided in Starkie's empirical work which focuses on road and railway track investment.) Further, the approach once again emphasises user benefits but does not allow for external factors, especially the environmental effects of transport on non-users (Button, 1980).

8.8   Assessing the effect on national income

It has been suggested that rather than expand financial surplus by a comparability ratio, or force some form of common pricing on all sectors of transport, an entirely different measure of the net value of investment, applicable to all forms of transport project irrespective of ownership, may be preferable. The effect of transport on national income, for example, could be used as a substitute for the combined consumers' and producers' surplus generated (for example, see work by Bos and Koyck (1961) and Friedlaender (1965) on trunk road appraisal). However, besides the practical difficulties involved in estimating the change in national income associated with alternative transport investments, the measure throws up an additional problem that involves the more fundamental question of whether the national income approach really does offer a reasonable and acceptable guide to the relative desirability of alternative investments. (We should perhaps note at this stage that national income, in this context, refers to the accountancy concept used in macroeconomics rather than the wider notion of national income referred to by Wildavsky in the chapter.)

We can consider Figure 8.6 and assume that demand will not shift following a change in capacity. Further, if we assume the transport undertaking acts as a monopolist in its pricing policy, then we can see that an investment that reduces marginal costs from MC_1 to MC_2 will increase social surplus by *abcdef* in the diagram and profits by *(abidef)* − *(gcih)*. The reduction in costs will also produce a higher national income. If the Laspeyres index is used (that is, the change in output valued at the pre-investment price), the rise will be measured as *lijk*. If the Paasche approach is favoured (that is, the change in output is valued at the post-investment price), however, the addition to national income is found to be only *lidk*. There is no reason for the social surplus measure to correspond to the national income measure (or for different estimates of the latter to correspond) except in rather unrealistic circumstances. Nor indeed need it correspond to the profit generated. Of more practical importance, there is no reason why alternative investment possibilities will be ranked consistently by the different methods.

The reason that social surplus and national income measures (and, indeed, financial measures) need not correspond, nor rank consistently, stems from the fact that they measure entirely different things. Social surplus both includes leisure benefits emanating from a project and explicitly incorporates allowances for the diminishing marginal utility associated with the increased consumption of travel. The national income measure does neither: it concentrates exclusively on goods and services traded in conventional markets and assumes either a fixed pre or post-investment price level. Mohring (1976) has demonstrated that the only time the two types of measure yield identical numerical results is '*If* a change takes place which increases the output obtained from a given set of primary resources, and *if* the primary resources allocated to market activities do not themselves change, and *if* the same pricing rules are used in consumers' surplus as in national income change benefit calculations' (emphasis original). Clearly, this means that the national income measure is likely to differ in practice from either the financial or social surplus measure of benefit and, hence, is simply an alternative method of ranking and appraisal, different but not necessarily superior. Given the practical difficulties of estimation in most advanced economies its usefulness seems limited. In less developed countries, though, it may be seen as a more viable appraisal technique if distributional and welfare considerations are felt to be of secondary importance to boosting the national product (see Chapter 10). Transport projects that help stimulate national income growth in these circumstances may be given priority over others.

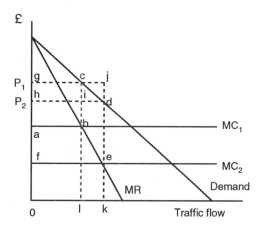

Figure 8.6
The national income change approach to transport investment appraisal

8.9   Comparability in practice
The practical problems of incomparability between investment in different transport sectors has not gone unnoticed by UK and other transport authorities. The problem is particularly acute in publicly owned inland inter-urban transport where government policy in the UK, for example, initiated in 1968 an administrative structure which distinguished among different types of service, some of which must show a financial return and others a social return. While the recent moves towards privatisation and deregulation (see Chapter 11) have rather blurred the distinction, the problem of allocating resources between commercial and social transport services remains.

Certain measures have been introduced in the UK that attempt to standardise some elements of appraisal procedures across the two groups. Since the late 1960s, for example, discounting techniques have been employed in all sectors (UK Treasury, 1967) using a nationally stipulated rate of discount. Some minor changes in the basis of calculation have taken place subsequently (for example, UK Treasury, 1978) but such techniques remain the main tool of appraisal. The differences among sectors are really just the actual items discounted; in one case

it is simply the fare revenues while in the other it is user benefits (usually calculated in terms of the financial value of the money, accident rate and travel time
changes associated with the investment).

The official position, until recently, was that, although there may be a need to
take distributional or environmental factors into account when doing *either* type
of calculation, the pricing policies pursued mean that revenue may be equated
with social surplus in the financially based calculation. Comparability then
becomes unnecessary. The rationale behind this view was summarised by the
Department of the Environment in evidence to a UK House of Commons Select
Committee (1974), the argument being that although 'the mechanics of assessment differ ... in ordinary circumstances British Railways pursue a policy of market pricing which ensures that *most benefits to users are fully reflected in the revenue collected*' (emphasis added). The Select Committee was not convinced,
however, that inconsistencies did not remain and advocated the establishment of
an Interurban Directorate to tackle the problem.

The Leitch Committee in the UK, which looked specifically at trunk road investment (UK Department of Transport, 1978), examined comparability in more
detail and recommended that consistency could only be achieved if those undertakings employing financial techniques extended their analysis to embrace the
wider social-surplus-based procedures of appraisal. As we have seen the type of
CBA envisaged, however, is somewhat more comprehensive and transparent than
that currently used for road investment appraisal in the UK which concentrates
solely on user benefits. Further, to gain an even greater degree of consistency,
there is a need to bring port and airport investment into the general CBA framework and widen the scope of appraisal away from the purely financial aspects
which tend currently (with some significant exceptions) to dominate decision-
making in these spheres.

While the notion of common CBA techniques being applied throughout the
publicly controlled inter-urban transport system may have certain apparent
advantages – in Germany and some other European countries it is used for all
inter-urban road, rail and waterway analysis – the Leitch study recognised the
private ownership of coastal shipping and pipeline limits the degree of
comparability. Essentially, the widespread use of CBA within the publicly owned
sector (which, in fact, goes beyond the road/rail situation considered by Leitch)
may produce consistent investment decisions within this sector but does not
determine the optimal size of public *vis-à-vis* private sector investment. In effect
very limited progress has been made towards a common method of economic
assessment for road and rail investments in the UK, and some other countries,
despite the findings of the Standing Advisory Committee on Truck Road
Appraisal (UK Department of Transport 1986), that:

> It is possible to have a consistent approach to economic assessment along the lines
> we have recommended which is equally appropriate to the evaluation of road public
> transport investments.

8.10   Further reading and references

Winston (1991) provides a good survey of efficiency in transport infrastructure
provision. The available technical literature on investment appraisal is immense.
Mishan (1988) is a classic volume on cost-benefit analysis and is almost
encyclopaedic in its coverage – it is hard going! A more accessible and very clear

discussion of investment appraisal is to be found in Pearce and Nash (1983) and this provides possibly the most suitable follow-up reading to this chapter. It also contains useful case-study material. Button and Pearce (1989) provides a discussion of the problems of defining the exact boundaries of a transport investment appraisal and, in particular, the requirements of different institutional bodies involved in an investment decision. Specific consideration of investment in transport infrastructure is to be found in Adler (1987) which is particularly strong on approaches which are relevant in Third World countries. Button (1979) provides a brief résumé of alternatives to the conventional CBA approach and has an extensive set of references. Wood (1993) provides a clear account of the development of transport infrastructure appraisal procedures pursued in the UK.

References

Adler, H.A. (1987), *Economic Appraisal of Transport Projects*, Washington, World Bank.
Baumol, W.J. and Bradford, D.F. (1970), 'Optimal departures from marginal cost pricing', *American Economic Review*, 60, 215–83.
Bos, H.C. and Koyck, L.M. (1961), 'The appraisal of road construction projects; a practical example', *Review of Economics and Statistics*, 43, 13–20.
Button, K.J. (1979), 'Models for decision-making in the public sector', *OMEGA*, 7, 399–409.
Button, K.J. (1980), 'Some comments on Starkie's method of allocating interurban road and rail investment', *Regional Studies*, 14, 333–5.
Button, K.J. and Pearce, D.W. (1989), 'Infrastructure restoration as a tool for stimulating urban renewal – the Glasgow Canal', *Urban Studies*, 26, 559–71
Commission on the Third London Airport (1971), *Report*, London, HMSO.
de V. Graaf, J. (1975), 'Cost-benefit analysis: a critical view', *South African Journal of Economics*, 44, 233–44.
Foster, C.D. and Neuberger, H.L.I. (1974), 'The ambiguity of the consumer's surplus measure of welfare change', *Oxford Economic Papers*, 26, 66–77.
Friedlaender, A.F. (1965), *The Interstate Highway System: A Study in Public Investment*, Amsterdam, North-Holland.
Friedlaender, A.F. (1981), 'Price distortions and second best investment rules in the transportation industries', *American Economic Review, Papers and Proceedings*, 71, 389–93.
Gorman, W.M. (1955), 'The intransitivity of certain "criteria" used in welfare economics', *Oxford Economic Papers (new series)*, 7, 25–35.
Harrison, A.J. and Mackie, P.J. (1973), *The Comparability of Cost Benefit*, Civil Service Occasional Paper 5, London, HMSO.
Hicks, J.R. (1940), 'The valuation of social income', *Economics*, 7, 105–24.
Hill, M. (1968), 'A goal achievement matrix for evaluating alternative plans', *Journal of the American Institute of Planners*, 34, 19–29.
Joy, S. (1964), 'British Railways' track costs', *Journal of Industrial Economics*, 13, 74–89.
Kaldor, N. (1939), 'Welfare proposition and interpersonal comparisons of utility', *Economic Journal*, 49, 549–52.
Lichfield, N. and Chapman, W. (1968), 'Cost-benefit analysis and road proposals for a shopping centre – a case study: Edgware', *Journal of Transport Economics and Policy*, 2, 280–320.
Little, I.M.D. (1950), *A Critique of Welfare Economics*, Oxford, Oxford University Press.
McGuire, M. and Gain, H. (1969), 'The integration of equity and efficiency criteria in public project selection', *Economic Journal*, 79, 882–93.
Mishan, E.J. (1967), 'Interpretation of the benefits of private transport', *Journal of Transport Economics and Policy*, 1, 184–9.
Mishan, E.J. (1974), 'Flexibility and consistency in cost-benefit analysis', *Economica*, 41, 81–96.
Mishan, E.J. (1988), *Cost-Benefit Analysis* (3rd edition), London, Allen & Unwin.
Mohring, H. (1976), *Transportation Economics*, Cambridge, Mass., Ballinger.

Nijkamp, P. and van Delft, A. (1977), *Multi-criteria Analysis and Regional Decision-Making*, London, Martinus Nijhoff.

Parker, P. (1978), *A Way to Run a Railway*, Haldane Memorial Lecture.

Peaker, A. (1974), 'The allocation of investment funds between road and rail: a conversion factor linking financial and surplus rates of return', *Public Finance*, 75, 683–735.

Pearce, D. W. and Nash, C. A. (1983), *The Social Appraisal of Projects – A Text in Cost-Benefit Analysis*, London, Macmillan.

Prest, A.R. and Turvey, R. (1965), 'Cost-benefit analysis – a survey', *Economic Journal*, 75, 683–735.

Quinet, E. (1993), 'Can we value the environment', in Banister, D. and Button, K.J. (eds) *Transport, the Environment and Sustainable Development*, London, E. & F.N. Spon.

Samuelson, P.A. (1961), 'Evaluation of social income, capital formation and wealth', in F.A. Lutz and D.C. Hague (eds), *The Theory of Capital*, London, St Martins.

Simon, H.A. (1959), 'Theories of decision-making in economics and behavioural science', *American Economic Review*, 49, 253–83.

Skitovsky, T. (1941), 'A note on welfare propositions in economics', *Review of Economic Studies*, 9, 77–88.

Starkie, D.N.M. (1979), 'Allocation of investment to inter-urban road and rail', *Regional Studies*, 13, 323–36.

UK Department of Transport (1978), *Report of the Advisory Committee on Trunk Road Assessment (Leitch Committee)*, London, HMSO.

UK Department of Transport (1986), *Urban Road Appraisal: Report of the Standing Committee on Trunk Road Appraisal*, London, HMSO.

UK Department of Transport (1989), *COBA 9 Manual*, London, Department of Transport.

UK Department of Transport (1992), *Assessing the Environmental Impact of Road Schemes, Report of the Standing Committee on Trunk Road Assessment*, London, HMSO.

UK House of Commons Select Committee (1974), *First Report from the Expenditure Committee Session 1974, Public Expenditure on Transport*, HC 269, London, HMSO.

UK Treasury (1967), *Nationalised Industries: A Review of Economic and Financial Objectives*, Cmnd 3437, London, HMSO.

UK Treasury (1978), *The Nationalised Industries*, Cmnd 7131, London, HMSO.

Wheaton, W.C. (1978), 'Price-induced distortions in urban highway investment', *Bell Journal of Economics*, 9, 622–32.

Wildavsky, A. (1966), 'The political economy of efficiency: cost-benefit analysis, systems analysis and program budgeting', *Public Administration*, 26, 292–3.

Winston, C. (1991), 'Efficient transport infrastructure policy', *Journal of Economic Perspectives*, 5, 113–27.

Wood, D. (1993), 'Environmental quality and value for money in British roads policy', in D. Banister and K.J. Button (eds), *Transport, the Environment and Sustainable Development*, London, E. & F.N. Spon.

9   Transport Planning and Forecasting

9.1   The development of transport planning

The preceding chapters have concentrated primarily upon pricing and investment decisions for individual modes of transport in isolation – the pricing of public transport, urban car-users, etc. Little has been said about the coordination of pricing and investment decisions across whole sectors of transport. Coordination, as Adam Smith pointed out, will come about automatically in a perfectly competitive market framework where marginal cost pricing principles are universally applied. Indeed, there has been considerable emphasis on coordination through the market in the development of inter-urban transport policy in countries such as Britain and the USA from the late 1970s as we see in Chpater 11. Concern over safety is the now often considered to be the main interest of the authorities and, within a quality licensing framework, competition both within and among inter-urban modes is often encouraged. There is, however, generally, either by central or local government, some plannning of infrastructure provision in most countries and, indeed, at the international level there are coordinated plans for motorway and high speed rail development within the EC and other such groupings. The main objective in these cases is the avoidance of duplication, especially in relation to major development projects with a long period of gestation, and the adoption of a high degree of technical consistency.

In other areas of transport activity, and particularly in the urban context, it is often felt, although as we see in Chapter 11 this feeling has declined somewhat in recent years, necessary to introduce a high degree of planning and central/local government intervention to improve the overall efficiency of local transport provision. The role that transport may play in other spheres of economic activity is one reason for this (improved transport, for example, may form part of a social welfare policy and is currently seen as central to the revitalisation of local economies in depressed inner city areas), but a more general explanation may be found in the magnitude of the imperfections of the urban transport markets. The justification for urban transport planning in this context was usefully summarised some years ago in a UK policy document, *Transport Policy* (UK Department of Transport, 1977):

> The many activities concentrated in urban areas must be accessible to people and the economic and social life of cities depends on enormously diverse and complex patterns of travel and destination. Yet there is not enough road space in large towns and cities for people to travel as much as they like and how and when they like. This in

itself can be one source of grievance. Another is that intrusion of dense traffic brings
objectionable and sometimes intolerable noise, fumes and vibration.

We have already seen, in Chapter 5, the extent of the external effects of
transport and subsequently considered ways in which they may be tackled
individually. A comprehensive marginal pollution pricing regime combined with
comparable social investment criteria would ensure optimality. Political
resistance to such an approach combined with disquiet over the possible
distributional repercussions and the practical problems of implementation have so
far tended to rule out the full-scale use of market mechanisms to regulate the
urban transport sector. This does not mean that the pricing mechanism is not used
but rather that it forms part of a much larger package of policy instruments which
are combined with the intention of improving the overall efficiency of urban
transport in meeting the objectives of society.

The history of urban transport planning in the UK is comparatively short,
originating in the recognition that urban life-styles and cities themselves would
change once ownership of private cars became widespread. The physical planners
of the immediate pre- and post-Second World War periods were concerned with
redesigning cities and transport infrastructure to meet the requirements of a
motor-car age. Abercrombie, in the County of London Plan of 1943, for example,
typified much of the philosophy of the period in his proposals for the university
quarter of Bloomsbury and the area around Westminster where he advocated the
application of the precinctual principle. Traffic was to be diverted around these
areas on good quality, arterial roads, with the precincts served by a limited number of local, access routes. While this idea, which was American in origin, was
never applied to the two sites studied by Abercrombie, the broad principle was
employed in the post-war reconstruction of Coventry.

The 1947 Town and Country Planning Act institutionalised planning by making anyone wishing to develop land seek permission from the local authority. The
basis for decision making regarding land use changes were a series of proposal
maps which traced out proposed land uses for an horizon of ten years or more.
The 'Town Map' was a legal document which both took time to prepare and
required cumbersome procedures to be gone through prior to changes being accepted.

The system had the advantage that it allowed land to be set aside for schools,
residential development and so on but only limited land was allocated to road
construction. Further, since funds were not always available for rapid construction programmes, in many places where land was allocated for transport corridors
it led to blight and lack of maintenance of buildings which might at some unspec-
ified future date be taken for road building. These were particular problems since
a central theme of the physical planning approach to the urban transport problem
was that traffic congestion could be alleviated by improving the local transport
network.

As traffic grew alternative solutions were sought. While the initial approach to
urban planning had been a narrow one, two important developments occurred in
the 1950s and 1960s which strengthened the concept. First, although some
planners, such as Abercrombie, took a broad geographical view of urban problems the focus of most early planners tended to be local, seeking piecemeal
solutions to specific traffic problems. In the 1950s there was a widening out.
Local highway authorities were encouraged by central government to produce
joint plans for local road networks and the joint plans produced by the authorities

in the Manchester area (the SELNEC Highway Plan of 1962) and by the Merseyside area authorities (in 1965) bear witness to the success of this policy.

Secondly, and not entirely independent of coordinated highway planning, came the recognition of the strong links between land use and transport planning. The *Buchanan Report* (UK Ministry of Transport, 1963) provided firm evidence of the need to coordinate the two areas of planning. Buchanan was particularly concerned about the environmental cost of traffic, and argued that urban road networks should not be expanded to the extent needed to reduce congestion to some pre-defined levels, as was then the accepted practice, but rather changes in transport and urban land-use systems should be assessed in terms of the costs of reducing congestion while maintaining some pre- defined environmental standard. If the costs of expanding the transport network without violating the environmental standard prove excessive to the community then traffic must be restrained until the environmental limit is attained.

Once it became recognised that not only was there a need to consider objectives other than simply congestion in transport planning, especially since transport is an integral part of a much wider urban economic system, it became apparent that physical planning needed to be replaced by a more comprehensive planning framework. The coordinated approach which resulted embodied 'structure planning' which sets out policies for the development of land, transport and the local environment. The Town and Country Planning Act of 1968 embodied the idea of structure planning while the creation of the Department of the Environment in 1970 integrated overall responsibility for urban and transport planning in one organisation. The 1968 Transport Act created a number of Passenger Transport Authorities in major conurbations which were given responsibility for public transport operations within their areas. The PTAs were themselves committed to drawing up policies (within a year) and plans (within two years) to provide 'a properly integrated and efficient system of public transport to meet the needs of [the] area'. While the commitment to draw up structure plans necessitated liaison and coordination between local planning and highway departments and the PTAs, in practice land-use, road-building and public transport responsibilities remained separate – indeed in some cases the agencies had different boundaries. The Local Government Act, 1972, integrated the existing PTAs, plus three newly created ones, into a reformed local government structure. The Act placed further emphasis on the need for coordinated transport planning in urban areas and each urban authority was compelled to produce a Transport Policy and Programme (TPP) setting down the strategy and objectives which were being followed. The TPPs have been used since 1975 as a means of assessing the level of central government financial aid to local urban transport undertakings (via the Transport Supplementary Grant) and emphasis has been placed on integrating transport planning with the wider issues of land-use planning and social policy in the area. The aim of this structure, therefore, has been to distribute grants to reflect local transport needs, and to reduce central government control.

The move to structure planning which still forms the basis for local transport policy today, resulted in two major changes in the types of approach adopted by local transport agencies. First, there has been a trend towards more structured and phased planning; the Tyneside Study of 1968, for instance, produced an immediate action programme, a transportation plan for a fifteen-year horizon and a general urban strategy plan to the end of the century. The TPP framework encourages a continual monitoring and up-dating of plans within a rolling framework. Secondly, planning is no longer viewed simply in terms of investment but now embraces the short-term management of existing resources. In part this may be a reflection of the changing objectives of urban transport planning but it is also the consequence of a greater economic awareness in planning that there is an opportunity cost associated with all actions involving the employment of scarce resources.

9.2   The theory of transport planning

The movement away from physical transport planning to structure planning in the 1960s increased the economic input into the transport planning process, although the development of modern planning methods must be attributed mainly to civil engineers, statisticians and mathematicians rather than economists. One of the main problems of urban land-use/transport planning is the enormous range of possible options available, although this is much less of a difficulty in a country such as Britain, where urban land-use patterns are established and not susceptible to rapid change – in such cases one is seeking the optimal transport system for the existing urban structure. A sequential approach to urban transport planning may, therefore, be appropriate (UK House of Commons Expenditure Committee, 1972) with four different levels of planning taking place, namely,

(1) design of broad land-use plan;
(2) design of strategic transport plan;
(3) design of detailed land-use plan; and
(4) design of detailed transport plan.

(There may be some feedback between (3) and (4) in the sequence.)

The transport planing process itself is a complex process which entails far more complex institutional and technical issues than can be fully considered here. In general, it can be broken down into a number of stages, each involving a certain amount of economic input to it. There is no firm or accepted best-practice method of drawing up a transport plan, different agencies favour different detailed approaches. Broadly, however, the process may be typified by the various stages set out in Figure 9.1 but this must be seen very much as a stylisation, intended rather more to show where economics can contribute to the transport planning process, than as a representation of any actual planning procedure. A few comments are justified on each of the stages.

Goals and objectives

As we have seen above the objectives of urban transport planning tend to change over time; periods where there is an emphasis being placed upon social and environmental considerations often being followed by a focus on improving the efficiency of the system. The general objectives of policy need to be made specific to permit trade-offs among alternative goals at a later stage of the planning process. The economist's contribution at this stage is that of a balancing agent, often counteracting engineering pressures for the emphasis of the plan to be on improving traffic flow or adopting capital-intensive solutions to environmental problems. The notion of 'opportunity cost' is essential if resources are to be used efficiently. He may also act as a sieve, pointing out the incompatibility or contrary nature of certain goals. Since goals and objectives are often formulated at the beginning of the planning exercise before full information on existing transport problems have been obtained, they may be redefined after later stages in the sequence.

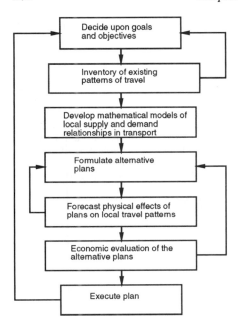

Figure 9.1
The urban transport planning process

Inventory of existing transport system
Information is gathered about the nature of the local transport system and travel patterns both by sampling and counting people actually in the act of transport and by obtaining information from firms and households about their travel behaviour and requirements. Additional information is often extracted from official sources such as the Census, the National Travel Survey and the Family Expenditure Survey. The types of surveys conducted and the questions asked have changed over the years as a result of important developments in transport forecasting. As we see in later sections much more emphasis is now placed on understanding why people travel rather than on modelling flows of traffic. Consequently, more detailed information of household characteristics is now sought although the greater efficiency of modern measuring techniques means that the actual sample size has tended to fall (from over 10,000 households in the large studies of the late 1960s – the last substantial household survey in the UK, that of the West Yorkshire Transportation Studies, sampled 12,322 addresses – to considerably less than 1000 today).

The broad-brush approach has given way to seeking greater insights into representative travel behaviour. One reason for this is that the types of planning issue under review have changed with time and in particular the large road building programmes have tended to be replaced by traffic management and public transit policies. But modelling has also evolved. The development of stated preference techniques in recent years has in particular furthered our understanding of the underlying nature of travel decisions. Quite clearly, since the basic aim is to seek

information on existing conditions of supply and demand for urban transport services, economists can contribute to formulating the types of questions to ask.

Mathematical simulations of the local transport market

The following sections look at modelling and forecasting techniques, and in particular their economic underpinnings, but it is important to emphasise at this stage
the basic requirements of the simulation models. Transport markets are complex
and to produce models which replicate all their details is both difficult and, more
importantly, likely to be too cumbersome for later forecasting work. Heggie
(1978) suggests that the prerequisites of a good transport model are that it:

- assists in understanding and explaining behaviour;
- aids policy formulation; and
- provides robust predictions.

The models of travel and transport demand are used for forecasting; therefore it is
important that the explanatory factors can themselves be predicted with some
degree of certainty. The models are also used to assess the effects of different
planning options; thus it is important that they are simple to use and permit the
effect of several alternative strategies to be explored. One of the major limitations
of early models was that they were cumbersome to manipulate, limiting the
possible policy options which could be assessed.

Formulating alternative plans

The complex and wide-ranging effects of any change in an urban transport system
makes it very difficult in practice for more than a limited number of detailed plans
to be fully formulated. A comprehensive plan consists of a package of projects
and schemes, and for a large city the possible combinations forming such a package is immense. In some cases only one planning alternative is drawn up in detail
after a preliminary sifting of other possibilities at an earlier stage in the planning
process. Usually the planning alternatives considered are a little more numerous
and, besides the 'do-nothing' situation, which may act as a bench-mark, generally
involve at least one public transport orientated package, one private transport-
based proposal and probably one rather more central alternative, offering a mix of
private and public transport (witness, for example, the Merseyside Area Land–
Use Transportation Study of 1969). Since the plans themselves are later
evaluated, this approach should not be as restrictive as it appears. Following the
forecasting and/or the evaluation stage new light may be shed on the detailed
effect of alternative plans, and new compromise packages of projects emerge.
Without feedback of this kind it would be quite possible, given the vast range of
alternative plans which are feasible for most large cities, to miss the potentially
most beneficial alternative.

Forecasting the physical effects of alternative plans

Transport forecasting is looked at in detail in sections 9.3–9.6, the modelling and
forecasting stages being both central to the planning process and having a very
substantial economics component. The key aspect of forecasting is that it provides
the planner/decision-maker with useful information about the *long-term*
implications of plans, emphasising in particular those areas where there are significant differences in the consequences of the alternative plans. Given the fact
that transport is going to exist in the urban setting, irrespective of the plan

adopted, and providing a 'do-nothing' option is assessed, then it is the *relative*
performance of plans which is important. Additionally, it is important that the
final decision-makers are aware of the underlying assumptions of the forecasts so
that they can assess the reliability and strengths of the traffic forecasts. To this
end, most forecasts are now presented as a range of likely outcomes under
alternative assumptions. Table 9.1, for example, sets out the official UK traffic
forecasts to the year 2025 under both a set of low growth assumptions and a set of
high growth assumptions.

Table 9.1
Forecasts of car traffic in Great Britain to 2025

Year	Low	High
1980	100	100
1990	106	110
1995	118	130
2000	129	149
2005	140	168
2010	150	186
2015	161	203
2020	171	219
2025	182	234

Source: UK Department of Transport (1989)

Economic evaluation
The economic evaluation of plans normally involves employing some variant,
albeit in a less formalised format, of the cost-benefit analysis approach outlined in
Chapter 8 (Truelove, 1992). The comprehensive nature and emphasis on distributional effects which characterises the Planning Balance Sheet makes it a particularly attractive technique in the urban planning context. It is also sufficiently
'open' to permit the various consequences of plans to be related directly to the
objectives of the planners. With traditional cost-benefit analysis, not only are
there problems of placing monetary values on many items but also the final output of a single net present value of benefits is often viewed with suspicion by
members of the urban community. General practice involves the inclusion of
public participation at the evaluation stage, often in the form of public inquiries.
In some cases – such as the Layfield Inquiry into the Greater London Development Plan (UK Department of the Environment, 1973) – such inquiries can result
in quite substantial revisions of the plan to be adopted. Evaluation of something
as complex as a transport plan is, by necessity, a political process but economists
can assist the decision-maker by ruling out plans which are *clearly* inferior to
others while at the same time giving a systematic presentation of the pros and
cons of the final short-list of alternatives. The inherent value judgements built
into all forms of CBA make it a powerful aid in evaluation, but it is unlikely ever
to provide an automatic, purely technical decision-making calculus, indeed it is
debatable whether such a mechanical approach is to be desired.

Implementation
While it is often possible to implement some parts – usually traffic management components – of a transport plan almost immediately upon acceptance, other components – usually those involving infrastructure changes – are much longer-term in nature. It is important, therefore, that actions are phased so that costs are kept at a minimum. Additionally, over time objectives change and 'errors' in forecasts become apparent and this may necessitate revisions of the plan. Consequently, there are feedbacks from the implementation stage back to the early stages of the planning process; in other words modern planning is seen as an on-going, rolling process of adaptation and change. It is often important, in this context, to ensure the maximum flexibility in the implementation programme.

The preceding paragraphs have painted a thumb-nail picture of the transport planning process, highlighting the role economics can play. It is thin on detail and hides many of the subtleties of the planning exercise: readers interested in this specific aspect of transport economics are strongly advised to refer to one of the excellent texts now available on the subject. The following sections consider the economic problems of transport modelling and forecasting. These areas, together with plan evaluation, have become increasingly the preserve of economists and involve the application of modern microeconomic theory.

9.3 Modelling and forecasting
To conduct successful planning exercises it is essential to have reliable forecasts of the probable effect of different policy options. General qualitative assessments can often provide useful insights into the effects of different policies but good planning decisions require that we have more exact information of the detailed quantified relationship between travel and transport and the factors that influence them. Engineers, for example, need projections of future traffic flows when designing roads and other infrastructure. Recent years have witnessed a substantial growth in work attempting to specify and calibrate econometric travel demand models, a trend strongly encouraged in the UK by the introduction of structure planning in British urban areas in the late 1960s and the need for major transport planning agencies to produce statements of 'Transport Policies and Programmes'. In the US the increased role of the federal authorities in funding both inter-state transport facilities and local, urban transit systems had a similar effect. The need to allocate large sums to durable transport infrastructure schemes in the Third World motivated the World Bank to pursue a similar course. More recently still, the general move towards more careful project appraisal at the micro level has led to the development of stated preference techniques employing market research style procedures to transport forecasting.

Having noted the growth of work in the field it is only fair to point to the limitations of what has been forthcoming. A study of 41 road schemes in the UK concluded from a comparison of actual and projected flows that only in 22 cases were the actual flows within 20 per cent of the original forecast. Of the remainder, flows ranged from 50 per cent below to 105 per cent above the original estimate (UK House of Commons Committee of Public Accounts, 1988). The forecasts for the M25 London orbital road, for instance, were that on 21 of the 26 thre-lane sections the traffic flow would be between 50,000 and 79,000 vehicles a day in the fifteenth year whereas the flow within a very short time was between 81,400 and 129,000. It is not only with road traffic that problems arise. Pickrell's (1989) study of grant programmes funded by the federal Urban Mass Transportation Administration in the USA found that all ten urban public transport projects examined produced major underestimates of costs per passenger (for example, the costs for the Miami heavy rail transit were 872 per cent of those forecast, for Detroit's downtown people mover they were 795 per cent and for Buffalo's light rail transit project they were 392 per cent). While inaccurate costing was one element of the problem, the forecast patronage in all cases was over-optimistic (see Table 9.2). Indeed, only the Washington heavy rail transit project experiences actual patronage that is more than half of that which was forecast. Some of the differences can be explained by difficulties in predicting future values of explanatory variable such as demographic changes, automobile costs and the service level which the public transport service would offer, but Pickrell argues that important questions must also be raised over the structure of the models employed, the ways in which they were used and the interpretation of output during the planning process.

Table 9.2
Forecast and actual rail transit ridership in a number of US studies*.

| | Heavy rail transit projects | | | Light rail transit projects | | | | $DPM^\dagger$ projects | |
	Wash-ington	Balt-imore	Miami	Buffalo	Pitts-burgh	Port-land	Sacra-mento	Miami	Detroit
Forecast	569.6	103.0	239.9	92.0	90.5	42.5	50.0	41.0	67.7
Actual	411.6	42.6	35.4	29.2	30.6	19.7	14.1	10.8	11.3
% difference	−28	−59	−85	−68	−66	−54	−71	−74	−83

* A heavy rail transit project for Atlanta was also examined but no passenger forecasts were made.
$\dagger$ Downtown people mover
Source: Pickrell (1989)

It is quite clear from these findings that forecasting traffic is far from easy. While these problems are diverse and some rather technical, a number of general comments on the application of econometric analysis to transport forecasting highlight the difficulties that have been encountered in constructing travel demand models.

First, transport is by its nature a derived demand but equally, as we have seen in Chapter 2, it interacts with land use and location patterns. There is, therefore, a logic in developing a forecasting model which allows for these very close linkages. This is obviously not an easy thing to do but it is unlikely that reliable long-term forecasts will be forthcoming if transport and land-use models are treated in tandem rather than developed within an interactive framework. Indeed, using the type of interlinked land-use and transport model set out in Figure 9.2 it was shown that interactive effects over time account for a significant portion of the economic benefits of a transport scheme. A useful survey of work in this area is contained in Berechman and Gordan (1986).

Moving on to the actual transport modelling framework, traditional micro-economic analysis specifies a demand relationship relating quantity demand to price and assumes that this relationship only changes (that is, shifts) when factors other than price vary. In transport demand analysis it is fairly easy to incorporate the 'shift' variables into a modelling framework because their values are essentially determined outside the transport system (for example, income changes or changes in taste). The control 'price' variable is much more difficult. As we have seen, price is a broad concept in transport, embracing time, comfort and other factors, in addition to simply the monetary cost of a trip. While generalised cost offers one method of reflecting the multi-dimensional nature of the price variable there is a tendency in forecasting work to employ changes in the ease of access as a proxy for price. Accessibility is nothing more complicated than an index that reflects the ease with which people can achieve the various activities they wish.

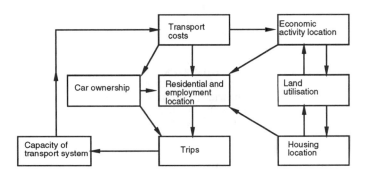

Source: Webster *et al.* (1988)

Figure 9.2
Urban land-use and transport interaction model

Transport systems are extremely complicated, comprising many modes of travel, varieties of routes and combinations of different potential travel patterns. The sheer number of links and possibilities in any non-trivial transport network has inevitably resulted in simplifications having to be adopted by forecasters to permit calculations to be reduced to manageable proportions. Further, the 'product' being offered by the transport system is also unique in that a passenger kilometre at a particular point on the network at a specific time may be performing a completely different function to another passenger kilometre at another time and at a different point in the system.

While not always designed to handle the land-use/transport interaction effects, these latter types of problems have resulted in the emergence of three broad types of forecasting framework, each with its own characteristics and each with its particular advantages and defects. Each of these has many variants but they can generally be thought of as sequential, disaggregate and interactive frameworks. They are looked at in turn. While the discussion is couched primarily in terms of forecasting the demand for person movements, much of the traffic carried by the transport system is freight. The demand to move commodities differs quite substantially from person movements in the sense that is, normally, unidirectional while person trips are usually circular (that is, from home to work to home). The types of forecasting frameworks used to look at goods traffic are, however, essentially the same as for person movements, modified usually only in terms of the actual variables used (for a survey of work in the field of urban goods traffic demand forecasting see, Button and Pearman, 1981, and Pitfield and Whiteing, 1985). The three main approaches are now reviewed in turn.

9.4   Sequential travel demand forecasting

Sequential models attempt to reduce the complexity of travel demand forecasting by breaking the complicated patterns of demand for travel into, usually, four sub-models. First, the trip generation/attraction model (the trip-end model) is used to forecast the number of trips originating and ending within predefined geographical zones of the study area (these might be countries in international travel studies or smaller areas within a city in urban land-use studies). The total zonal trips are then 'distributed' between origin-destination pairs of zones. Thirdly, for each flow between different zones, a modal choice model is calculated to explain the split of traffic between the alternative forms of transport available. Finally, the traffic flows between each pair of zones and by each mode of transport are assigned to specific routes on the transport network. In the context of freight modelling the parallel sub-models represent transactions, flows, means change and network assignment, with an industrial location model added to make the links between industrial activities and freight vehicle movements explicit. A vehicle loading sub-model is also sometimes added to shift the emphasis from the vehicle to the consignment.

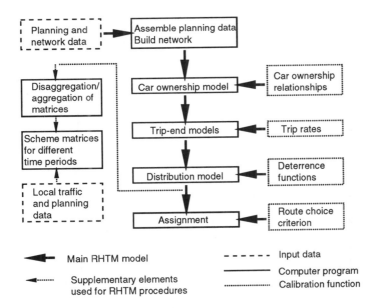

Figure 9.3
The Regional Highway Traffic Model

Figure 9.3 provides an example of the sequential approach as developed by the Regional Highway Traffic Model team in the UK and developed to assist specifically in national road planning. Mode choice sub-models are excluded because of the dominant position filled by motor-car traffic. The approach set out is particularly useful in distinguishing between the data analysis, computer simulation and calibration aspects of the overall modelling and forecasting process.

The sequential framework may, therefore, be seen as moving from aggregate to disaggregate forecasting with each successive sub-model in the sequence acting as a check on the one following. In econometric terms the sequence is recursive. Attempts have been made (for example, in work forming part of the appraisal of the Greater London Development Plan) to introduce feedbacks from later to earlier sub-models in the sequence on the grounds that one cannot really forecast, say, mode choice without knowing probable levels of congestion on each route and this latter knowledge only becomes available after the assignment stage. The transport model sequence is usually preceded by a land-use forecasting model which attempts to describe the effect of changing land-use patterns on transport. Ideally, because land use is itself partly affected by transport conditions, there should also be feedbacks from the assignment sub-model to land-use patterns but to date this has proved to be practicably impossible.

Trip-end sub-models are usually estimated on a household basis using either multivariate regression techniques or category analysis. The former statistically relates the number of trips made by households to the socio-economic characteristics of the households (for example, income, number of residents, car ownership, social status, etc.) and the type of environment in which they are located. The concentration on the household is now widely accepted as standard practice to reduce statistical problems that appear when data is grouped excessively (for example, by geographical zone). Category analysis is simpler, involving the construction of a multi-dimensional matrix with each dimension representing a socio-economic variable stratified into a number of discrete classes or categories. For example, households may be divided into four income classes, three car-ownership classes and two locational classes, giving in total 24 categories of household, each with its own average trip-generation level. Forecasts are obtained by predicting the number of households falling into each category at the target date, and multiplying by the relevant average trip generation rate. The total zonal trips in the example above would be predicted as:

$$T = \sum_{k=1}^{24} n_k r_k$$

where n_k is the future number of households in category k, and r is the corresponding trip-rate.

Revealed preference approaches to trip distribution models are of two broad types. Growth factor models involve extrapolating existing patterns of trips between alternative origins and destinations with projected trip-end estimates acting as constraints on the total number of trips leaving or entering any individual zone. They are little more than mechanical procedures based upon past behaviour patterns and suffer, in particular, from inabilities to allow for new zones being created. They have also gone out of favour because they require a substantial amount of data input.

The second group, simulation models, are more overtly economic in their nature. The gravity model is the most commonly used member of this group and has the attraction of having a precise economic interpretation (Cochrane, 1975).

Gravity models differ in form but all exhibit terms reflecting the relative attractiveness of different destinations and terms that measure the effect of impedance caused by the nature of the transport system. In early work, attractions were specified simply in terms of population size but in more recent studies a multiplicity of factors have been included, frequently varying with the journey purpose under consideration. Similarly, the crude notion that distance is a full reflection of impedance has given way to the incorporation of various forms of generalised cost measures.

The interactive version of the gravity model takes the form:

$$T_{ij} = T_i T_j A_i A_j B_j f(C_{ij}) \tag{9.1}$$

subject to $A_i = \{\sum_j T_j B_j f(C_{ij})\}^{-1}$ and $B_j = \{\sum_j T_i A_i f(C_{ij})\}^{-1}$

where: T_{ij} is trips between zones i and j;
$\quad\quad\quad T_i$ is the total number of trips originating in zone i;
$\quad\quad\quad T_j$ is the total number of trips destined for zone j;
$\quad\quad\quad C_{ij}$ is the generalised cost of travel between zones i and j; A_i and
$\quad\quad\quad B_j$ are 'fuzz factors' – sometimes justified as indices of inverse accessibility – to ensure that total trips distributed across the whole study area originating from i do not exceed T_i and those destined for j do not exceed T_j.

This doubly constrained model assumes that trip-makers are competing for a limited number of opportunities in any specific zone and has clear applications to modelling the demand for work or school trips where job and educational opportunities can be assumed independent of the transport system. In many cases only one constraint (either T_i or T_j) is imposed; for example, with inter-urban freight demand one is often only interested either in the way movements fan out from a city or depot or in the way they converge on it. Urban non-work demand models are also often based upon origin-constrained models with less concern about destinations. On other occasions it may prove necessary to relax the constraints to facilitate easier fitting of the models – constrained versions of the gravity model usually requiring specific computer software for calibration. An alternative simulation model considers the opportunities available in different zones to meet the needs of travellers.

The intervening opportunities model assumes that people try to keep their trips as short as possible and only lengthen them if nearer destinations do not prove acceptable to their needs. Individual residents in a given zone are assumed to consider opportunities for the location of their conduct of specific activities (residence, work, shopping, etc.) at various places, starting from the base zone and fanning out to other zones in increasing order of difficulty in reaching them. Each time an opportunity is considered, there is a given, constant chance that it will be selected. The model takes the general form:

$$T_{ij} = T_i \{\exp(-LV_j) - \exp(-LV_{j+1})\} \tag{9.2}$$

where: V is the possible destination just considered;
$\quad\quad\quad L$ is a constant representing the probability of possible destination being accepted (if considered).

While this type of approach has an intuitive appeal, it does suffer from the problem that, empirically, L seems to vary with V rather than remaining constant. Adjustment techniques to correct for the 'wandering' of L values are available but their use seems to violate the notion of constancy. Empirical studies indicate that the results obtained using the intervening opportunities model are no better than those from gravity models. Attempts to develop the opportunities framework by considering competing rather than intervening opportunities (by basing the underlying probability function on the ratio between the trip opportunities in a zone and its competing opportunities) offer no improvements in a forecasting context but complicate the estimation process considerably.

In some instances, as for example with inter-urban road traffic forecasting in the UK, the tradition is to employ a 'fixed trip matrix' which assumes that the total number of trips (that is, the trips generated and attracted) is unaffected by the new transport scheme. The total traffic, which may well grow due to changing socio-economic conditions, is simply redistributed as a result of the change in transport policy or infrastructure investment. If new traffic is generated, however, this result may prove distortive. In Figure 9.4 D_I represents the true aggregate relationship between the cost of travel and the traffic flow. As a result of, say, a road investment the cost of trip-making falls from P to P_I with traffic increasing to F_I. Assuming that there has been no shift in demand due to changing income or other socio-economic factors, the traditional model would assume that demand had remained fixed at the all-traffic flow – in other words that the implied demand curve is D. This means that the benefit enjoyed by the generated traffic $(F_I - F)$ and represented by the shaded area in the diagram would be excluded from the subsequent appraisal stage. This is another reason why there are often feedback links which, in this case, result in the trip end models being rerun incorporating some allowance for this generation effect.

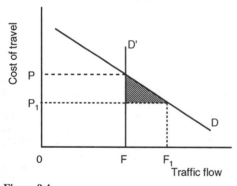

Figure 9.4
The fixed trip matrix

Modal split models allocate traffic flows to particular types of vehicles. In some cases, for example, with urban freight transport or long-distance international passenger transport, one mode so dominates a particular sphere of transport activity that no mode choice sub-model is required although this is exceptional. The traditional method of splitting origin-destination traffic flows by mode involves the use of diversion curves. These show the proportion of traffic likely to

favour a particular mode given its relative cost (or other) advantage over alternative modes. If we are concerned with two forms of transport, *a* and *b*, then a
typical model might be,

$$\frac{T_{ij}^a}{T_{ij}^a + T_{ij}^b} = \frac{1}{1 + e^{-\lambda(C_{ij}^b - C_{ij}^a)}} \qquad (9.3)$$

which yields a diversion curve of the form seen in Figure 9.5. Normally a series
of curves are estimated by sub-dividing the travelling population (for example, by
income) and modes (for example, by service ratios).

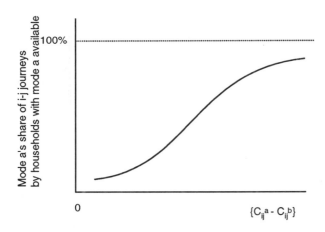

Figure 9.5
Diversion curve of traffic between modes '*a*' and '*b*'

   In some studies mode choice is modelled prior to distribution using trip-end or
interchange models. The former are often used in highway-orientated origin and
destination studies where the emphasis is on car travel with public transport being
treated as little more than a residual to be subtracted from the trip-end predictions
prior to assignments being made. The emphasis on variables such as car ownership and income, and the general neglect of public transport characteristics, limits
the usefulness of this approach in urban transport planning. Interchange models
are more commonly used in public transport feasibility studies and, consequently,
concentrate on comparative time, cost and service differentials between competing modes. Models of this type take the form:

$$T_{ijm} = a_o X_{ij}^{a_1} (F_{ij}^M)^{a_2} (F_{ij}^b)^{a_3} (H_{ij}^M)^{a_4} (H_{ij}^b)^{a_5} \qquad (9.4)$$

where X_{ij} is a matrix of exogenous economic and social variables;

F_{ij}^M is the financial cost by mode *M;*

H_{ij}^M is the time cost by mode M; and

the superscript b indicates the money/time cost by the best mode.

Models of this type have a foundation in economic theory (Quandt, 1970) but estimation of parameters $a_1 - a_5$ pose serious statistical problems.

The final sub-model, route assignment, compares the travellers' preferences for routes with the characteristics of the routes available. Early approaches relied upon diversion curves similar to those used in modal choice work but the development of minimum-path algorithms combined with improved computing facilities has permitted the introduction of more sophisticated techniques. A major problem in assignment is the possible need to constrain traffic flows on each link in the transport network to the capacity of the link. If the capacity constraint is omitted then an 'all-or-nothing' assignment results and no allowance is made for the congestion which accompanies high traffic volumes (see Chapter 5). In reality, travellers use all routes, both the initially cheap and the not so cheap, especially when overall cost differentials are small. The introduction of capacity constraints permits this to be reflected in the model by adjusting link speeds (and hence costs) as the assignment proceeds and congestion levels rise.

In summary the sequential method of forecasting broadly involves developing a series of mathematical models taking the general form:

$$T_i = f(X_i) \; ; \; T_j = f(X_j) \tag{9.5a}$$
$$T_{ij} = f(T_i, T_j, C_{ij}) \tag{9.5b}$$
$$T_{ijM} = f(T_{ij}, C_{ijM}, C_{ijM}') \tag{9.5c}$$
$$T'_{ijMP} = f(T_{ijMP}, Ci_{jMP}, C_{ijMP}') \tag{9.5d}$$

where the prime notation refers to alternative modes (M') or routes (P'). Clearly, the series of calculations required to calibrate this set of equations places tremendous strains on the data base available and, in most studies, large and expensive surveys are needed to gather the necessary information. Also, as pointed out above, it is difficult to incorporate the desirable feedback from assignment and other stages to trip generation so that quality of service variables are adequately and consistently reflected in each sub-model of the sequence. Statistically, while it is possible to test the significance of the individual models in the sequence it is not possible to undertake statistical tests of the overall recursive system. Disaggregate models have been developed to avoid some of these problems and to approach more closely to the basic decision-making unit, the household (Ben-Akiva and Lerman, 1985).

9.5 Disaggregate modelling

The substantial data input required to calibrate satisfactorily the sub-models and the difficulty of transferring models once estimated from one data area to another, combined with dissatisfaction with the basically mechanistic and physical nature of the sequential approach, has resulted in an alternative mathematical approach being developed (see Quandt, 1976). This disaggregate method of travel demand forecasting emphasises the economic-psychological influences on travel behaviour at the individual household level. The idea is that households are utility-maximizers who, mainly for mathematical convenience, are considered to make travel decisions in isolation from other activities. The emphasis is on short-run decisions rather than long-run mobility decisions. Small stratified samples of households (about 700 or so) provide the data input into the models which tend to be probabilistic, rather than deterministic, in nature (that is, they forecast the probability of particular household travel patterns rather than the average number and type of trips to be undertaken). A personal disaggregate model of trip-making would be of the general form:

$$P(f,d,h,m,r) = P(f)P(d/f)P(h/f,d)\ P(m/f,d,h)\ P(r/f,d,h,m) \tag{9.6}$$

where $P(f,d,h,m,r)$ is the probability that an individual will undertake a trip with frequency (f) to destination (d) during time of day (h) using mode (m) and via route (r) out of a choice set comprising all possible combinations of frequencies, destination, time of day, modes and routes available to the individual. For actual planning or assessment, the forecasts produced from such models must be aggregated up to the level of the geographical zone – it is the inter-zonal level, for example, which determines the level of public transport demand. While there are claims that the approach can be used in comprehensive transport planning its main role to date has been in policy assessment (for example, looking at car pooling proposals, pollution controls, public transport subsidies, etc. – see Ben-Akiva, 1977).

Broadly, disaggregate models are characterised by two main features. First, they explicitly recognise that travel decisions emerge out of individuals' optimising behaviour and, if it is pointed out that the final goods consumed as a result of travel are normal, then at a very minimum the demand for travel ought to be related positively to disposable incomes and negatively to the prices of transport services. Secondly, most have their origins in the 'attributal theory of demand' associated with Lancaster (1966). This approach to human behaviour assumes that people desire to maximise a utility function which has, as its arguments, commodity attributes rather than the quantities of the actual goods consumed. In other words, if we represent the amounts of attributes by the vector z, the amounts of commodities (in this case travel alternatives) by the vector x, posit a utility function, $U(z)$, and a production of attribute function, $G(x)$, which reflects the attributes of different travel alternatives, and assume that potential travellers are constrained by income, y, and the price of travel, p, then we can reduce the problem to solving:

max $U(z)$ (9.7)
subject to $z = G(x),$
                $x \geq 0,$
                $p.x \leq y.$

As an example, if one is considering air transport between the UK and the USA, then the alternative commodities would be the different fare-packages offered by the airlines, and the attributes of each would be characteristics such as money costs, speed, period of advance booking, timing, type of aircraft, on-plane service (food, drink, films, etc.), stop-over regulations, required length of stay at destination, etc.

Direct attempts have been made to apply Lancaster's theory at the aggregate level by Quandt (1970) and associates in the context of abstract mode modelling. At the inter-urban level Quandt and Baumol (1966) attempted to construct an abstract mode model for air, bus and car journeys between sixteen city pairs in California using cost and time (both absolute and relative) as the determining attributes, but the results were inferior to those obtained from more conventional trip-distribution models. Howrey's (1969) study of air travel out of Cleveland produced an abstract mode model with correct signs, significant coefficients and a good overall fit to survey data. However, while its explanatory power proved statistically superior to a conventional gravity model it turned out to be inferior in terms of *ex post* forecasting quality. Talvitie (1973) concentrated on developing the framework to handle intra-urban travel while Baumol and Vinod (1970), by combining the attributed theory of demand with an inventory theory of goods handling, have adapted the approach to deal with urban freight transport demand.

While some of the calibration problems which were associated with the early aggregate abstract mode models have been resolved (see Quandt, 1970), it has been the introduction of disaggregate approaches which has marked the greatest advances. The major advance in this context was the realisation that each individual has a different utility function, partly because of quantifiable differences in their personal characteristics but also partly because of random factors. While the heterogeneous nature of the population poses serious problems, the work of Domenich and McFadden (1976) in modelling the random factors, and especially their theoretical work on justifying the use of 'multi-nomial logit models', forms the basis of much modern disaggregate analysis. The forms of disaggregate model that have been developed along these lines, and the range of applications to which they have been applied, are many.

Most of the recent work on disaggregate modelling has centred on mathematical and calibration issues and there is no intention of taking discussion of such matters any further in this book. The mathematical complexity stems from the fact that one is looking at discrete choices – that is, whether a person makes a trip or not – and this involves complications not normally encountered when considering continuous functions. A good indication of the current direction of work is to be found in the collection of papers contained in Ben-Akiva and Lerman (1985) although the reader should be warned that many of the contributions have a substantial mathematical content.

9.6 Interactive and stated preference modelling

While the sequential and disaggregate approaches to transport demand analysis concentrate on developing sophisticated mathematical simulations, recently there has been a growth of interest in 'behavioural realism', and an emphasis on 'understanding the phenomenon' (Dix, 1977). This has been tied in with the greater use of stated preference techniques which we have already encountered in Chapter 5 in the context of contingency evaluation procedures. This latter approach which to adopt Kroes and Sheldon's (1988) definition, is 'a family of techniques which use individual respondents' statements about their preferences in a set of transport options to estimate utility functions', is often claimed to be helpful when:

- there is insufficient variation in revealed preference data to examine all variables of interest;
- there is a high level of correlation between the explanatory variables in a revealed preference model making statistical estimation of parameters difficul;:
- a radically new technology or policy takes the analysis outside of the realms where current revealed behaviour is relevant;
- variables are not easily expressed in standard units (for example, when the interest is in the effects on demand of less-turbulent travel by air).

The aim of interactive modelling is to develop models that get closer to the essential decision process underlying travel behaviour. Rather than simply incorporate variables such as household status in mathematical models because the statistical 'explanation' of the model appears to be improved, interactive modelling seeks to explain why status affects travel behaviour. Theoretically, travel is seen as one of a whole range of complementary and competitive activities operating in a sequence of events in time and space. It is seen to represent the method by which people trade time to move location in order to enjoy successive activities. Generally, time and space constraints are thought to limit the choices of activities open to individuals. The technique is, still far from fully developed but it has been applied only in a relatively limited number of small-scale forecasting studies (for example, by Jones, 1978, in the UK to school bus operations and by Fowkes and Preston, 1991, to new local rail services; and by Phifer *et al.*, 1980, in the USA to energy constraints).

The emphasis of interactive models is upon the household (or individual) as the decision-making unit. Ideally, an interactive model should exhibit six main properties (Heggie, 1978):

(1)   It should involve the entire household and allow for interaction between its members.
(2)   It should make existing constraints on household behaviour quite explicit.
(3)   It should start from the household's existing pattern of behaviour.
(4)   It should work by confronting the household with realistic changes in its travel environment and allowing it to respond realistically.
(5)   It should allow for the influence of long-term adaptation.
(6)   It should be able to tell the investigator something fundamental that he did not know before.

In general, the approach is typified by a fairly small sample and careful survey techniques, often involving such things as 'board games' (such as the 'household activities travel simulator' (HATS) developed by the Oxford University Transport Studies Unit) or other visual aids, frequently computer based, to permit households to appreciate the full implications of changes in transport policy for their own behaviour. In a sense it represents an attempt to conduct laboratory experiments by eliciting responses in the context of known information and constraints. The HATS approach, for example, was to confront a household with a map of the local area together with a 24 hour 'strip representation of coloured pieces' showing how current activities of the household are spread over space and throughout the day. Changes to the transport system were then postulated (for example, reduced parking availability in the local urban centre) and the effects on the household's activities throughout the day were simulated by adjustments to the strip representation. In this way changes in the transport system could be seen to influence the entire 24 hour life pattern of the household, and apparently unsuspected changes in 'remote' trip-making behaviour can be traced back to the primary change. It makes clear the constraints and linkages that may affect activity and transport choices. The emphasis is on the micro-unit with the aim of being able to develop fairly simple models which permit much clearer insights into the overall effects of transport policy. By asking respondents to trace the effect of changes in transport provision on the entire set of activities undertaken during a day (or week), information on important travel intentions can be seen and the relationships between travel and non-travel activities become explicit.

More recent studies have adopted rather more sophisticated experimentation procedures, often involving computers, which provide for greater flexibility and easier interaction with those being 'interviewed'. While this aspect of the approach has been refined important technical issues remain regarding using the information gathered from stated preference type experiments for forecasting. There is still, for example, much to be learned about why some households give strategically biased responses; in particular there are difficulties in handling habit, inertia and hysterisis in an experimental framework. At a more technical level, Bates (1988) points to our lack of knowledge about the error structures associated with stated preference data and the particular problems of pooling data across individuals.

In contrast to the more traditional revealed preference schools, advocates of this approach, however, point to both the specific recognition that travel is a derived demand and the fact that transport policies have qualitative, as well as quantitative, effects on people's lives. In the longer term, when operational models are more fully developed, the framework may offer the much-sought-after basis for integrating land-use and transport planning assessment. In the short term the approach has offered useful insights and a method for cross-checking the validity of conventional statistical analysis of behavioural data.

9.7   Further reading and references

Heggie (1972) offers a useful extension to this chapter by setting out in more technical detail the methodology of transport planning and by outlining some of the basic techniques. Truelove (1992) is a very readable account of how transport planning developed and operates in practice in the UK, and Deakin (1990) discusses some key US issues. Bayliss (1992) offers a perspective on the approach to transport planning in the developing world, and Timberlake (1988) provides useful case study material. Jones (1977) provides a terse but very useful guide to the contribution that economics may make to the transport planning process and also sketches out in more detail than has been possible above the various methods of transport demand forecasting. The set of papers edited by Hensher and Stopher (1979) referred to in the text offers useful overviews of transport modelling and forecasting, while Ortúzar and Willumsen (1990) is an up-to-date text on the subject – the mathematics in both is at times formidable but a careful and selective 'picking' through the pagers should prove invaluable to a reader specifically interested in this branch of transport economics. Kroes and Sheldon (1988) offers a good introduction to stated preference approaches to forecasting.

References

Bates, J. (1988), 'Econometric issues in stated preference analysis', *Journal of Transport Economics and Policy*, 22, 59–70.

Baumol, W.J. and Vinod, H.D. (1970), 'An inventory theoretical model of freight transport demand', *Management Science*, 16, 413–21.

Bayliss, B. (1992), *Transport Policy and Planning: An Integrated Analytical Approach*, Washington, World Bank.

Ben-Akiva, M. (1977), 'Passenger travel demand forecasting: applications of disaggregate models and directions for research', in E.J. Visser (ed), *Transport Decisions in an Age of Uncertainty*, The Hague, Martinus Nijhoff.

Ben-Akiva, M. and Lerman, S.(1985), *Discrete Choice Analysis: Theory and Application to Travel Demand*, Cambridge, Mass., MIT Press.

Berechman, J. and Gordon, P. (1986), 'Linked models of land use – transport interactions: a review', in B. Hutchinson and M. Batty (eds), *Advances in Urban Systems Modelling*, Amsterdam, North-Holland.

Button, K.J. and Pearman, A.D. (1981), *The Economics of Urban Freight Transport*, London, Macmillan.

Cochrane, R.A. (1975), 'A possible economic basis for the gravity model', *Journal of Transport Economics and Policy*, 9, 34–49.

Deakin, E. (1990), 'The United States', in Barde, J.-P. and Button, K.J. (eds), *Tranport Policy and the Environment: Six Case Studies*, London, Earthscan.

Dix, M.C. (1977), 'Report on investigations of household travel decision making behaviour', in E.J. Visser (ed.), *Transport Decisions in an Age of Uncertainty*, The Hague, Martinus Nijhoff.

Domenich, T. and McFadden, D. (1976), *Urban Travel Demand – A Behavioural Analysis*, Amsterdam, North-Holland.

Fowkes, A.S. and Preston, J. (1991), 'Novel approaches to forecasting the demand for new local rail services', *Transportation Research*, 25A, 209–18.

Heggie, I.G. (1972), *Transport Engineering Economics*, Maidenhead, McGraw-Hill.

Heggie, I.G. (1978), 'Putting behaviour into behavioural models of travel choice', *Journal of the Operational Research Society*, 29, 541–50.

Hensher, D.A. and Stopher, P.R. (eds) (1979), *Behavioural Travel Modelling*, London, Croom Helm.

Howrey, E.P. (1969), 'On the choice of forecasting models for air travel', *Journal of Regional Science*, 9, 215–24.

Jones, I.S. (1977), *Urban Transport Appraisal*, London, Macmillan.

Jones, P.M. (1978) 'School hour revisions in West Oxfordshire: an exploratory study using HATS', *Technical Report*, Oxford, Oxford University Transport Studies Unit.

Kroes, E.P. and Sheldon, R.J. (1988), 'Stated preference methods: an introduction', *Journal of Transport Economics and Policy*, 22, 11–26.

Lancaster, K.J. (1966), 'A new approach to consumer theory', *Journal of Political Economy*, 74, 132–57.

Ortúzar, J. de Dios and Willumsen, L.G. (1990), *Modelling Transport*, London, John Wiley.

Phifer, S.P., Neven, A.J. and Hartgen, D.T. (1980), 'Family reactions to energy constraints', *Transportation Research Board Conference Paper*, Washington.

Pickrell, D.H. (1989), *Urban Rail Transit Projects: Forecast Versus Actual Ridership and Costs*, Cambridge, Mass., US Department of Transportation.

Pitfield, D. and Whiteing, A.E. (1985), 'Forecasting rail freight flows in Britain', in Button, K.J. and Pitfield, D. (eds), *International Railway Economics*, Aldershot, Gower.

Quandt, R.E. (ed) (1970), *The Demand for Travel: Theory and Measurement*, Lexington, Heath-Lexington.

Quandt, R.E. (1976), 'The theory of travel demand', *Transportation Research*, 10, 411–13.

Quandt, R. E. and Baumol, W. J. (1966), 'The demand for abstract transport modes: theory and measurement', *Journal of Regional Science*, 6, 13–26.

Talvitie, A.P. (1973), 'A direct demand model for downtown work trips', *Transportation*, 2, 121–52.

Timberlake, R.S. (1988), 'Traffic modelling techniques for the developing world: case studies', *Transportation Research Record* 1167, 28–34.

Truelove, P. (1992), *Decision Making in Transport Planning*, Burnt Hill, Longman.

UK Department of the Environment (1973), *Report of the Panel of Inquiry into the Greater London Development Plan*, London, HMSO.

UK Department of Transport (1977), *Transport Policy*, Cmnd 6836, London, HMSO.

UK Department of Transport (1989), *National Traffic Forecasts (Great Britain) 1989*, London, HMSO.

UK House of Commons Committee of Public Accounts (1988), *Road Planning*, London, HMSO.
UK House of Commons Expenditure Committee (1972), *Second Report: Urban Transport Planning*, House of Commons Paper HC.57 (I–111), London, HMSO.
UK Ministry of Transport (1963), *Traffic in Towns*, London, HMSO.
Webster, F.V., Bly, P.H. and Paulley, N.J. (eds) (1988) *Urban Land-use and Transport Interaction*, Aldershot, Avebury.

10   Transport and Development

10.1   Transport and economic development

Economists have long been concerned with assessing the links between changes in the transport sector and the evolving pattern of economic development within the area served. While the importance of transport in economic growth and development has never seriously been questioned, its exact role and influence have been subjected to periodic reappraisals. The underlying problem is, however, a more general one in that our understanding of what causes economic development is poor. This point was very clearly made nearly by Kindleberger (1958) over a quarter of a century ago:

> We have suggested that there is no agreement on how economic development proceeds and have implied that this is because the process is not simple. There are many variables involved, and there is a wide range of substitutability among ingredients – land, capital, and the quality and quantity of labour, and technology can substitute for one another, above certain minima, although there are at the same time certain complementary relationships among them. The will to economise and organisation are probably the only indispensable ingredients. For the rest, none are necessary, and none sufficient.

The interest in the topic, though, is not purely an academic matter; public concern with regional disparities in economic performance and the considerable differences in national economic prosperity between the 'North' and the 'South' has brought forth efforts to stimulate growth in lagging economies by investing in various forms of infrastructure. The form and scale such measures should take, and indeed their general desirability, are matters of practical interest. In consequence, while Kindleberger is still correct in that our knowledge is in many respect very limited, efforts to clarify the situation continue.

Traditionally, it was argued that transport exerted a strong positive influence on economic development and that increased production could be directly related to improved transport. In the UK context, for example, over a century ago, Baxter (1866) argued that 'Railways have been a most powerful agent in the progress of commerce, in improving the conditions of the working classes, and in developing the agricultural and mineral resources of the country.' Fifty years later we still find Lord Lugard (1922) writing, 'the material development of Africa may be summed up in the one word – transport'. Perhaps the strongest advocate of the positive role of transport, however, is Rostow (1960) who in accounting for economic growth maintains that 'The introduction of railroads has historically been the most powerful single indicator to take-offs. It was decisive in the United States, France, Germany, Canada and Russia.'

A broader brush approach is adopted by Andersson and Stromquist (1988) who claim that all the major transitions in the European economic systems were accompanied (or initiated) by major changes in transport and communications infrastructure. Four main transport and logistics revolutions can be distinguished:

- the period from the thirteenth century, in which water transport emerged as a new logistic system connecting cities along the rivers and coastal areas (the Hansa economy);
- the period from the sixteenth century (the Golden Age), characterised by a dramatic improvement in sailing and sea transport and by the introduction of new banking systems which stimulated trade to the East Indies and West Indies (with Lisbon, Antwerp and Amsterdam as major centres);
- the period from the middle of the nineteenth century, marked by the Industrial Revolution, in which the invention of the stream engine generated new transport modes thereby creating new market areas such as North America;
- the period from the 1970s which is marked by increased information and flexibility; just-in-time systems and material requirements planning have evolved within this framework.

Positive linkages between transport provision and economic development can be divided between the direct transport input and indirect, including multiplier, effects. Good transport offers low shipping costs which have permitted wider markets to be served and the exploitation of large-scale production in an extensive range of activities. Hunter (1965), for example, postulates a causal linkage between low-cost transport and economic growth – the Industrial Revolution was successful because of a prior revolution in transport technology. Similarly, Owen (1964) argues that a widening of domestic markets through improved transport services is a necessary prerequisite for national economic development. Further, most undeveloped countries are, for a variety of geographical, economic and historic reasons, dependent upon international trade and an expansion of this trade is an essential prerequisite for growth. In these circumstances the provision of efficient port facilities will, according to this school of thought, positively assist development.

The indirect effects stem from the employment created in the construction of transport infrastructure and the jobs associated with operating the transport services. Further, there may be multiplier effects stemming from the substantial inputs of iron, timber, coal, etc. required to construct a modern transport system and which, at least in the context of development in the nineteenth century, were supplied by indigenous heavy industries. Transport also often provided some initial experience of business for many industrialists of the period. The potential multiplier effects for third world countries today are likely to be substantially less given the growth (itself a function of improved transport) of international trade and tied development aid. Additionally, the technical expertise required to engineer and plan modern transport systems is often unavailable in less developed countries and must be bought from more advanced nations.

This causal view of transport and economic development has become less credible in recent years. The econometric work of Fogel (1964) in the United States, for example, offers evidence that American growth in the nineteenth century would have been quite possible without the advent of the railways – waterways supplying a comprehensive transport system at comparable costs. The view that the railways were the motive force behind American economic development has given way to a weaker position, namely that good transport permits economic expansion.

Economic development is, thus, now generally seen as a complex process with transport *permitting* the exploitation of the natural resources and talents of a country; it is, therefore, necessary but not sufficient for development. Transport can release working capital from one area which can be used more productively as fixed capital elsewhere, although a necessary prior condition is the existence of suitable productive opportunities in potential markets. Public infrastructure in this sense should be set in the context of the availability of private capital; many parts of the world, for example, would not benefit from more transport infrastructure because of the lack of private resources (Biehl, 1991).

Looked at from a slightly different perspective, improved transport can help overcome bottlenecks in production and thus further foster economic expansion (Blum, 1982; Rietveld, 1989). This is, for example, the underlying position taken by Vickerman (1987) and Button (1990) when examining the regional impacts of the Channel Tunnel. A difficulty, of course, if this true is that the bottleneck may be some distance from the region and superficially appear unconnected with it. Accepting this caveat, the basic view of this school of thought, whereby transport is seen more as a facilitator than a generator of development, is usefully summarised by Ahmed *et al.* (1976):

> In many developing countries the inadequacy of transport facilities is *one* of the major bottlenecks to socio-economic development and a national integration. Often the lack of transport makes it difficult to introduce other social infrastructure such as education and medical services. The dissemination of the modern techniques and inputs of agricultural production and the linking of agriculture to other sectors of the economy through the market is hampered by the absence or inadequacy of transport facilities. As a result of these and other factors, the productivity of agriculture – the dominant sector in developing economies – is deplorably low. (Emphasis original)

While the approaches sketched out above ascribe a positive role to transport in economic development, albeit in different ways, there is a feeling among some economists that an excessive amount of scarce resources sometimes tend to be devoted to transport improvements. As with any scarce input it is possible to define an optimal provision of transport to facilitate development so that resources are not wasted by being drawn from other activities where they may be more productive. At a given point in economic development, a country requires a certain level of transport provision so that its growth potential is maximised – hence there is an optimum transport capacity for any development level. It has been argued, however, that there are economic forces that tend to lead to an excess of transport provision (especially high cost infrastructure) at the expense of more efficient and productive projects. More specifically, Wilson (1966) has pointed to the lumpiness of transport capital which together with its longevity and associated externalities makes it particularly difficult to estimate future costs and benefits. Consequently, decisions to devote resources to transport are not easily reversible or readily corrected.

The political acceptability of transport is highlighted by Hirschman (1958) who feels that the sector attracts resources quite simply because it is difficult for mistakes (of an economic nature) to be proved even after major projects have been completed. Also development planners tend to be mainly concerned with allocating public investment funds and it is, therefore, natural that they should claim transport, communications, energy, drainage, etc. as being of overriding and fundamental importance. Further, given the industrial composition of wealthier developed countries with an established heavy industrial base, tied aid for transport schemes has a firm attraction. Those adopting this rather sceptical approach to the role of transport, therefore, accept that an adequate basic transport system is an obvious *sine qua non* for modern economic development but question whether the opportunity costs involved in further improving transport are necessarily justified.

The empirical evidence has not always been very helpful in sorting out these rather diverse ideas concerning the links between transport and the environment as can be seen from the summaries of studies conducted in industrial countries set out in Table 10.1. The objective of the following sections is to consider in a little more detail the role transport can play in economic development at successively different levels of aggregation. The coverage of this large topic is certainly not claimed to be comprehensive. We look first of all at the general problem of stimulating economic growth in the third world before proceeding to consider the problems of formulating a common transport policy to foster the economic growth ambitions of the member states of the European Community. At a more micro level there are also questions concerning the ways in which transport provision can stimulate economic growth within certain parts of a country or for a given urban area.

While the discussion of transport and economic development has been sectionalised for expositional convenience it is important to emphasise that in practice considerable trade-offs may be necessary between, say, devising a transport policy to stimulate national growth and one designed to assist the development of specified backward regions. The poorest countries especially often feel they must attempt to increase their national income. Indeed, if one were to accept the 'growth pole' approach to economic development, then national growth is attempted by concentrating effort in several strong regional centres. Hence, interregional inequality of growth is an inevitable concomitant and condition of growth itself. Consequently, although it may be possible to design a national transport strategy or investment programme that assists in the maximisation of national economic growth, it may need modifying to ensure that an acceptable degree of equity is retained among the different regions of the country.

10.2 Transport economics in less developed countries

Transport investment forms a major component of the capital formation of less developed countries, and expenditure on transport is usually the largest single item in the national budget. Up to 40 per cent of public expenditure is devoted to transport infrastructure investment with substantial supplements coming from outside international agencies such as the World Bank or in direct assistance from individual countries. At one level it is important to know whether this is, in aggregate terms, the most practical and efficient method of assisting the poor countries of the world while at another level it is necessary to be able to assess the development impact of individual transport schemes.

Broadly, transport may be seen to have four functions in assisting economic development (Fromm, 1965). First, it is an obvious factor input into the production process permitting goods and people to be transferred between and within production and consumption centres. Because much of this movement is between rural and urban areas it permits the extension of the money economy into the agricultural sector. Secondly, transport improvements can shift production possibility functions by altering factor costs and, especially, it reduces the levels of inventory tied up in the production process. Third, mobility is increased permitting factors of production, especially labour, to be transferred to places where they may be employed most productively. The fourth factor is that transport increases the welfare of individuals, by extending the range of social facilities to them, and also provides superior public goods such as greater social cohesion and increased national defence.

Table 10.1
Summary of findings looking at transport and development in industrialised countries

Author	*Geographical scale*	*Infrastructure*	*Conclusions*
Botham (1980)	28 Zones (UK)	Changing nature of highway	Small centralising effect on employment
Briggs (1981)	Non-metropolitan counties (US)	Provision of highways	Presence of interstate highway is no guarantee of county development
Cleary & Thomas (1973)	Regional level (UK)	New estuarial crossing	Little relocation but changes in firm's operations
Dodgson (1974)	Zones in North (UK)	New motorway	Small effect on employment
Eagle *et al*. (1987)	87 counties (US)	New highway expenditure	No increase in employment
Evers *et al*. (1987)	Regional level (Netherlands)	High-speed rail	Some effect on employment
Forrest *et al*. (1987)	Metropolitan areas (US)	Light rapid transit	Property blight - good for urban renewal
Judge (1983)	Regional level (UK)	New motorway	Small economic impact
Langley (1981)	Highway corridor (US)	Highway	Devalued property in area
Mackie *et al*. (1986)	Regional level (UK)	New estuarial crossing	Small overall effect
Mills (1981)	Metropolitan areas (US)	Interstate highways	No significant effect on location patterns
Moon (1986)	Metropolitan areas (US)	Highway interchanges	Existence of interchange villages
Pickett (1984)	Local districts (UK)	Light rapid transit	Properties close to the line benefit
Stephandes (1980)	87 counties (US)	New highway expenditure	Could affect employment - depends on county's economy
Stephandes *et al*. (1986)	87 counties (US)	New highway expenditure	Some positive association with employment
Watterson (1986)	Metropolitan area (UK)	Light rapid transit	Modest growth in land use
Wilson et *al*. (1982)	Regional level (US)	Existing highways	Transport affects location decisions but not development

Note: I would like to thank Scott Leitham for permission to make use of his unpublished table.

Transport economists have made significant contributions in assessing in detail the role that transport may play in assisting economic development in third world countries. At the microeconomic level they have developed techniques of project appraisal that permit a more scientific assessment of the costs and benefits of individual transport projects to be conducted. Many of the techniques of investment appraisal employed in the developed parts of the world (see Chapter 8) are applicable in third world conditions but local situations often require changes of emphasis. This is not surprising considering these techniques were devised to look at transport systems based almost entirely upon mechanical modes while head-porterage and canoes still account for the greatest proportion of goods movement in many less developed countries. The basic data are also often not so readily available or reliable in the third world as in most developed countries thus limiting the precision of any analysis. Nevertheless, the development of investment appraisal techniques of the type set down by Little and Mirrlees (1974) permit consistent analysis across investment alternatives both within the transport sector and between the transport sector and other areas of economic activity. Such techniques emphasise the importance of estimating appropriate shadow prices for both inputs into transport and the benefits derived from it. In particular, the shortage of foreign exchange suffered by many less developed countries is highlighted while it is recognised that higher levels of under-employment and unemployment require adjustments to the wage costs of labour. (The shadow price of labour being estimated as any lost production by diverting it from elsewhere in the economy – which is usually negligible – plus an allowance for the disutility associated with the work in the transport sector.)

At the macroeconomic level economists have pointed to the general influence that appropriate transport planning can have in assisting overall economic development. While it may be argued that ideally one should expand transport provision to balance developments elsewhere in the economy, this is not always possible. The balanced growth approach maintains that if transport services are inadequate, then bottlenecks in the economy will curtail the growth process, but if the services are excessive this is both wasteful, in the sense that idle resources could be earning a positive return elsewhere in the economy, and can become demoralising if the anticipated demand for transport does not materialise relatively quickly (see Nath, 1962, for a general defence of the balanced growth model). Hirschman (1958) takes a somewhat different view, arguing that the relationship between economic development and the provision of social overhead capital, such as transport, is less flexible than members of the balanced growth school believe.

In Figure 10.1, the horizontal axis shows the provision and cost of social overhead capital (which is normally provided by the public sector and will embrace transport as a major component) while the vertical axis measures the total cost of direct productive activities (which are normally undertaken on purely commercial criteria). The balanced growth approach assumes that *DPA* output and *SOC* activities should grow together (i.e. along the growth path represented by the ray from the origin), passing through the various curves from *a* to *d* representing successively higher amounts of *DPA/SOC* output. Hirschman, however, argues that less developed countries are in practice not in a position to follow such a path – partly because of the lack of necessary expertise to ensure the balance is maintained and partly because of inherent indivisibilities in the social overhead capital schemes available. Consequently, growth is inevitably unbalanced and may follow one of two possible courses; one based upon excess capacity of *SOC* (i.e. path $A=>A_1=>B=>B_2=>C$) the other upon a shortage of SOC (i.e. path $A=>B_1=>B=>C_1=>C$). If a strategy of excess SOC capacity is preferred it is hoped that this will permit DPA to become less expensive and encourage investment in that sector. Alternatively, with the second approach, DPA expansion occurs first and DPA costs will rise substantially. As a consequence considerable economies will be realised through the construction of more extensive SOC facilities. The actual effectiveness of the alternatives depends upon the strength of the profit motive in the DPA sector, and the responsiveness of the public authority in the SOC sector to public demand.

The type of transport provision most suited to developing economies is often of as much importance as the aggregate level of provision. Many developing countries tend to spend scarce development funds on prestige projects, especially international air transport, to demonstrate visually their capacity to emulate the performance of more developed nations; in other words X-efficiency is sacrificed for a modern, if superficial, image. More critical is the way in which funds are spent on internal transport provision and, in particular, whether there are advantages in concentrating limited capital resources in either the road or rail modes.

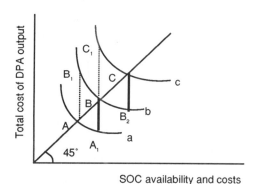

SOC availability and costs

Figure 10.1
Balanced and unbalanced growth of social overhead capital and direct productive activities

The appropriateness of different modes often depends upon the geographic–demographic nature of the country. Most less developed countries may be categorised as one of the following (Fromm, 1965):

(1)   densely populated tropical lands;
(2)   tropical land with low population density;
(3)   mountainous, temperate lands with a low overall density of population but a concentration on a coastal plain or altiplane; or
(4)   thinly populated desert areas with population concentrated along irrigated channels.

The appropriateness of different transport modes changes according to the type of country under consideration, thinly populated, tropic lands having different transport problems to highly urbanised countries with high population densities.

While the railways were important in the development of nineteenth-century economies and characterised colonial development in many countries the emphasis in recent years has switched to the provision of adequate road infrastructure. This is particularly true in areas where a skeleton of roads already exists and resources can be devoted to improving and extending an established, if rudimentary, network. This approach may be especially fruitful if it links isolated agricultural communities both with each other and with the more advanced areas of the economy. Millard (1959) argues that, unlike developed countries, in third world nations 'the benefits from road construction are almost entirely in the form of new development from traffic which the new road will generate'. The effect is not purely on immediate output but can stimulate a propensity for further development. Wilson (1966) strongly supported road development in third world countries for this reason, arguing that 'Investment options might usefully be analysed in terms not only of their direct economic pay-off but also in terms of their influence on attitude' and that 'The educational and other spill-over effects of road transportation appear to be greater than those of other modes of transport. This is especially significant at low levels of development.' Having said this, however, there is a danger if integrated planning is not pursued that while improved road facilities may stimulate the agricultural economy, the new links between rural and industrial-urban areas could lead to increased polarisation in the spatial economy with an enhanced geographical, as well as sectional, dualism resulting.

Externally, improved port and shipping facilities permit less developed countries to export their products to wider markets, although, as we see below, there are some dangers here. Since the demand for shipping services is derived from that for the final product we can illustrate the benefits to LDCs from reducing maritime shipping costs by looking at the quantities of exports from a third world country and the imports into the market of a Western economy. Figure 10.2 shows a back-to-back diagram (after Shneerson, 1977) where S_i, D_i are the supply and demand schedule for the commodity in the developed country and S_j, D_j the supply and demand in the less developed nation. Demand for imports and supply of exports is obtained by subtracting horizontally the domestic supply from demand. The demand for imports (exports) at each price being the difference between quantity supplied and demanded assuming domestic and import commodities are perfect substitutes. D_e and S_e in Figure 10.2 are derived in this fashion – the vertical difference between these curves then represents the demand for shipping shown as D_s. (If shipping charges were zero, for example, then the free trade equilibrium would be Z.) Suppose actual shipping rates were P^1, then at that rate the price of imports from country i confronting country j is seen to be P_m^1 (the cif price) while the cost of exports to country j would be seen in country i to be P_e^1 (the fob price). Country i would then import an amount ab equal to country j's (our less developed country's) exports of AB.

There is now an improvement in shipping services; this may take the form of better port facilities or more efficient ships or it may be administrative (e.g. relaxation of high conference shipping rates). The effect is that shipping costs fall to P^2 resulting in exports from country j rising to CF to match the higher imports of cf into the developed country i. Trade has expanded for the less developed country. The benefit of this trade to the two countries is represented by areas in the figure. Area adc is the extra consumption enjoyed by the developed, importing country as a result of the fall in the cif price while bef is a positive production effect resulting from a contraction of country i's relatively high-cost industry. The areas

ADC and *BEF* are the symmetrical benefits to the less developed country. (Interestingly the sum of these benefits can be measured directly as the area *WXY* under the demand curve for shipping services.)

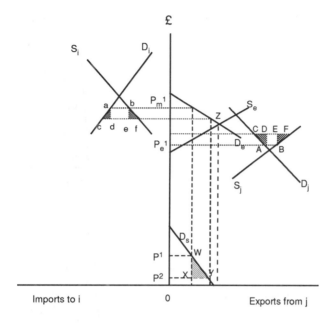

Figure 10.2
Welfare gains from improved shipping services

While it can be demonstrated that improved shipping facilities can aid development it should be noted that the analysis is crucially dependent upon the elasticities of demand for goods in developed and underdeveloped countries and the relative costs of supply. This often poses serious problems for less developed countries, as pointed out by UNCTAD (1969), with the LDCs often paying much of the costs of transport, that is:

> For many of the world's agricultural products, on which developing countries rely for much of their export earnings, supply elasticities are low in the short run ... Although overall demand elasticities for most of these commodities are also low, the elasticity of demand facing the individual supplier or the whole group of suppliers in a single country is likely to be relatively high, unless that country is the only source of supply, and there is no ready substitute for the commodity ... *The supplier in these cases therefore normally bears the bulk of the transport costs.* (Emphasis added)

In practice, the world is also a little more complicated, with trade involving not simply the production and transport sectors but also the system of international finance operating.

One of the practical problems experienced by many less developed countries has been the fact that shipping lines have combined in conferences to regulate prices and thus have often led to shipping costs – which are often borne by the less developed countries – being higher than in a free market situation. There are also arguments that the existence of non-pricing competition within conferences in itself produces a much higher quality of service (and *ipso facto* cost) than would prevail without collusion (Evans and Benham, 1975) and that this is again detrimental to third world countries. Empirical evidence produced by Devanney *et al.* (1975), looking at trade between the East Coast of the United States and Chile, Columbia, Ecuador and Peru, suggests that the conference system on these routes pushed up shipping rates by about $20 per ton in 1971, most of which would have been borne by the poorer countries.

It is not surprising that in these circumstances UNCTAD has negotiated a Code of Conduct for Liner Conferences which allocates maritime traffic on 40:40:20 basis with 40 per cent of the trade allocated to the merchant marine of each of the trading nations and 20 per cent to cross traders (see Neff, 1980, for more detail). This is intended to give underdeveloped countries the chance to reap some of the financial rewards from shipping and also exert a more immediate influence on their own development. In 1978, for example, third world countries were in the disadvantaged position of only having 8.6 per cent of the world deadweight tonnage of shipping but generating over 30 per cent of the bulk cargoes and over 90 per cent of the tanker cargoes. In the short term lack of capacity may prevent some nations from enacting the full implementation of the Code. Zerby (1979) has estimated, for instance, that of the 26 less developed countries he studied only nine had merchant fleets large enough to handle 40 per cent of their exports in 1975 and only fifteen had sufficient capacity to handle 40 per cent of imports (third world nations physically export about twice as much as they import – i.e. 440 million tons compared to 242 million tons in 1973). Attempts to expand the fleets of less developed countries to fulfil 40 per cent of the market will, therefore, result in excess capacity in the fleets of the developed countries but more importantly, given the imbalance in the volume of imports and exports, attempts to meet 40 per cent of shipping demand both into and out of LDCs will lead to a 50 per cent excess capacity within their own fleets. Zerby, therefore, feels 'that a rigid adherence to the 40–40–20 principle is likely to be an extremely costly method of reducing the developing countries' dependence on conference services'. Only with cooperation both between the developed and underdeveloped nations and between the LDCs themselves, Zerby argues, will benefits be reaped.

10.3 EC transport policy
A number of national groupings have emerged in both the developed and less developed world where countries have come together into loose economic unions with the aims of fostering their common economic interests. The European Community is one example, the North American Free Trade Area is another. Each has its own priorities and has set about achieving these in its own way. The development of transport policies within the framework of the European Community provides some indication of the importance which is increasingly being attached to transport by these groupings and also to some of the problems of creating pan-national transport policies.

The objective of the European Community is 'to promote throughout the Community a harmonious development of economic activities, a continuous and balanced expansion, an increase in stability, an accelerated raising of the standard of living, and closer relations of the member states'. While not central to the policies of such unions, coordinated transport policies can facilitate the easier attainment of their basic aims. The difficulties of agreeing on a 'Common Transport Policy' by such unions are numerous. Each member state has its own set of transport objectives which must be modified to conform with commonly agreed goals and objectives and each has its own sets of institutions and policy tools which may conflict with the criteria favoured by the grouping as a whole. Many countries in Europe have traditionally used transport subsidies to protect specific industries or regions, but this may run counter to Community objectives of increasing overall economic efficiency or be thought to result in undesirable redistributions of welfare.

The EC provides a useful illustration of the problems of devising an international transport policy designed primarily to foster economic growth. Attempts to formulate a Common Transport Policy can be traced back to the inception of the older European Coal and Steel Community (ECSC) which, in the Treaty of Paris, explicitly laid out a number of basic requirements regarding comparability of transport charges for carrying coal and steel, publication of rates and the use of discriminatory transport charges during a transition to eventual harmonisation. The Treaty of Rome (signed in 1957) confirmed many of the policies of the ECSC (although not publication of rates) and contains a specific remit for 'the activity of the Community [to include] ... the adoption of a common policy in the sphere of transport'. While the acceptance of the desirability of a common policy came early, the detailed development of such a policy has been much slower (Button, 1979). Early ECSC agreements on non-discriminatory cost-related rail tariffs for intra-Community traffic were possible because existing market distortions tended to spread evenly across members and no single country suffered significantly from their removal. Where areas of the former West Germany were seen to suffer as a result of such changes specific subsidies were authorised. Subsequent developments in ECSC and EC policy have been less easy.

(1)   While the early ECSC policy was concerned primarily with rail transport, the broader EC policy must encompass all forms of inter-urban freight transport. European railways are heavily regulated and normally state controlled making coordination of policies relatively easy. Historical and institutional factors – especially the small size of most operating units – make the regulation of road and water transport more difficult.

(2)   There are two broad schools of thought about transport policy within the Community. Countries such as West Germany tend to favour a 'social service philosophy' with transport seen as subservient to wider economic objectives and rigidly controlled to achieve these wider aims. Other countries, notably the Netherlands, argue for a 'commercial philosophy' with the free market determining capacity and price. As the debate over a Common Transport Policy has developed it has become increasingly difficult to find common ground upon which to hang measures.

(3)   The EC has periodically incorporated new members and this has resulted in the need to reconsider the direction of policy as the balance of views has shifted. The membership of Eire, Denmark and Great Britain in 1973, for example, meant that questions of cross-frontier traffic were effectively superseded by more fundamental questions concerning international trade. It also meant that the commercial philosophy was given added support – the UK being an extreme liberal. Subsequent expansions bringing in

Greece (in 1981), Spain and Portugal (in 1986) has added to the diversity of attitudes.

(4)   The administrative structure of the EC means that the Commission is responsible for policy formulation while the Council of Ministers is responsible for adopting regulations. This results in a rather lengthy decision-making process with the Commission formulating many policies that are never adopted. Additionally, the Commission sees its role to be in 'active' policy formulation, designing a framework which prevents transport from distorting the other markets for goods and services. This conflicts with national transport policy formulation which tends to be 'reactive' and responsive to specific problems as they occur. This can lead to difficulties if the Community's policy prevents members responding to specific transport problems within their own boundaries. In such cases members may accept Community policies but operate them half-heartedly and ineffectively (Gwilliam, 1980).

Until 1972 most policy initiatives within the EC tended to follow attempts of the ECSC to define detailed operational guidelines. Emphasis, for example, was placed on pricing policies and considerable attention was focused on the idea of 'forked tariffs'. This meant the establishment of upper and lower haulage rates within which the actual carriage rate must be set. The underlying idea was that the upper limit would prevent monopoly exploitation of consignors while the lower floor would contain any tendency towards excessive competition among hauliers. Initially, from 1968, a scheme with a 23 per cent fork was applied to a limited range of commodities subjected to international carriage but a subsequent extension did not materialise. The determination and enforcement of such rates proved impossible and this, combined with the logical inconsistency of trying to prevent monopoly exploitation and super-normal competition simultaneously, led to the adoption (from 1975) of simple reference tariffs. Similarly, there was an initial presumption that intra-Community road haulage capacity would need regulating to ensure free competition among members' fleets unhampered by national policies of protection. The existing bilateral agreements were thought excessively restrictive. A Community Quota of 1200 licences was established in 1968 with the intention that this would gradually expand to replace the bilateral system. Unfortunately, the Quota only expanded slowly and by the end of the 1970s it was estimated that 95 per cent of international road freight within the EEC was still carried on bilateral terms.

The limitations of the early phase of a Common Transport Policy were realised in 1973 when the EC Commission Member for Transport said, 'Without wishing to detract from progress already achieved, particularly when it is reviewed in relation to existing difficulties, we must nevertheless frankly and objectively admit that very few of the aims of the Common Transport Policy have been achieved.' The so-called 'New Impetus', which followed a rapid expansion of intra-Community trade and coincided with the enlargement of the Community in 1973, changed the emphasis from detailed regulation and control of individual transport modes towards the setting of more general guidelines and the establishment of an institutional framework within which transport could operate with maximum efficiency. Progress was, however, slow. The Quota was retained (with periodic small expansions) and earlier proposals to unify quality licensing arrangements (both in terms of managerial and operational licensing) were adopted. Uniform working hours were introduced. All Members charge road users at least the short-run marginal road track costs they incur (calculated on common principles) although, as we have seen in Chapter 4, this hardly represented a movement forward since such policies were already being pursued by all Members anyway.

Significant changes to the EC's transport policy emerged in the mid-1980s as, initially, the European Parliament and Commission began to put legal pressure on the Council of Ministers to meet their obligation to create a Common Transport Policy and as, later, the Single European Market initiative took form (Button, 1992). The latter laid particular stress on both deepening and widening existing transport policy. The argument for cabotage, liberalisation of market entry and easing of frontier crossing, for instance, extended policy in an area where considerable effort had already been expended. The argument for freer maritime markets and the liberalisation of air passenger transport could be seen as a widening of transport policy into areas which had not previously been viewed as integral to the Common Transport Policy.

As one may have anticipated, the change in approach has not been easy (for example, see Button and Swann, 1989, for a discussion of aviation policy) but change certainly has occurred. The outcome of the measures designed to lubricate the EC economy and to allow the benefits of a Single Market to be realised, has been a general withdrawal of intervention, both at the national and Community level, from many transport markets. From 1997, for example, EC airlines will be free to operate anywhere in the Community. Equally, there is a gradual phasing in of cabotage in road haulage and the right of any EC railway to operate anywhere within EC territory is leading to a liberalisation of land transport markets. Cabotage is also being initiated, with some limitations, in the maritime sector. Overall, transport is now regulated more within the framework of the Community's competition policy rather than as a 'special sector'. Coupled with these measures on regulation, the EC has also been active in creating an administrative structure both to help coordinate national transport infrastructure investments and to provide additional funding for projects of 'Community interest'.

Finally, in the past decade there have been major developments in EC regional and infrastructure policy which has witnessed considerable monies being channelled through agencies such as the European Investment Bank and the European Regional Development Fund to fund transport projects. Indeed, from 1987 to 1991 the EIB invested ECU 12 billion in infrastructure while some 80 per cent of ERDF funding between 1975 and 1989 went on infrastructure projects; a great amount of this money is going to the transport sphere. For example, in 1991 ECU 2.632 billion of EIB financing was for transport projects.

10.4   Transport and regional development
The inter-regional spread of economic activity within a country is of major concern to national governments. Geographical variations in unemployment, income, migration and industrial structure are of importance because they both result in spatial inequalities in welfare and, in many cases, reduce the overall performance of the national economy. For these reasons, Britain has pursued an active economic policy for over half a century in an attempt to stimulate economic activity in depressed areas and to contain damaging explosive growth in prosperous regions. The policies, which have varied both in intensity and in form over time, have generally concentrated on giving direct financial assistance to industry and on improving the mobility of labour. In addition there have been attempts at improving the economic infrastructure of the so-called development areas, with

specific emphasis being placed on providing better transport facilities. The policy of biasing transport investment in favour of depressed regions has been subjected to considerable debate (Gwilliam, 1979, Giuliano, 1989). In the UK scepticism about the effectiveness of such a policy as a regional economic development aid was initially expressed by A.J. Brown in a Minority Report of the Hunt Committee Inquiry into the Intermediate Areas (UK Department of Economic Affairs, 1969) and was supported by the findings of the Leitch Committee (UK Department of Transport, 1978) and by Parkinson (1981). A common thread in these studies is that in a country such as the UK where infrastructure is already relatively comprehensive, transport is seldom an important factor explaining disparities in regional economic performance. It is now accepted by many developed countries that transport policy motivated by regional policy objectives must be pursued with circumspection and that, in many cases, improved transport facilities may prove counterproductive for development areas.

A simple hypothetical example illustrates the difficulty (see Sharp, 1980). We have two regions, A and B, producing a single homogeneous commodity. The centres of the regions (see Figure 10.3) are M miles apart and the commodity can be transported over the area at a constant money cost per mile of $f–t$ per ton. The markets served by the regions differ, however, because it costs £C_A to produce a ton of the commodity in region A and £C_B a ton in region B. Consequently, and assuming no production centres exist between the regions, a distribution boundary can be drawn (shown by the dashed line in the figure) which is m_A miles from the centre of A and m_B miles from the centre of B (where $m_A + m_B = M$). The boundary is determined by the relative production costs of the regions and the costs of transport (i.e. $C_A + tm_A = C_B + tm_B$). Basic manipulation of the algebra gives the form:

$$m_A = 0.5 \left\{ M + \frac{C_B - C_A}{t} \right\} \tag{10.1}$$

If, therefore, production is relatively cheaper in region A then m_A will increase if infrastructure reduces the cost of transport. Thus if A is a depressed area then transport improvements could assist in expanding its potential market and, therefore, generate more income and employment but region A must be a low cost producer for this to be automatically true. If region B is the depressed one, then quite clearly investment in improved transport will only worsen the regional problem by contracting the market area served by the region. Indeed, at the extreme (where $(C_B - C_A) > Mt$) region B may be forced from the market entirely by the expansion of the low-cost region's market area.

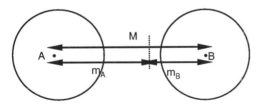

Figure 10.3
Market areas served by regions A and B

Of course, the model is a considerable simplification. Regions do not normally, for instance, specialise exclusively in the production of a single commodity but produce a range of goods. Thus a transport improvement, while damaging certain industries, may increase the competitiveness of others. The final effect of the improved transport facility will then depend upon relative production costs between regions and the importance of transport *vis-à-vis* production costs in the overall cost functions for the various commodities. Further, costs of production may vary with output and thus (following the 'infant industry argument') it may be beneficial to reduce transport costs if the government's regional policy also involves using grants and subsidies for encouraging the establishment of decreasing cost industry in a depressed area. Supplementary measures of this kind may be necessary if the depressed area is sparsely populated and, to be successful, its industry needs to penetrate the markets of other, more populous, regions to benefit from scale economies. It should be noted, however, that in these circumstances transport improvements *must* be accompanied by other regional aids if the natural gravitation of decreasing cost industries to centres of population is to be counteracted. Additionally, transport costs tend not to increase linearly with distance because of discontinuities and fixed cost elements in the overall cost function (see Chapter 3). Consequently, the influence of any transport infrastructure improvement is much more difficult to predict than the simple analysis implies.

In summary, there is no general case for thinking that investment in transport infrastructure will automatically improve the economic performance of depressed regions. In a country such as Britain, where the transport cost differences between the least and the most accessible regions is only about 2 per cent for all industries (Chisholm and O'Sullivan, 1973), the effect of transport investment on regional policy is, in general, unlikely to be substantial. This is particularly true if indus- trial location is, as many suspect, influenced by objectives other than cost minimi- sation (for example, on satisficing principles) or where there is a high degree of X-inefficiency.

While in Table 10.1 a number of important studies are cited, it is nevertheless true that empirical evidence on the specific regional effect of transport policies is scant and that which is available is often weakened by the difficulties of isolating transport effects from the effects of other regional policy measures. By conducting a counterfactual exercise Botham (1980) suggests that road investment in Britain between 1957 and 1972 had little effect although there was some tendency for it to have a centralising effect on the distribution of employment in the country. At a more micro level, Linneker and Spence (1991) conclude from their study of the impact of the M25 motorway that while it has improved accessibility (and regional market potential) much of this has subsequently been eroded by generated traffic. Work by Balduini (1972) attributes the creation between 1958 and 1970 of 53,000 jobs in the heavily depressed Mezzogiorno in Italy to the building of the Autostrade de Sole. This study, however, does not allow for the substantial range of other aid measures then operative, nor for intra-regional movements between sub-regions adjacent to the new facility and those more distant. A study of the high-speed TGV rail system in France by Bonnafous (1987) suggests that, while facilitating development, the overall impact has been small.

10.5 Transport, urban development and redevelopment

Changes in transport technology have, over time, exerted a strong influence upon the shapes and forms of the urban areas in which we live. The development of steam locomotion in the second half of the nineteenth century substantially improved inter-urban transport and permitted urban growth. Local, distributional services evolved much more slowly leading, in most cities, to a concentric pattern of development around the main rail (or occasionally port) terminal. The wealthy tended, because they could afford transport which was available, to live in the outer rings of housing while industry, being dependent upon good inter-urban transport, and the working class poor concentrated near the urban core – the CBD (the upper element in Figure 10.4; see also Chapter 2). The introduction of motorised local public transport (initially the tramcar and later the omnibus) followed by the motor car encouraged the growth of an axial pattern of urban land use with the former succession of concentric rings of housing being extended (star-like) in ribbon developments along the main road arteries (see lower element of Figure 10.4). Finally, the widespread adoption of the motor car, combined with improved road systems, limited traffic restraint and more efficient road freight transport has led to the growth of multi-nucleus cities where there are numerous sub-centres and suburbs – Los Angeles is often cited as the extreme example. While this simplified account of urban development misses many important subtleties it serves to highlight the historical role which transport has had in shaping urban growth.

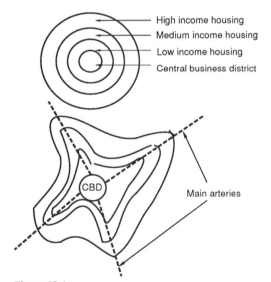

High income housing
Medium income housing
Low income housing
Central business district

CBD
Main arteries

Figure 10.4
Transport and concentric city development and axial city development

More recently, the difficulties of most large urban areas in the United States and Europe have not been ones of containing or moulding growth but rather of reversing decay. The concern once focused on the role of transport in urban development has been, since the early 1970s, transformed into concern for inner city revitalisation and redevelopment. As can be seen from Table 10.2 there were substantial outflows of population from the centres of virtually all major cities from the 1960s. This has been accompanied by an even faster exodus of industry. The result of this has been a decay in inner city public economies (the tax base of such areas has fallen while the composition of the population has become increasingly biased towards the old, disabled and poor) and unemployment (not only have firms left faster than population but also it has primarily been manufacturing industry which has left leaving behind large numbers of unemployed, unskilled workers). The causes of the decline of inner city areas are complex (see Button, 1978), regional and urban planning policies are partly responsible but there have also been changes both in the life-styles aspired to by the population (urban life becoming less attractive as incomes have risen) and in the production functions confronting industry (the land-output ratio in particular has been rising). Improved personal transport, especially higher car ownership levels, has also encouraged more commuting from more distant suburbs.

Official policy to counter the decline of the inner city areas and to stimulate the redevelopment of urban cores has incorporated a substantial transport component. For example, the white paper, *Policy for the Inner Cities* (UK Department of the Environment, 1977) made specific reference to the fact that 'Commerce and industry in inner areas need to be served by transport conveniently and efficiently' and points to the need for local authorities 'to give weight to the implications for local firms when designing traffic management schemes to improve access for central traffic, to ensure efficient loading and to provide adequate and convenient parking'. Additionally, it is argued that movement, notably in terms of journey-to-work trips, needs to be made easier especially for certain groups of travellers.

Table 10.2
Net migration from British cities 1966–76

| City | Decline in population | |
	Number	% of total population
Glasgow	205000	21
Liverpool	150000	22
Manchester	110000	18
Inner London	500000	16
Birmingham	85000	8
Newcastle	40000	12
Nottingham	25000	8

At the theoretical level, the bid-rent curve analysis set out in Chapter 2 would seem to imply that cheaper and better public transport would lead to a spread of cities (i.e. the residential bid-rent curves would shift up and to the right) while traffic restraint policy would lead to greater concentration of economic activity at the urban core. As Goldstein and Moses (1975) have shown, however, this type of analysis rests upon the assumption of a single central business district with no allowance for possible competing suburban centres. This is unrealistic in the context of most modern conurbations. Figure 10.5 depicts a more typical urban situation with a major urban centre – the Central Business District (CBD) – serving as the focal employment point dominating the suburban centre to which it is linked by road.

The urban centre is itself served by good local public transport with people for up to B miles away travelling into work by bus. The situation is one of equilibrium, with every household achieving the same utility level. Workers may opt for one of three main employment/residential location choices:

(1)   live within the immediate commuting area (radius B) and travel to work at the CBD by bus;

(2)   live outside of the immediate commuting area and travel to work at the CBD by car; or

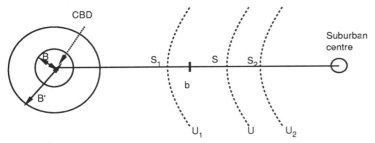

Figure 10.5
The impact of traffic restraint and public transport subsidies policy on the urban core

(3)   commute to the sub-centre by car.

In this situation – and excluding residents of the city who elect to take a fourth option, namely working at home – the boundary U will separate those workers employed at the core and those with jobs at the suburban centre. This state of affairs is one in which no household can improve its utility by changing its place of work, residential location or mode of transport. We now assess the impact of two alternative strategies on the economy of the central core area of the city.

(1)   The generalised cost of car travel in the central city area is increased, say, by either higher parking charges or the imposition of road pricing. This will tend to cause a rapid decline of the urban core in this model. Higher motoring costs will cause the immediate commuting belt to widen out (say to a radius of B' in Figure 10.5) with a reduction in real income for those living $(B'-B)$ miles from the CBD. This will encourage more people either to work at home or to cease to be active in the labour force (if there are other cities in the economy, there may also be some out-migration), leading to a decrease in the labour supply function at the CBD. Also car travellers confronted by higher costs will seek work at the suburban centre shifting the employment boundary to, say, U_1. The increased competition for jobs at the sub-centre will depress real income there leading, once again, to a general reduction in the overall labour supply in the city. Generally, therefore, traffic restraint in the CBD makes labour conditions less favourable which will, in the long term, make non-core sites more attrac-

tive for industry. The empirical fact that skilled labour tends to be more mobile (both between jobs and locations) is likely to magnify this effect on industrial location.

(2)   A subsidised express bus service running in bus-only lanes is introduced from a depot at location *b* to run non-stop into the urban core. This is unlikely to have an effect on those using the existing commuter public transport services around the CBD although, if fewer car trips and less congestion result, the speed of their journeys may rise – but if the service is, in general cost terms, cheaper than car travel this will widen the employment market for the urban core. Former car travellers from as far out as S_2 will find that by driving to *b* and transferring to the express service they reduce the overall cost of travelling to the CBD. Consequently, the boundary marking employee catchment areas will shift to U_2. People living to the left of U_2 will find their real income has risen as a result of lower transport costs (indeed, many people to the left of *b* may drive out to the depot to catch the bus into the core) and the labour supply function at the core will have shifted out, making the CBD a more attractive place for industry. People formerly inactive or working at home may also now find it attractive to seek employment at the CBD. The labour supply for the sub-centre has fallen, and wages will have to rise to generate the real income increase anticipated by employees there. In the long term the sub-centre will become less attractive for employers.

This theoretical analysis suggests that while one common effect of both the traffic restraint policy and the public transport improvement policy is to increase local bus service utilisation, the long-run effects on the distribution of population and economic activity are likely to be quite different. Goldstein and Moses (1975) argue, therefore, that even if transport policy in itself cannot cure the malaise of inner city areas, improved public transport provision can at least slow down the decline.

10.6   Further reading and references
An up-to-date, if rather difficult-to-obtain, survey of what we understand about the links between transport and economic development is contained in Slater (1992) while Dugonjic (1989) reviews the influence of transport on regional inequalities. The importance of transport in encouraging the development of third world economies is looked at in Prest (1969) which offers a good, general, if dated introduction to the subject. Little and Mirrlees (1974) is difficult, but fruitful reading, and provides a comprehensive treatment of investment appraisal (including transport) in less developed countries. The EC periodically publishes pamphlets outlining changes in its transport policy, but for further analysis of the philosophy underlying the Common Transport Policy and also for some critical comments on its more recent developments, see Button (1992). Transport and regional policy is well assessed in the much-cited papers of Gwilliam (1979) and Sharp (1980), both of which contain careful theoretical arguments outlining conditions where transport policy may affect regional economic performance as well as reference to a body of applied literature. Giuliano (1989) and Nijkamp (1986) offer some useful theoretical discussion of the links between transport and land-use patterns while Transportation Research Board (1990) contains a collection of articles linking transport and development.

References

Ahmed, Y., O'Sullivan, P., Suiono and Wilson, D. (1976), *Road Investment Programming for Developing Countries: An Indonesian Example*, Evanston, Ill., Northwestern University.

Andersson, A. and Stromquist, U. (1988), 'The emerging C-society', in Batten, D.F. and Thords, R. (eds), *Transportation for the Future*, Berlin, Springer.

Balduini, G. (1972), *Autostrade et Territorio in Quadermi de Aulostrade*, Rome.

Baxter, R.D. (1866), 'Railway extension and its results', *Journal of the Statistical Society*, 24, 549–95.

Biehl, D. (1991), 'The role of infrastructure in regional development', in R.W. Vickerman (ed), *Infrastructure and Regional Development*, London, Pion.

Blum, U. (1982), 'Effects of transportation investments on regional growth: a theoretical and empirical analysis', *Papers of the Regional Science Association*, 49, 151–68.

Bonnafous, A. (1987), 'The regional impact of the TGV', *Transporation*, 14, 127–37.

Botham, R.W. (1980),'The regional development effects of road investment', *Transportation Planning and Technology*, 6, 97–108.

Button, K.J. (1978), 'Employment and industrial decline in the inner city areas of British cities: the experiences of 1962–1977', *Journal of Industrial Affairs*, 6,1–6.

Button, K.J. (1979), 'Recent developments in EEC Transport Policy', *Three Banks Review*, 123, 52–73.

Button, K.J. (1990), 'The Channel Tunnel – the economic implications for the South-East of England', *Geographical Journal*, 156, 187–99.

Button, K.J. (1992), 'The liberalization of transport services', in Swann, D. (ed), *The Single European Market and Beyond*, London, Routledge.

Button, K.J. and Swann, D. (1989), 'European Community airlines – deregulation and its problems', *Journal of Common Market Studies*, 27, 259–82.

Chisholm, M. and O'Sullivan, P. (1973), *Freight Flows and Spatial Aspects of the British Economy*, Cambridge, Cambridge University Press.

Devanney, J.W., Livanos, V.M. and Stewart, R.J. (1975), 'Conference rate making and the west coast of South America', *Journal of Transport Economics and Policy*, 9, 154–77.

Dugonjic, V. (1989), 'Transportation: benign influence or an antidote to regional inequality?', *Papers of the Regional Science Association*, 66, 61–76.

Evans, J.J. and Benham, A. (1975), 'A forked tariff system for liner freight routes}, *Journal of Transport Economics and Policy*, 9, 62–6.

Fogel, R. W. (1964), *Railroads and American Economic Growth, Essays in Econometric History*, Baltimore, JohnS Hopkins University Press.

Fromm, G. (1965), 'Introduction: an approach to investment decisions', in G. Fromm (ed), *Transport Investment and Economic Development*, Washington, Brookings Institution.

Giuliano, G. (1989), 'Research policy review 27, new directions for undestanding transportation and land-use', *Environment and Planning A*, 21, 145–159.

Goldstein, G.S. and Moses, L.N. (1975), 'Transport controls and the spatial structure of urban areas', *Papers and Proceedings of the American Economics Association* (87th Meeting), 85, 289–94.

Gwilliam, K.M. (1979), 'Transport infrastructure investments and regional development', in J.K. Bowers (ed), *Inflation, Developipient and Integration – Essays in Honour of A.J. Brown*, Leeds, Leeds University Press.

Gwilliam, K.M. (1980), 'Realism and the Common Transport Policy of the EEC', in J.B. Palack and J.B. Van der Kamp (eds), *Changes in the Field of Transport Studies*, The Hague, Martinus Nijhoff.

Hirschman, A.O. (1958), *The Strategy of Economic Development*, New Haven, Conn.Yale University Press.

Hunter, H. (1965), 'Transport in Soviet and Chinese development', *Economic Development and Cultural Change,* 14, 71–72.

Kindleberger, C.P. (1958), *Economic Development,* New York, McGraw-Hill.

Linneker, B.J. and Spence, N.A. (1991), 'An accessibility analysis of the impact of the M25 London orbital motorway on Britain', *Regional Studies,* 26, 31–47.

Little, I.M.D. and Mirrlees, J.A. (1974), *Project Appraisal and Planning for Developing Countries,* London, Heinemann.

Lugard, F. D. (1922), *The Dual Mandate in British Tropical Africa,* Edinburgh, Blackwoods.

Millard, R.S. (1959), 'Road development in the overseas territories', *Journal of the Royal Society of Arts,* 107, 270–91.

Nath, S.V. (1962), 'The theory of balanced growth', *Oxford Economic Papers,* 14, 138–53.

Neff, S.C. (1980), 'The UN code of conduct for liner conferences', *Journal of World Trade Law,* 14, 398–423.

Nijkamp, P. (1986), 'Infrastructure and regional development: a multi-dimensional policy analysis', *Empirical Economics,* 11, 1–21.

Owen, W. (1964), *Strategy for Mobility,* Washington, Brookings Institution.

Parkinson, M. (1981), *The Effect of Road Investment on Economic Development in the UK,* Government Economic Service Working Paper No. 43, London.

Prest, A.R. (1969), *Transport Economics in Developing Countries,* London, Weidenfeld and Nicolson.

Rietveld, P. (1989), 'Infrastructure and regional development: a survey of multiregional economic models', *Annals of Regional Science,* 23, 255–74.

Rostow, W.W. (1960), *The Stages of Economic Growth,* Cambridge, Cambridge University Press.

Sharp, C.H. (1980), 'Transport and regional development with special reference to Britain', *Transport Policy and Decision Making,* 1, 1–11.

Shneerson, D. (1977), 'On the measurement of benefits from shipping services', *Maritime Policy and Management,* 4, 277–80.

Slater, D.W. (1992), Transportation and economic development: a survey of the literature', in Royal Commission on National Passenger Transportation, *Directions,* Volume 3, Ottawa, Royal Commission on National Passenger Transportation.

Transportation Research Board (1990), 'Transportation and Development Conference', *Transportation Research Record,* 1274.

UK Department of Economic Affairs (1969), *The 'Intermediate Areas',* London, HMSO.

UK Department of the Environment (1977), *Policy for the Inner Cities,* Cmnd 6845, London, HMSO.

UK Department of Transport (1978), *Report of the Advisory Committee on Trunk Road Assessment* (Leitch Committee), London, HMSO.

UNCTAD (1969), *Level and Structure of Freight Rates, Conference Practices and the Adequacy of Shipping Services,* New York, United Nations.

Vickerman, R.W. (1987), 'The Channel Tunnel: consequences for regional growth and development', *Regional Studies,* 21, 187–197.

Wilson, G.W. (1966), 'Towards a theory of transport and development', in G.W. Wilson, B.R. Bergmann, L.V. Hirsch, M.S. Klein (eds), *The Impact of Highway Investment on Development,* Washington, Brookings Institute.

Zerby, J.A. (1979), 'On the practicability of the UNCTAD 40–40–20 code for liner conferences', *Maritime Policy and Management,* 6, 241–51.

11   The Regu

11.1   The broad issues

A comprehensive chapter concerned with the regulation of transport activ must inevitably involve some overlap with other areas of transport economics. Space, for instance, has already been devoted to policies for containing pollution and for the control of traffic congestion. Transport, however, has been a sector which has been subjected to various forms of regulation throughout history and this in itself justifies a more specific examination. Just why have regulations been imposed and how have they operated? Equally, there are different ways in which transport is supplied with differing degrees of public-sector participation in ownership – the ultimate form of regulation. Just why this occurs and how it differs between countries raises a further set of economic questions.

Besides the general issues of regulation and ownership of transport, there is also the fact that in recent years there have been significant changes in the way in which many countries approach these policy issues. We have seen, for instance, a considerable relaxation of long–standing entry and price controls in markets as diverse as US domestic aviation and UK bus transport and it is a trend which is extending to the new market economies of the post-communist states. We have also seen extensive privatisation of transport facilities (for example, the British Airport Authorities in the UK) and operations (for example, Air Canada). Private-sector involvement at a second tier is also growing with the franchising out of operations (for example, London's bus services) and the greater use of private-sector funds in the financing of infrastructure investments (for example, the Channel Tunnel and French TGV network). The subject, therefore, is an important one and is likely to remain so for some time to come.

The objective of this chapter is not to describe all of the changes in regulation and ownership of transport which have taken place, although some of the more important developments are reviewed, but rather to explore the economic arguments underlying the various positions which policy-makers have taken. Some contextual historical information is helpful in doing this. Initially, however, a little time is spent looking at the various economic theories of regulation and setting trends in transport policy in the context of these theories.

11.2   Theories of regulation

Economists have long recognised that markets may, in practice, suffer from serious imperfections, indeed some discussion of this has been set out in previous chapters. Most obviously, these imperfections, or market failures, could adversely affect the users of transport services, perhaps because fares would be

lly high or the service offered dangerous. But equally, they may harm
ties through, for example, generating excessive environmental pollution
redatory pricing behaviour of incumbent operators may reduce the poten-
ability of other firms wishing to supply transport services and thus deter
from entering the market.

A wide range of arguments, some of doubtful economic logic, have been
awn into debates over transport regulation. Broadly the types of market failure
which have attracted most attention embrace:

- *The containment of monopoly power.* This was particularly so in the case of
  the railways, which dominated inland transport for nearly a century from the
  late 1830s but while some monopoly power still persists today in certain areas
  of transport activity, technical advances across a range of transport modes have
  reduced the potential for pure monopoly exploitation, at least in most developed countries. More common perhaps is the fear that suppliers of transport
  services may combine in cartels to limit output and prevent new entrants coming into the market.
- *The control of excessive competition.* Unregulated competition may limit the
  quality of service offered to customers and result in instability in the industry –
  in technical terms there may be no 'sustainable' equilibrium. The actual problem is not competition *per se* but rather the possibility that externalities may
  result or that certain sections of the community may not be provided with adequate services. Additionally, in some instances, notably road haulage and inter-urban passenger transport, the potential for conditions of monopolistic
  competition developing also pose problems of possible excess capacity being
  supplied.
- *The regulation of externalities.* Imperfections in the market mechanism may
  result in transport activities imposing costs which are not directly included in
  the private sector's decision-making – pollution and congestion being the main
  causes for concern. This subject has been explored more fully in Chapters 5
  and 7.
- *The provision of public goods.* Because certain items of infrastructure, such as
  roads, are thought to exhibit public goods characteristics (that is, non-exclud-
  ability and non-rivalness) their provision, it is argued, would be at best inadequate without government intervention. The degree to which such infrastructure should be seen as conforming to a public good, however, often depends
  upon the initial policy in place – for example, it is relatively easy to exclude
  cars from a road if wished.
- *The provision of high-cost infrastructure.* The sheer cost and long pay-back
  period, combined with possible high levels of risk, makes it unlikely that all
  major pieces of infrastructure would be built or expensive transport engineering research undertaken without some form of government involvement.
- *The assistance of groups in 'need' of adequate transport.* As was seen in
  Chapter 3 this embraces the notion that, for a variety of reasons including
  faults in the existing pattern of income distribution, effective demand is not an
  adequate guide to transport resource allocation and wider, social criteria
  should, therefore, be sought.
- *The existence of high transactions costs.* While free markets may theoretically
  be capable of optimising output this may involve high transactions costs.
  Drivers confronting each other on a road could bargain as to who has right of

way but a simple rule, say giving priority to the left, is likely to prove more efficient.

- *The integration of transport into wider economic policies*. Land-use and transport are clearly interconnected and some degree of coordination may be felt desirable if imperfections exist in either the transport or the land-use markets. Additionally, intervention in the transport sector may form part of a wider government macroeconomic strategy (for example, price controls or investment programmes) or industrial policy.
- *The need to reflect the genuine resource costs of transport*. In the case of certain finite, non-renewable resources (for example, mineral fuels) the market mechanism may fail to reflect the full social time preference of society. The government may, therefore, intervene to ensure that the decision-maker is aware of the true shadow price.
- *The improvement of transport co-ordination*. Because there are numerous suppliers of transport services, inefficient provision may result if their decisions are made independently. There is also the prospect of duplication of transport facilities and consequential wastage of resources, without some degree of central guidance.

Of course most official policies claim to cover a range of different problems although conflicts may, and do, emerge. For example, policies designed primarily to contain externalities may have adverse effects on income distribution or could run counter to a national economic policy that is pursuing a course of maximising gross national product. Similarly, measures to ensure that adequate high-cost research is conducted may mean conferring monopoly powers on private suppliers (for example, through the patent system or in terms of government contracts to purchase the fruits of a new technology). Consequently, there is an inevitable blurring across these justifications for government involvement when various policy measures are discussed or introduced. Even more uncertain than the exact justification or objectives underlying some policies is the exact effect the different policy tools employed by policy-makers is likely to exert.

The instruments of transport policy are sometimes broken down into those which, adopting US jargon, are aimed at economic regulation and those at social regulation – quantitative and qualitative regulation in the English vocabulary. The former are concerned with controlling the amount supplied in transport markets, who supplies it and the price which consumers pay. Social regulation specifies the nature of the transport services provided relating, for instance, to vehicle design, maximum emissions levels, driving hours, training of personnel, etc. In practice there is an inevitable overlap between the two sets of instruments. Limiting market entry, for example, can contain many adverse environmental effects of transport while strict quality controls can act to contain competition.

It is perhaps more useful, therefore, simply to provide a listing of the various policy instruments under the following general headings:

- *Taxes and subsidies*. The government may use its fiscal powers either to increase or to decrease the costs of various forms of transport or services over different routes. Or, indeed, the cost of transport in general. It may also influence the factor costs of transport inputs.
- *Direct provisions*. Local and central government are direct suppliers, via municipal and nationalised undertakings, of a wide range of transport services.

They are also responsible for supplying a substantial amount of transport infrastructure, notably roads, and supplementary services, such as the police.

* *Laws and regulations.* Government (and to a lesser extent, local authorities) may legally regulate the transport sector and there has grown up an extensive body of law which, in effect, controls and directs the activities of both transport suppliers and users.
* *Competition policy and consumer protection legislation* It is useful to distinguish general industrial legislation, governing such things as restrictive practices and mergers, and consumer protection legislation, covering such things as advertising, which embrace all forms of activity in the economy and not just transport. Obviously they apply to transport.
* *Licensing.* The government may regulate either the quality or quantity of transport provision by its ability to grant various forms of licences to operators, vehicles or services. The system of driving licences also influences the demand for private transport.
* *The purchase of transport services.* Various non-transport activities of government require the use of transport services. Hence, by means of its position as a large consumer government may exert a degree of countervailing power over transport suppliers.
* *Moral suasion.* In many instances this is of a weak form, usually being educational or the offering of advice on matters such as safety (for example, advertising the advantages of the wearing of seat belts) but it may be stronger when the alternative to accepting advice is the exercise, by government, of others of its powers (for example, the refusal of a licence or withdrawal of a subsidy).
* *Research and development .* Government may influence the long-term development of transport through its own research activities. These are, in part, conducted by its own agents (for example, the Transport Research Laboratory) and, in part, through the funding of outside research.
* *Provision of information.* The government through various agencies offers certain technical advice to transport-users and provides general information to improve the decision-making within transport. Many of these services are specific to transport (for example, weather services for shipping) while others assist the transport sector less directly (for example, information on trading arrangements overseas).
* *Policies relating to inputs.* Transport is a major user of energy, especially oil, and also utilises a wide range of other raw materials and intermediate products. Government policy relating to the energy and others of these sectors can therefore have an important bearing indirect on transport.

It seems logical, therefore, that if such market imperfections can be identified it is in the 'public interest' to intervene and reduce their distortive effects. This is not a particularly contentious view. Difficulties arise, however, not from the notion of public interest as such but rather to the degree to which intervention can, in practice, produce public benefit. In the 1970s, as we see below, a growing body of opinion emerged that regulation had become excessive and no longer served the public interest. In particular, the ideas of the Chicago School of economists questioned the motivation underlying the actions of regulators – most notably that they tend to act as rational economic entities and pursue policies aimed at furthering their position rather than necessarily that of the public interest. Others considered the power of the regulated and argued that because of their control of information flows (for example, regarding cost data which is needed to regulate fares) and their power to lobby there was a tendency for them to capture the regulatory process.

Even if regulation is initiated in the public interest it is not free from problems. Ideally, policy-makers like to match one policy instrument with one objective but this is seldom possible in transport. The problems of interdependence of objectives have already been alluded to but, in addition, the instruments themselves frequently have diverse effects. Taxation policies to reduce the use of a specific mode of transport may prove regressive while licensing to contain externalities may result in quasi-monopoly powers being given to certain suppliers. Actually forecasting, monitoring and appraising the effects of alternative policy instruments also usually proves difficult. Transport policy is pursued through a package of instruments and policy changes usually resulting in several of these instruments being varied in their intensity at once. The effects of such changes is also only likely to be fully felt after a lag as agents in the transport market gradually respond and adjust to the new situation. In the short term a road haulier, for instance, may do little in response to higher fuel taxation (save pay the additional money) but in the longer term he is likely to modify the method of operation employed and, in the very long term, he may even change the type of vehicle fleet used. Even if one could isolate occasions when a change is made to a single policy instrument it is unlikely that the full effect could be recorded before further changes take place. Finally, there is the problem of determining the counter-factual – the course of events which would have ensued if policy had not been changed. Government is frequently reactive in its approach – suggesting that changing circumstances are already observable by the time policy is enacted – but on other occasions policy changes represent initiatives and actually anticipate change. One can never simply assume that events would have continued on the course set prior to a major policy change.

It now seems appropriate to examine the various landmarks and phases of transport policy. This is intended to highlight the way in which transport policy has evolved to match both the changing technical and organisational structure of the sector and also the differing attitudes of society to transport over the past century and a half. It is in no way intended as a comprehensive piece of economic history. While much of the focus is on the UK situation, changes elsewhere in the world, and in particular in the USA, are also examined. The 'story' is also slanted in favour of the more recent developments.

11.3 Priorities in transport policy

The anti-monopoly phase, pre-1930
Government has always taken some interest in transport. Historically, military, political and fiscal factors were the prime motivation but over the past century and a half this concern has broadened out. Previously, it was not the efficiency of the transport market which was the principal concern but rather the insurance that adequate transport was available to permit the fulfilment of the major commitments of defence, administration and internal stability. The Industrial Revolution placed greater emphasis on the need for an economically efficient transport system which, combined with the rapid technical changes that took place in transport during the later years of the eighteenth and, more importantly, the early decades of the nineteenth centuries, resulted in rather more official intervention. (Indeed, even the Duke of Wellington called for a National Transport Plan for the UK at one stage.) While much of the early involvement was to permit canal and railway

facilities to be constructed, there was also a political awareness of the potential monopoly powers which canals, but railway companies in particular, could exercise. The 1844 Railway Act in the UK, for example, gave government the option of purchasing newly formed companies after 21 years (a power never exercised) and maximum rates were normally included in the enabling acts. In all, over 200 regulatory acts were passed before 1930 to appease public concern about the private control exercised over the monopoly of the railway companies. By the 1920s the railway companies had to publish their rates, were subject to common carrier obligations, were not allowed to show undue preference, had to present accounts in a prescribed manner and were subjected to controls over wage bargaining. An element of social service obligation was also apparent in some of this legislation with, initially, railway companies required by law to provide specified cheap services and, subsequently, workmen's tickets.

This type of situation was not unique to the UK. At the extreme, the majority of Continental European countries, partly for strategic reasons but also in part because of their general approach toward natural monopoly, had developed their rail systems as public enterprises from the outset. The USA, while fostering private ownership and finance, had passed its first legislation on rate regulation in 1856 and the Interstate Commerce Commission came into being in 1887. Equally, in Canada the inherent advantage of the railways led to concern about the abuse of their powers, including discriminatory practices, and to the passing of the Railway Act of 1903.

The anti-competition phase, 1930–45

The advances in road haulage and passenger transport in the period after the First World War substantially eroded the near-monopoly that had been enjoyed by the railways for the previous eighty or so years. The nature of road transport, and especially the relative ease of entry, and low capital requirement necessary, changed the towards the regulation of dangerous operating practices and 'excessive competition'. The political pressures of the railway companies, still hampered by numerous restrictions on their commercial freedom, to contain cheap road transport added emphasis to the debate. Besides the financial strains on the regulated railway industry, fears were expressed that excessive competition produces dangerous operating practices and results in inadequate and unreliable services for those situated away from the main transport arteries. The Salter Conference which reported on road haulage in 1932 found that 'Any individual at present has an unlimited right to enter the haulage industry without any regard to the pressure on the roads or the existing excess of transport facilities ... This unrestricted liberty is fatal to the organisation of the industry in a form suitable to a carrier service purported to serve the public.' (It should perhaps be said that the composition of the Salter Conference – it was made up of railwaymen and representatives of *established hauliers* – may have coloured its conclusions!)

The legal manifestations of this policy were the passing of the Road Traffic Act, 1930, and of the Road and Rail Traffic Act, 1933, which introduced, respectively, quantity licensing into road passenger transport and public road haulage. In addition to trying to temper the competitive environment of road transport the operation of the licensing system for road passenger transport also encouraged the provision and cross-subsidisation of unprofitable social bus services by virtue of the method of licence allocation. Other measures designed to produce greater equality in the operating conditions encountered on the roads and railways included relaxation of certain constraints on railway pricing and the introduction of minimum wage rates and specified employment conditions into the road haulage industry.

Elsewhere a plethora of similar regulations were appearing. In the US, federal legislation was introduced controlling coastal shipping (1933), inter-urban bus operations (1935), road haulage (1935), airlines (1938), inland waterways (1940) and freight forwarders (1942) and many states also tightened their regulatory regimes. Canada initiated regulations over its aviation industry under the 1938 Transport Act and encouraged coordination, rather than competition, between its main railway operators under the 1933 Canadian National–Canadian Pacific Act.

Central control and nationalisation, 1945–51

The years immediately following the end of the Second World War saw, under the newly elected Labour government, a period of reconstruction and an industrial policy emphasising the nationalisation of industry. The 1947 Transport Act, for the first time outside of war years, brought a substantial part of the British transport system under direct government control. (Although it should be pointed out that peace time nationalisation was not entirely new nor a Labour Party monopoly and, indeed, the British Overseas Airways Corporation was formed in 1939 by a Conservative administration.) The objectives of the 1947 Act were clearly stated, namely to 'secure the provision of an efficient, adequate, economical and properly integrated system of public inland transport and port facilities'. The earlier success of the London Passenger Transport Board gave credence to this view and the British Transport Commission (with five functional executives) was established to emulate this success. It was given the responsibility of coordinating the newly nationalised railways, long-distance road haulage, sections of public road transport, London Transport and publicly owned ports and waterways.

Unfortunately, the BTC was given no rules of economic behaviour as guidelines. It was recognised that, for the railways to compete efficiently, a much closer price–cost relationship was required but it was impossible for a new set of freight charges to be set before 1955 and, in the meantime, the BTC was impotent to direct traffic to the mode for which it thought it was best suited. The difficulty was compounded by the fact that consignors had a free choice of transport mode, and that own-account road haulage vehicles were free from government control. Further, the 1947 Act had little opportunity to work because of, first, the lack of sufficient time needed to develop the necessary administration and to reorganise the newly nationalised undertakings and, secondly, the inadequate funds available to carry out the necessary investment required in the rail sector.

A competitive framework, 1951–64

The period of successive Conservative administrations between 1951 and 1964 witnessed a movement away from a regulatory approach to transport coordination towards one based upon competition, that is, by making use of 'the natural interplay of economic forces'. A policy of decentralised control was pursued and, under the 1953 Transport Act, the railways were freed from many of their long-standing statutory obligations (for example, they were relieved of the status of 'common carrier' and the burden of having to publish their rates and charges). Large sections of nationalised road haulage were also returned to private ownership. The basic argument for this competitive approach was that even if integration in the fullest sense were practicable, it would result in a large, unwieldy machine, ill-adapted to meet with promptitude the varying and instant demands of industry.

The culmination of these policies was the 1962 Transport Act which freed the railways from most of their remaining legal constraints, regionalised their boards, separated their overall administration from that of road haulage and recognised that commercial viability required some rationalisation of the rail network. Nationalised road haulage (which was composed of British Road Services and several specialist undertakings) was given terms of reference requiring it to perform as though it was a 'private enterprise concern'.

The general policy of 'coordination by competition' pursued by the Conservative government met with considerable problems after 1962. The railways and public transport in general ran into increasing financial difficulties while public concern began to grow about both the need to provide additional road space for the growing number of motor vehicles and the actual environmental effects of this growth, especially on urban areas. The established method of providing social services by cross-finance from profitable services ceased to be financially viable. Further, there were questions arising concerning the most appropriate ways of exploiting new transport technologies, especially containerisation.

Controlled competition, 1964–74
The Labour administration elected in 1964 undertook a series of detailed policy studies in transport which culminated in the 1968 Transport Act. This, in conjunction with the 1968 Town and Country Planning Act, attempted to produce a policy based upon 'controlled competition' (see Munby, 1968). It hoped to combine the advantages afforded by the automatic processes of the market mechanism with those of direct control. The policy was comprehensive, setting up authorities (Passenger Transport Authorities) to control and coordinate urban public transport, devising new systems of quality licensing for road haulage, providing specific finance to support socially necessary transport, drawing up a national road-building programme and reconstructing the accounts and activities of the railways. It used all means of policy: market measures, such as taxation and subsidy, as well as 'administrative' measures such as licensing and the establishment of new institutions. The Act was also liberal in the sense that the framework of legislation and licensing which was introduced was intended to provide a basis for 'fair' competition, leaving the actual coordination of modes, in the majority of sectors, to market forces. The PTAs were introduced in the major conurbations to control urban public transport, but this was in a market where externalities are widespread and competition felt to be unlikely to solve problems of congestion and environmental decay. The inter-urban market was left to competitive forces with intervention limited to preventing excess instability or dangerous practices.

The Conservative government returned to office in 1970 pledged itself to the repeal of many of the clauses in the 1968 Act although, in practice, few of the measures they found exceptionable – such as quantity licensing for long-distance road haulage – had in fact been implemented (see Button, 1974). Indeed, the 1972 Local Government Act set up authorities which logically extended the PTA concept and further integrated the long-term planning of overall urban development. The Civil Aviation Authority, which was set up in 1971, rather than reversing the philosophy of the 1968 Act, was designed to control operating practices and improve the stability of the sector. As the Minister said at the time, 'There are close links between the economics and the financial health of the airlines and the safety of their operations and between operational safety, air worthiness, air traffic control and navigational services.'

The search for efficiency, 1974–80

The policy emphasis of the Labour government from 1974 to 1979 was spelt out in *Transport Policy* (UK Department of Transport, 1977). They were, 'First, to contribute to economic growth and higher national prosperity ... Second, to meet social needs by securing a reasonable level of personal mobility.... Third, to minimise the harmful effects, in loss of life and damage to the environment, that are the direct physical results of the transport we use.' In many ways the policies, which reduced government expenditure considerably, moved further towards the free market than the 1968 Transport Act, with greater emphasis now placed on allocative efficiency. Although government expenditure on 'roads and transport' fell from £3820m to £3023m per annum (at 1978 prices), between 1974 and 1978, this does not mean official intervention was ignored. The 1974 Railway Act, for example, had already introduced the idea of a 'Public Service Obligation' and subsidies were made available to provide services 'comparable' to those existing at the time of the legislation. Methods of allocating public monies were also modified with the introduction of transport supplementary grants and the need, from 1974, for the production of transport policies and programmes by local authorities to demonstrate the evolution of coherent local transport policy. This latter idea was later extended in the 1978 Transport Act to embrace public transport services (the Public Transport Plans) at the shire level. But, on the other hand, grand strategies for road-building were replaced by piecemeal assessments emphasising a further shift from the active policy of the Labour administration of the 1960s to rather more reactive policy-making (Gwilliam, 1979).

The emphasis on allocative efficiency and market mechanisms was further strengthened in the 1980 Transport Act introduced by the Conservative government returned the previous year. Quantity licensing in the express coach sector was abolished and free competition (with quality controls) was permitted. Further relaxation of sharing and lift-giving laws also allowed more opportunity for private transport to offer limited forms of public service in rural areas, while policies of denationalisation have resulted in sales of limited amounts of publicly owned transport assets to private industry. (It is interesting to compare this trend towards both reactive policy-making and a greater reliance on market forces with the developments in the EC Common Transport Policy discussed in Chapter 10.)

The age of regulatory reform, 1980 to date

The past fifteen years witnessed major reforms in transport regulation. While there are marked national differences in the nature and pace of change, this process has, in the case of public transport modes, been characterised by moves toward more liberal regimes and a withdrawal of government from the ownership of transport operating companies. In contrast, there has been an increasing emphasis on the containment and the management of automobile use both on environmental grounds and because of congestion problems .

The liberalisation measures which have been adopted not only represented legal reforms, but also embraced *de facto* changes in interpretation and enforcement of regulations. In addition, they have extended across national boundaries with, for instance, the removal of institutional barriers to free transport operations being an explicit element of the EC's 1992 initiative. Whereas previously the majority view was that, because of scale economies and the potential for serious market failure, it was in the public interest for government to take an active role in regulating the industry, the prevailing wisdom is now that intervention failures are often potentially more damaging than market imperfections.

The generality of the regulatory trends across industrialised countries raises questions concerning the underlying causes of change. Certainly, in more recent years one can point to the demonstration effects exerted mainly by the deregulation of US domestic aviation but there also seem to be more fundamental issues which need addressing.

The first American economists to oppose regulation did so for a straightforward reason. Most subscribed (and still do) to the basic theorem that welfare is maximised when the price of each good or service equals its long-run social marginal cost but evidence mounted in the 1950s, 1960s and 1970s that regulatory agencies caused prices to diverge from long-run social marginal costs, rather than converge to them. Economic studies of US aviation provided a cornerstone in this debate. It was the combination of direct evidence that the Civil Aeronautics Board kept long-haul, high-density fares high and evidence of low fares in the unregulated intra-state markets in California that provided the first evidence that deregulation of intercity air passenger transportation was justified. Indeed, in the case of airlines, the California markets provided evidence against airline regulation, evidence which could be understood not only by economists, but also by the general travelling public (Table 11.1).

By the mid-1960s, a strong case existed for transport deregulation in the US but there was much research needed to get a full picture: for example, early studies disagreed as to whether the costs of excess rail capacity resulting from closure regulation were high or low. A number of subsequent studies considered these issues, as well as the more basic issue as to how high the social loss from transport regulation was in the USA.

There were also theoretical developments in economics which encouraged deregulation. The Chicago models of regulation made it clear that the public interest is not necessarily served by regulation. However, these models also implied that existing regulations were the result of a rational process, and by the interpretation of some they could be thought to work against deregulation, because they implied that regulation was itself a result of social optimisation. Nevertheless, subsequent analyses have extended the analysis to indicate how it could indeed explain regulatory reform. The reason is that changes in technologies, markets and the balance of political power among different groups can easily stimulate regulatory reform, even in a Chicago-type model (Keeler, 1984; Button, 1989b).

Another theory which supported deregulation was that of contestability (Bailey and Panzar, 1981), which asserted that with sufficiently easy entry and exit in a market (there are no sunk costs but there are lags in matching price cuts), even a natural monopoly could have a zero-profit, competitive outcome. The model, however, served more as an after-the-fact rationale for deregulation than as a stimulus, because it was only developed after deregulation occurred in most US industries. Furthermore, subsequent empirical evidence for the US airline industry has not fully supported the contestability hypothesis (Morrison and Winston, 1986).

The resultant changes which have taken place across the world since the mid-1960s have not been uniform either across countries or modes. Part of this stems from the different starting points which existed in the early 1970s. In very general terms, the USA led the way in legal change with a rush of liberalising measures during the 1970s and early 1980s which removed much government control from its domestic transport system – see Table 11.2. Other countries have followed the trend, in part because of demonstration effects which indicated significant benefits from change, but in some cases because of the direct impacts of changes in the US – Canada, for example, was so affected.

Table 11.1
Results of US studies of domestic aviation regulation

Study	Data	Comparisons	Conclusions
Caves (1962)	CAB routes	Structure, conduct & performance	Problems with the industry's performance which required changes in the regulatory structure but did not oppose regulation
Levine (1965)	Intrastate & CAB routes	Fares	Regulation caused higher fares and resulted in lower load factors
Jordan (1970)	California & CAB routes in 1965	Fares	Regulation caused excess capacity, benefited aircraft manufacturers, labour unions & airline service suppliers
Keeler (1972)	California & CAB routes in 1968	Fares	Regulation created excess capacity which dissipated any profits from fares set at cartel level by the CAB
Douglas & Miller (1974)	CAB routes	Fares & flight frequencies	Regulation resulted in high fares & sub-optimally high qualities of service being offered
DeVany (1975)	California & CAB routes in 1968	Fares & flight frequencies	Regulation protected the consumer with fares set close to the output maximising level
Keeler (1978)	California & CAB routes in 1974	Fares	CAB regulation led to excess charges amounting to $2.7 billion per annum

Source: Button (1989a) which contains full references to studies cited.

In effect, the systems of Boards and Committees which regulated the industry have gradually had their powers curtailed and transport industries are increasingly being treated like other commercial undertakings. Where controls remain there has been a shift in their emphasis. In inter-state road haulage, for example, the 1980 legislation shifted the burden of proof for market entry from the applicant to the protester and this effectively eliminated the major entry barrier. It also created a zone of reasonableness within which rates could vary. Equally, with respect to freight railroads, the reforms gradually removed rate controls, allowed rationalisation and facilitated reorganisation, especially mergers.

This quest for efficiency has been emulated in the UK as, first, the 1980 Transport Act and then the 1985 Transport Act liberalised bus markets and

introduced new financial mechanisms for providing social services. *De facto* reform has been brought about in domestic aviation as the Civil Aviation Authority
has adjusted its position on licensing since 1982. Developments within the EC
mean that there will be further *de jure* changes as cabotage is phased in within the
Community by 1997. Indeed, as outlined in Chapter 10, the creation of a Single
European Market means that cabotage rights, albeit initially often in rather limited
forms, will extend across all transport modes within the EC. Similar changes occurred elsewhere with the domestic Canadian road haulage market, partly as a result of increased competition from the more efficient US carriers being liberalised
in 1987 and its aviation market, after some *de facto* changes in 1984, being
legally deregulated in 1988. Reforms of a similar nature ended Australia's 'two
airline' domestic aviation policy in 1990 but liberalisation of surface transport has
progressed more slowly. Gradually the effects of reform strategies, especially
through the influence of agencies such as the World Bank and Asian Development Bank, are also being felt in developing countries

Table 11.2
Major legal changes to US transport regulations 1976–89

1976	Railroad Revitalisation and Regulatory Reform Act – removed many regulations over rate setting
1977	Air Cargo Deregulation Act – initiated free competition fir air cargoes
1978	Airline Deregulation Act – initiated a phased removal of fare setting and market entry controls
1980	Staggers Rail Act – removed many regulations over line abandonment and gave further freedom in rate setting
1980	Motor Carriers Reform Act – increased entry and rate setting freedom and reduced the role of rate fixing bureaux
1981	Northeast Rail Service Act – enabled Conrail to abandon little-used lines
1982	Bus Regulatory Reform Act – eased conditions of market entry and exit and phased in re-laxation of rate controls.

The extensive public ownership of transport which existed in countries such as
Canada, Australia, Japan and most of Europe has meant that reforms here have
often also involved elements of privatisation. The privatisation process, while reducing the direct control of government, has stimulated the creation of new regulations, for example, to limit market power and to meet social objectives. Many of
these relate to quality of service, especially safety, and to the nature of ownership
(such as governing allowable foreign ownership of shares) but economic
regulations have also been imposed.

The sale of transport undertakings through stock market flotation (for instance,
British Airways and British Airports Authority) has attracted considerable
attention and raised large sums of money for the Exchequer (Table 11.3) but, in
fact privatisation in transport has taken a diversity of forms (Button, 1992). The
former National Bus Company in the UK, for instance, was broken up and privatised mainly through management buyouts. In France and Japan private money is
increasingly being used to finance railway operations through commercial loans
and investments. Open tendering for formerly publicly supplied bus services is
now widespread in the UK and franchising systems, albeit on a somewhat different basis, exist in a number of Continental European states. In a similar way,

Sweden has attempted to increase efficiency on parts of its railway network by separating operations from track and allowing private operating companies to tender for services – similar proposals are in hand in the UK for elements of its rail system.

Table 11.3
Transport privatisation proceeds in the UK

Undertaking	Year	Amount
National Freight Company	1982	£7 million
British Rail Hotels	1983	£30 million
Associated British Ports	1983/84	£34 million
Sealink	1984	£ 66 million
British Airways	1987	£892 million
British Airports Authority	1987	£1200 million
National Bus Company	1988	n.a.

11.4 Studies of regulatory reform

The impacts of recent reform have been extensively researched, but the impossibility of accurately guessing counterfactuals (what would have happened in the absence of regulatory change) leaves much room for debate. Furthermore, many markets have not yet reached long-run equilibrium. In particular, sectors such as the UK bus industry, US domestic aviation and international freight distribution are still in the process of merging and shaking out. Experience so far, however, provides some insights on the working of transport markets and the benefits and costs of regulation.

One important issue in the working of transport markets is that of contestability. Evidence so far indicates strongly that actual competition is considerably more effective in reducing market power than is potential competition. But even those sceptical of the contestability of transport markets nevertheless find evidence that the market power of firms in these markets is nowhere near strong enough to justify regulation. That is, it can be strongly argued that unregulated markets in transport function quite well by reasonable measures of market performance, compared with other sectors of market economies, and more efficiently than they did under regulation.

There is in fact a strong body of evidence that regulatory reform has substantially enhanced economic efficiency in the US and UK intercity transport markets, and that the benefits of that efficiency have been passed on to consumers, as we shall summarise below. The evidence on more limited experiments in deregulating markets in urban transport is not so clear.

Although almost all studies trying to analyse the effects of regulatory liberalisation for intercity transport in the US and UK find positive benefits from change, there is nevertheless some controversy around the proper methods for evaluating the costs of excessive regulation. Traditionally, regulation is seen to affect efficiency by imposing static deadweight loss, encouraging excess capacity, and stifling technological change. The implications of regulation, however, extend beyond these considerations. For example, regulatory change can have a dynamic effect on productivity change, rather than just a one-shot effect on static efficiency. Furthermore, regulatory change will likely redistribute income as well as changing productivity.

As regards dynamic shifts in productivity, there have been far fewer studies than of static efficiency. Nevertheless, some studies have been done, including for airlines and for US road haulage. Both conclude that deregulation caused an acceleration in the improvement of productivity in their industries, at least for a period (see Button and Keeler, 1993).

Concerning redistribution, existing studies clearly indicate that the effects of deregulation in this area are substantial Early work in the US, for example, indicated that deregulation of US aviation benefited the user by some $6 billion per year (1977 prices) with profits rising $2.5 billion (Morrison and Winston, 1986); subsequent mergers and structural changes have probably altered these figures. In the area of freight, US deregulation seems to have had powerful effects on efficiency and distribution. Winston *et al.* (1990) find $20 billion (1988 prices) in annual benefit to shippers and their customers. Yet investors in road haulage are estimated to have lost over $5 billion per annum, with losses of similar magnitude to labour employed in the industry. On the other hand, investors in railroads appear to have gained from deregulation. In some cases, such as UK buses and US railroads and airlines, there have been overall declines in wages from deregulation.

While the privatisation of transport supplying industries has been somewhat more recent than many other measures of liberalisation, the evidence seems to be that it has enhanced efficiency. In the case of air transport simple comparisons of productivity between the privately owned major US carriers in 1987 and the mainly state-owned European carriers indicate the former to be significantly more efficient (McGowan and Seabright, 1989). The privatisation of British Airways has unquestionably improved its productivity *vis-à-vis* nationally owned European rivals. Equally, the privatised UK bus companies have increased productivity. The application of more rigorous analysis to those transport industries still under public ownership tend to indicate that levels of subsidy and intervention in management decision-making lead to technical inefficiency.

In nearly all cases of liberalised regulation, there were concerns on the part of some observers that regulatory change would come at a cost to society in terms of safety and externalities, because the need of firms to minimise costs under a competitive market situation would require them to pay less attention to these considerations. Although it is always difficult to distinguish between long-run trends and short-run fluctuations in transport safety, nevertheless, considerable time has now passed since regulatory reform, especially in the USA. Virtually all evidence regarding deregulation and safety in the USA goes in one direction: there has been no change. In the case of airlines, perhaps the greatest concern of many, not only did deregulation not harm safety (in terms of fatalities per passenger-mile), but the trend towards increased safety did not significantly shift with the Airline Deregulation Act of 1978 – fatalities continued to decline at basically the same rate. Of course, to the extent that deregulation induced intermodal shifts in traffic, the effects could be complicated. But even here, the most evident effect is positive: low airline fares have induced passengers away from a less-safe mode (the private car) to the safer mode of air transport.

Effects of transport deregulation on the wider environment is at best ambiguous. Greater freedom of entry and exit has removed much excess capacity from markets everywhere; this goes for road haulage, airlines and railroads, in the EC and USA. Fuller planes, lorries, trains and railway track should be positive in their effects on the environment. Furthermore, to the extent that freedom of the railroads to compete in the US takes traffic from roads, that could be thought to be an environmental improvement as well. The major polluter in most contexts is the private car, and little if anything has been done to liberalise the market for car use.

What the recent phase of liberalisation has revealed is that, although less regulation may be beneficial, there is still a need for government intervention. A degree of 'reregulation' is already being considered by some although in practice the process is one of tidying up and adjusting to new circumstances. Specifically, it is concerned with removing serious market imperfections.

With some notable exceptions, the recent liberalisation of transport has tended to focus on operations. Transport infrastructure investment has in contrast continued to be controlled, and in many cases owned, by government. How to achieve optimal utilisation of this infrastructure and, specifically, the development of appropriate user-charging mechanisms which minimise distortions in liberalised markets is attracting increasing attention. At one level there are matters relating to investment coordination and policy appraisal, especially in the international market, which have attracted little attention from economists. At another level there is the matter of efficient use and financing. The separation of infrastructure from operations, as has been the tradition with road and air transport and is being considered by more countries in the context of railways, is seen as one approach to achieving greater efficiency. In North America recent history has seen monopoly passenger services (such as VIA Rail in Canada) hiring track capacity from freight companies. An alternative approach, however, is simply to offer available capacity to the highest bidder, although this can raise a variety of technical problems (UK Department of Transport, 1992). Sweden, however, has already gone some way in this direction (Hansson and Nilsson, 1991).

An alternative is to develop economic charging regimes. Important in this is the question of cost attribution. In terms of rail transport, the past fifteen years have seen considerable advances in cost allocation procedures. Equally, at airports, our improved understanding now provides a more rational basis for determining landing fees. With respect to road track cost allocation, studies in the US (Small *et al,.* 1989) and UK (Newbery, 1988) provide a similar foundation for more rational user charging regimes. Indeed, in New Zealand road freight transport taxation is on a broad user-costs basis. The basis is, therefore, now laid for more rational charging for infrastructure use.

The past two decades have witnessed a complete transformation in the way in which policy-makers think about regulating transport market. Part of this stems from wider developments concerning the perceived role of government *per se*, but the changes in transport have also come about because of particular concerns. The outcome has seldom been as predicted and certainly the more liberal conditions which now exist in most transport markets around the world are not without their problems. In general, however, the changes have afforded the opportunity for users to express their preferences through the market and for regulators to pinpoint specific distortions where intervention can be justified.

In summary, if there is a single conclusion to be drawn from the experience of regulatory reform in transport, it has been that reform has, in general, been an economic success. Though there have been areas in which the policies need improvement (antitrust, infrastructure, franchise arrangements, etc.), these are small matters of 'fine tuning' compared with the broad picture of overall success in improving the efficiency of transport provision. What has been lacking have been comparable reforms in the regulation of private transport use along the lines discussed in Chapter 7.

11.5   Coordination via the market, or by direction?

These very important facts emerge from the previous section. First, government finds the transport sector extremely difficult to handle; this is perhaps most clearly seen if one reflects on the fact that *major* pieces of transport legislation have appeared on the UK's statute books every seven or eight years during the past half-century (that is, 1930, 1933, 1947, 1953, 1962, 1968, 1974, 1980, 1985). These have been supplemented by numerous pieces of minor legislation. There have been substantial shifts both in the way that transport has been viewed and the type of policy approach pursued.

Secondly, the changes in policy have exhibited systematic swings between attempts at making greater use of market forces and a more comprehensive level of central control or direction. Intervention has always existed but the degree and nature of this intervention has differed according to whether more or less confidence was felt in market processes. Recent changes in policy, from the late 1970s, have reflected a greater market orientation while the nationalisation of the immediate post-war period followed philosophies of direction. The respective merits of market-orientated policies *vis-à-vis* ones of planned allocation of resources are subjects of considerable debate. While much of the discussion is political (often doctrinal) there is, nevertheless, an important area of economic controversy involved.

It is quite possible that in theory a variety of approaches with quite significant differences in their degree of market orientation could achieve the basic objectives of transport policy but the standard economic problem of integration or 'coordination' remains practically difficult. (Coordination is here used in its economic context and is best defined by Peterson, 1930, 'Coordination is the assignment by whatever means of each facility to those transport tasks which it can perform better than other facilities, under conditions which will ensure its fullest development in the place so found.') In practice, reliance is never placed entirely on the market mechanism to achieve the desired coordination, nor upon direction. The issue is rather one of degree and emphasis. It seems useful, however, to look initially at some of the arguments that are advanced for adoption of the extreme position.

The price mechanism is the main instrument of the market and offers an obvious method of coordination – each consumer being in a position to purchase transport services at the lowest cost. Arguments that transport is a public utility, on a par with street lighting or the police force, are dismissed by advocates of this school who point out that transport, unlike genuine utilities, would be provided even if government did not exist. There may be cases (for example, quasi-public goods) where government must act as the supplier, if provision is to be optimal, but providing the rules of marginal cost pricing are pursued no difficulties arise. If externalities exist then these can be handled adequately by means of ensuring that property rights are allocated according to fairly accepted rules while social difficulties associated with hardship should be tackled by lump-sum transfers. (At the extreme one may argue that income differences are themselves the result of market forces and should, therefore, be left.) The longevity of transport infrastructure and associated risks would be handled by insurance markets. Safety would be ensured by travellers/consignors selecting operators with good safety records or alternatively they may prefer a higher risk but at a lower charge for the trip. Perfection in the 'safety market' may require government intervention to ensure that users are cognisant of the dangers involved – in this sense information becomes the only 'merit good' to be provided in the transport sector.

Advocates of the market approach to coordination point to the automatic mechanisms involved and the freedom of the system from political manipulation. Hibbs (1982), in particular, suggests that the direction of resources by some overriding body is likely to be less efficient at coordination because 'The administrative mind is not likely to possess the qualities of imagination and flair that are necessary if the consumer's interest is to be served.' Cooter and Topakin (1980) produce evidence from the Bay Area Rapid Transit system of San Francisco that provides tentative confirmation of this type of bureaucratic hypothesis; namely, that the technostructure places *its* interest before that of customers. The validity of this view is, however, debatable and it has been suggested that the managers of any large undertaking, irrespective of the type of purpose they are charged to pursue, will be motivated by their own self-interest – in particular they will attempt to maximise their power and security. Self-interest at the expense of customer interest, therefore, seems to be a function of the scale of management rather than of ownership or the objectives which are set it.

But even if there are potential managerial problems associated with the central direction of resources, these may well be outweighed by the possible benefits. Strictly, planned resource allocation involves the direction of traffic as well as factors of production actually employed in providing transport services. In general, however, UK policy has seldom attempted to direct traffic, leaving the consumer free to choose his mode, route, service, etc. (There are exceptions such as one-way streets, barriers to lorry traffic, etc. but these are rather outside of the main thrust of the debate.) The most important case, where some degree of direction was intended, concerned the proposed introduction of quantity licensing into long-distance road haulage under the Transport Act, 1968. The broad argument here was that it was to the consignor's benefit to be directed to rail in certain instances because of his own misperception. ('Inertia and habit will play their part and some consignors may not even be aware of the advantage to them of the new rail services, nor of the true economic cost of their present arrangements', according to the UK Ministry of Transport, 1967). The difficulty with this line of argument, and possibly one of the main reasons the system was never implemented, is that the administrators, in making their allocation, may misperceive the priorities and needs of the consignor.

On the more central issue of service provision it has been suggested that without directed coordination it is often impossible or prohibitively wasteful for many of the wider goals to be fully achieved. Direct income transfers, for example, may rectify differences in the spending power of households but it is often a sub-group within a household (for example, housewives) whom one is trying to assist and direct transfers may not reach them. Further, with so many operators in the transport market, there are suggestions that technical coordination of services would be less efficient (for example, bus services would not act as local distributors to trunk rail services). Private firms may not be willing to undertake substantial capital projects because, unlike government, they cannot spread risk adequately, even where insurance markets do exist. In more simple terms, advocates of direction feel that it is likely to prove overall to be more efficient than an optimally maintained market environment.

Quite clearly the substance of these lines of argument is likely to vary among transport sectors. It is not surprising, therefore, that in general the allocative mechanism favoured for inter-urban transport (especially freight) is that of the market and of price while intra-urban transport tends to be subjected to considerable planning and control. The widespread occurrence of externalities, the more immediate distribution issues, the interaction of an imperfect transport market with that of an imperfect land market, etc. make it particularly difficult to remove the impedance that exists to the efficient function of a pure market for urban transport. One exception, which should be noted, to the dominance of the market in allocating inter-urban resources is the public provision of roads. Here, as we saw in Chapter 4, there are important differences between the way road and rail track costs are passed on to users. Comparable pricing policies are the clear market solution, but it is worth noting that increasingly economists have taken the argument further and have suggested that both sets of track should be publicly owned and then users should pay on an identical basis for the services rendered; a situation which exists with parts of Sweden's rail network and one actively being reviewed in the UK.

Finally, it is becoming increasingly apparent that the tools of direction or control are, in effect, so numerous, sophisticated and subtle that the distinction between market-orientated policy and control is rapidly ceasing to be a meaningful one. By manipulating price, licensing, operating laws and work conditions, the government is in effect directing resources and ultimately influencing the traffic patterns that evolve. The tools of policy outlined in section 11.1 are all, in effect, tools of direction but at the same time they may operate as tools to improve the workings of the market. Would road-pricing, for example, be extending the market to embrace congestion or would it be a direction of traffic? In this context the extremes of market versus direction cease to be helpful; one removes to a rather more basic debate concerning the desirability of goals and the relative merits of different policy tools for achieving them.

11.6 Further reading and references
The recent literature relating to transport regulation is extensive and the recommendations offered here are but a small sample of what is available. Button and Keeler (1993) offers a recent overview of transport regulation while Button and Gillingwater (1986) provides an historical perspective. Sets of papers setting out recent experiences of transport regulation across a number of countries and covering virtually all modes of transport are to be found in Banister and Button (1991), Button and Pitfield (1991) and Bell and Cloke (1990). In terms of mode-specific studies, Button (1991) contains papers on aviation, Winston *et al.* (1990) analyse the deregulation of US surface transport, Keeler (1983) is concerned with US railroads, Keeler (1991) focuses on US aviation and Dodgson and Topham (1988) provides studies of UK bus regulatory reform. Button and Chow (1983) offer a comparative study of US, UK and Canadian road haulage regulation. An interesting discussion of some of the problems associated with privatising transport infrastructure is contained in Gomez-Ibanez *et al.* (1991) and a useful overview of experiences with bus deregulation is contained in Meyer and Gomez-Ibanez (1991).

References
Bailey, E.E. and Panzar, J.C. (1981), 'The contestability of airline markets during the transition to deregulation', *Law and Contemporary Problems*, 44, 125–45.

Banister, D. and Button, K.J. (eds) (1991),*Transport in a Free Market Economy*, London: Macmillan.

Bell, P. and Cloke, P. (eds), (1990), *Deregulation and Transport: Market Forces in the Modern World*, London, David Fulton.

Button, K.J. (1974), 'Transport policy in the United Kingdom 1968–74', *Three Banks Review*, 103, 26–48.

Button, K.J. (1989a), 'The deregulation of US interstate aviation: an assessment of causes and consequences, Part 2', *Transport Reviews*, 9, 189–215.

Button, K.J. (1989b), 'Economic theories of regulation and the regulation of the United Kingdom bus industry', *Anti-trust Bulletin*, 34, 489–515.

Button, K.J. (ed.) (1991), *Airline Deregulation: International Experiences*, London, David Fulton.

Button, K.J. (1992), 'Privatization in the transport sector: some of the key issues', *Economisch en Sociaal Tijdschrift*. 45, 29–48.

Button, K.J. and Chow, G. (1983), 'Road haulage regulation: a comparison of the Canadian, British and American approaches', *Transport Reviews*, 3, 237–64.

Button, K.J. and Gillingwater, D. (1986), *Future Transport Policy*, London, Routledge..

Button, K.J. and Keeler, T.E. (1993), 'The regulation of transport markets', *Economic Journal*, 103.

Button, K.J. and Pitfield, D. (eds) (1991), *Transport Deregulation: An International Movement* , London, Macmillan.

Cooter, R. and Topakin, G. (1980), 'Political economy of a public co-operation – pricing objectives of BART', *Journal of Public Economics*, 13, 299–318.

Dodgson, J.S. and Topham, N. (eds.) (1988), *Bus Deregulation and Privatisation*, Aldershot, Avebury.

Gomez-Ibanez, J.A., Meyer, J.R. and Luberoff, D.E. (1991), 'The propsects for privatising infrastructure: Lessons from US roads and solid waste', *Journal of Transport Economics and Policy*, 25, 259–78.

Gwilliam, K.M. (1979), 'Institutions and objectives in transport policy', *Journal of Transport Economics and Policy*, 13, 11–27.

Hansson, L. and Nilsson, J.-E. (1991), 'A new Swedish railroad policy: separation of infrastructure and traffic production', *Transportation Research*, 25A, 153–60.

Hibbs, J. (1982), *Transport without Politics...?*, London, Hobart Paper 95, Institute of Economic Affairs.

Keeler, T.E. (1972), 'Airline regulation and market performance', *Bell Journal of Economics and Management*, 3, 399–424.

Keeler, T.E. (1983), *Railroads, Freight and Public Policy*, Washington, Brookings Institution.

Keeler, T.E. (1984), 'Theories of regulation and the deregulation movement', *Public Choice*, 44, 103–45.

Keeler, T.E. (1991), 'Airline deregulation and market performance: the economic basis for regulatory reform and lessons from the US experience', in D. Banister and K.J. Button (eds)*Transport in a Free Market Economy* London, Macmillan.

McGowan, F. and Seabright, P. (1989), 'The deregulation of European airlines', *Economic Policy*, 9, 283–344.

Meyer, J.R. and Gomez-Ibanez, J.A. (1991), 'Transit bus privatisation and deregulation around the world: some perspectives and lessons', *International Journal of Transport Economics*, 18, 231–58.

Morrison, S.A. and Winston, C. (1986), *The Economic Effects of Airline Deregulation*, Washington, Brookings Institution.

Morrison, S.A. and Winston, C. (1987), 'Empirical implications and tests of the contestability hypothesis', *Journal of Law and Economics*, 30, 53–66.

Munby, D.L..(1968), 'Mrs Castle's transport policy', *Journal of Transport Economics and Policy*, 2, 135–73.

Newbery, D.M. (1988) 'Road user charges in Britain', *Economic Journal (Conference Papers)*, 90, 161–76.

Peterson, G.S. (1930). 'Transport coordination: meaning and purpose', *Journal of Political Economy*, 38, 660-81.

Small, K.A., Winston, C. and Evans, C.A. (1989), *Road Works – A New Highway Pricing and Investment Policy*, Washington, Brookings Institution.

UK Department of Transport (1977), *Transport Policy,* Cmnd 6845, London: HMSO.

UK Department of Transport (1979), *Road Haulage Operator's Licensing: Report of the Independent Committee of Enquiry*, London, HMSO.

UK Department of Transport (1992), *The Franchising of Passenger Rail Services: A Consultation Document*, London, Department of Transport.

UK Ministry of Transport (1967), *The Transport of Freight,* Cmnd 3470, London: HMSO.

Winston, C., Corsi, T.M., Grimm, C.M. and Evans, C.A. (1990), *The Economic Effects of Surface Freight Deregulation*, Washington, Brookings Institution.

Index